MERCHANTS
of DECEIT

OPIUM, AMERICAN FORTUNE
& THE CHINA TRADE

RICHARD J. FRISWELL

HAMMONASSET HOUSE BOOKS
Clinton, Connecticut

hammonassethouse.com

Copyright © 2022 by Richard J. Friswell

All rights reserved under international and
Pan-American Copyright Conventions

Library of Congress Cataloging in
Publishing data

Fiction/Connecticut

I. Friswell, Richard J., b. 1945

II. Title

ISBN 978-0-9966169-6-6

Manufactured in the United States

Book design by Anne Marcotty

To Kathy
With gratitude and love,
For her wit, wisdom,
boundless patience and
keen editorial eye
:
For
My children and grandchildren,
with heart-felt love, affection
and hugs ;-)

"Opium has a harm.
Opium is a poison, undermining our good customs and morality.
Its use is prohibited by the law... However, recently the purchasers, eaters and consumers of opium
have become numerous.
Deceitful merchants buy and sell it to gain profit."

QAINLONG EMPEROR (KNOWN AS HONGLI),
6th in Succession, Qing Dynasty (in the year, 1793)

CONTENTS

PROLOGUE

February 1, 1862

I CANNOT ASSURE THE READER this accounting of my life is thoroughly authentic, since most memories fade over the years, clouded by time, they are vaguely recalled like pictures lining a dimly lit hallway. But, age and infirmity, I fear, may have caught up with me. Yet, some scenes, long past, were so profoundly unsettling they became etched in my mind, and are recounted with absolute clarity, even decades later. Such are the moments—or, more accurately, a collection of horrifying incidents—which I had been a party to during my years abroad as a principle in the China Trade.

If there is any value whatsoever contained in this narrative, it may be found in the striking, colorful journals I elected to maintain during my distant, long-ago world travels. In so many ways, I was propelled by happenstance of history to bear witness in an astonishing time and place. Some would argue that my immediate agency and personal choices in the dramatic unfolding of those encounters, in no small way, helped to define that chapter in world history. I could also argue that events in China—only much later labeled by the greater world as tragic—were well underway prior to my arrival in the 'Celestial Kingdom,' and that my only infraction was to take advantage of existing conditions in a manner that would favor me, my partners and investors back home. They all placed great faith in me at the time, expecting nothing less.

In the spirit of any proper introduction, I believe my story will be more easily understood, fair reader, if I beg but a few moments of your precious time in laying this brief foundation for the narrative, soon unfolding on these pages. The gravity and moment of these events bear more relevance in their telling (or re-telling) when presented with first-hand thoughts and actions of those individuals, including my own, who were directly involved. I therefore defer to the cast of characters with whom you shall soon become acquainted; and, in good time, as prudence and common courtesy would dictate... my own acquaintance, as well.

And, in that those accounts are thus assembled, here is our story...

~*Samuel Russell*

BOOK I
MIDDLE KINGDOM

1. I, Zhengrui

QING [PRONOUNCED 'CHING'] Dynasty, partial timeline, relevant in bold)
1722–1735: Yongzheng Emperor (known as, Yinzhēn), 5th
1735–1796: Qainlong Emperor (known as, Hongli), 6th
1796–1820: Jaiqing Emperor (known as, Yongyan, or Jai), 7th
1821–1850: Daoguang Emperor (known as Minning), 8th
1850–1861: Xianfeng Emperor (known as Yizhù), 9th

According to Zhengrui, Advisor to Three Generations of Qing Dynasty Emperors: Hongli, Jaiqing and Minning, Sixth, Seventh and Eighth in Succession, Sons of Heaven, Ancestral Reign since 1644 over the Timeless Celestial Kingdom.

I, ZHENGRUI, HAVE many concerns today, not the least of which are the health and well-being of my emperor, whom I have served as trusted advisor for many years. That trust was hard-earned, given our tumultuous past. Over many decades of service, I have accomplished much, including that of Grand Minister to this Son of Heaven, Minning. But, more on our current crisis in a moment.

First, though, a word-or-two as to how I came to be here: As a young man, thin as a bamboo shoot, lusting for a glimpse of the world beyond my isolated village, I first served the court of Minning's grandfather, Hongli. As the son of a Shandong nobleman, I won the attention of the most powerful men in the court's inner circle. It was near the time of the British mission in the Year of the Water Rat (English, 1793), the emperor, Hongli, made a pilgrimage to Shandong's Mount Tai—the so-called South Gate of Heaven—to climb the thousand steps and offer his *Fengshan* sacrifices, paying homage to the earth (at the foot of the mountain), and heaven (at the summit).

There I was, in the company of my father and his mid-echelon, government entourage, in their official role in attendance to the royal court. My excitement ran high, and at twenty years of age, I was willing to complete any task, no matter how insignificant. Qainlong Emperor, Hongli, took notice of my ambition and directed my father to have me sent to his palace staff in Beijing. There was much love between my father and me, but he could not say no to the emperor.

Once I had arrived in Beijing, my privileged background benefited me in two important ways: first, my youth enabled me to move with few restrictions despite the confines and strictly controlled setting of the fortressed Forbidden City; secondly, because of family ties, I managed to retain my masculinity, pledging fealty to the emperor, thereby avoiding joining the ranks of the hundreds of eunuchs, *huànguān* (宦官), in the service of the emperor's court, as conscripts, male consorts and household staff.

On one particular night, I remained veiled in shadow, observing Hongli, as he stood at the entrance to his sleeping chamber in the Hall of Mental Cultivation. Here was the world's most powerful man, now just a hulking silhouette in a darkened doorway. The scene reminded me of his beloved great gray crane, *Cāng lù* (苍鹭) as she might be, poised motionless beside the palace pool—on one stilt-like leg, yellow eyes fixed—ready to strike at a shadowy form just beneath the surface. Hongli's thoughts seem to have drifted away from our earlier conversation regarding the next day's official schedule. In the sanctity of this space, he was far removed from the hundreds of servants, soldiers, concubines and eunuchs asleep elsewhere on the sprawling grounds of his country retreat—and farther still from the Forbidden City, his sprawling fortress in the center of Běijīng (北京). Here and alone, the emperor's self-doubt and reflection could reign.

Two heavily armored guards, tall pikes in hand, stand motionless a few meters away, their expressionless faces obscured by highly polished, plumed battle helmets aglow beneath an auspicious full moon. A shrunken, balding 'ancient,' a long-time palace eunuch sits huddled under a lamp, flickering in a corner of the enclosed courtyard, a porcelain bowl cradled between his legs. If the emperor decides to relieve his bladder or move his bowels at any time during the night, this man is tasked to quickly whisk it away. But, Hongli is not aroused by any such need, at least not tonight.

Silence enshrouds the walls of the courtyard, except for the deep roll of thunder that follows flashes of lightning, briefly silhouetting distant hills. A single mourning dove's plaintive call from a nearby treetop matches the emperor's sullen mood. In the stillness, I watch his shoulders rise and fall with short, shallow breaths, a portent of anxious days ahead. With more than his share of aches and pains for eighty-two years, Hongli still holds his silk-robed frame erect, even when alone—a force-of-habit after decades of court functions and ceremonies where court minions looked to their sacred leader for evidence of strength and resolve. Too much rich food and a sedentary life while confined behind the walls of the Forbidden City make for his generous gut and round face. The few strands of hair remaining on his balding head shone like tangled silver threads in the moonlight. I can sometimes imagine him as he once was, leading a charge in a long-ago battle—adorned in his elegant leather armor while atop a fiery white stallion—a scene long-since faded from the memories of most.

Later, I stir from my sleep in a nearby chamber, sensing movement in the adjoining room. Hongli is stumbling from his bed. He, a recognized master of zhǔ (主), the ancient form of calligraphy, now sits holding a long-handled, ermine-bristle inking brush cradled into the curve of thumb and forefinger. His insomnia during these early morning hours, and the comforting, familiar feel of the brush-in-hand, takes the form of a burning resolve to frame an argument on paper, one his court scribes will later shape into a powerful warning to a presumptuous upstart. He labors at his drafting table with inking stone and brush until the sun's rays break over the top of the garden wall. By sunrise, the outline of a missive has taken shape, one conceived by the Sun God, Ruler of the Kingdom at the Center of the World—the Middle Kingdom, Zhōngguó (中国)— to be dispatched to a less worthy adversary, the 'barbarian' King George III, of England.

Hongli's firm stance against representatives from the Western world has helped to re-establish his power and authority in times of strife and faltering influence. Hongli was the first Qing monarch to be chosen through a secret system his father, the Yongzheng Emperor, Yìnzhēn, instated to prevent struggles over succession. And, like his father before him, strict rule means expanding and controlling borders, imposing order, and treating enemies with despotic efficiency. Under his own rule, the fifth in Qing dynastic succession since the sixteen-hundreds, many years of military expeditions and territorial conflicts have depleted the royal treasury, costing thousands of Chinese lives in the process. Hongli has managed to consolidate much of an unimaginably vast empire—including Outer Mongolia, Tibet, portions of Burma, Nepal, and even Viet Nam—far-reaching nation states—eventually subjugating, then demanding tribute to be sent to Beijing, the far-off seat of the Qing empire.

As years have turned to decades of rule, though, the aged Hongli has become disillusioned with power, relying heavily on He-shen, his highest-ranking, most favored minister. I watch in dismay as the day-to-day governance of the country is left in the hands of He-shen, while Hongli himself indulges in luxuries, and his favorite pastime, hunting. But, more recently, with increasing outside pressures being felt to trade with nations far beyond the boundaries of China, the absolute authority of the Qing dynasty—Hongli, in particular—was seen as weak and ineffectual. And, so with word that the English emissary to China is now in the country, intending to apply just that sort of international pressure to the Throne, Hongli senses opportunity, sending a eunuch in the early morning hours for He-shen, demanding his presence to devise a strategy.

The affairs of state in the Hall of Mental Cultivation are conducted in a modest low-ceilinged anteroom, a short walk from the residential wing. This dimly lit, heavily-paneled gathering space for official meetings possesses none of the elegance of the gilded, heavily-carved Dragon Throne Room in the Forbidden City. More a library and contemplative retreat than ostentatious showcase of Qianlong regal authority, Hongli's modest country retreat, and spaces such as this, are as far removed as possible from court politics, and the daily crush of responsibility in Beijing.

A highly polished black marble floor, scattered silk rugs and a row of thick-legged tables spread with scrolls waiting to be studied, fill one end of this long, narrow space. At the opposite end, on an elevated platform, a low-backed, rosewood chair is positioned, emblazoned with the image of a dragon, symbolic of the Qing dynasty. A red-silk, gold fringed seat cushion adorns this, the only chair in the room. Behind the modest throne, tall panels bearing images of cranes rising from tall grasses beside a stream, have been erected to frame the dais. Much of one side of the room lies in shadow. Diffuse morning light filters through rice paper shoji screens. It streams across the floor in wide yellow bands to the other side of this most private of chambers, a place where a dozen of the emperor's subjugates await his arrival.

At five feet-ten inches, Hongli projects an impressive figure for his eighty-two years. Known for his affability, he intends to communicate a different message this time—one that reflects his great concern for matters developing just beyond the gates of the city. So, for this particular meeting, he bedecks himself in conspicuous emblems of authority: a loose robe of imperial yellow silk, and a cap of black velvet topped off with a red ball. It is adorned with a peacock's feather, the peculiar distinction of Mandarins of the first class. He wears silk boots embroidered with gold, and a sash of blue girds his waist. He strides commandingly into the room, taking his seat in the high-back, teak and gold throne of his ancient ancestors. With that, every man drops to his knees, kowtowing (叩 *kou* 'knock,' 頭 *tou* 'head,') on the room's cold stone floor. In more formal or ceremonial settings, this reverential gesture would be repeated many times; but here, the emperor's staff is only expected to demonstrate their devotion with a single kowtow, before proceeding with the task that has brought them there.

"A new form of invader has arrived on our shores and strategies have to be discussed," Hongli proclaims.

He-shen is the first to rise but cannot speak until spoken to. After years together, he is referred to by the emperor as *Chih-chai*, his 'courtesy name.' As the court's long-standing Grand Secretary, his importance is belied by his physical appearance. Imposing in neither height nor build, his movements beneath layers of cobalt blue and red silk robes seem those of a doting old man. His small hands are nearly hidden beneath long, flowing sleeves, his thin lips frozen in a kind of semi-smile, making It difficult to imagine the extraordinary influence he wields in the Qianlong court, or his central role in addressing the gravity of this crisis.

"We have fended off attempts by foreign devils in years past...the Dutch, other English pretending to speak for their kings. Tell me, Chih-chai, of the barbarians' progress, this time," Hongli says. "Do they still intend to engage me?"

"Yes, Excellency," He-shen replies, "the delegation is even now in country, at the mouth of the Pei Ho, asking for permission to move inland. They departed England in the ninth month, last, with three vessels, two heavy with barbarians and their tribute, the third, a warship. Within days, the fools were inundated by gales and sought shelter in their very own land, just a few miles from where they had departed. The gun ship was lost, but the emissary mission was able to carry on. Now, six months later, after much misadventure, they are here, Excellency."

"I am told by our Portuguese court missionaries, who regularly travel south to Macao, that they want us to assign them an island!" Hongli says, incredulously. "Could that kind of insolence from the gray-eyed ones possibly be true?" With that, those gathered in the room can't help themselves, chortling quietly behind raised hands.

"Yes, Excellency," He-shen replies, "it is true," his modest smile growing into a broad grin.

Hongli listens in amazement. "They seek to persuade me of *what*, precisely?"

"In the future, they hope to anchor their English trading ships nearby, to be better able to bring us the playthings of their culture. They sense we are in desperate need." With that, He-shen points to the sunlit side of the room, and the bright row of multi-colored flowers in an adjoining garden.

"We remain grateful to the long-departed Dutch for their tulips, however." And with that, the men standing nearby can no longer restrain themselves, bursting into raucous laughter.

Hongli manages a short, mirthless snort, but quickly shifts the mood to one of concern. "We'll have to be on guard at all times. These barbarians are divisive, if nothing else. They'll try to impose themselves into our affairs, with diplomacy and spies. Our nation has long been a mystery to the West, a condition I have every intention of preserving."

"Diplomats and spies, surely," says He-shen. "But scientists and scholars, too, will be with the group. Their English ships are stocked with books on Chinese history, and tutors are helping to sharpen their wits and tongues on the journey with a Mandarin phrase or two. They hope to impress."

'Yes, yes," says Hongli, his voice now filled with frustration. "Guard our tea plants and mulberry bushes with your life while they're here. Some are very likely to find their way into British holds before they depart for home. The rack and a slow knife to any of our own who assist in their efforts."

"There is the matter on our meeting, Excellency," He-shen cautiously adds. "As they approach, we should select a location far from here at the summer residence, and terms of the meeting. The lead man, a nobleman named Macartney, wishes a direct meeting.

"If they regard my throne, I can indulge that, however briefly," Hongli says.

"But, Excellency, they have made it clear...*he* has made it very clear, he will not bow before you." With a tremulous voice He-shen lets the phase deliberately hang in the air momentarily, until the full impact of the British demand sinks in.

"We are pre-eminent in the world, our culture knows no equal. Many have come before this House from all corners of the world, paying tribute with gifts for the Throne. Why should they not?"

"They don't see it that way. England has grown powerful over many years, and see themselves as our equals," He-shen pleads.

"They have decades; we have centuries...no, tens-of-centuries to our credit, and all we need is already here for us. We are a nation fulfilled, replete with riches: silk, minerals, fair climate, farms and cities, beautiful women...culture...well-being." His voice trails off as he considers the consequences of such an audacious demand."

"I understand your concern and take your point, Excellency. They would argue they have their kings, as we have our emperors, and traditions for presenting themselves before their king that hold sway in both settings, as well. I would suggest I deal with that part of their demands as they draw nearer, and negotiate a compromise, if possible."

"Tell them I will not meet unless they're prepared to recognize our superiority to their culture, and let us also decide where to meet. My hunting lodge north of the Great Wall, in Chengde, is where I traditionally go this time of year. Let's plan a meeting there, on neutral ground. I don't want the barbarians anywhere near here, tainting the soil of our ancestral home."

And with that abrupt conclusion to the meeting, Hongli stands, directing Chih-chai and his assembly of scribes to move to the other end of the room. There, they turn their attention to the task that kept the emperor awake for most of the night. The men gather around the long table, preparing ink and paper to draft a response, as dictated by Hongli, himself. It is to be addressed, personally, to the English king, and presented to the British emissaries who were, even at that very moment, slowly working their way from the coast after a months'-long journey, hoping to soon find themselves in his imperial presence.

≈

THE FOLLOWING IS an account of the travels and actions of the barbarian intruders into the heart of the Celestial Empire by Lord Macartney and his mission, reported to Hongli by palace security forces, as told by subordinate, Zhengrui, assigned to monitor and record their movement.

Excellency: The Macartney mission reached Beijing by their calendar on 21 August 1793. They were escorted to a residence north of Beijing, near the Old Summer Palace. In the party are two skilled negotiators, the brothers Staunton, Thomas and George. They were not permitted to leave the premises for the duration of their stay. Wanting to be closer to our political center, Macartney received our official permission to move to a different residence in Beijing, which they had hoped would eventually house their embassy after the meeting with His Excellency. A small group of us will take responsibility for the future meeting, as we remain in regular contact with Macartney's men as they move throughout the region. The tribute brought by their mission is stored amongst other tribute items in the throne room at the Old Summer Palace. Macartney, the Englishman, expressed his delight and gratitude to be allowed the first English to visit. His men worked tirelessly, for days, assembling and arranging many gifts. The most important item, a small orrery, is so complex, it takes eighteen days to assemble.

Having left that planetary model and other gifts behind at the Old Summer Palace, about seventy members of the mission—among them forty of their soldiers—depart for Beijing on 2 September, heading north towards Jehol, where they hoped Your Excellency would be awaiting. The mission proceeded alongside a road reserved for you alone, stopping each night at one of the lodges prepared for your travel party's use along the way. Guard posts punctuated the route at roughly five mile intervals, and Macartney commented on the large number of troops working to repair the road in preparation for your return to Beijing later in the year. He is not aware that many of the 'workmen' along the way are actually our soldiers, prepared to go into prompt action if the English happen to forget their place as guests in our kingdom.

The English crossed our Great Wall at Gubeikou, where we greeted them with ceremonial gunfire and several companies of troops from the Eight Banners of the imperial military. We later learned that William Alexander, who remained in Beijing, expressed regret at not being able to see this spectacle for himself. Under Macartney's orders, we permitted Lieutenant Joshua William Parish of the Royal Artillery to survey the Wall's fortifications with his men. It was a transparent intelligence-gathering effort on the part of their mission. But, just as in the classic dance of sworn enemies, the mongoose and cobra, we managed to assess their capabilities and weaknesses, just as they measured ours.

They must think us very naive, Excellency. Some of their men, meanwhile, took bricks from the Wall as souvenirs, an appalling gesture of disrespect. As you know, past the Great Wall the terrain becomes more mountainous and difficult for their men's horses to traverse, slowing their progress. The Macartney entourage finally arrived at the outskirts of Chengde on 8 September 1793. At that time, I was delegated—as the 'son of a diplomat'— to go to the Englishman, Staunton George, and explain through a linguist the terms and conditions under which we will meet *their* delegation. I nervously agree, but will be unable to speak with their leader, Macartney, who determined such planning to be below his station as leader.

"Please to be advised," I say, "that His Excellency, Qianlong Emperor, will be journeying to his country hunting lodge in Chengde in the next few days. This is his ritual tradition each year on the date of his birth. He generously consents to meet you there."

Perhaps having heard of potential conflict on this matter, Staunton George coolly replies: "Our delegation is here as the official representative of our king, and we hope to meet as equals. And I do not expect to be negotiating such matters of gravity with a mere *boy*."

"You would be advised to accept my good faith effort," I reply with mock impertinence, "to find common ground and 'accept all ceremonials of the Court which may not commit the honor of your Sovereign or lessen your own dignity,' and not to let any 'trifling punctilio' get in the way of your mission."

"It is those very trifles that will help to dictate the nature of our meeting," he replies.

"The emperor has met other dignitaries in this way and in this place," I patiently explain. "He has consented to do so in years past for the visits of Amursana and the Sixth Panchen Lama, and will do so again, for you, a no-less distinguished guest."

"There is the matter of the kowtow, though," Staunton George counters. "Neither the king of our great land, nor do his representatives of the most powerful nation on earth, supplicate themselves before any foreign leader, let alone prostrating ourselves on a stone floor and knocking our heads nine times, or whatever foolishness he might be used to."

"But the practice is time-honored," I explain patiently, "and shows respect and admiration for the throne and all that symbolizes the Sons of Heaven, without equal. The kowtow is necessary when meeting your emperor, but also when receiving imperial edicts from his messengers. You should be showing *me* the same respect at this very moment."

"Let me be clear, he is not *my* emperor, he is yours," Staunton George says, his voice growing more shrill. "We have gifts we wish to present to him, on behalf of our king and our nation..."

"From our perspective, these are not 'gifts,' but tribute to His Excellency. Your Englishman, Macartney, is viewed merely as a 'conveyor' of tribute, not a 'legate of the sovereign,' as he has repeatedly described himself. Qianlong has experienced much annoyance in this repeated designation. When he is to hear of this refusal, he will grow increasingly impatient, and consider canceling the meeting altogether."

"The Portuguese and Dutch merchants in *Kwang-tung*—what they have named Can-*ton*—might have acquiesced to these vulgar rituals, but we regard them as slavish and humiliating; and we will always choose to leave the room when such practices are being carried out by them."

I caution the English mission that their Macartney, "would be regarded a boor and a laughingstock if he does not perform the ritual of kowtow when the time comes.

"For our delegation, then, this is a real sticking point. We consider the status of the two sovereigns—George III and the Qianlong emperor, Hongli—to be equal in station and influence, and cannot concede the request."

"In the face of your refusal, then, I am sorry to say the meeting cannot occur. It is a shame you have come all this way..."

It seems we are at an impasse, frustration showing on our guests' faces, when another English steps forward and signals Staunton George to join him outside the room. They are gone for some time, only returning when our tolerance is almost gone.

Staunton George takes a deep breath and speaks, new-found patience in his voice: "Now, Zhengrui, I ask you to agree that Lord Macartney cannot perform a single prostration, let alone the nine typically called for. This action runs contrary to our culture, in the same way you might not expect your emperor to venture beyond the walls of the palace to parade himself openly before his subjects. We accept that it is just not done here."

"Can we agree that our legate, Lord Macartney, will genuflect before the emperor as he would before his own sovereign, touching one knee to the ground," offers another Englishman. "This is a sign of respect, in much the same way it would be in our nation, and a concession to the position the emperor occupies in yours?"

A long period of silence follows, while I and my associates cast our eyes, first at one another, then the floor. "I must consider this, I reply tentatively, "and discuss it with His Excellency."

Reading promise into our delay, Staunton George then eagerly adds, "We would hope that the emperor, or any Chinese official of equal rank, were they ever to be in the presence of an image of our sovereign, would be expected to do the same before a portrait of our George III."

My anger flares once again, Excellency, as I quickly reply to the English, "I will bring your first proposal to my emperor, but not the second. With all your foolish idolatry and pomp, you are expecting too much, then." And with that I stand, and the meeting quickly adjourns.

THE MUCH-ANTICIPATED MEETING with my emperor, Hongli, finally takes place twelve days later, by their counting on 14 September 1793. The British had set off from their residence at the Hour of the Ox, in darkness, arriving at the imperial encampment, in the pre-dawn hour of the clumsy, hot-tempered Tiger. The ceremony is held in the imperial tent, a large yellow, domed yurt, with the emperor's throne in the center of a raised platform. Hongli and his royal party arrive at the auspicious hour of the Dragon, beneath a slanting sun, to preside as khan over the proceedings. He is borne high on a plinth by a dozen men, along with countless priests, courtiers, armsmen, attendants, standard-bearers, and household staff—all clad identically in blue and yellow robes. Several dozen attendees stand expectantly at the entrance to the yurt, including Lord Macartney, his mission staff, various foreign visitors, the viceroy, and the emperor's very own first-born, Yongyan, Prince Jai of the First Rank—the future Son of Heaven. The aged Hongli wishes him present, as his eventual successor to the throne, signifying the young prince will be playing a key role in the future of China trade relations with the West.

After much positioning and maneuvering, Macartney is beckoned to enter the tent along with the main British delegation, and their Chinese interpreter. The others, an entourage of more than one hundred, wait outside. Lord Macartney steps up to the platform first, lowering his knee once, before stepping forward to exchange ceremonial gifts with Hongli. He then presents the emperor with a letter from King George III, petitioning him to allow the establishment of a mission in China, the assignment of a permanent port to be used by the English for trade and repairs, and the beginning of active commerce between the two nations. He is followed by delegates, brothers George and Thomas Staunton. As Thomas had studied the Chinese language, the emperor beckons him to speak a few words. The British are followed by other envoys, about whom little needs to be written for this report. An elegant banquet is then held to conclude the day's events. The British are seated to the emperor's left, an honorific position in Chinese culture and one I can only hope they appreciate.

In some respects, the meeting is a success, in that both the imperial court and the British sought compromise to allow the event to occur. As we return to the Summer Palace, Hongli leans to me to say, "Zhengrui, you honored your emperor by keeping the hungry barbarians at bay. They will leave with a full stomach, but empty handed. They will return home believing they have scored a victory. The document they carry with them will explain our boundaries clearly. We have no need for their inventions, or their goods. But, we cannot trust going forward. Do you understand?"

"If I may, Excellency, the English are fools to have traveled so far to demand so much from us. The most dangerous part, though, is that they are unaware of this, believing they depart as victors in their quest."

"Zhengrui, we must not let them out of our sight. Once they have safely departed in their ships, waste no time traveling to Canton, where they will most certainly stop. You will meet with its governor-general. We will need to establish precautions to account for their every move. Their world view differs greatly from ours. They wish to fill any void where they believe one to be found. Their insistence in our acceptance of their material objects is no less dangerous than the imposition of their missionaries' orthodoxy. Unless they are contained, they will conspire with the Portuguese and perhaps even the Americans, and others, like the Dutch, to gain influence. Caution them against doing so in order to avoid further trouble. Also, include Secretary He-shen and my son, Jai, in your planning. I wish them both to understand what is at issue here."

"I understand my mission, Excellency. And the document you have prepared?"

"When they are safely aboard in Pei Ho, and about to depart on the tide, present them with the document we have prepared, explaining my reasons in greater depth, and direct them to deliver it without delay to their king, George."

I do as my emperor directs, and include excerpts of the document here, as placed in the hands of Lord Macartney and Staunton George:

You, O King, live beyond the confines of many seas, nevertheless, impelled by your humble desire to partake of the benefits of our civilization, you have dispatched a mission respectfully bearing your memorial. Your Envoy has crossed the seas and paid his respects at my Court on the anniversary of my birthday. To show your devotion, you have also sent offerings of your country's produce.

I have shown your agents high favor and have allowed them to be introduced into my presence. To manifest my indulgence, I have entertained them with a banquet and given them numerous gifts. I have also caused presents to be forwarded to the Naval Commander and six hundred of his officers and men, although they did not come to Peking, so that they too may share in my all-embracing kindness.

As to your entreaty to send one of your nationals to be accredited to my Celestial Court and to be in control of your country's trade with China, this request is contrary to all usage of my dynasty and cannot possibly be entertained.

Your proposed Envoy to my Court could not be placed in a position similar to that of European missionaries in Beijing, who are forbidden to leave China, nor could he, on the other hand, be allowed the liberty of movement and the privilege of corresponding with his own country; so that you would gain nothing by his residence in our midst....

I have but one aim in view, namely, to maintain a perfect governance and to fulfill the duties of the State. Strange and costly objects do not interest me. As your Ambassador can see for himself, we possess all things. I set no value on objects strange or ingenious, and have no use for your country's manufactures.

I have expounded my wishes in detail and have commanded your tribute Envoys to leave in peace on their homeward journey. It behooves you, O King, to respect my sentiments

Do you reverently receive them and take note of my tender goodwill towards you! A special mandate.

.. Should your vessels touch the shore, your merchants will assuredly never be permitted to land or to reside there, but will be subject to instant expulsion. In that event your barbarian merchants will have had a long journey for nothing. Do not say that you were not duly warned.

2. Aftermath

This, according to Legate Zhengrui, loyal Qianlong servant and witness to events in the years following British decampment from the Celestial Kingdom:

FOLLOWING THE ENGLISH delegation's departure, Hongli calls for a meeting of He-shen, Prince Jai, and his other trusted advisors.

Hongli is pacing angrily when his court arrives. "How *dare* these barbarian call for the opening of trade. And they want a small unfortified island near Chusan as a residence for their traders, storage and outfitting of ships! I sent them packing with my thoughts on a permanent British embassy in Beijing. *Hah!* Their George should tremble, obey and show no negligence, if he's as clever as they say. Subjugation...yes, subjugation, like the rest who travel great distances for my counsel."

"But, we learned much about their capabilities, Excellency," He-shen says.

"And they of ours. Did you see how they observed, making notes and renderings in their journals. They'll be back, Chih-chai, I can assure you, British will not take no for an answer."

"But, tell His Excellency that his communique is strong, decisive, his limits clear," someone in the gathering offered to He-shen, never presuming to speak directly to the emperor.

"We never should have allowed the foreign devils to lay claim to any part of our shore. This was my ancestors' doing, and I am dealing with the consequences. We have our own trouble, controlling our borders to the west and south—the Mongol Zunghars, Russian Kazakhs, the Jinchuan Tibetans—all sapping our military strength, our purse, to say nothing of our morale."

"They have been controlled, Excellency," He-shen says, lowering his eyes to the floor, his voice now more pleading than assured.

"Sixty years on the throne, now. I am tired, very tired. I commanded you to manage this English problem, Chih-chai." Hongli's eyes are bulging now, his face scarlet with anger and frustration, as he repeatedly points at He-shen.

"Be assured, Excellency, I will take steps," He-shen demurs, ever the supplicant in the presence of his emperor. "Our flank remains weakest at Macao and Canton; but our influence in the surrounding provincial region is great, the river heavily fortified. We will take steps to limit their presence there. And know, that at such a great distance, Beijing will remain safely remote to the dangers posed by these foreign devils."

≈

IN THE YEARS following those events, I witness many changes behind the fortress walls of Beijing's Forbidden City. And when the history of the Qing Dynasty is written, it will reveal the story of Qianlong Emperor, Hongli, Fifth in Succession to the Qing Dynasty, greatly weakened by his advisor, He-shen—the very person he had most counted on.

Also, it must be told that two years following his fateful meeting with the British delegation, the emperor grants one final meeting with Western representatives, a delegation from the Dutch East India Company. Unlike Macartney and his minions, the Dutch, who traveled in 1795 to celebrate the sixtieth anniversary of Hongli's rule, agree to kowtow before His Excellency. As a result, they are much feted by the Chinese for their apparent compliance with conventional court etiquette. This diplomatic overture plays to the emperor's vanity and Chinese world view, going a long way toward winning the Dutch representatives the favor they hope for in trading relations. Yet, history may reveal that it serves only to further weaken the Qing Dynasty's authority and control over its vast empire.

At the same time, Hongli makes the decision to relinquish the power of his throne to his only surviving son, Jai, the following year—that of the auspicious 'Dragon' pictured on the Qing imperial banner. Because of his advanced age, he had long exhausted his interest in governance, pledging at the beginning of his rule not to serve longer than the sixty-one years of his grandfather, the Kangxi Emperor. So, the Qianlong Emperor relinquished the throne at age 85 to the 36-year-old, Jiaqing Emperor. Jai functions as regency emperor for three additional years, until his father's death in 1799.

≈

THIS CHAPTER IN our nation's history would not be complete however, without inclusion of the saga of 'trusted' palace advisor and confidant to the Qianlong Emperor, He-shen. It must be said that Hongli devoted most of his life and long rule attempting to live up to his grandfather's reputation as despotic and ambitious. Hongli's military adventurism and rebellions at the farthest reaches of the kingdom, aggressive construction of residences and gardens for his personal use, and embezzlement and corruption within his ranks, depleted a national treasury estimated at seventy-five million taels at its peak in 1775, far surpassing those of any predecessors. Eventually it became impossible to reverse the dismantling of every level of government, along with increasing foreign pressure and internal unrest.

In the same year as the emperor's death, it is revealed that He-shen's self-serving motives were setting a precedent that would continue to weaken and corrupt future Qing dynasties for decades. Only after his father's death, is Jaiqing able to act. In the second month of 1799, He-shen is arrested. He is declared guilty by an imperial edict and condemned to death by slow slicing, lingchi (凌遲), also known as 'death by a thousand cuts.' In this form of execution, a knife is used to methodically remove parts of the body over a period, eventually resulting in death. Our emperor spares He-shen this horrible death out of respect for his half-sister Gurun, Princess Hexiao, and instead orders him to commit suicide, zishā (自杀), by hanging himself with a rope of golden silk in his home. This spares his family disgrace. At the time of his death, it is determined that the emperor's long-time, valued advisor had amassed a fortune. The combined value of his land, estates, gold, silver, jade and other holdings far exceeded the total treasury deposits of our nation at that time.

3. Opium Eaters & Sorcerers

IN COMPARISON TO his father's extensive sixty-one-year reign on the throne, seventh emperor of the Manchu-Qing dynasty, Jai-qing Emperor, the so-called Yongyan, reigned only briefly—just twenty years—reflecting a growing loss-of-control over the Chinese people by the Qing dynasty. He has not care for himself in the way his father had, becoming quite obese. This would have the effect of shortening his life; but that was yet to be. Early in his reign, and in the wake of the He-shen scandal, Jai searches for a man he can trust as his chief consul. As my destiny, *mìngyùn* (命运)would have it, I am selected and promoted to Senior Consul, a powerful role where I hope to serve my emperor to the best of my ability. But I soon discover that Yongyan's desire to outshine his father falls prey to events—some of his own creation, some well beyond his ability to control.

During his reign, Jai-qing faces internal disorder, with the large-scale White Lotus and Miao rebellions, as well as an empty imperial treasury. Jai spends much time and treasure engaged in the pacification of the empire and the quelling of rebellions, even as he endeavors to return China to a level of prosperity and power known to his ancestors. But, a far-greater threat arrives on our shores from distant nations. The scourge of opium, *yāpiàn* (鸦片) proves impossible to control for many reasons: its appeal to the common man, who find its powers irresistible; to the mid-level autocrat, drawn in by the seduction of sudden riches; to the foreign devils who continue to push larger and larger quantities of the foul substance into our cities and villages over the objection of my emperor. All of these forces prove too much to bear. Thousands of tael of silver are drained from our nation as payment for the yāpiàn smuggled from Turkey and British-controlled India during these years. And, as Western nations grow richer, the Chinese culture and economy steadily decline.

Efforts by officials to curb opium imports through regulation of consumption only results in increased drug smuggling by European and Chinese traders, as corruption runs rampant. In 1810 as frustrations grows, Jai issues an edict concerning the opium crisis, declaring:

> *Yāpiàn has a harm. Yāpiàn is a poison, undermining our good customs and morality. Its use is prohibited by law. Now the commoner, Yang, dares to bring it into the Forbidden City. Indeed, he flouts the law! However, recently the purchasers, eaters, and consumers of opium have become numerous. Deceitful merchants buy and sell it to gain profit.*
>
> *The customs house at the Ch'ung-wen Gate was originally set up to supervise the collection of imports (it had no responsibility with regard to opium smuggling). If we confine our search for opium to the seaports, we fear the search will not be sufficiently thorough. We should also order the general commandant of the police and police-censors at the five gates to prohibit opium and to search for it at all gates. If they capture any violators, they should immediately punish them and should destroy the opium at once.*
>
> *As to Kwang-tung [Canton] and Fukien [Fujian], the provinces from which yāpiàn*

comes, we order their viceroys, governors, and superintendents of maritime customs conduct a thorough search for opium and cut off its supply. They should in no ways consider this order a dead letter and allow opium to be smuggled out!

Another threat to the Qing Dynasty comes in the form of Christian missionaries. They had, of course, been living and working in Macao for more than a century at the time of my emperor's reign. Jesuits of the Catholic faith had even been allowed to live and teach in the heart of our nation, Beijing. But, their actions and movements are strictly controlled to exclude any contact with Chinese. But, with the arrival and increased influence of Western nations in the Pearl River region, great numbers of 'religious' from other branches of the faithful are increasingly proselytizing in Canton, Hong King, Fukien, Shuntak, and more far-flung locations.

In 1811, Jai institutes The Great Qing Legal Code, with one statute titled 'Prohibitions Concerning Sorcerers and Sorceresses,' with specific reference to Christianity. His edict cites cautionary language first drafted by his father, Hongli:

"Ever since the beginning of history, sage Emperors and other wise rulers have bestowed on China a moral system and inculcated a code, which from time immemorial has been religiously observed by the myriads of my subjects. There has been no desiring after heterodox doctrines."

Jai's edict goes much farther in terms of its restrictions, threatening to sentence Europeans to death for spreading Catholicism among Han Chinese and Manchus. Christians who do not repent their conversion are sent to Muslim cities in Xinjiang, to be given as slaves to Muslim leaders and military commanders.

But all of this is to little-or-no avail, as the influx of *yāpiàn* and missionaries continue unabated, inundating the shores of the Celestial Kingdom. While residing at the summer palace, the mountain resort in Chengde, I am at bedside, to witness Jai's death in 1820. History records his death clouded in mystery and uncertainty. I can attest to the fact, though, that a lifetime of poor habits, ill health in later years and an overall resignation to his own failure to secure and protect his People from the ravages of changing times, all contributing to his early demise. At sixty years, he was not only an old man before his years—but a *defeated* old man—who wished to finally join his ancestors.

His successor, Daoguang Emperor Minning, is now the eighth Emperor of the Qing dynasty. As elder statesman, now, I will continue to serve, elevated to the role of Grand Secretary at the side of my beloved emperor. He will rule for thirty years, his reign marked by additional external disaster and internal rebellion, as I shall later explain.

≈

WITH THE PASSAGE of time, it is only in the reign of Minning that I learn of Lord Macartney's earlier impressions of His Excellency, Hongli. It was revealed in his published accounting, which has been widely disseminated to the amusement of many around Macao and the Western factories in Canton:

"The Empire of China is an old, crazy, first-rate Man of War, which a fortunate succession of able and vigilant officers have contrived to keep afloat for these hundred and fifty years past, and to overawe their neighbours merely by her bulk and appearance. But whenever an insufficient man happens to have the command on deck, adieu to the

discipline and safety of the ship. She may, perhaps, not sink outright; she may drift some time as a wreck and will then be dashed to pieces on the shore; but she can never be rebuilt on the old bottom."

In that same year, 1820, at the request of the imperial palace regarding unusual shipping activity in the Pearl River, far south of Beijing, reports are received of a new American vessel, *Fame*, clearing Macao Roads under the command of Captain Joshua Rathbun. After years of inactivity on the part of the Americans, this raises concerns. On board are a cargo of cotton goods and miscellaneous raw materials for trade, and a young Connecticut man hoping to make a name for himself as an agent in the China trade, Mister Samuel Russell.

BOOK II
BEND IN THE RIVER

4. July, 1801, Death Comes Home

PA DIED THIS WEEK. He was six-and-thirty, and I, just twelve. He passed at night, in bed, without a whimper to alert Ma that something might be wrong. Doc said it was likely his heart, yet he was a powerful man right up to the end. That day, Ma woke early to set the kitchen fire goin', carefully slipping out from under the blankets, so's not to disturb him. When some time passed and the sunlight was starting to slant, pale and cool, through the kitchen window, she went back up to wake him. She found him, cold as ice, still lying on his side as he always did, one big, curled hand protruding out from under the covers. Ma's clipped, high-pitched cry at that moment had me running to the room to see the matter. She was shaking him and pleading for Pa to wake up, but I could tell she knew the fact of it and was pleading with God, I guess, to bring him back to us.

We waked him in the front room of the house, and lots of good folks came to pay respects. They told me, now than John Russell was gone, I'm the man of the house, and at twelve, how did I know any better? We buried him on the hill in the Vine Street Cemetery near town. The sun streamed down bright on that summer day, slanting in hazy bands from between some fat clouds, like heaven was coming right there to carry him up. They lowered the pine box into the ground with a prayer or two and then it was over.

We live on a spare acre-and-a-half not far from town, not land enough to farm... too much to let go t'seed. Now the oldest of the brood, I would have to go to work to support Ma, sister Lucy and baby brother, Edward. 'Your father, Johnny, he was a good man,' they told me when I started going into town in the following days, looking to run errands...what have you. 'He cared about folks and was patient with everybody...'a good Christian man,' they said, and how, 'he barely had time enough to live his life.' My memory will be of a big, tall bear-of-a-man, who looked taller somehow when he was all decked out in his ship captain's getup. Nothing fancy, mind you, just a dark coat with brass buttons and tan breeches, high black boots and a tricorn' left over from the old days. He captained 'tween here in Middletown and the Indies, carrying lumber and cheese, soap and potatoes to the big ol' estates down there. Sometimes horses, mules and other animals, too; but he didn't much care for them horses, since some died on route and had to be thrown over the side.

What he saw down there, on those plantations, shocked and saddened him. He spoke of it often. We've never been a slave-owning family, in recent years though lots in town have been. Some still hold onto that which they believe is theirs, resigned to freeing the Negroes only when they're good and ready. State law now says folks here can't buy or sell Africans. Those that were here in '92, must be set free when they reach majority, which is still some years off for many; particularly those born when their parents were property of fancy families, right here in Middletown—lawyers, doctors, preachers, big farms, mostly—they kept 'em on.

The Russell clan has never been in favor of slavery, an 'abomination,' Pa called it. He would speak up when he was home from the Indies, trying to let people know how shocking it was to see hundreds a' Negro men, women and children laboring under the hot tropic sun, no water, food, comforts. The abolition movement has gained ground around here, with more-n-more important people speakin' out against 'forced servitude,' as they politely call it. Pa was always at those meetings, though many others couldn't speak their mind, at the risk of losing some of their business with slavers, here in town. Times're changin' now, but slowly, though.

But it hadn't always been this way.

5. Rescue

PA TOLD ME that one day, back in '88—soon after he was married—about a well-out-fitted sloop that tied up at the Middletown docks one hot summer day. It was rumored to be out of New York City. A wealthy merchant here in town had gotten a contract for dried fish, onions, and lumber, very much in demand in those places down in the islands. The vessel arrived dockside—towed the last hundred yards by two teams of oarsmen in heavy skiffs—to take on that consignment. But first, it had to discharge its current load. The word had passed as to what to expect and feelings in town were running high, like I said. Pa and his brother Jacob went to the docks and were stunned by what they witnessed there.

On that particular day in July, Pa asked Seth, our long-time farmhand, to take him and Uncle Jake by way of town to see for themselves the event rumored to be taking place that very afternoon—the arrival of the slaver, *Speedwell*, at the docks.

"If your father're alive today, he'd nevah be lettin' you do this, Johnny," Seth said as they came in sight of town.

"Its alright to be looking around, I'd guess. No harm in standing with the rest of the gawkers, is there?"

"Still, an' all. This is dangerous times and no knowin'. They'd as soon break out and riot. You'd be in the middle of it all. Nowhere to go but into the river. No day fer a swim, I'd say," Seth argued.

"Father'd let me come to town to trade with him all the time," my father argued. "Negroes always about. Never no harm."

As the wagon came down the long rise leading into town, Seth cautioned them: "It's different this time Johnny. There'll be some upset folks, them's against all this slavin'. Politics, religion, all mixed up nowadays. You can get out now, but be back right here for me by three sharp, got me?"

They agreed and leapt off the back gate of our hay wagon as soon as it turned the corner of the old Meriden Road, south onto Main. As it pulled away, Pa said he heard a snap of the reins and Seth's sharp "giddy-up, he-*ah*!" Whether intended as a last word to the men to take care, or just to spur on the team, the two men couldn't be sure.

The course gravel of the wide downtown thoroughfare was hot from the scorching sun, searing the skin on the backs of their necks as they walked down Main. Rumors were floating about that slavery was to be outlawed in the state and curiosity seekers weren't about to let the blistering heat stop them from what might be the last specta-cle of a long, inhumane part of town history. They hustled to where a narrow band of shade would offer some relief, working their way toward the river front, to the docks where they'd transacted business so many times before.

My family had traded on the docks for many years, sending New England pro-duce and manufactured goods to under the "Russell, Co." label by way of packets and sloops to parts south and to Europe for years. The Russell name was splashed on boxes and sacks stacked all over the waterfront, familiar to most who did business here.

Middletown ranked right up there with New York, Newport and Boston as a good place to do business, away from the sea by a mere two-score miles, and an easy reach to cities and towns around the region. My pa had come here since he could remember, loading and unloading the wagons with *his* pa for a few pennies, and generally making himself useful, while learning something about the world of trade tied to the Russell name.

In their haste to get to the river, they took a shortcut through the back yard of wealthy merchant and ship-owner, Richard Alsop. The cool grass in his groomed, backyard gardens was a temporary respite for their burning feet. They moved so quickly through the deeply-shaded space that Mrs. Alsop—or some well-dressed woman gathering flowers there—glanced up, sensing movement out of the corner of her eye. "*Hallo*, someone there?" she asked of no one in particular, her voice shrill and tremulous. But, just as quickly as they both had trespassed, they was gone, the telltale *click* of the rear gate latch the only evidence of an incursion.

That clever diversion soon brought them to Parsonage Street, the side road leading down to the river, and the nearby docks. The masts of *Speedwell* were now visible a mile south, at the river bend. She had been waiting down river, at anchor for hours, for the crucial few moments when the tide was slack. Now, sails had been doused, except for a single triangular, aft-most spanker to allow the captain steerage at the great wheel. The massive packet, its three masts towering over trees lining the riverbank, was being guided by a team of oarsmen in a pair of heavy lapstrake whalers—so-called pilot boats—cordoned to the ship's bow by a series of thick lines. The rowboats and their eight-man crew, their backs straining under the effort, were slowly towing the *Speedwell* through the narrow river channel toward town, where the massive vessel would then be secured at dockside.

Then a scramble at water's edge, as men moved in frantic patterns along the length of the dock, readying lines to cast to the approaching packet. Barrels and bales had been rolled and stacked in out-of-the-way locations, making way for the important cargo about to be off-loaded from *Speedwell* dark hold. The gangway was blocked, tackled, and swung from its usual resting place in the tall grass nearby, to be positioned on board the vessel once she was lined in. Pa and Jacob studied this frenzied energy, until their eyes alighted on a single, stocky figure, standing pensive and unmoving, amid the dockside activity swirling around him. He had materialized, virtually unnoticed, from his house on Main Street—perhaps by carriage—but, judging from his labored breathing, he must have walked the short distance in the oppressive heat, to personally assess the cargo as it came ashore.

Slave dealer and Middletown scion, Dr. Thomas Walker gazed fixedly on the approaching vessel, to the exclusion of all else. Silent and unmoving, his stern face seemed cast in permanent shadow beneath his wide-brimmed hat. Standing barely five feet, four inches, with thick legs heavy as tree trunks, corpulence and a life of excess defined his overall appearance. Generous folds of skin spilled over his tight, high collar, glistening with sweat in the July sun. His bloated hands protruded from beneath the cuffs of his waistcoat, pale and smooth from idleness; his neatly manicured fingers, like fat sausages, tightly clutching the gold tip of a walking stick in the one, a bound ledger held high against his barrel-like gut, in the other. As he continued to stare down river, this slave dealer's round face and deep-set eyes registered no apparent emotion; the florid tones of his skin displaying the chronic effects of a rich diet, and too much in the way of wealth and privilege from his tradecraft: a commerce in human beings.

Within moments of the *Speedwell* coming to rest at the dock, the gangway was lowered into place. Men moved with haste to secure lines and clear the way for Dr. Walker to step aboard. For anxious moments, he could be seen conversing with the captain and first mate, his ledger open. After moments of animated conversation, the ponderous grated midship hatch was lifted and moved aside, revealing a dark, featureless abyss below.

Two crew, pistols in hand and bandannas tied over their mouths and noses, descended into the darkness. Those standing nearby soon became aware of a horrifying stench drifting up from below decks, carried on the light summer breeze and settling on the docks like an imagined Satan's plague. It was the smell of death, mixed with all manner of human effluence, stale and rotting food and putrid, vomit-infused seawater. Before any sign of life could appear from these depths of hell, another blast of hot, fetid air spewed forth, descending on the assembled crowd, driving some to flee in horror; others' eyes to water, retching and attempting to cover their faces with jacket sleeves; more still to draw closer, their morbid curiosity and thirst for entertainment triggered by the expectation of a spectacle unparalleled in recent months.

After a long delay, the first of scores of black-skinned skeletal figures began emerging, one-after another in a seemingly endless procession, from the cavernous mid-ship hatch. Chained together and bound in hand shackles, each semi-naked figure bore only the faintest semblance to humankind. Some men, and all the women—a few gripping the hands of small children—attempted to cover themselves, preserving what modicum of modesty remained. Weighed down by their shackles, they slowly worked their way down the gangway to the docks. On men and women alike, skin the color of coal hung from emaciated frames. After weeks in near-complete darkness, tear-filled eyes were straining to adjust, as each stepped out into blinding sun. Silence prevailed among the crowd gathered nearby; although a few young men—mere boys, really—taunted and jeered the Black cargo, further adding to their misery and humiliation.

Dr. Walker stood nearby, visually inventorying his purchases, performing—one would guess—mental calculations about prices and profit with each emerging Black body. Pa could hear talk of the numbers of dead or dying—too many to ever know for certain—thrown overboard during the long passage across the Atlantic. For the moment, though, unfazed by the pervasive odor, Walker's motivation and primary concern was to see all of his surviving prized possessions safely transferred to the local jail until auction time, some days hence.

The frightened human assembly, numbering about sixty, was shoved and forced into a cluster, at the point where the road leads from the docks to the center of town, the courthouse and its basement gaol. The prurient mob, larger now, stood and stared in partial disbelief, speculating on how so disheveled a group of Negroes could ever be of productive value, with countless more already working in the fields and farms of Connecticut, and even farther north, in New Hampshire and Vermont. These Black men, weak and frightened, returned the stares, wondering what to make of this brash, hostile new world they'd suddenly been thrust into so unwillingly.

As the stream of African humanity emerging from the ship's hold slowed, Pa and Jake drew closer to the scene, appalled by the spectacle. Rage washed over them as they witnessed Negro boys about the age of their own children being cruelly shoved and corralled into a trembling dockside huddle. Next, the slow-moving, gravely ill and near-dead struggled into daylight from the darkened hold. They stumbled and blindly fell, only to be struck on their backs and heads by two of Walker's henchmen, as they struggled to regain their footing. Fear was etched in their eyes, grief, pain and loss evident in their stooped posture. A Negro boy soon emerged on deck, supporting an old man—perhaps his father, or other elder, as they both flailed to regain their bearings on deck.

Suddenly, Pa's body became electrified with energy. "Jake, you wait here. Don't *move* for anything or anyone. I'm not sure what I'll do, but I just can't stand and watch this horror. Keep an eye out for me, please."

Jake replied, shocked by Pa's sudden decision to put himself in harm's way, "You can't go in there. Seth'll be waiting for us and warned us..."

But, by then, Pa was out of earshot, on his way to the *Speedwell*. Without thinking but filled with indignation and a sudden sense of some ill-defined objective, Pa raced down the dock to the rope walk, where new coils were neatly tied off and stacked. As he had done countless times in the past, he heaved one large length over his shoulder, returning to the gangway. Without hesitating—as though on some urgent errand—he ascended the ramp to the deck of the *Speedwell*, the large bundle partially concealing his face.

"Where you goin', fella?" asked a disembodied voice. Turning slightly, he saw one of Walker's men looming nearby, cudgel in hand.

Without breaking stride, he replied, turning only slightly toward the man, "Coil a' line the quartermaster ordered, sir. Needs it below for repairs."

The man lunged toward him, in a failed attempt to grab his shirt sleeve. "Damn shit," he muttered. But, the man remained distracted by other, more immediate nearby events, as Pa quickened his pace, finding a set of stairs leading forward, deeper below deck. Walker's man, cursing below his breath, but otherwise preoccupied, quit the chase to return to his post.

Once his eyes had adjusted to the darkness, Pa found himself alone in the part of the boat that served as galley and mess quarters for the crew. His mind raced as he considered what Seth or Ma might say if she knew he was behaving so impulsively...even stupidly. He didn't even know, *himself*, what he was out to accomplish, now that he was below decks. Any crew he might encounter would consider him an unwelcome interloper, as he moved deeper into blackness bound to be laden with danger, even death. Still, he pressed on, hands shaking, gut twisted into a knot of fear and anticipation.

≈

INTENT ON INVESTIGATING this repugnant scene, he moved aft, through a low doorway into the crew's bunking area. There he found a lantern hanging from a gimbaled hook, still burning. 'That's lucky for me,' he mumbled, as he unhooked the light and held it high, edging his way further into the lower recesses of the vessel, finally encountering a barred door, the entrance, he suspected, to the cargo hold. Shadows swung wildly around him as he struggled to hold the lantern and simultaneously release the bar from across the door. It finally fell with a heavy thud. Pushing the door inward toward pitch blackness, he ducked through the opening, the dull glow of his dying lantern held out at arm's length.

As the cramped, low-ceilinged space materialized out of the dimness, he stared in disbelief at the scene. Light slanting in from the deck above quickly faded, too weak to permeate the thick atmosphere of this man-made hell. The stench was unbearable, forcing him to jam a hanker-chief against his nose and mouth. The heat of this hellish place was so great and the odor so repulsive that it seemed quite impossible to move farther into the confines; but the horror of imagining a dozen or more disheveled corpses, men, women, even children, lying shoulder-to-shoulder on crude wooden

racks was even more unnerving. Wooden bowls, shapeless rags and discarded man-
acles and fetters were scattered throughout the near-airless space. The only words
that came to mind were recalled from his schooling: *medieval dungeon*—a sight centu-
ries-removed from anything even remotely familiar to him.

Still, he edged deeper into the hold, a dream-like state of detachment arising from
the sensory shock of the scene and paucity of oxygen. He was struck most forcibly by
how any human being could survive here, let alone multitudes packed in and wedged
together so tightly, row upon row of shelves—barely three feet high—jammed
against the bulwarks. The temperature, he would guess, was more than one-hundred
degrees. It was impossible to imagine how the numbers that survived had managed to
do so, given these appalling conditions.

Looking for any sign of life, he peered into the narrow spaces, nothing more than
makeshift prison cells installed between decks, with men and boys apparently confined on one level, women and girls on another. Space was so confining that each captive would have been unable to turn to one side or the other, forced to live without
being able to sit upright for a rough ocean voyage of three weeks or more.

Pa's hands shook as the lantern finally went dark, Desperate now, he managed to
call out, "Hallo, *hallo*? Is anybody still here?"

Nothing. He cocked his head to one side, to better detect a response. Silence perme-
ated the blackness.

"If there's anybody alive, move, make some noise," he called out in a raspy whisper,
so as not to be detected by crew overhead. "Let me know *somehow* if you can hear me."

Heavy footfalls resonated on the deck above. Suddenly, the heavy oak hatch was
dropped back into place with a *thud*, and the faint shaft of light permeating the hold
disappeared. He stood frozen in place, listening expectantly. Fading threads of conversation meant that the men who commanded this effort were moving away from the
ship, and into town with their captives.

He was about to turn and leave, when, from the darkness, a weak voice called out,
"*Amul solo. Amul solo. Waaw, Waaw.* Please, yes, yes."

"Hallo! Yes, where are you?" Pa whispered into the darkness, shocked that anyone
could still be alive here.

"*Salaamaalekum, Salaamaalekum. Amul solo! Waaw. Amul solo!* Please, Yes. *Please!*"
came the reply.

He frantically followed the sound of the voice, stumbling through the darkness to
the remotest corner of the hold, head stooped, groping at whatever he could find in the
gloom to keep from slipping on the ooze he felt shifting under his boots. Cracking his
head on a beam, he leaned down farther into the blackness until barely upright. Hands
outstretched, making contact, at last, with what he hoped was just a warm leg.

Moving in closer to where he believed the figure's head might be, he asked, "Can you
walk?" not fully expecting an answer. He felt for chains around ankles or wrists. None!

"Please," the voice said again, in broken English. Perhaps sensing rescue, the
despondent figure raised a frail arm and dropped it on Pa's shoulder. It felt bone-thin,
nearly weightless. But the signal was clear: 'Save me, please.'

As Pa struggled to lift the limpid survivor from a shelf on which he lay, the person
groaned, struggling to find footing for the first time in weeks. Gripping him by his rib
cage for support, Pa's arm nearly encompassed the man's entire upper torso. "*Waaw,
Waaw, Amul solo*" he kept repeating, as if to 'say, yes, yes, please, let's go.'

He half-carried, half-dragged the frail fellow back across the confines of the hold, through the low door into the crew's quarters and back into the ship's mess, where he finally got a clearer view of the person he had extracted from the nightmarish hole. Judging from his bone structure, Pa was amazed to see that it was just a *boy*, perhaps fourteen or fifteen, but only slightly taller than some local boys half his age, and fragile as a bird.

Momentarily fatigued and dazed by the magnitude of what he had just done, Pa settled the boy onto one of the benches in the mess, to buy time and consider his next move. He knew he would have one chance—though a very slight one—to get this youth to safety, out of reach of the slavers and their sympathizers in town. Seth, he considered, was soon returning in the family wagon, to pick up Jake and him up for the trip back to the house. If he could just get the boy to the wagon, then home, they could all strategize about what to do next.

Pa stuck his head out from below deck, seeing that the docks were now largely deserted. Most had gathered to follow the grim parade of captives and Walker's army of henchmen to the town hall jail. A dozen yards up the pier, Jake had remained as instructed, half concealed behind a stack of burlap sacks and coils of rope, intently surveying the scene for any sign of his brother. Using a series of hand signals, Pa let him know what he needed next. Both men understood instinctively that they would have only a fleeting moment—a *single* chance—to accomplish their plan.

≈

MOMENTS LATER, BOTH men emerged on deck, a burlap sack with the *Russell* name imprinted on the side, slung over Pa's shoulder. They made their way down the gang plank slowly and, unchallenged, walked with deliberation north along the waterfront piers, then into the deep shadows of the rope walk roofline until they reached the Avenue of Buttonwood Trees, located only a short distance to Main, where Seth and the wagon, as agreed earlier, would soon draw up to meet them.

It would be another hour before Seth was due to arrive. Until then, they had to remain concealed with their 'parcel' behind the wood pile next to the Mortimer house, the rope merchant's place. Hopefully, they would go unnoticed. Pa gently lowered the boy to the ground and released the sack from around his head and shoulders. What the full light of day revealed was a shocking example of a human being. The boy's body was skeletal-like, his black skin drawn back around his mouth and cracked lips, white teeth protruding gruesomely, as in death. His globular eyes appeared dull and unfocused, hair an orange cast now, from malnutrition. Sores covered most of his upper torso, and his chest heaved, as if every breath were his last—a fragile wisp of humanity living on borrowed time. It occurred to the brothers that if this young man did not receive medical attention, he would soon be dead.

'Focus his attention, keep him engaged,' Jacob said. 'Don't let him die here, after all this," he pleaded. Pa attempted conversation. Gesturing to his own chest, he slowly mouthed, "My name is John. What is yours?" With that, he pointed to the boy partially revealed in the sack.

Silence.

"What...is...your name?" he repeated slowly, continuing to thump his chest and the phrase, *John, John...*

More silence. Gradually, the boy's blank stare shifted to focus on their dirt-smeared, sweaty faces. With extreme effort, he mumbled, "*Adama, Maa ngi tudd... Adama...Adama.*"

"Adama?" Pa repeated, delighted to have a response, "Adama here," he gestured toward the boy, "John, here," again tapping his own chest, while smiling broadly to show pleasure at the boy's response.

The would-be rescuers carefully peered over the wood pile, surveying the tree-lined street leading up to Main for any sign of Seth and the wagon. "God, will he *ever* get here," Jacob cursed under his breath. Speaking more to himself than his charge, and hoping to muster the needed courage, Pa explained, "Adam, I'm gonna get you out a' here. We're taking you to my house where we'll get you some *help*...some *food*," he said, gesturing to his mouth with the universal symbol for sustenance. "And then, maybe to safety." At the moment, he wasn't certain how he was going to accomplish all of this; but he clearly wasn't thinking long term, only minute-by-minute.

At the strike of three on a distant church tower, Pa gestured to Jake to stay low and quiet, as he sprinted for the daylight of Main Street hoping to spot Seth and the wagon waiting nearby. Sure enough, the sight Seth's arrival gave him a burst of confidence. Without a word, he hoisted himself onto the seat next to Seth and pointed the way down Buttonwood, and the nearby woodpile. "Just go, Seth! I'll explain along the way."

As he explained the situation on the way to their hiding spot, Seth's eyes grew larger and unblinking, as fear and amazement washed over his face. "Hell and damnation, Johnny, what have you gone and done? Three hours in town and all hell breaks loose." He 'Yee-awed" the team to pick up the pace, wanting, for sure, to be anywhere else other than in this spot at this moment. "Wait till your missus finds out about this. You just wait, Johnny."

Once at the foot of Buttonwood, Pa jumped down and went to locate Jacob and the boy. They were relieved hear that the wagon was nearby as they swept the boy up, concealed in his burlap disguise, and onto a bed of hay in the back of the wagon.

"Jërëjëf! Jërëjëf! Amul solo, Amul solo. Thank...thank, please...please," Adam kept whispering. "Shhh, Pa signaled, his finger to his lips. "Let's get out of here," he signaled. "Jacob, you ride up top. Take it slow, Seth. This guy is fragile."

"Let's go home."

≈

WHEN THE WAGON pulled into the yard and the family learned what Pa and Jake had done, they were thrown into a tizzy, unable to contain their disbelief. Abigail scolded him no end for the risk he and Jacob had taken. "Here I am, working my fingers to the bone, and you decide to bring this kind of trouble into the house. Johnny, I can't understand you, sometimes."

But, despite my future mother's misgivings and her anger at Pa, the fragile child was immediately taken in. He was carried into the side room off the kitchen, where a spare cot for the seasonal farm hand, or occasional traveler was put up for a night or two. Ma soon took charge, as was her nature. She had my grandma fetch water from the well and proceeded to offer small sips. "Not too much at once, it'll kill him," she cautioned. "Seth, go get Doc Miller. Tell him to hurry. He can be trusted with this." Hesitating momentarily, she then said, "Jake, you git goin', and summon Pastor Wilkins to come here right quick. We got to figure out how to git this boy to safety."

Without much ado, the Russell clan had always solidly stood with the free-men movement. Though always appalled by the scene in town when slavers arrived, we maintained our distance while going about our business in town. That kind of complicity was wrong, clearly wrong, but practical matters had to be the order of the day back then, if for no other reason than to make ends meet in a hostile, unforgiving time.

Looking back, I think Pa's actions to save this one child from almost certain death finally cracked open the pent-up frustration my kin was all feeling, but had no way to express. Ma, Pa's dearest "Abby," the rest of the family, Seth and the others, were secretly thrilled, I think, that they now had a chance to make a difference—to take action against this abomination called slavery. In other words, Pa didn't get sent to the woodshed for what he had done.

Five days later, after the news was passed along, some men from Simsbury, a half-day's travel out of Middletown, came to see the boy and talk about getting him to safety, somewhere north of here. The Pettibone Tavern, in Simsbury, Connecticut, was part of network of free-men sympathizers who secretly moved Negroes to safer parts of the country. "We're doin' it at some risk between some helpful folks, mostly at night," they explained.

After the men left, Ma explained to those in the household "We're sworn not to tell a soul for the next several weeks, but once Adam's stronger, emancipationists will be takin' him north to the Berkshire Hills of Massachusetts, maybe even Vermont or Canada, where he can live with some helpful folks, maybe do some farmin', and figure out what happens next. Havin' a black face *anywhere* now a-days means you can be kidnapped and sent south. There's bounties for that sort'a thing. Hunters on the lookout everywhere. A law gives 'em the right to grab any Negro they see walkin' free. But he'll have a chance out there, at least."

"Abby," Pa said later that night when they were alone, "that boat was a terrible place. I think I did right. Sorry to make such a mess a' things."

"You did right, took a stand," she replied, "good thing I weren't there, I'da had you by the wrist and dragged you home. You put Seth's neck on the line, too. Think about that next time you and your fool brother want to do something crazy like this."

"I hope Adam's gonna be fine," Pa said with a wry smile, undetectable in the darkness of the bedroom. "What's right is right."

After Seth's chores, he visited with Adam each day. He, along with Ma, taught him some rudimentary English, and, in return, Adam taught them a bit of Senegalese. In his *Wolof* tongue, Adam would point to Mrs. Sage come-a-visitin' with her new baby girl, back then still swaddled, and lying in the copper basin atop the kitchen table, "*rafet na*, beautiful," he would say. Then he held up a sequence of fingers to express, "*Adama fukk ak ñeent*," signifying fourteen. Ma read to him from a school primer and showed him a map of the world, pointing to the place where he came from, then tracing her finger across the flat blue ocean to this spot in America. She learned that his belief was Mohammadism, and that the Abraham of our Bible is the very same Abraham in his *Koran*. He explained how he was gathering firewood at the edge of his village when he was taken by kidnappers from a rival tribe, who brought him to the white men at the boat. Other people from his clan were taken too; and that he didn't know if his parents were dead or alive.

I'm certain Ma came to think of him as one of her own. "I'm going to miss that boy," she would say to Pa and the others, hiding a tear as she went about cooking or mending, or sat at the kitchen table sipping a cup of tea.

Once Adam was stronger, Seth took him out to the stables, but only after sunset, to groom the horses and feed the chickens. Everything amazed the boy: the arc of the Milky Way against a black velvet sky; or the bright oranges and reds of the foliage as fall settled on the New England landscape. He greeted each new thing with equal amounts of curiosity and joy. Adam taught Seth how to use a sling shot to knock a can off the rail fence at twenty paces, and how to contrive a drinking cup from a squash leaf.

As the weeks and months passed Adam gained strength. Ma's cookin' and Doc Miller's regular visits had their positive effect. At harvest time, when the air turned crisp, the men with kind faces came to take him away. Trepidation shone on his face, not for what was ahead, but for the loss of what he had come to know as his home. He, and our family finally parted with bountiful tears and many good wishes, knowing that his fate would be uncertain. "*Jàmm ak, jàmm ak*, Goodbye, Goodbye", he kept repeating, as the wagon grew distant on the long dirt road leading from the farm, the small black figure sitting in the back, surrounded by piles of boxes and carpets— meant to hide him, if need be. All strained to keep eye contact as the wheels of the departing buckboard kicked up more and more dust. Adam's flailing arms and broad grin was the last image to fade from view as he ventured out into the world.

My family later learned that Adam was apprehended by bounty men on the Vermont Road, near Brattleboro, and sold onto a rice plantation near Charleston, South Carolina. It was considered unlikely he would survive in those heat-soaked, disease-ridden fields, under the watchful eye and whip of a cruel task master. No word of his fate was ever received at our farm, but Adam almost certainly would have succumbed—one of many countless young Black lives—to the ill intentions of the few among us, motivated to possess others less fortunate in the name of profit.

≈

JUST ABOUT ONE year after that incident, on the twenty-fifth of August, 1789, I came into the world. With Pa gone to sea to the West Indies for months at a time, Ma's daily labor included another mouth to feed, and her new-found day-to-day cares for me meant that our extended family—and, eventually I—would have to share in household responsibilities. Memories of Adam and his time with us would soon faded but were never forgotten. As soon as I was old enough to appreciate what had transpired, Pa would regale me with the story of Adam's rescue, until I was able to recount in detail his exploits and the remarkable boy that Adam had become during his time with the Russell family.

The years inevitably passed, and the cusp of a new century would prove to be eventful for me: Pa died in what seems a lifetime ago; his heroics and the *Speedwell* slave ship boy had come and gone from our lives, as manhood and responsibility were suddenly thrust upon me. Because of my family's stories, my eyes had been opened to the senseless cruelty of slavery in the world; but also, to the genuine goodness found in some people. I was to discover an inner strength and focused determination I would come to rely on. Slavery came in many guises in those days. And little could I know that the scene unfolding in the Russell household years before, as Adam was taken from the bosom of our family simply because he was black, would impact my future wealth and actions in important ways. Greed and enslavement—of different, but no less insidious guises—were destined to ensnare me.

6. Aftermath

IT IS THE YEAR 1811. The mantle of winter falls mercilessly on the New England landscape. Thick shrouds of gray-blue snow drape the fields behind the house, weighing down branches groaning in protest with every blast of northwest wind. The hills rising above the town are crowned in gleaming caps of swirling white, their jagged granite cliffs and spare copses protruding like bones from torpid flesh. That morning, I had gone to the Middletown docks at the bend in the Connecticut River, which the Wangunk natives call *Mattabesset*, for 'the end of the carrying place.' At this abrupt elbow on the river's course, still some twenty-four miles north of where it spills into the Atlantic, a determined four-knot current temporarily slows at the bend, sweeping large branches and other debris down river from the hillsides of Hartford County and even as far north as Massachusetts' high country, against the near bank south of town. Still, life teems in my hometown, this 'carrying place,' where ships from every part of the world tie up at our waterfront piers.

Since the middle of the last century, Middletown has afforded cargo vessels a deep, safe harbor, far removed from the angry Atlantic, rivaling the largest northeast coastal cities of New York, Newport and Boston with our accumulated wealth, secure anchorage, and commercial influence. The riverfront docks and boat-building yards lay dormant now, in the face of winter's fury. Smaller vessels are hauled ashore on Chatham's opposite bank to avoid the crush, anticipating spring's inevitable ice flows. Larger sloops and schooners, their towering spars whistling in the harsh wind, are securely lashed to piers, immobilized like hapless insects encased in amber. The flat, wind-swept mantle of ice covering the Connecticut River cracks and booms under the effects of an anemic January sun, resounding like cannon shots through the town. I often glimpse a dark, relentless current flowing beneath this gale-washed scene, forcing tons of razor-sharp ice shards up-and-over the riverbanks in massive heaps of crystalline blue, building up as tall as a man. Spring thaw will inevitably sweep them away.

Before I bundle up for another short walk to town each day, I join with Ma and my sister Lucy and baby Edward for a short Bible reading, a recitation of poetry or an article from the local paper, along with my chores.

"You take care, Sammy, them streets aren't as quiet as they used to be."

A fading voice adds, "And bundle up, catch a death if you're not care..."

"I will," I call back over my shoulder, even as a harsh blast of light and cold takes hold of my senses. In my mind's eye I imagine a vista of Long Island Sound far to the south of here, a flat expanse of gold and blue, aglow under a low-riding winter sun. And maybe, in my mind's eye, I can even spy the high cliffs of Spain and Portugal tumbling down into an angry sea, disguised for now as a distant, low blanket of scudding clouds somewhere out over Long Island Sound.

While the docks are quieter on this January day, lots of business continues as usual. Undaunted by winter's deep freeze, goods are being taken by wagon to markets in Hartford, or for the day-long trek to New London, or even Newport, Rhode Island, where they're loaded onto open-water vessels. In recent years, the risk of hostilities with England over Atlantic merchant trade routes and western territorial disputes, means that our trade with the West Indies has become the focus of intense commercial activity. Always pragmatic, these long-established routes offer the least risk of impressment or naval confrontation for shippers, to say nothing of shorter round-trips, in addition to rapid profits.

Farmers converge from all directions bringing turnips, potatoes, and ropes of onions to the docks for transport to West Indian plantations, feeding slave and master, alike. Barrels of salted fish, beef and pork, hay, bricks, oats, cracked corn, rope, lumber, nails, and livestock are positioned on our busy docks, waiting to be on-loaded to barks and packets for southern passage. Vessels returning are laden with rum, sugar, molasses and tropical fruits for quick sale at dockside auctions, directly from the hold. Not so many years ago—and not just to Middletown, but throughout the Northeast—brigs belonging to prosperous, local ship owners returned with a cargo of slaves, acquired along that insidious 'Middle Passage' between Africa's west coast, White land holdings in the West Indies and the United States' East Coast.

I can't visit the waterfront on any day without thinking of Pa and Uncle Jacob's daring rescue of Adam, the time he spent with my family, healing and learning what Ma had to teach him about the Western world, his eventual capture by those bounty men and kidnappers, and his almost certain death in the rice fields of South Carolina. Those very lessons also taught *me* to keep my eyes wide open to the many dealings—both legitimate and illegitimate—undertaken by men living behind fashionable facades on *any* main street in New England, Middletown being no exception.

≈

IN THE YEARS since that incident in '88, as I've grown to manhood, I've busied myself with becoming indispensable to many of the powerful men living behind those same fancy doors on Main. As runner and delivery boy, I prove myself trustworthy and capable to handle cash bank deposits, transfers of legal documents and bills of sale to lawyers and other businesses, even bartering transactions with merchants, always to the favor of my employer. Even though I'm still young, I'm no 'gentleman of four outs,' as the expression goes. No '*wit, money, credit or manners*' certainly doesn't apply. No funds to speak of, but wit, credit and manners have all served me well in my many face-to-face interactions—on the docks and in the corridors of power.

This morning, I've been summoned for an early meeting in the richly paneled, heavily draped front room of the Joseph Alsop house, on the Old Meriden Road. As a partner with Chauncey Whittlesey and Samuel Wetmore (a cousin of my grandmother), their trading company has clients far-flung throughout the world. Now that I've reached majority age, I hope I might be of more value to them than merely stoking office fires, copying letters, collecting wharfage bills-of-lading, *et cetera*.

I ascend the steps to the wide porch leading up to the heavy front door. There, I reach up for the brass knocker cast as a clenched fist, rapping confidently three times. Soon, a faint commotion on the other side—then steps—and a young Negro girl answers.

"Mister Russell?" she asks, politely.

"Yes, here to see Captain Alsop. Would you kindly give him my calling card?"

"Come in, please," she says. Taking my coat and hat, she adds, "You can wait right here. The captain will be with you shortly."

I note that the young woman carries herself with more than the usual amount of deference, a particular halting style suggesting an underlying insecurity or sadness. As she departs, I also note she doesn't entirely turn her back to me, hinting at a degree of training or expectation for behavior in the presence of men, dating from another period—with its lingering culture of servitude.

Soon, Captain Alsop appears, slowly descending a long curved staircase from the second floor. A tall, impressive figure, his demeanor is that of a man of wealth and authority. His eyes are lively, but project a cool detachment. A faint aura of tobacco surrounds him, and a hint of Bay rum—a luxury toiletry item secured in the West Indies, I would guess—emanates from his freshly-groomed face.

After a bit of small talk about the winter's day, he invites me into the dining room, where we sit opposite each other for what seems an eternity, while that same young Negro woman appears, placing a cup of tea and sweet cake before each of us. She is delicate, with long black hair pulled back, secured neatly atop her head. Her sweet round face, the color of mocha, and deep green eyes, like ocean pools, suggest a mixed-race heritage. She carries her youthful figure, full, but athletic and graceful, with a particular melancholy noticeable in her halting mannerism. Without raising her downward gaze or uttering a word, she steps back, pausing momentarily. "That will be all, Ti," Alsop says coolly, turning his attention to deliberately study the girl as she departs the room. In that moment, it is as though I'm suddenly not present at the table. A chill runs down my spine as I consider this awkward scene.

I'm now aware that a fire crackles in the nearby hearth, freshly set with a log or two. Ornately framed portraits of Alsops, likely going back generations, line the walls. A tall clock in the corner, heavily embellished with cornices and filigree, patiently metes out endless seconds, then suddenly springs to life to chime twice, on the half hour. I'm aware that my gut is twisted in knots for what might happen next.

"Sam," Alsop finally says slowly, but without diverting his attention from the closed kitchen door, "you've got quite a name and reputation for yourself around town."

"Yes sir, I would hope it's a good one," I say laughingly, encouraged by the tone of what I'm hearing thus far.

"My partners and I would like to retain you as an apprentice at the store. Learn the trade from the inside. Participate in some of the deal-making. Get your feet on the ground as a trader, agent, broker, what have you," Alsop explains. "What part of the merchant trade do you think you might be interested in?"

"New England goods, I'd guess. Things I know well," I say, "cotton, nankeen, farm produce, horses, lumber...things from here in demand elsewhere."

"There're ships available to be filled here, goods traded elsewhere; then stocked with high profit items that fetch a pretty pound-or-two, once back here. Coast of Europe, Africa, parts south and east," Alsop says, an edge of excitement in his voice. "I've seen all the possibilities from the deck of my ships. There're fortunes to be made for our company, and for an ambitious young man like you, if you choose wisely."

Alsop abruptly stands and walks to the dining room window. From this high-ceilinged room, the massive window frames extend nearly to the floor. The view is of stately High Street, the roof peaks and spires of downtown, and the river, beyond. He suddenly bellows, "Ti, in here!" With that, the same young woman quickly appears from behind the kitchen door. She stands, motionless, head bowed, a few feet from Alsop's back. Without turning from the widow, he demands, "Were you listening to us from out there, Ti? Were you? Tell me the truth, now."

"No sir," Captain Alsop, I was doin' up some a' them dishes from th' morning.

Swear." Ti's hands, clutched into fists against her apron, are trembling now. Her chest rises and falls with each short, irregular breath. Her gaze never leaves the rich Persian-carpeted floor.

Alsop hesitates, as though assessing the veracity of her explanation. Finally, he turns, and with a mirthless smile, says, "Ti, don't be rude, this is my guest, Mister Russell. Say hello to Mister Samuel Russell," Alsop offers ominously. "We might be see-ing more of him here. Remember that, will you?" And with that, Ti shoots me a hasty glance, as though to lock in the image of my face for future reference. I smile back at her; but, instead of reciprocating, only fear fills her eyes as she quickly looks away.

"Ti, we're almost done here. When Mr. Russell leaves, I'll be taking my afternoon bath. Heat my bath water and have it ready. I'll be going to the office for dinner with the partners tonight. You'll be available when I return sometime after nine, is that clear?"

"Yes, sir, Captain Alsop. I'll be puttin' a kettle a' water on the fire right away." Ti shoots me another glance, a flash of softness in her face this time, then, once again, quickly leaves the room.

"Niggers do best when you're clear about tellin' them what to do," Alsop says, pick-ing up a small Chinese vase from its stand on a side table. He glances down at it, but his gaze and thoughts are elsewhere. "Ti's been trained well and knows what I need. Did you notice how I did that? Be smart and ambitious, and life can go this way for you, too. It's a privilege that comes with success. Do you understand what I'm telling you here, Russell?" Alsop asks. He then slowly returns the vase to its stand, appearing to signal the riches that could be mine if I can learn to be a good company man.

It is all too clear to me, masking a level of revulsion rising in my gut, as I blandly answer. "Yes, sir." I thank Captain Alsop profusely for the opportunity to be part of his organization and as I rise to leave, I calmly ask, "Shall I come to the offices on Monday, then?"

"Yes, of course," he says dismissively, in a tone that suggests this meeting is finally over.

Before I'm barely out the door, I hear Alsop as he walks through the house on his way to the kitchen, railing, "Ti, where're my robe and slippers? You were the last to have them."

As I pace out my steps to the street, I am in a state of shock and disbelief. I've had a glimpse of a lifestyle I can never condone, especially among a class of men I aspire to become. I believe I've just been offered the opportunity to become a slave trader; or, at the very least, to receive the necessary guidance to acquire and manage a young female 'captive'—with all of the attendant 'privileges' deriving from that.

At this moment, as I'm walking home, I am already clear that I won't be staying long in this current position. And much to my amazement and dismay, I'm already formulat-ing plans in my mind's eye for altering Ti's circumstances, rescuing her from this unten-able position of oppressive servitude, to put her, as my father once did, into the hands of our friends, the emancipationists. Despite a brisk winter wind, my blood boils with indignation in the same way it must have for my father, decades ago.

7. Deliverance on Main

BY SPRING OF the following year, 1812, I'd decided to resign my appointment to the firm of Whittlesey, Alsop and Wetmore, and enter into a modest lease on Main Street: endeavoring to own make my own way as an agent for goods sold on the international market. But this couldn't occur until I kept the promise to myself to extract Alsop's Ti from her circumstances. I make seemingly innocent inquiries around town and confirm what I'd suspected. During last trading season, the good captain had made a surreptitious purchase of a "young female African, fulsome bodied and in good health," as he had specified, while trading in Antigua. He arranged the purchase at a premium price, so that he might hand-select his acquisition prior to the sale in St. John's public square. She was swiftly spirited aboard his vessel and confined to his quarters for the three-week journey home to Middletown There she was quietly ensconced in the unheated room at the rear of the house. Above the objections of Alsop's wife and family, Ti had been in his service for several months when I first encountered her in the dining room on that winter's morning.

On the day I call at Captain Alsop's home to let him know of my decision to leave his firm, I have an ulterior motive: I want to encounter Ti again—since it had been several months since that eventful breakfast. But, I'm not sure she will recognize my face and voice when we again meet. Once again on the granite steps, I ring and am greeted at the door by Mrs. Alsop, who bids me enter. I present my card and ask if I may have a few minutes with the captain. As I wait in the foyer, my true intention is to get as close as possible to the kitchen at the back of the house, where I might encounter Ti busy with her usual duties. I edge my way toward the dining room, as voices and footsteps resound from the rooms above. Any sudden effort on my part to enter the back area of the house unannounced will only startle and frighten the girl, further defeating my attempt to win her trust and confidence.

Just as I decide to chance it, I hear the captain descending the stairs. He appears pale and disheveled, a consequence of a fever malady for which, it was rumored, he had been bled and treated with herbals, but with little positive effect. This morning he wears a rumpled white shirt, collar still upturned and askew, hair uncombed in a gray jumble atop a shiny, balding pate. His breeches drape low on his hips, revealing a generous paunch. He seems annoyed to see me, even though I had indicated the previous day that I wished to call on him for his counsel today. He ushers me into the dining room, where we stand momentarily. He is shifting from foot to foot, as he attempts to shove his shirt tails into his trousers, hoping to appear a bit more composed, I would guess. I can read in his actions that he is uncomfortable in my presence, perhaps because he had heard of my imminent departure from others in the community of men now known to both of us.

"You look unwell, captain, may I call for a glass of water for you?" I'm hoping for a reason to call Ti to his aid.

"No, I am fine, sir, thank you. But, let us get to the point. You have news for me, I understand," Alsop grumbles.

"Yes, Captain," I say. "I've decided to enter into business for myself. The moment seems opportune and I am here to express my gratitude for all you've done for me in recent months." As I speak, my eyes dart nervously toward the kitchen door, hoping for some glimpse of the girl.

"Well, sir, there is room enough for another in this busy market, and I'm sure you will find opportunity. Just remember where your start came from, and I caution you, *not* to do my company any harm. I will be merciless with you if that is ever the case," Alsop cautions. I appear to take the threat in stride, assuring him I mean no harm to his endeavors.

After exchanging some small pleasantries, I thank him again and assure him of our understanding. As the captain gestures to lead me to the front door, I feign a sudden coughing spell, hoping to break the mood and seize the moment I've come for.

"Good Lord, man, I'm the one who is supposed to be ill here," Alsop says, impatiently. Suddenly he turns from me and bellows, "Ti, water out here. Bring some water for Mister Russell."

A moment later, Ti emerges from behind the kitchen door, flustered yet steady-handed, as she approaches to hand me the glass. As I take it from her, Alsop pulls back a window shutter, momentarily preoccupied with activity on the street in front of the house. I use this moment to place my hand over Ti's and gain eye contact. A warm smile and kindly eyes are my only means to conjure a momentary connection with this poor girl, letting her know, non-verbally, that I mean no harm and that, 'she can place her trust in Mr. Samuel Russell.' She makes fleeting visual contact as I move my hand slowly away, and quickly leaves with a breathless, "Yes, sir."

I read a lot into that simple reply, praying she wants me to know my gesture has been received and understood. "Thank you, Ti," I call after her, as much in gratitude, as to have the tone of my voice recognizable to her, if and when we're to meet again.

As he opens the door, Alsop takes the glass from me. "Good luck in your ventures, young man, and remember my advice, keep your friends close, and your enemies closer." With that he shuts the door behind me, with more than a resounding *bang!*

≈

THE RESCUE IS to take place on that very same black, moonless night in May. This time, though, Seth is my willing accomplice, as we ride our two drafts to the edge of the field behind the Alsop house. The group of men and one woman from Pettibone Tavern are standing by at my house. This must be a lightning strike if she is to be handed off to the emancipationists. But, unlike the emaciated Adam of years ago, no long recuperation will be necessary, here. In Ti's case, we anticipate that an alarm would soon be raised by the captain and his friends, with a search for the missing girl ensuing within hours.

"Seth, bring the blanket and sack," I say. "She may be wanting to carry some of her personals with her. She's not knowing we're coming, and we'll be working without benefit of light, so don't do anything to alarm the girl, promise?"

Seth dismounts and gathers up the 'tools of our trade' in his arms, as we move quickly through the broad field toward the house. Our way is lit only by an arc of stars overhead, as we become like shadows, cutting a straight-line path through a blanket of parchment-pale, knee high grass. Once at the back gate, we cringe as the hinge makes creaking sound, as we slowly work our way to the back door. It too, groans in protest, as we slip in, hoping not to alarm Ti, causing her to cry out in fear. Once in the small anteroom, I whisper, "Ti, are you awake, its Mr. Russell. Ti, can you hear me?"

The room is pitch black as I feel my way along the wall to where I believe her bed might be, below the one small window in the tiny room. I sense Ti stirring as she awakens from slumber, suddenly sitting up in alarm. Crouching down to eye level, I repeat, "Ti, its Mr. Russell. Don't be afraid. I've come to get you out of here. Do you want to come with me? No harm will come to you, I swear. There are *good* people who want to take you to a safe place."

I can dimly make out Ti's form in the bed, sitting upright now, a thin blanket pulled up to her chin, framing her round face and bright, wide eyes. I know her mind must be racing at this moment, a mixture of fear and disbelief.

Not wanting to touch her and cause further alarm, I speak in low tones in the direction of the indistinct figure. "Ti, you mustn't make a sound. If you come with us, you will be safe, I promise. Please, come with us and be done with this nightmare you're in."

I'm hoping Ti recalls my warm smile and demeanor in the foyer earlier that day, and that she will decide to trust me and finally move from the bed. I sense that precious moments are flooding by. It will only be a matter of time before the captain senses a faint disturbance under his roof raises the alarm, as only a homeowner familiar with every tell-tale or suspicious sound, might.

"Mr. Russell, what you want a' me?" Ti finally asks. But even as she speaks, she is finally standing to peer out the window, in a futile attempt to assess the danger...the risk of responding to my pleas. "You want me to go wit' you and leave this place, Mr. Alsop, the lot of 'em? They'll have my hide, Mr. Russell."

"Not if you act now," I urge. "Get dressed quickly, get your things and I'll take you to a place where no bad people will find you. Then, off to a better place and good people who will care for you. Please, Ti, time is wasting."

"You goin' git me beat, or worse killed, Mister. Russell." And with that, Ti begins to tear up. If she doesn't act soon, I might have to choose between carrying her out the door over her protestations, or abandon the effort, as the risk of discovery for us all is becoming too great. "Please Ti, I mean you no harm, only help. We must *go*."

After an eternity, she begins to move. "I'll get my stuff, not much, shoes and such. Where you say you takin' me?"

"Out this door, through the yard, Ti. There are horses waiting in the back to take us to my house. There are friends there to bring you to another town called Simsbury, where you can be safe. Please hurry, Ti, we haven't much time," I say, my heart thudding against my chest, expecting the kitchen door to open at any minute, a knife-fine shaft of anemic yellow light silhouetting the looming figure of Captain Alsop, demanding, "What's going on here!"

Finally comprehending and willingness to trust me, Ti moves about in the dark, sweeping various sundries off a tabletop into the sack. I throw a blanket over her shoulders as we head out the door to where Seth is waiting. Hastening through the darkness to the horses, Seth quickly hoists Ti up into my saddle; once Seth is mounted, I swing up behind TI, holding her steady in my arms as we finally head out to the safety of my homestead—the horses moving at a brisk canter. There, a group of family and accomplices anxiously await. The sun won't crack the eastern horizon beyond the river for another two hours. By then, Ti will be on her way to a new kind of freedom, one she probably hasn't known in her all-to-brief lifetime.

Captain Joseph Alsop will awaken the next morning to find the spare bed in the cold room off his kitchen empty, his prized Ti inexplicably gone; his evening's dinner dishes still stacked, unwashed in the soapstone tub; his usual morning routine of toast, eggs and a carefully peeled, exotic St. Croix orange, disrupted; his afternoon bath and other indulgences now a distant memory. I take a certain quiet satisfaction in knowing that the good captain's various appetites will go unabated, at least for the foreseeable future.

8. Wild Hills & Uneven Ways

'TI' WAS EVENTUALLY taken by the emancipationists to the new, free state of Ohio, where she now lives safely with an Amish farming family. We learn she has taken their surname, Miller, and will hopefully find happiness there. I and my new business, on the other hand, are being held 'captive' by other forces—namely, an embargo by British naval forces along the Connecticut coastline. In what some are calling the 'Second Revolution,' war has been declared in '12, by our current president, Monroe, against English interests on the high seas and in our territories to the north and west. Some are even suggesting our state, along with other New England states, secede from the Union, to avoid the hardships in ship building and commerce that have befallen our Northeastern economy.

While this issue of federal versus states sovereignty over such matters as declaring war and consigning state's militias for international conflicts is being hotly debated in towns, taverns and capital hallways throughout the region, my reputation in Middletown for competency as a trader continues to grow. Through my business connections, I have been invited to travel to New York City—a demanding two-day journey by coach from here—to meet with an established firm with business to conduct in Europe. I am eager to see this rapidly growing New York town and witness, for myself, the arguments on both sides of the heated debate, for-and-against a return to conflict with the English, our principal trading partner across the Atlantic.

Travel along Connecticut's roads and turnpikes is greatly improved of late, with miles of newly laid thoroughfares between major cities now in place. A public carriage-and-four can move with relative comfort for its confined passengers over modern roads that once were little more than narrow, winding pathways. Crowned surfaces, drainage ditches, cutting and filling to eliminate the steepest grades, and gravel surfacing are now more common than in the past. Many of these roads are privately developed and managed 'turnpikes,' meaning that our coachman has to stop every ten miles-or-so, to pay a tavern keeper, merchantman, or farmer use-rights for passage on a few miles of smooth roadway.

Intricate webs of old farm roads still crisscross these byways, creating the opportunity for unscrupulous travelers to bypass tollgates by detouring temporarily onto any one of these 'shunpikes.' I am happy to report that was not the choice of my current conveyance, and I and my fellow travelers arrived in Stamford, Connecticut at the end of our first day's travel at Webb's Tavern, on Bank Street, just off the Post Road.

The tavern keeper hastens to the porch, projecting a beaming smile—the very picture of a warm welcome—as the coach rounds up and our driver throws his reins to the waiting hostlers. I and my fellow excursionists briefly refresh at the well, preparing for a tolerable good meal of chops, bread and ale, before I write this journal entry; then retire to a shared down-feather bed with another traveler for the night, lacking as I do, sufficient funds for a room of my own.

An early break-fast consisting of a warm bowl of milk, bread and honey and sausages has us on the way to our destination, the City of New York, and busy Fulton Street, on the East River. We arrive in lower Manhattan in a chilling deluge, driven by a late spring ocean gale off North River Bay. I am greeted by the harsh sting of rain as I step from the coach, quickly soaking my waistcoat and trousers. I am not prepared for this sudden turn in conditions and fear I won't make a favorable first impression on my host, Josiah Daggett, of the Sanford & Daggett firm, who'd assured me in our correspondence he would be here to greet me. I seek shelter under the eve of a nearby building, water still dripping from the rim of my hat. I scan the busy waterfront for anyone who might be moving with deliberation toward this rag-tag, water-soaked collection of passengers, along with our disarrayed pile of luggage and parcels littering the curb.

Through the downpour, I make out an indistinct figure purposefully working his way through the crowd toward us. Amid the tumult on the docks, he dodges and weaves through the dense tangle of dock workers, merchants, and wanderers, like a needle through cloth. As he nears the coach, he expectantly surveys the small cluster of passengers. I take that as my cue to ask, "Sir, are you sent by Mr. Daggett?"

He turns, "Yes, I have been...Mr. Russell?"

My escort approaches. His wide-set eyes, now fixed on me, are almost too large for his face. A single arched eyebrow and pugilist's nose are distinctive, barely safe from the rain under his broad-brimmed 'John Bull.' "Mr. Edwards, sir," he proffers, "Aaron Edwards to retrieve you and show you to our offices. Do you have baggage?"

"Just a small valise, sir. I have it here," I say, and retrieve it from the heap. We shake hands, immediately making our way into the heart of the city.

As we walk the teeming streets of the city, I ask, "The pace of things here is a dizzying change from the Connecticut countryside. Are you a New Yorker?"

"I've come and gone a number of times, but always gravitate back. This is where the opportunity lies in this modern world. We're adding new neighborhoods every year. Growing north on the island by leaps and bounds. Pretty soon, no room left for farms and grazing sheep, except maybe up Alms House way."

"Do you work with Mr. Daggett?"

"Only on occasion. He's brought me into the firm to do some legal work. You'll be meeting with the partners today...putting some plans together for China trade. They're in need of reliable representation over there. You've a good reputation, Russell. Word's out. If it comes together, I'll be drafting the agreement."

"I'll be needing to get to the hotel after the meeting. The St. George, on Beckman?"

"I'll bring your bag there during your meeting, if you wish."

Mr. Edwards' willingness to please...to be at my service in so many ways...is a curiosity, a small concern, but I'm ready to concede I don't yet fully understand this sprawling city or his place in the organization.

Once assembled in the room with Josiah Daggett and his principles, we speak of their need to have an agent in Europe, and Canton, China, particularly. I express favor for any arrangement and spell out my generous terms: a mere 1.5% commission on any goods I represent for them, and, as supercargo, the ability to determine fair market for finished cotton goods sold, and other expenditures for materials deemed appropriate for sale upon the return voyage. Aaron Edwards is not in the meeting, but stands outside the door, ready to escort me to the hotel as soon as we are finished.

"Mr. Russell," Josiah says, "I suggest we discuss the details of our immediate plans for the vessels currently loaded in North River Bay and adjourn for now. There's dinner planned at the home of a client. I wish for you to meet him. Big in the seal fur trade, but wants to branch out, as well. He's a convivial fellow, with a good head for trade. Mr. John Jacob Astor's the name. Perhaps you've heard of him? Mr. Edwards will pick you up at the St. George at seven, sharp."

I try not to let surprise and delight register on my face at the news of a proposed meeting at the home of Mr. Astor. "I will be ready," I say, matter-of-factly.

Once at the hotel, I make a quick meal of oysters and fresh bread in the dining room. After an exhausting day-and-a-half on the road, the ale I order to wash dawn the lot tastes very good, indeed. Time in my room consists of some short note-taking, a welcomed nap on a luxurious city mattress, a splash of cold water to the face, and a change of shirt and cravat in preparation of the evening's event. Mr. Astor has earned a reputation as a skillful businessman and wily trader, his markets extending all the way to the West Coast. I look forward to meeting him, at last.

~

MR. EDWARDS IS already waiting in the lobby of the St. George when I come down from my room just before seven. We climb into a hired hack and travel the muddy streets of Manhattan to Mr. Astor's seventy-acre property, spanning the distance between 42nd and 46th Streets, on the banks of the Hudson. Vast expanses of well-groomed lawn, undulating fence lines and grazing cattle mark the entrance to his estate, as the carriage eventually pulls up to a magnificent, covered entrance to his home. The two-story property, constructed in the Palladian style, is aglow with candle light, as white-gloved doormen and servants attend our every need. I eventually find myself in the grand space that would serve as our dining room that evening.

I catch Mr. Daggett's eye and move through the crowd to thank him for the invitation. "Yes, Samuel. Come please. I want you to meet our host and some of his guests."

John Astor is a small man, solidly built, with generous locks of chestnut-colored hair hanging across his brow. Though he emigrated from Germany as a teen, he retains his native accent. His Christian names, *Johann Jakob*, however, have long since been abandoned. He greets me warmly, asking if I might take a few minutes to talk with him privately before the evening's event ends. Naturally, I agree. This opportunity seemed particularly auspicious, given that my assistant, Thomas Boggs, had explained prior to my departure from Connecticut, that his own efforts to solicit a meeting with Mr. Astor on my behalf, had been greeted with a terse note in return, simply stating that Mr. Astor was 'not accepting letters at this time.' Considering that fact, I have trouble believing my good fortune, or contain my excitement—to meet with one of the richest men in America—a moment that calls for a celebratory glass or two of champagne from one of many silver trays being passed among the crowd by household staff.

As I move to the edge of the noisy room for a breath of fresh river breeze coming through the open doors, I happen upon three similarly inclined young ladies, standing nearby.

"Ladies, if I may be so bold, I am Samuel Russell, recently arrived from Connecticut, and I feel somewhat adrift in this gathering. Are you from New York?"

"Well, yes and no, sir," the oldest of the trio replies, "I'm Abigail Winston, guardian for my orphaned nieces, Mary and Frances Osborne. Their parents died in the West Indies, while tending their property there. My husband is a solicitor in the service of Mr. Daggett. These young ladies are here for some weeks away from their schooling." She gestured toward the two young women, as each extended a brief curtsy in my direction.

Placing my hand to my waistcoat, I nod slightly, "It is my pleasure ladies."

"Did you say Connecticut, Mr. Russell? Which part?" Mary, the elder-appearing of the two, asks.

"Middletown, miss, a small but prosperous town on the river, there."

"Quite astounding, sir," says Mrs. Winston, 'these young ladies are also from Middletown. I am surprised you do not know of them, or at least the family."

"The name Osborne is well-known in my town," I say. "But, if I may be so bold, these two young ladies most certainly came of age while I was absent, pursuing business interests in Europe, and elsewhere. Their beauty would certainly have come to my attention if I had been about the social scene there, of late."

"A coincidence, indeed," said Frances. "We also know the name Russell, with many 'Russells' in town and throughout the region. There's a cousin with connections to Yale College, I believe. Mr. Russell has an excellent reputation in Middletown, as he has worked for a well-known there, before leaving for Europe on behalf of those interests," she explains, turning back to Mrs. Winston.

I briefly consider the fact that they seem so well acquainted with my efforts, when the youthful Mary asks, "And what brings you here, sir?"

"Some of those same business interests, I'm afraid." I find myself directing my comments largely to the attractive, Miss Mary Osborne, whose sparkling hazel eyes and broad smile I found arresting. "I can assure you, I will look forward to acquainting myself with the changing scene in my modest hometown from now on. May I ask, in Mrs. Winston's presence, if I may call upon the Osborne ladies once we are all back in Connecticut?"

"That will be a matter for Mary and Frances to decide...will it not, ladies?"

Mary speaks first, "We would be delighted, sir."

"And with that, ladies, I must beg my leave," as Mr. Astor's assistant's catches my attention from across the room. "It has been a distinct pleasure." I extend my hand to each, with an extra moment's lingering attention to Mary, as I take her gloved hand in mine.

9. The Astor Proposal

THE PANELED LIBRARY where Mr. Astor and I meet is separated from the social gathering by a pair of heavy double doors, which he draws shut behind me. One entire wall of the large room is lined with bookshelves, catalogued in neat leather-bound rows, extending to the ceiling. Their gold-embossed spines are aglow in the paneled study's warm candlelight. "The greatest authors of our civilized world are here at my fingertips: Ovid; Shakespeare; Homer; Dante; Hobbs, Locke" Astor says, reaching up to remove a volume..."knowledge is power, Russell, don't ever forget that. People come and go; money is made and lost. Intelligence and the ability to know *where* to find wisdom is something that can't be taken away."

"I've had great interest in the work of John Locke. His principles of individual rights and social contracts. My small library at home doesn't offer much, however," I offer.

"Let me show you this, young man," he says, leading me to a far wall, there opening the glass doors of a crowded cabinet full of various objects, most novel to my eyes. Arranged seemingly at random on dusty shelves are ancient animal skulls and bone fragments, yellowed with age, rocks of variable sizes, some with small faded labels attached, swatches of multicolored fabric, frayed by time, a grimacing, nail-studded totemic figure, looking to be of primitive African origin, an iridescent-winged butterfly pinned to a pedestal under a glass dome, heaps of exotic, patterned sea shells, and fragments of shale and schist, bearing imprints and markings of long-extinct ocean creatures.

Among these curiosities, Astor reaches in to slowly withdraw a weathered booklet from behind a row of small, fragile bird's nests. Once in his hand, he carefully turns to its mid-section, carefully unfolding a bound, crudely drawn map. A dark red line courses its way across the printed terrain represented by a series of tightly spaced, concentric lines. In his faint German accent, he explains, "This represents an accomplishment which I might be the proudest of in my career. It is the westward route identified by a team of explorers financed by me in '11, when I established a Columbia River trading post at Fort Astoria, the first of its kind on the Pacific coast. Back then, I sent a team of men from St. Louis to find the best route to that outpost. They were gone for two years...lots of hardship; but they blazed a passable trail through the Rockies, a south pass, which will make it a hell-of-a-lot easier for men to reach the west coast in the future."

"Northwest country...isn't that King George's neck of the woods?" I ask.

"Those bastards, yes!" They're thick as thieves out there. Have to guard against them every day. Then, the war. That has bolloxed up the works for me, as well. Slowed things down, which is why I want to talk to you."

My heart leaps at those words, but I maintain my outward composure. "That little matter of trade seems close to being resolved," I say. "The English seem to know they already have their fingers in too many pies."

"Samuel, in business, you have to look ahead. My teacher in school used to say,

'*Wo geht die Zukunft hin?*' which means 'Where does the future go?' Much of what the future holds rests with planning today. I have large shares in the seal fur market. Will that last? What is next? I can't know for sure; but if I'm to continue on this path, I have to have more than one tool in my box." Astor hesitates for a minute, resting his hand on my shoulder, looking beyond the library windows to darkening skies over the Hudson. "Come, come outside with me."

We step out onto the estate lawn, sloping into the darkness toward the riverbank. Under a moonless landscape, the Palisades on the opposite bank tower like innumerable cathedral spires beneath a dazzling Milky Way dome, spanning an ink-black sky. Before us, the broad Hudson, like slow-moving quicksilver, flows silently to the Atlantic. Dim city lights mark the distant tip of Manhattan Island. A dozen iron foundries along the river's banks—their white-hot blast furnaces growling—belch heavy black smoke and orange sparks into the cool, June night air.

"This is beautiful," I say, awe-struck by the panorama.

"Yes, but it's also telling us a story about the future, if you know not only *where* to look, but *how*." Astor says. "See those masts by the dozens, ships tied at the docks. They're trade vessels from everywhere...moving cargo in and out of the city all day. All well-and-good. But see those ship in the Reaches, sitting well outside the channel in darkened waters? Now spot the dozen-or-so pilot boats coming and going without running lights, if you can," he adds. "It looks like business is over for the day. At this moment, though, those smaller crafts running in darkness are transacting business, thousands in silver bullion credits, all in paper form, held by New York banks."

"What's the cargo?" I ask.

"People...slaves. *Slaves*, Samuel. Fresh from Africa and, for those that survive, on their way to the Trades, without ever setting foot on dry land."

"But slavery is illegal here, I say, naively.

"Let's say, 'frowned upon'...at least in New York. Abolitionists have been agitating to set the Africans free since the war with Britain. Some Blacks already are. But it's thought best for all in high society to do it behind the backs of their city friends and neighbors. The reality is that slavery is going to disappear, soon enough."

"My father fought it tooth-and-nail in Connecticut. I have clear memories of the stories he told me. Why, I myself...."

Astor did not wait to hear me out. "The point, my boy," he interjected, "is that those who stake their fortunes on products which depend on free labor are doomed to fail in the long run. Read the future by reading the facts in front of you. This slavery business *has* to be clandestine in order to work. Its days are numbered. For that reason, I won't go near it any longer." After a moment to consider his own point, he adds, "Come inside, now, we'll catch a death out here, night vapors and all that."

Once inside, Astor and I sit as we finally get to the point of his meeting. "I'll be looking at my options over the next few months, but I want you to consider a strategy for yourself. One that can benefit both of us. It's been rumored that you're being considered for a posting in China by some of your Providence and New York accounts. Another successful venture or two in Europe as supercargo and my guess is that you'll have earned your way to a China station.

"Thank you. But I have no intention..."

"Wait, please. Just hear me out. The British are making a killing with Turkish paste from Afyan Province. It's finding its way into China and London, thanks to their network. I'm planning to load ten tons of it onto my packet, *Macedonian*, soon, and deliver it to Canton in the next few months. It'll be buried under furs, with none-the-wiser. If that works, I'd rather have an American agent than a Brit working for me there in the future.

"Mr. Astor, I can't allow this conversation to continue. I'm honored that you'd consider me for this project, but my principles and my objectives *don't* include illicit activity."

"But this is fair trade. Opium's not illegal, just frowned upon by the Chinese government. The people are craving it and our job is to provide it. It can't be our problem that a few million Chinamen would rather go to an opium den everyday than work at some dull, repetitive job. Remember what I said earlier: consider the future in light of what you are seeing today. Opium is the future of American business in China. I would like to think I can count on you."

I decide at the moment it was best to move beyond the discussion, which could easily devolve into argument. "Thank you for your insights, Mr. Astor. I will certainly consider them carefully."

"We should be getting back to the party, Samuel, but for the nonce..." And with that, Astor returns to his bookshelves, where he removes a slender red leather-bound book. "Here, Samuel, a gift for you. It so happens I have two copies of this treatise, one of Locke's best, *The Second Treatise of Government*. Take his message to heart, young man, there is nothing wrong with fortune, as long as you can turn a portion of it for the public good."

"But, sir, I also can recall from my school and church studying at that Locke additionally calls upon us to regard ourselves all as equals in the eyes of God, and, reciting more-or-less from memory, that we may not 'subordinate or destroy another of our own, as we might the animals of lower rank.'"

"Well put, Samuel. You're a bright young man. Rejoin my guests and give my proposal some consideration. Time and acquired wisdom can only work to your favor and advantage, I trust."

As I stand to leave, I hesitate at the door, turning to Astor with one last question. "Mr. Astor, I have been bothered by something all day. It's a fine point for sure, but one I can't seem to clear from my mind. It's about the man who accompanied me here tonight, Mr. Edwards. He seems competent, well trained, and amiable, but assigned to menial tasks, like escorting me around town, and attending to my minor needs. He says he's a lawyer, with responsibilities at Daggett's firm. But..."

"You mean *Aaron* Edwards? If you were local, you would be well-aware of him. He is, in fact, Aaron Burr, late of several European cities hiding from creditors, recently returned to New York to find work as a solicitor. His reputation was ruined by the Hamilton affair—killing a decent man—and the ensuing trial. Case dismissed, but still *persona non grata*, as it were. He's back with friends who are supporting him, the Eden widow and her children, an old client who paid his bills. He assumed his mother's maiden name, 'Edwards,' in the hopes that people would forget. They haven't, but he is tolerated within our ranks. Good lawyer, perhaps, but a past he can't shake. Be kind to him, my advice. He needs any friend he can get."

~

AFTER MY UNSETTLING meeting with Astor and a brief goodbye to the Osborne women, Mr. 'Edwards' appears in the vestibule of the Astor house to accompany me back to the St. George. I say nothing to him about my earlier conversation, but the sad facts of his life help to explain some of his obsequious behavior I found so unsettling earlier in the day.

I return to Middletown two days later, a new contract relationship with New York's Sanford & Daggett tucked in my breast pocket. Feeling empowered by my success, I take time to call on the Osborne family, and particularly the lovely, nineteen-year-old, Miss Mary. We discover our shared interest in nature and literature, not to mention our affection for one another. I don't really understand her attraction to me, "I'm lantern-jawed, with too-large a nose and early receding hairline," I say, in protest to her compliments often aimed in my direction.

"But you're kind and patient. Love is not rational, Russell," she replies. Six months after we first met at the Astor home, on a splendid Connecticut autumn day in 1815, we are married. Mary and her sister, Frances move to the Russell house at the edge of town. The following year, a son, George Osborne Russell is born.

Our time together is blissful. Now, some four years later, she is expecting our second child. At this crucial time in our marriage, I am called upon by my new partners in Providence to sail to Canton, China, to establish a new office. With my departure in 1819, I never suspect it is to be the last I will ever see my dear Mary.

BOOK III
BOCA
TIGRES

10. Supercargo

"FUNNY, TA' ME, you look a bit like a fish outa' wahtah, all gussied up, an' all," a voice chides me as I walk up the gangway.

"Them city threads won't do ya much good in a blow...wash overboard, sink like a rock," adds another.

"Tell ye sumpin, sire, get seasick and heave on *my* deck, you'll be on them knees with a bucket an' stiff brush till it shines aggin," comes a dismembered voice from the spars as I approach Captain Rathbun to report for our departure as supercargo.

"Don't mind them. They mean no harm" Captain Rathbun says. "Just the gauntlet the crew make every new man run when we're fixin' to shove off. Their breeches in a knot over all they have to do and you get to kick your feet up and enjoy the view."

"I've heard it all before...don't mind," I explain.

"They're tough, hard-drinking Irishmen, the lot of 'em," Rathbun adds, "the finest deep-water sailors in the world. 'Bout half—mebee ten...twelve, a' these 'packet rats' been with me for years. Needed to press fifteen more for this trip. Likely as not, some of 'em were pissed and befuddled in some god-forsaken alley or brothel last night before we were done scuttlin' the bottom of the barrel."

"Some come to us from boarding houses where they'd run up a bill, can't pay. My man here in town, Gardner, gets invited to a boarding-house proprietor's birthday party, with dancing girls and plenty of liquor. Next thing I know, they're bound out; been scuttled. Proprietors then collect money for delivering unconscious sailors to the next outbound ship. Most men don't fight it. They're as inclined as not to cut and run this town for a few dollars, three squares, and as many miles of ocean water 'tween them and the constable as possible 'fore anyone realizes they're gone."

I'm standing beside the ship's master, Joshua Rathbun, looking out at the deck and rigging of the schooner, *Fame*, as men scramble in every direction in preparation for departure. The captain's a tall, impressive figure—second generation commander and one who, by his appearance, elicits a sense of confidence and good judgment. A narrow bridge of the nose cuts a sharp line between deep-set, dark blue eyes. A high forehead and receding hairline, together with generous 'chops' running along his jawline, add a look of regal determination to his overall countenance. He can most always be seen holding a riding crop, which appears to serve little purpose here, except to add emphasis to his commands when he raps it against any nearby object—seemingly without realizing it.

"Safe journey from Connecticut, I assume?" he says, as though not expecting any other answer than, 'Yes, thanks.' "Again, my apologies for the men," he clips.

"I've done this a few times before. They'll figure out I'm good enough to have around. Give them time," I say. Then turning to the loudest of the bunch, I keep the good-natured joust in play when I shout up toward the crew in the rigging, "I got barnacles growin' in places *you've* never seen and a backbone stiffer than any backstay. Gimmee time to settle, an' we'll be havin' pigs' knuckles and harf a' grog and you'll be wishin' you had three, the likes a' me, in any storm."

I'M ON THE docks at Fox Point, in Providence, Rhode Island, at the head of Narragansett Bay, to board the Carrington & Butler Company-owned vessel, *Fame*, under the command of Joshua Rathbun, for a long, round-about journey to China. We're loaded with a thousand bales of cotton and bundles of rough-cut Nicaraguan lumber for sale in various European ports. My task, according to my Providence employer, is to fetch the best price in Spanish dollars, '*species*,' for those goods, then sail directly to Canton with that silver trove to establish our business there.

I drop my bag on deck and follow First Mate Ryan Morgan below to inspect the cargo. I duck my head to enter the dingy hold, two decks down, where tons of goods are lashed, acting as ballast for the thirty-day European ocean trek. Cotton dust hangs in the air—a fine mist that clogs the throat; the darkened crawl space is rank with the stale smell of bilge water and the acerbic odor of fresh-cut timber. The bales are bound to skids, six inches off the ship's bilge planking to discourage inevitable rat nesting. The teak is secured to posts amid-ship to avoid shifting, once underway.

Rathbun yells down from on deck: "Morgan will show you to your bunk when you're done down there. We'll sup in my quarters at six bells. Mr. Morgan, make sure our supercargo knows to dress for the occasion," he adds, jokingly.

"Will do, sir."

"Let's go Ryan. I want to write a letter before we cast off in the morning, and while I'm still sober. I've been to just a few of these fetes and will be needing my wits about me when I put pen to page," I add.

My 'quarters'—for it is that in name only—more closely resembles an oversized coffin, than any ordinary space fit for ease of movement. Barely wider than the reach of my arms and hardly a foot longer than my six-foot height, it consists, inboard, of a wooden sleeping platform covered with a poplin and horsehair mattress. A course blanket and pillow, yellowed and flattened by years of use are piled at the end of the bed. On the opposite wall—against the ship's bulkhead—is a small writing table designed to drop down from its wall housing. From a sitting position on my bunk, I can easily reach the desk. Two deep shelves take up the corner of the space, as well as a narrow hanging closet. There, a set of oiled rain gear is already in place. A single brass lantern is suspended from a gimbaling hook above the desk, its whale oil wick tainting the air with a musty odor to this windowless confine, one that will serve as my home for the next several months.

I lower my writing desk in these cramped quarters, setting pen to paper to hastily write to my wife:

My Dearest Mary-

I've not been gone but a few hours, and I'm already missing you desperately. The overnight journey was not without peril. We stopped to exchange horses once on the Post Road in Westerly, and the inn keeper there had to be aroused from a drunken stupor to meet our coachmen, and only reluctantly offered my fellow travelers and me any form of refreshment. I arrived in Providence just after dawn, so hungry, I could have eaten a cow! Fortunately, the cook on Fame provided me with coffee and a stack of toast and jam.

There is some good news, however. My modest cabin, in the secure aft-most quarters of Fame, will be far-removed from the steady heave-and-fall of the ship's bow in open seas. And, I'll be sleeping with my feet facing forward, so if we run aground, or strike something in the night (fallen timbers always possible at sea), my legs will take the blow, sparing me a more severe injury to the head.

I'm hoping Mary will find some comfort in these vague assurances, and other triv-
ials related to my carriage ride to Providence and preparations for our departure on
the next morning's tide. My heart aches for her in her current condition, and the harsh
reality that I was denied the opportunity to have her present to see me off. It would
have been small consolation, but a moment that could have meant so much to us both.

I saw how grief-struck you were when I left Middletown yesterday. I know you were
never pleased with my decision to go, but you put on a brave face and reluctantly
accepted it. I had so hoped you could accompany me on the ride to Providence—a city
you've never seen.'

'But, the ride would now prove to be much too rough, given that you're so far along.
Your weakened condition with this second baby has me so concerned, in spite of Frances
being present to help with daily chores and George's care—our rambunctious two-year
old, constantly on the move.

My last image of her was standing beside the coach, with little George in Frances's
arms. She finally gave in to bitter tears, streaming down her pale cheeks as the coach
departed Main Street depot. It was a sight no man wants to see and one that long persisted in my mind's eye, well past Rhode Island and beyond.

I swear to you, dearest Mary—and to myself—that I will return before you realize I was
even gone, and will write so frequently, you will soon tire of me, even though I might be
half-a-world away.'

> Your loving husband, Samuel

~

I DISEMBARK *FAME* in the failing summer's light as clouds thicken to the southwest,
to take a short, wind-blown walk to the carriage depot. There, I pay a small fee to the
ticket master to insure my letter would be on the next coach to Hartford, with a stop
in Middletown. I've included a small piece of parchment doused with my shave cologne
inside the envelope, and place one last kiss on the back of the envelope before handing
it over to the dispatcher. I fight back tears as I return to the ship by way of rain-slicked
cobble alleyways.

Once back at my digs, and with a quick splash of cold water to the face—at precisely seven in the evening, or six bells, signaling the first of two 'dog', or night watches—I knock on Rathbun's spacious state room door, as requested, for dinner. I am soon
greeted with a grand *halloo* and an extended hand proffering a stem of port wine. A
gathering of men sit at a small table in the center of the room, the lights of the city and
harbor glowing through a bank of windows at the stern of the vessel.

Once seated, I sip from the glass of the rich, red-brown liquid, raising my eyebrows
as it hits bottom, sending a rush of sweet heat throughout my body. Watching my
response, Rathbun says, "That Oporto's liquid gold. Been traveling with me three year-
a'-more. Keep the cask bunged in the mess. Siphon off a finger or two when I feel the
urge. Have the hide of any crew that touches it. Captain's personal keep an' they know
it. They'd prefer a good stiff glass of Jamaica, at any rate. Rockin' of the ship seems to
make this better with age," he says, holding the glass to eye-level. "Fine, eh?" I agree
with a big smile, nod and sip again.

≈

RATHBUN'S GENEROUS ACCOMMODATIONS are fitted out with rich walnut and mahogany paneling. Four modest wooden Doric columns stand at the corners of an arched ceiling, with four brass-barred skylights tracing the ceiling's gentle curve overhead. A large, forward-facing leather-topped desk, covered at that moment with bills of lading and supply logs, occupies a large portion of the room, separating us at the dining table from the broad transom's bank. On the starboard side, a row of book-cases, also finished in classical style, containing rows of books and journals, secured in place by fiddles, to guard against dislodging in rough seas. Fat, leather bound vol-umes with gold embossed titles like *Travels in Egypt*, *Polwele's History of Devonshire* and *Manners & Customs of the Russians* suggest a man of erudition who has seen much of the known world.

On the room's port side, an array of tubes containing rolled navigation charts for every quadrant of the earth's surface, nautical instruments, and the current ship's log stand at the ready beside a tilt-top charting table. A locked gun case on the wall, nearby, contains several muskets (enough for each officer of the ship), two blunder-busses for crowd control (mutiny?), and any number of side-arms (piracy?). A match-ing set of American-made flintlock pistols—presentation pieces engraved and inlayed with pearl and silver—are displayed in a glass case above the navigation table.

Beneath the charting table, a large tabby cat lazes complacently in a shallow basket. Her eyes are closed, but ears twitch at every unexpected sound from the captain's table. "That's *Cleo*, after Cleopatra. Found her wandering a souk in Alexandria one day. Skin and bones, she was. Turns out, she's a great mouser, ratter. Put her in the hold at night. Does the trick," Rathbun notes when he sees my eyes focusing on this unusually rotund creature. "She'll get a scrap or two when we're done. Doesn't miss a trick, better believe."

My eyes then wander to a darkened corner, where I discern the captain's bed cham-ber in a far corner on the port side. He'd a gimbal compass installed in his bedroom, to monitor *Fame's* course at any time of the night or day, 'without going up on deck,' he explains. "I have never seen this before," I say, thinking: a sure-fire reflection of his competence as a ship's commander.

Polished brass fittings and silver-trimmed decanters shimmer in the evening's can-dle and lamp's light, as the aromas of hot wax, gun oil, old books and the evening's meal sitting nearby beneath burnished copper domes, hang in the air.

Captain Rathbun speaks above the fray, rapping his crop on the table top for atten-tion: "Gentlemen, may I introduce Mr. Samuel Russell, supercargo for this little adven-ture of ours. His job is to make money for the company and spend it wisely; our job is to get him to-and-from without incident."

He then makes the rounds of the table: "Ryan Morgan, First Mate." Morgan looks across at me expectantly, knowing we just shared a few minutes below deck, inspecting cargo. I nod in his direction. He is bright-eyed, flushed with enthusiasm and perpetual energy, it seems—a trait of one always anxious to please. He carries a thick tangle of chestnut hair above a broad, sun scorched face, a pale white scar running the length of his left cheek. Morgan is young, just now coming of age in the relentlessly cruel and dangerous world of ocean sailing. If he is prudent and chooses his assignments well—like many capable men who have gone to sea before—he will likely have a future as a ship's captain.

Next, "Second Mate, Michael Faircroft." His lowered eyes make momentary contact with mine. I sense he'll be the silent one on this journey. Broad shouldered and with powerful hands, Faircroft shows every sign of coming to his position through a series of life's hard knocks. A face deeply scarred from childhood pox, he appears as the 'survivor' in his private world; a man who has learned to mask his emotions—someone of few words—relying on instinct to guide his actions. He will be hard to know, but reliable in a crisis and a good sailor. Rathbun relies on Faircroft as 'officer of the night watch,' a coveted role, only calling on the captain when tough choices must be made. I will come to rely on Faircroft's seamanship and look forward to knowing him better as we spend this next period of months confined to a cramped vessel.

"Last, but not least, Third Mate, Patrick Haskell," who offers me a quick smile. A thin, nervous creature, his skin appears stretched to breaking over high cheek bones. His deep-set eyes fix on me from their dark orbits. His weathered, crane-like neck reveals bundles of tendons and blood vessels which flex around bone structure when he moves. He seems a soul older than his years—a survivor. He has had years at sea, and as he tells it, 'close to death many times—the scurvy, fever, malaria, and one-or-two encounters with Barbary raiders off the African coast.' A gentle smile and reserved manner suggest a man who has found a place for himself in the world, even if the fates deal him a short, perhaps painful, life.

Will there be a ship's surgeon aboard?" I ask.

In response, Rathbun nods in the direction of Faircroft. "Served on the Navy brig, *Argus* in '12, under Commandant William Allen," he says. "Assigned to the ship's surgeon there. Barbary scum a bigger problem than the Brits for us back then. Tripoli blockade, skirmish at Derma...saw enough blood and brains on the deck for a lifetime. Picked up enough to know what to do, so I guess I'm the man you're looking for."

With that, Morgan leans in to add, "Michael's a boon for us, for sure. Good to know he's around with his bandages and salves. Just don't break a leg, Mr. Russell, or ol' sawbones here'll be feedin' the sharks with those spare parts a' yours."

When the laughter subsides, Rathbun stands with lifted glass, "Before we sup, I would like to propose a toast to our Mr. Russell, to a safe journey, and to our lady, *Fame*, who has carried us safely to every corner of the world." A series of 'huzzahs' and 'hiphips' momentarily reverberate around the room, as Cleo slowly lifts her head, glancing in the direction of the table through heavily-lidded eyes, signaling her annoyance at the disruption.

And, as if on cue, the men at my table now bow their heads, as Rathbun continues: "*May God send this good ship to her desired port in safety and may He guard and protect all the souls embarked on this voyage. I pray that he may take kind care of us and our beloved families during our absence & may we all be returned in safety, in the name of God's goodness.*"

Cleo is out of his basket now, making the rounds unseen beneath the table, her massive belly brushing repeatedly over my boot tops and against the cuff of my britches. "This must be some form of get-acquainted ritual," I whisper to Morgan. Aware of Cleo's mischief beneath the table, I stifle a smile as Morgan explains, "She's friendly to all new-comers. If she thinks you're ignoring her, though, she can turn on you like a rabid dog, however. Just warning you. On a serious note, though, "Rathbun always recites a prayer," he further explains, "as do many other captains I've served with. And his recitation will be entered verbatim, as a talisman, into the ship's log.

IN MY ROLE as a supercargo, or trading merchant on board *Fame*, under Capt. Rathbun, I'm responsible for a hold-full of cotton bales brought from the Carolinas, through New York; and two tons of jungle timber from the tropics. I'm acting on behalf of the shipping firm of Misters Carrington & Butler, first traveling to merchants awaiting in Europe. We then sail to the Iberian Peninsula, where I hope to successfully negotiate a sale in the northwest port city of La Coroña, Spain or Lisbon, Portugal. If terms are not favorable, we then sail north to Amsterdam, where markets may be better.

Our final port o' call is Gibraltar, where any unsold goods are bartered for silver. I am then under instructions to secure those silver proceeds, continue on to China and establish my agency, Russell & Co. acting on behalf of my employer in Providence. I will not be owning goods, simply acting as a broker to acquire good markets, and buyers, then purchase tea, porcelain and silks with those proceeds for the return trip to Providence, Newport, or Boston.

Gibraltar, a British colony, is an ideal port to re-stock ship's stores before leaving for China—a journey of four-to-five months, depending on sea conditions. *Fame*'s larder is inventoried with only the best that money can buy:

Salted beef, 3 barrels
Pork, 2 barrels
Beer, 12 barrels
Water, 27 hogsheads and 12 casks of 18 gallons each
Bread, 54 loaves
Butter, 220 lbs
Oatmeal, 10 bushels
Peas, 8 bushels
Flour, 600 lbs in 4 barrels
Suet, 82 lbs in 1 barrel
Raisins, 100 lbs in 2 barrels
Rum, 4 half hogsheads, 126 US gallons
Vinegar, 1 hogshead
15 dozen waxed eggs
Catalan oranges, fresh and sugared; apples, dried and fresh; grapes; lemons; limes, 5 bags, mixed
Turnips, squashes and potatoes, 20 bags
12 pullets; 6 piglets, 10 caged grouse.

Cook once again issues strict orders to keep Cleo away from the fowl cages, as her past history provides enough evidence of the death and destruction she can cause.

≈

WITH THE SPANISH coast now fading from view off the stern, Gibraltar's summit is our lingering reminder of civilization, as it sinks beneath the horizon. We bear away, China-bound at last. I find myself on *Fame*'s forecastle, a fresh southeasterly breeze broadly abeam, the sound of hands at station overhead, setting tops'ls, lashing free lines, urgently hailing and barking to one another high above-deck on ratlines and gyrating spars.

I turn aft to study Joshua's stance at the helm. He's barking orders, eyes fixed on the sky and the precise alignment of sail and line needed to drive the hull efficiently through mounting seas. While long weeks or even months of sailing still lie ahead, a commander's instincts are perpetually aimed at maximum performance from his vessel. Every moment spent at sea subjects ship, crew, and cargo to constantly changing conditions, placing all at risk of damage, injury and loss of life. Urgency—the unspoken watchword—is top-of-mind on board any vessel in open waters.

"Mr. Morgan, have your men slack the second stays'l. Standby the halyards. Attend the luff in the main topgallant, now, please."

He replies after a second or two, "Made."

"Thank you."

"Mr. Haskell, prepare the chip log. In two minutes, and on my count, prepare to cast."

Haskell secures the chip and knotted line from a trunk on the quarterdeck, standing at the ready by the taffrail. "On my count," says Rathbun, "cast!"

With that, Haskell gives the length of timber a high toss into the trailing sea, well out of range of the swirling eddies of the ship's wake. He calls out the knots tied in the line every seventeen feet as they quickly pass through his hands: "One...two...three..."

"Stop," says Rathbun, frowning. "Three knots in ten seconds. I want six-to-seven in this fresh blow by noon sighting. Mr. Morgan, fine tune the rig and make it happen, please. Studdingsails to be set on both sides, a kite between masts if you wish. Take the helm. Now that we're well underway by four leagues, I'm going below for my first entry of the day."

And with each fine adjustment to the rigging, a slight sensation of greater speed. White water rises and slams against the bow with increasing intensity and frequency, only to slip alongside, fanning out toward the cobalt blue horizon in roiling ribbons of foam. Half a world away, a remote and ancient civilization unknowingly awaits our arrival.

≈

DATE: JUNE 18, 1819

My Dearest Mary

Since posting my last letter to you with the Gibraltar harbor master, I want to undertake a more detailed epistle relating the many details that might be lost to memory during this next, protracted phase of my journey to Canton.

I am desperate for your arms around me and I must say that I am haunted by questions of my wisdom in agreeing to this expedition, since it means such a prolonged separation from you, darling George, our next child and the rest of my family. I sometimes worry I might never see you all again or feel the warmth and sweetness of your kiss. Fortune is an unforgiving mistress, brooking no ambivalent emotions when it comes to acting on behalf of our future well-being. And, it is for that reason, and by example for our son, that I chose to leave behind kith and kin in search of fortune. Riches are to be found in the Celestial Kingdom, wealth beyond imagining, as I have learned. A short tenure in this hostile land so far from you, and I hope to return with the means to accomplish our every dream.

The first leg of the trip, as I have mentioned in the letter, should have arrived for you. It describes my thirty-eight-day crossing to Europe, which transpired without major incident. I met with our contacts there and sold our goods at a favorable price. I took to heart the partners' warning that I not be too glib or revealing about competing interests among them, playing one against the other very effectively, I believe. An early victory in this long saga!

Captain Rathbun has set a course due south, straight to the Canaries, off the African coast. Thence, we turn toward South America, riding a favorable, prevailing westerly three-thousand miles across the Atlantic. This first southward leg might seem counter-intuitive, but centuries ago, European explorers happened upon these trade winds, and we are still benefiting from them today.

The wonders of nature constantly surround us every day. Unfamiliar fishes with massive pectoral fins are disturbed by our presence, breaking the surface of the water on the bow, to skip or 'fly' above the waves to some safe distance yards ahead. These so-called sea robins, with their deep pumpkin-coloration, linger near us, hoping for scraps from the galley, I would guess. Cook turned the tables and would haul a few aboard in his net. Under his knife they were a spare, bony treat—a welcomed alternative, though, for the crew from his usual offerings.

Petrels and albatross, large sea birds with immense, unwavering wingspans drift high above the spars, our constant companions as we course onward. Astoundingly, numbers of butterflies and common birds—wrens and swallows—alight on our rigging for hours or days at a time, blown out to sea by high winds and facing certain death in these unforgiving elements. On moonless nights, with black waters peaking all around us, the vast expanse of stars arrayed in the heavens are sufficiently bright to light our way on deck. A glowing, water-borne path of lime-green light trails behind toward the horizon from whence we'd come, an eerie chemical marker created by thousands of minuscule sea creatures agitated by our passing vessel.

Rathbun's crop is tapping at my door, and I'm being called to dinner. I will resume this letter as soon as I am able. Till then, my love flying over the waves to you and the family...

With Deep Affection, Samuel

11. Hell Arrives Uninvited

DATE: JULY 1, 1819

AN UNEVENTFUL PASSAGE from Europe brings us to anchorage in the South American post of São Vincente. The deep harbor and civilized town serve as a destination-of-choice for American and British vessels heading to-and-from China. There are ample supplies of goods and services for ships in need of resupply and repair, and for crew looking for relief and distraction on shore. English is spoken here by many of the natives, especially those who have come to rely on Yankee dollars and English pound for their income.

After days ashore, partaking of the food and sights in the nearby frontier city of São Paulo, I return to the familiar motion and sounds of the ship, instilling in me the discontent and fear that arise only from the anticipation of our journey through dangerous waters. The crew had apparently had their fill of rum, beautiful *mulattas* and loose women—so called, *mulheres de má reputação*—in this familiar waystation for vessels heading to Pacific waters.

Fully provisioned for our longest and most treacherous leg of the journey, we weigh anchor under a blistering sun and flat, linen white skies, piloting from *Baia de Santos*, finally re-entering the massive rolling swells of the South Atlantic. The crew is stepping smartly now to set tops'ls and stays'l, to move us along into open water. There, we track with a prevailing tail wind, sweeping southward along the coast, toward diminishing latitudes. This route will eventually carry us through perilous Drake Passage, well south of *Tierra del Fuego*'s archipelago, and, eventually, into the broad Pacific.

DATE: JULY 5, 1819

THE MIDDLE PART: A sun sighting by Captain Rathbun indicates we have crossed the Tropic of Capricorn, 23° south of the Equator today, meaning that on this, the eighty-sixth day of our journey, unsettled seasonal weather will prevail. This is providential because Drake Passage still lies many nautical miles ahead, waiting to greet us with uncertain forecasts, perhaps including threatening seas. One small grace is that we will not be skirting this notorious realm of ice and snow, in that we are at the cusp of the hemisphere's winter season, as they are inverted in these climes. And while the worst of conditions don't prevail, danger remains a real prospect.

DATE: JULY 8, 1819

THE LAST PART: At evening mess, the captain stood to address us all, explaining to officers and crew, alike, that our course would take us into the Scotia Sea, east of Argentina's Islas Malvinas—known to the English as the Falklands. It is a wind-swept, sparsely populated archipelago some distance off the continental shelf. There, a rough-and-tumble fishing settlement can be relied upon if trouble arises, but landfall such as that should be steered clear of, since uncontrolled encounters with land are far more perilous to sailing vessels than most threats posed by open waters. He also informed us that the vessel is currently at a latitude, south of the equator, a distance equal to that of New England to its north.

DATE: JULY 28, 1819

THE FIRST PART: Barely making way under clear skies and calm seas. Currents, at least, in our favor toward Tierra del Fuego, still 300 nm S. Full t'gallants configured in hopes of catching a rising morning breeze, sails slack as ship lolls in flat seas. Spotted many varieties of sea birds skimming the surface, two-hundred miles due east of Puerto Santa Cruz, Argentina. Masts of ship *Dolphin* astern of us for last two days. At midday, day three, we shortened sails to allow her to lay by, allowing exchange of certain supplies. Hailed by Captain Luke Gallagher with request to deliver mail bag to Canton, as *Dolphin* now diverted to Hawaii and Northwest territories to take on otter furs and pine board.

My previous passages to Europe had acquainted me with conditions at sea, and to have confidence in the skill of captain and crew to deliver myself and cargo to our destination. But, whether by reputation or fact, the motion and color of the undulating waters of the South Atlantic around *Fame* feel different. Massive walls of icy-cold water lie ahead of us, rolling out in an endless progression toward the southern horizon. Though incomprehensible from a landside perspective—or even aboard ship making a passage between two familiar landfalls—the vast, untamed waters of the South Atlantic present an unfathomable reality when you find yourself surrounded by it.

First, is the striking color of the heaving depths as the bow plows forward as I stand at the rail, peering into it. It is of the deepest blue—like the infinite depths of the heavens soon after sunset, before night truly sets in. This is the lapis blue of the Madonna's robe in a Renaissance painting; the blue of a stained-glass window in Paris's Sainte-Chapelle; or the shifting purple-blue shades captured in the facets of a sapphire.

Even in the best of conditions, mounds of seawater rise to heights of forty or fifty feet, taller than the mainsail spar. In their slow succession, each gently lifts our vessel with vertiginous effect, only to slip under our hull, to rolling off toward distant shores. Our following breeze teases the crest of each swell, fashioning these monsters with a delicate trim of lace. These gentle giants will be our benign companions for days to come, only to turn deadly if weather and sea states deteriorate in the reaches of the southern-most tip of the South American continent—Chile's *Tierra del Fuego*, the 'Land of Fire'—named by those who have survived the passage, 'the End of the World.'

And the ocean's depths remain unknowable, inconceivable to those of us who live most of our lives on *terra firma*. The water's crystal clarity allows me to stare down several hundred feet into the heart of the sea; yet the ocean floor is still thousands-more feet below the location where I stand on deck, constantly shifting my stance and gripping firmly any solid feature within reach. Well beneath me, I imagine hulking leviathans feeding on creatures that live their short lives never knowing the light of day. Hundreds of leagues yet farther down, ghoulish monsters of the depth with eyes aglow and spiny appendages swim in endless circles with murderous intent. At this moment, but for the grace of God, I stand on the precipice of certain death—separated only by a fragile array of posts and beams—three miles above this mysterious briny domain.

DATE: AUGUST 2, 1819

After more than a week on a S or S-by-SW course—day 58, since first leaving Gibraltar—our compass rose swings to ordinal west as we run the length of the Drake Passage (so named after the 16th century circumnavigator), and Cape Horn, the dividing line between Atlantic and Pacific. A dark shelf cloud—looking like a massive tidal wave suspended in the sky looms to the east. Increasingly, fractured layers of ominous black clouds threaten to obliterate whatever trace of restless blue sky has followed us for most of the last five days.

It is said that animals can sense an imminent change in weather. No one can know for sure. But, perhaps stirred by subtle changes in barometric pressure, or actions of the ship in restive seas, large and perpetually dozing Cleo is now afoot, carefully exploring the nooks and crannies on the middle deck. She moves furtively from point-to-point, crouched low on her haunches, as though some savory morsel might be skulking around every corner. Usually eager for human contact, instead, at this juncture, Cleo has entered her primal state—vestiges of a jungle cat on the hunt.

THE CAPTAIN REMINDS me that a brisk wind, so long as it doesn't exceed Force 11 (below hurricane at 60 knots), is a level that the ship could easily withstand when properly sheeted and battened down. In fact, he assures me, a 'brisk blow' will only hasten our passage to the safer regions of the South Pacific. I remain confident of this fact, even as masts emit a ghostly low groan and the rigging begins to whistle around us. Routine conversation becomes difficult in the rising din. It's hard describing to someone who's not sailed in open waters, the noise level that sea and ship, together, creates—elements of one working to counteract and defeat the force of the other. It is surely a campaign of will between man, machine and the sea, as features of the ship are controlled by the skill of its crew, working in unison, to bring the mounting powers on nature—wind and water—to heel.

The crew is sent aloft to strike the Royal and T'gallant yards, and the T'gallant masts, to reduce weight and windage aloft. A single forestaysail remains in place, to improve course stability by keeping the ship's stern aligned with the source of the wind. Backstays are doubled to ensure that yards are not torn from their masts. Men aloft move down to the fore and main tops'ls, reefing them to a fraction of their fair-weather size. Rapidly mounting winds and spray force the dark figures clinging to the ratlines high overhead, to swing and jostle at every deep dive of the ship's bow into the next trough.

Regardless, they edge along the yard lines to reef or stow most of the sail area, leaving enough for the ship to continue making way in the storm; without movement forward, the rudder would be rendered useless—and without steerage the vessel could find itself abeam the breaking waves, only to be rolled like a dog in freshly mowed hay. Another worry amid a massive following sea like this, is being overtaken by a monolithic wave coming in over the taff-rail, flooding the decks with possible damage or loss of helm, spars, sails or injury to crew.

As the foredeck rises to meet the next assault, tons of airborne sea water and salt spray obliterate the gunnels and sprit, inundating the decks with seething foam. Our oilskin slicks are of no avail, as each new wall of sea water finds its way into our head gear, collars, cuffs and boot tops. Commands are shouted to crew overhead by first, Ryan Morgan and Captain Rathbun, "Hold fast, mates, *hold fast*," while the third, Haskell, with that hour's helmsman's watch, holds tight to the massive, ungainly wheel, straining to make way against the forces of wind and current capable of driving us onto the rocky lee shore, close by. Being driven miles off course in conditions such as this—not 'tracking true'—is not uncommon for shallow-keeled commercial boats like *Fame*, designed to enter the shallow waters of rivers and estuaries to conduct trade. Haskell struggles to hold a course to south-of-west, a so-called "safe quadrant," over-correcting away from the distant charted coastline; a compromise destination that can be made up later, once in calmer waters.

As conditions worsen to Force Ten, winds exceeding fifty knots, waves are building to sixty feet, with overhanging crests, the surface of the sea is embroiled with white blown foam. The ship is complaining actively: every seam and joint, every stanchion and pedestal groaning; every line and tackle crying out under the strain of each roll and yaw. Visibility lessens to a few feet as blinding sheets of rain pelt our cheeks with a force, feeling like volleys of bullets. I have not known the sounds of pitched battle, but as we plow forward into the jumbled sea state, the resounding blast of each wave striking our bow must resemble the deafening roar of blazing cannons pitched against bitterly opposing armies.

I have lost track of time, as we contend minute-to-minute with the building crisis on deck. Has it been a few minutes, or hours since the tumult began? I cannot say. But survival and safety are foremost in everyone's mind. To go below now would be unthinkable. Conditions below deck are chaotic—even dangerous— as unsecured items become lethal missiles. The mind's disorientation to basic notions of up and down, left and right can be so overwhelming, that *mal du mer* would overtake all but the most seasoned sailor.

With the companionway leading below decks sealed, I have no choice but to remain topside, gripping a mid-ship rail with all my strength. Spindrifts of salty air swirl across the deck, soaking my face and hair. Crew, similarly affected, are stationed at various key stations on the perimeter of the deck, in case they need to scramble aloft, re-securing some part of our rigging or reduced sail. At one point, during the melee, a slop bucket breaks loose, careening athwart ship. As much to prove myself a worthy crewmate, as to intercept this wayward object, I creep on hands and knees in driving rain across an undulating deck, to intercept and re-secure it. Not exactly an heroic deed in this moment of crisis, I nevertheless feel I've contributing to the cause. Later, as lines, having slacked in the rain, are hauled and refastened, I lend my hands and strength to the team effort. There is little else I can do, except step up to the task when rare moments arise.

≈

THE SKY OVERHEAD is now an unbroken, horizon-to-horizon sheet of leaden gun metal gray cloud cover, except for a low, narrow band of sickening yellow-green light spanning the eastern skyline. Mid-day light dims, masquerading as early evening. Wind gusts are blowing relentlessly above sixty knots, wave heights trailing past us reaching seventy feet, or more. Slender threads of foam course down the concave face of every wave, agitated by relentless winds. As each mountainous crest passes below us, the entire ship lifts, and surges forward, the bow momentarily burying itself in the ink-black tumult, the stern, with its massive wheel housing, lifting suddenly with vertiginous effect. The sea's surface around us is a chaotic scene of short, choppy waves randomly colliding, a sign of dangerous cross currents. From the helm, the bow is no longer visible in driving wind and spray. And yet we plow on, *Fame* holding its own against these unyieldingly harsh conditions.

Captain Rathbun shouts over the torrent of wind and wave for his second to relieve Haskell at the wheel. Michael Faircroft, who had been forward, lashing a tattered remnant of sail to the deck, rushes aft, across a gyrating deck and up the steps to the quarterdeck. As he crosses the short distance between top step and wheel, the large spanker, or fore-to-aft mounted gaff sail flying behind the helm, suddenly catches an opposing gust and jibes, swinging wildly to the opposite side with a loud '*crack*.' Faircroft ducks, instinctively.

In that moment of confusion, a massive wall of black, foam-filled sea water breaches the bulwark and entire deck on the port side. In a matter of a second or two, Faircroft is swept over the side. A short cry of despair, and desperate clutching for any secure object between the stairway rail and the gunnel is all the crew can later recall witnessing. Faircroft is thrust into the roiling cauldron by the power of the wave, and likely drowns immediately, disappearing into the chaotic scene around us. Rescue at sea is nearly impossible under the best of conditions, as hundreds of yards will separate a man overboard from his mates in a matter of seconds; and before the ship's course can be reversed, long intervals of time will have passed—enough for a panicked sailor to lose any sense of control and be swallowed into the depths.

Without hesitating, and without so much as a glance over the side, Rathbun takes the helm to spell the missing man. There would be time enough to mourn and remember later. For now, the survival of the ship and its remaining crew and cargo is paramount. Hours pass (or is it minutes? days?), as the storm tracks in the same direction as *Fame*, extending its duration and potential damage to the ship. Dead-of-night falls, as conditions remain dangerously perilous for a crew functioning on the verge of fatigue. *Fame* plows ahead into the darkness, as massive waves emerge, seemingly from nowhere, crashing over the deck and soaking its crew, again and again.

The stays'ls and outer jib are now torn to ribbons, all but decimated by the gale. Reefed mains hold steady, while masts and yards perform steadfastly, and decks are no longer constantly awash. When conditions allow, every square inch of the topsides will be swabbed, with seaweed and other debris jettisoned. A sense of order and discipline to crew, deck and fittings will be the order of the day.

With first light-of-day and a crew gone without sleep for nearly two days, conditions begin to slowly ease. Skies brighten, seas subside, and a noon sighting has us comfortably through Drake Passage and into Pacific waters. The nearly five-hundred-mile passage is complete in just over thirty hours, meaning our speed over ground (total of wind, current and storm surge, combined) has our vessel averaging eighteen knots over the seabed, for the duration of these calamitous events. For this, we are relieved and satisfied. But now, all are hungry and tired. Cook slaughters two pullets to feast our survival and success. The captain orders a ration of rum to be issued in remembrance of our lost crew member, Michael Faircroft, and to our bravery in the face of potential calamity. But first, some much needed rest and the opportunity to dry our gear in the warm southern sun.

≈

Dearest Mary,

This document may never reach you; not because I am not willing to send it along through the usual channels, rather because so much time will transpire before those of us confined on board Fame will ever see signs of life again. By then, the matters reported here, which seemed so urgent at the time will have been surpassed by other, more pressing and timely events. Please be assured though, that every word was set down with you in mind, so you may have a window into my heart & frame of mind, assured that my life continues to revolve around my undying affection for you and our future together.

With warmest affection, Samuel

12. Day 80, Paradise Scorned

WE ARE MAKING good time now, careening on a tight reach through the turquoise waters of the South Pacific, a fresh wind on our starboard quarter. Should conditions continue to favor us, the captain estimates we could make China coastal landfall in 3-4 weeks. As yet, 18° south of the equator, we have another port-of-call, Levula, one of a cluster of islands called Fiji—hundreds of specks on the chart—a remote tropical archipelago atop a volcanic ridge protruding from the so-called, Koro Sea. With time on my hands, I was able to study older charts, which mark these as "Bligh Islands," so named as the H.M.S. Bounty, and Captain Bligh, himself, who sailed this route decades ago to distant Batavia, near the Indian sub-continent.

This small, but critically located waystation surrounded by coral reefs was appropriated by the China-bound British in the previous century for the nearby prolific whale hunting, its abundance of aromatic sandalwood, and just as importantly, its abundance of the valuable sea cucumber, or *beche-de-mer*. It's gathered from the sea bottom by native divers with the remarkable ability to hold their breath for sustained periods of time. Their harvest is then dried, packed, and sold by the English to the Chinese, who consider it a delicacy for soups and as a stimulant to heighten ardor. A single delivery of dried sea cucumber could be worth thousands to my clients back in Providence and, as for me, a spell on dry land would be most welcomed at this stage of our westward trek.

On our approach to Levula, on Ovalau Isle, the island of Wakaya—notorious home to a rumored, human flesh-eating tribe—lies to starboard; to port, eighteen miles away, is Makogai, known locally as the outcast, leper island; and on the horizon, like delicate blue jewels, are Ngau, Mbatiki and Nairai—profiles of mountainous jungle and sugar-white beaches, evoking images of sequestered bays and buried pirate plunder. We carefully tack our way under reduced sail through crystalline, azure waters, the helmsman deftly avoiding numerous barrier reefs, a dangerous gauntlet of unchartered coral outcroppings just beneath the surface, into Levula Harbor. Dozens of outrigged, dugout canoes, manned by one or two, vigorously head out to meet us, even before we have dropped anchor. Their vessels are piled high at the prow with coconuts, mango and bread fruit. Each man hopes and expects we will lean over the rail to exchange a few pence for our first taste of lush fruit in some weeks. We, on the other hand, are too busy securing the boat to sit at anchor for some days, gesturing wildly toward the beach to the dozens of boats now surrounding *Fame* that we intend to negotiate, but only once ashore.

Our skiffs are soon lowered, as Captain Rathbun and I, Morgan and a select number of trusted crew row ashore to report to authorities, and to track the *beche-de-mer* processors; but not before warning the men that cannibals are rumored to reside in the mountains here. The captain explains that unless they're willing to pay with their lives, gambling on the prospect of an exotic meal or eager female companionship, their mates—or they themselves—might end up on someone's dinner plate. "They carry knives in their hair, men, be aware!" For the time, the rest of crew are confined to quarters and assigned to sail mending and storm repair.

Levula, with a low line of grass-roofed structures, sits beneath the blazing sun, among the towering coconut palms and mango trees of a gently-curving, white sand beach. Behind it, a line of steep, seemingly unassailable gray-green mountains rise to meet heaps of cumulus clouds and soft blue sky. Dense tangles of tropical jungle impinge on the boundary of a rustic village settlement, a slender thread of life caught between the looming shadows of untamed wilderness, and an equally unruly sea that can be roused to fury *sans* warning. A long-running stone wall, not quite as tall as a man, separates the village from the beach front. As we approach, just off our bow is a small contingent of children eagerly anticipating the beaching of our crafts.

Towering and motionless at the center of the scrum stand two imposing figures. The tallest by a foot-or-so, wears a long black cassock, his tanned, weathered face shaded by a large, broad-brimmed black hat. He grips a staff, tall enough that a carved figure at its top rests against his cheek. I spot a long-neglected plait of tangled silver hair streaming down his back, as he turns to calm the young ones. The other man, bedecked in bone necklace and arm bands, is clothed in scant tribal garb, his dark, leathery skin mostly exposed to the elements, except for a loin cloth, a *malo*, knotted in the front, with a portion streaming to his knees. He wears a turban-like headdress and holds a short, heavily-carved war club, presumably symbolizing his position of authority in the village.

"Welcome, I'm Father Andreus, of the Methodist mission here," says the former, even as we were still hauling the skiff to a spot above the tide wrack. "This is Nauvilou, local leader in the village. Your masts were spotted two days ago by our fisherman and we've been expecting you."

Nauvilou gestures with arms extended, uttering a few phrases in broken English, as might be the custom, since so many English and American boats pass through here.

"Joshua Rathbun, here, sir, captain of *Fame*, and this is Mr. Samuel Russell, of Connecticut, in America. We hope to anchor in the Pearl River by mid-month, next; but if a crop of *beche-de-mer* might be had, we would be happy to settle on a price, effect some repairs to our vessel, and enjoy your hospitality for a brief respite before moving on."

"Let's get you on your way, then," Andreus said, as he gestures with a sweep of his hand toward the village center.

As we edge our way into the village, our every movement is met by crowds of men, women and children, eager to size up this boatload of new visitors, offering us trinkets and crafts in exchange for an unspecified amount of pocket change. Our destination: the ersatz customs house, a British-built stone and masonry building with red-tiled roof near the village center. There, we'll pay port fees and the necessary considerations to the locals in order to secure a contractor to assist with resupplying *Fame* for the last leg of our journey.

"I wouldn't bother," says Father Andreus with a faint smile, "that building has been abandoned for years. I suggest you deal with Nauvilou directly. His terms will be agreeable, as he wants you to feel welcome here. I will speak to him later to assure him you intend to be generous, but fair."

Joshua listens, his eyes narrowing as he takes in Andreus's direction. The only sign of his discomfort with the arrangement—his riding crop repeatedly tapping his right knee. "This pirate is going to want a piece of everything," he utters as an aside to me.

Before we're able to conduct business, though, we're led onto the balcony of a small grass cottage, where a gathering of locals perform a dance, shuffling and stooping in unison in a tight circle to the rhythms of drums and cymbals. The villagers are relishing this opportunity to celebrate, and we show our appreciation with broad smiles and hands raised in thanks. In an apparent effort to impress, Andreus leans to within earshot of me, shouting above the din: "Before we arrived here in '95, native Fijian customs were debased and primitive. Earned the name, 'Cannibal Isles.' The chiefs looked at Christianity like an intrusion, with much to lose and little to gain; but we endured with our preaching at great personal risk. Eventually we want them to find 'Yesu,' cut their hair, cover their bodies...with Tonga-style *sulus*, change their marriage and funeral rituals. They call it *lotu*; we call it God's work. But mostly they listen because we bring Europeans—like you—on ships, to their humble marketplace, with opportunities for them to obtain powerful articles."

"Referring to what?" I say, keeping the conversation going without appearing to ignore the display, and not wanting to miss this opportunity to learn more about this unfolding scene.

"Guns, sir, rifles and powder speak volumes to these people...steel axes, tools, knives. A means to win skirmishes against other tribes. Barbarism is never far from their minds. They're rumored to eat human flesh; but fact is, the taste of enemy blood is an expression of hatred for the enemy and ennobles these men in battle. Nothing more than that. But don't be deceived, they've been known to strangle a widow and throw her body on a husband's funeral pyre, or to decapitate their victims, mounting heads on pikes in the village. Piles of corpses ready for human consumption is much considered a rumor spread in the West to justify sailing here, guns loaded, to control the population, to take what's theirs... a paradise 'wasted on savage cannibals,' they claim."

We know of a handful of expatriate Europeans and Americans scattered about the islands—social outcasts and opportunists who were allowed to stay, and now trade and barter with passing vessels for Western goods—looking for any way to survive— even advance their position—in these far-flung tribal societies. Soon enough, we'll be off to a remote jungle location to meet up with one of these survivors. In particular— he's a Brit, name of James Hanover—with a native sobriquet earned by sailors passing through as Driftwood, 'Driff' to the villagers. We ask Nauvilou if he can take us to him, hoping to learn his price for a dozen chickens, goat jerk, pickled eggs, tack, breadfruit, coconuts and a local 'beer,' *Okolehao*, made from the plant root of the *ti*. But we're told that encounter with 'Driff' will have to wait.

For now, a glance toward our anchorage reveals men high in the spars, suspended over the ship's sides, making much-needed repairs and refits after that storm and additional weeks at sea. Two pistol shots from the captain's side arms, however, signals time for half the crew to come ashore for limited leave. The other designated half are to stand deck watch, with their shore leave slated at first light on the morrow. A silent raid by dark of night for any unsecured object—all essential to the effective operation of the vessel—is always a possibility, necessarily to be avoided.

Nauvilou let it be known through Father Andreus that we're to be feted this night with a "lovo," made by building a large fire around a heap of stones, then burying leaf-wrapped iguana, chicken, and fish prepared with sauces and herbs to steam under old sail tarps. Charred yams with sweet pumpkin-colored flesh and a strong fermented coconut drink will complete the feast. About twelve crewmen have now eagerly joined in, enthusiastically scanning the tumult surrounding them and the evening's preparation for any opportunity for female company or a possible flagon of alcohol. Tension runs high between these two groups of men—natives and sailors—until we are encircled by villagers and shown seats on the ground nearby, where they make it clear, we're expected to remain.

Black-robed Father Andreus sits on a mat in a place of honor, positioning Rathbun, First Mate Morgan and I, on mats to his left, with Nauvilou and the tribal elders to his right. Andreus's eyes narrow, growing steely as he carefully scans the gathering. The crew is scattered in small contingents around the mounded, below-ground oven, eager to engage in this exotic setting. The bare-breasted women are separated as a group, preparing other foods, conversing playfully; but not interacting with the men, and certainly not with us, the foreigners here tonight. Andreus seems to be taking a smug pride in the fact that his unspoken 'rules of order,' however imposing they may seem to this open, trusting people, is having the effect of damping down any dangerous co-mingling of the sexes, as an unspoken energy stirs fitfully in the smoke-filled air, enshrouding the riot of stars arching across the heavens.

In time, Captain Rathbun rises to speak to the crowd through Andreus as his interpreter. He shouts above the clamor, "Thank you, and let me speak for all of us from the American vessel, *Fame*, how much we appreciate your hospitality here tonight." Things quiet, but only slightly. Rathbun's face is aglow with the flickering light of the open fire. The women giggle with embarrassment and amazement at this tall man with his tight uniform and awkward gestures. "Let me say that it is an honor to be with you at this feast, and as we depart tomorrow..."

Suddenly, a woman's scream erupts in the darkness, and in the back of the assembly, several men, including one of our crew, stand up, unidentifiable in the tangle of flailing arms silhouetted against the reed huts. A flash of metal—likely a knife blade—briefly glints in the firelight. One figure bolts from the scene, choosing a path between buildings and out into the darkened jungle. Three others leave, apparently in hot pursuit. Rathbun and I rise, standing beside Andreus, imploring the crowd to stay calm while we sort out what has just happened. A tribal elder rises, shouting above the din, explaining in his rapid-fire tongue that the 'white' reached over in the darkness to touch the breast of a girl, his daughter.

Andreus asks her to stand and confirm that this is the case. A willowy, dark-skinned woman-child, showing all the signs of a youthful, blossoming beauty, slowly steps forward, head bowed, tears streaming down her cheeks. 'Yes,' she nods when asked by Nauvilou if this is true. No translation is necessary. Her pain, and the rage of the assembled crowd are palpable. Again, Nauvilou raises his hands and demands reason to prevail, while elders from the village and the captain sort out the facts, taking the time to find and punish the crewman in accordance with regulations.

Rathbun turns to me. "This is a very unstable situation right now. I suggest we retreat to the boat for the night and let daylight cleanse the scene of this anger. Retribution here can be ugly. By headcount, the missing crewman is apparently Reilly, a kid who may not have known any better. With luck, he's found his way back to the beach and may be hiding in the bushes, waiting for us. We'll pick him up there and confine him to quarters until we can figure this out. I just hope those fellows quit the chase and return to the village."

I agree, and we offer our thanks and assurances that we'll stay on the case until the question of what happened can be addressed and handled according to ship's rules. With that, we all move directly to the beach, hoping to find Reilly there and to row the

short distance in the moonlight to where *Fame* swings placidly at anchor. We search
the length of the beach, calling out for Reilly, but without luck. Reluctantly, we decide
it's best to depart; and once back on board, explain to the assembled crew that night
watch should keep a particular eye on the beach. "Look for any sign that Reilly may be
signaling, or even attempting to swim the half-mile to our retracted boarding ladder.
Come and wake me if there's anything," Rathbun instructs. Concern, bordering on fear
can be read in the expressions on many faces among the crew.

≈

THE NEXT DAY, at first light, the captain prepares a small contingent of trusted men
to return to the village. In spite of the crisis now looming, we must secure provisions
for the ship, and purchase the chests of dried slugs—one of our principle reasons for
putting in at Levula. This transaction, one key to the profitability of the trip, is my reason for accompanying them. Rathbun advises extreme caution as we lower the skiff,
reminding me and the crew that the scene we're returning to may still be a tinderbox
of anger and resentment. "Moderate your actions and comments, men, and stay close
by. We're here to find Reilly if we can, transact our business and be on our way with
the noon tide."

The captain stands at the prow of the skiff, scanning the beach and village for any
signs of unrest as we edge closer to the village. As we near, a low-slung, dark object
appears near the water's edge, a slender shaft, like a flag pole, rising from it at mid-
point. Rathbun directs the crew to row in that direction. As we approach the wave
line and jump ashore, our eyes are fixated on the form—now clearly identifiable as
Reilly's naked body lying prone, baking in the heat of a tropical sun. His bloated face
and lifeless eyes point seaward. A spear protrudes from his back. Flies swarm above
the corpse. A sand crab, harboring in the victim's gaping mouth, suddenly skulks
away, a bit of flesh in its claw. We slowly approach, to discover that his body is covered
head-to-toe with dozens of small knife wounds and streaks of encrusted blood. A single, palm-sized square of skin has been cut from his back. Tales of tasting the flesh
and blood of the enemy immediately come to mind.

Slowly surveying the horrific scene, the body clearly has been awash for several
hours. Reilly's face, hands and feet are blue, his torso a deathly gray white; his hair, a
tangle of seaweed and small stones washed there by a lapping tide. Blackened ligature
marks, like macabre bracelets, are still evident on his wrists. The spear shaft, as tall as
a man, protrudes from between the ribs, having entered behind his heart. From some
distance away, a single set of footprint in the clear sand leads to this point. It becomes
clearer that a likely scenario has our man slowly tortured by his captors, prodded with
knife points, partially splayed, then set free to run the length of the beach, naked,
before being brought down by a well-placed spear to the back. His protracted suffering would have been agonizing, but in the end, a sudden spear point to the heart would
mean Reilly was dead before he hit the sand.

"Good God," Rathbun finally says, hand covering his mouth and nose, his facial
expression not concealing his revulsion to the scene. "This boy did not deserve to die
in this way...no one does. This is intended to be a warning to all of us. We must proceed
with caution and get our business done quickly. We can't be out of here soon enough."

We are standing in a semi-circle at water's edge, still at a small distance from the
body, its left hand and arm now floating in wavelets of a rising tide. It's as if we fear it
might suddenly re-animate, springing up to reveal its gruesome, desiccated underbelly.

Somewhat naively, I offer up a suggestion. "Should we ask Father Andreus to come and offer last rites before we bury the body, Joshua?"

"That would be unwise," Rathbun says, thoughtfully. "He's probably the one responsible for this. He resents intrusion into his little fiefdom, here. That was clear from his conduct last night. We're invaders and disruptors. He sees us as the face of Western corruption and greed. Reilly went beyond the limits of Andreus' version of propriety, and he paid with his life. I wouldn't be surprised if he ordered this."

"Not to be trusted, then," I add, since Joshua's logic for Andreus's involvement makes absolute sense.

"When you spend as much time at sea as I do, everything is possible, says Rathbun. "We can't bury him here. The grave would be exhumed the minute we left, and they'd take delight in dismembering his body. You two," the captain says, pointing to his crewmen, "go back to the boat, secure a square of sail and line to wrap and tie the body up. And be sure to weight it with stones from the beach. He's coming with us. In good time we'll do a proper burial at sea. There'll be an extra ration for you for doing it. Step lively..."

With that, Joshua places his booted foot on the back of the corpse and pulls the spear from the rotting flesh of Reilly's back. With a broad sweep of his arm he throws the bloodied shaft to the ground. Without further comment, we walk to the village and on to our business for the day.

~

ON THE WALK through Levula this time, we are largely ignored. People go about their business as though we're invisible. Far from the novelty status we enjoyed just twenty-four hours ago, we are now viewed as pariahs. 'Be on your way' is the unspoken message, one being received loud-and-clearly by our nervous contingent. Nauvilou had earlier promised that he would have Driff available for our negotiation today. We approach Nauvilou's hut, where two men with machetes stand close to the curtained doorway. Joshua gestures toward the opening with his hand, and a mumbled, 'here?' as though to ask permission to enter. The two men step back but are otherwise unresponsive. I wonder who else will have to pay with their lives for a few chickens, coconuts, and cases of sea slugs? The captain, second and I lower our heads to enter the darkened interior.

Except for a few narrow, dusty shafts of light angling through slits in the woven reed walls, the space is illuminated too dimly to make out any detail. Finally, after a moment of dazed silence, we perceive Nauvilou and a bedraggled white man sitting side-a-side at the far end of the space. A low table is before them. On it, a knife, and an unlit oil lamp. Joshua speaks first: "Are you the man they call Driff?"

Silence.

We move closer. Rathbun speaks again in a firm voice, belying his ongoing concerns as to the dangers inherent in this meeting. "We wish to purchase supplies for *Fame*, a quantity of slugs, and be on our way. Can we accomplish that now?" Driff leans forward into a dull shaft of light. His physical appearance is alarming. A nest of tangled gray hair makes his head appear twice the normal size. He sits cross-legged on a low stool. His face is masked behind an equally chaotic mustache and beard, hanging in a tangled cluster of braids to mid-chest. He is shirtless, his deeply tanned, oddly wasted arms hang from a sunken, skeletal frame. His age is hard to know—anywhere from forty to seventy years. His trousers, held at the waist by a frayed hemp cord, are ragged and stained, trailing off in shreds below the knee into the darkness. Incongruously, a large gold ring bearing a heraldic design of some kind, adorns the last finger of his bony left hand. In the dim light, his steady gaze beneath overshot eyebrows: pale blue, cold and piercing.

He finally speaks: "I am aware of your needs. Nauvilou has told me that you want fresh meat, vegetables, eggs, and other sundries, for the balance of your journey. I can provide these for you. This is my price. I have no need for specie. Your silver is of no value to me." With that, he unfolds and slides a piece of paper across the table. Scrawled in lead pencil is the following:

A large barrel filled with-
Canvas duck (10 yds)
Rope (200 yds)
Saw
Hammer
Awl
Cooking pot, large
Cleaver or other heavy knife
Weapons, with shot and powder
Tobacco
Rum
Magnifying glass
Journal paper and ink
Bandages or cotton for wrapping wounds
Blousing shirt, white

Rathbun and I study this list of supplies. We expected something like this, but not to the extent of such demands on our ship's stores. "This is in the extreme. Our vessel doesn't carry surplus for many of these items. It would represent a hardship for crew on the next leg of our journey," I say emphatically.

"These are my demands," Driff says calmly.

Joshua momentarily turns away, briefly catching my eye. The message of disgust is communicated through the expression on his face: 'he's done this many times before, and we don't have any damn options.'

"Specie would be less dear than what you're asking here," Rathbun protests, dropping the paper back on the table. "And someone needs to explain the incident during the night that cost my crewman his life." The captain now throws all caution to the wind, his rage and frustration finally burning through, as he looks past Driff to Nauvilou for a response. Yet another conspiracy of silence hangs heavily in the room. The tribal chief's expression is inscrutable, as if to say, 'there is nothing to discuss here. Best that it be complied with, or more trouble might follow.'

"Bring these things to me before the sun peaks," Driff interrupts, "and I will have your goods and twenty cases of *beche-de-mer* on the beach. I survive here because I deliver to my clients, and I survive because I know what I need to survive. These are the same self-preservation rules you swear by in that place you're going. They apply here, as well. I'm sure you understand."

Joshua snatches the list from the table, and we abruptly stand. As we turn to leave, Driff adds, as if to taunt the captain one last time, while curling the corners of his mouth into a broad, mirthless grin: "Those pistols on your belt. They seem fine

Philadelphia-made pieces. They would suit me just *fine*." Joshua instinctively places his hands on his pieces, as if to protect them from Driff's prying eye.

"Before we go, I have a question for you in return," Joshua says, exuding sarcasm. "Is that ring on your hand something you secured by the same game of extortion you're playing here?"

Driff extends a skeletal hand into the sunlight, his thin fingers frail as a spider's web. "No, Captain," he says slowly, admiring the object as if for the first time. "This was a gift to me from a grateful pirate king. He obtained it from an English noble traveling a tea cutter to China, on a journey like your own. Unfortunately for that gentleman, however, he relinquished it to the pirate with his finger still attached.

"Outlandish!" Joshua says, more to himself than to me or the second, as we leave the hut to return to the beach. "How dare that greedy son-of-a-bitch strip us of our essentials for the sake of his vanity?"

Having misspoken in the past, I hesitantly offer: "We're two or three weeks from Canton. Barring an emergency, can we consider ourselves well enough fitted-out for the rest of the trip without some of these things? Anything can be replaced when we get to port. The cost to us seems manageable when measured against the safety of the ship, crew and profit to be had from those piculs of slugs."

"I just want to be out of this hell-hole as soon as possible," the captain says. "But I take your point. Let's head back and inventory his list against our stocks to determine what we can safely spare. I don't want to roll over and play dead for that chumpy bastard. We've got some room to negotiate. There's already one dead body to explain here, for Chrissake!"

~

BACK ON BOARD, a barrel is rolled out on deck, as we begin to gather the items Driff has demanded. Reilly's body is now on a bench in the cool lower hold, the 'repair shop' where some of the items on Driff's list are kept. The closed-off area is now the scene of activity. The tarp covering Reilly's body is drenched in briny seawater to stave off decay; but, despite that, the stench is finally reaching the upper deck. The pervasive smell of death adds urgency to the task of completing the transaction. Nevertheless, resentment builds among crew, as they see the captain's willingness to strip the ship of certain essentials to satisfy the demands of this jungle madman. "Let's get this done, gentlemen," Joshua says. "We've a noontide to sail on and I want to be well on our way and not look back."

With that, there is a loud rapping sounds on the side of the ship. A disembodied voice calls out, "Permission to come aboard, Captain?" Peering over the rail, Rathbun sees Father Andreus standing in a small boat, his staff at the ready to rap again, if need be. He is waved aboard and minutes later, Andreus's tall dark figure stands amid the men filling the barrels.

"Driff has sent me to confirm your agreement and to extend good will from Nauvilou before your imminent departure. If we can confirm the contents of the barrel before it's sent ashore, unpacking it there won't be necessary."

"Everything is here, except for the pistols he so admired. These aren't negotiable. I've included one of the ship's blunderbusses—horn-shaped barrel, scatter shot. You can stuff anything down there on a charge of powder: rocks, nails, old bones for all I care. But not my pistols. Then, a hesitation and a question: Why can't Driff be here, himself,' Rathbun asks?

"Sir, you don't understand...nor would you have any way of knowing," Andreus says, appearing to welcome the chance to ease the tension. "The gentleman is not easily able to get around. He has no legs from the knees down, the result of an unfortunate chain of events. Mr. Hanover came to us years ago—'97, I think—one of few survivors of a schooner in pursuit of seals off the coast of the great southern continent. Their ship was trapped in ice for months. It's told they ate some of their own to survive, though few did. When at last they were freed from the floe, they brought their injured here. Hanover was near death, feet and ankles blackened from frostbite. After a week, their ship suddenly left in the night, gone except for the abandoned Mr. Hanover."

"Our medicine men had a plan. We fed him copious amounts of *kava* till he was passed out, then soaked his blackened legs with more and hacked them off at the knees. They were infected with maggots for days, but with salves and herbal teas he survived. Now he moves around with leather caps on his stumps, but never very far from his hut. I guess you could say, he's now one of our own. So, in that regard," Andreus adds slowly, adding a sly smile, "I will be speaking for him."

Andreus' eyes move rapidly between the items on deck, Rathbun's face and the crew's activity around him. In my view, he is on edge and uncomfortable at this moment. The question of what he really wants, is soon answered.

After taking a long breath in, Andreus slowly speaks: "Captain Rathbun, or may I call you Joshua, I have some details regarding the unfortunate death of your mate. I wonder if I might offer some comfort to you and his family to know of his bravery in the end. I can only imagine the value this information might have for those who knew him." Andreus let that last phrase hang in the air, allowing its full import to register, his gray eyes coming to rest somewhere on deck between where the two men stand.

"That might be helpful," Joshua says, a cautionary edge in his voice as I watch his anger grow. "How much, you son of a bitch? How much for your story?"

"Sir, I beg your patience and indulgence. I don't ask for myself, but a small consideration to assist my ministry with these heathens...work I have devoted my life to. Five pieces of silver could sustain my work here until another gentleman with your sense of propriety and generosity were to come to our shores," Andreus says, a false tone of supplication and pleading in his voice.

"Very well," Joshua snaps, "tell me about Reilly's death, but be quick about it. I want to be done with this."

Andreus begins slowly—but for the horror of it all—as if he were telling a bedtime story for children: "Reilly was a brave young man in the end. He hid for hours, but the treetop creatures revealed his hiding place with their calls of alarm to the men in pursuit. They tied and tortured him, expecting that he would weep and cry out for mercy. Knife points to the flesh were not enough to break him. He remained steadfast. Finally, a piece of his flesh was cut out and he fainted from the pain. Before dawn, they released him on the beach, with the intent that he would run back and raise the call to you on deck. But, alas, a brash young man raised his spear, and that was the unfortunate end of young Mr. Reilly."

"And how do you know all of this, you bastard. Were you there? Were you *there* for the whole thing?" Joshua shouts, barely able to control himself.

"Them's weren't monkeys screaming last night, Cap'm. I've heard enough of 'em over th' years to know the diff'rence. Them's was Reilly's screams," protested a crewman from somewhere on deck.

Feeling frustrated and disgusted in the face of this obvious manipulation of emotion, Captain Rathbun turns to me and asks from aside, if—as supercargo for this venture—I would be willing to commit funds to resolve the conflict? I agree and go to his quarters, retrieving five pieces from the specie chest. "Let's be done with this whole matter, then" he says, dropping the coins into Andreus' open palm, dismissively turning his back on the distasteful scene. He then barks an order, "Block the barrels to the skiff." Turning to me, then, Joshua says, "Samuel, take a second skiff and go to the beach with these men to inventory the goods coming to us. Check the barrels for contaminants and return within the hour. You...and you," he says, turning to the crew as he begins to move about the deck, "to the top gal'nts. We're wasting a fair breeze. Make ready to weigh."

With that call to action, and a clear indication that our captain was finished with him, Andreus—specie in hand—slips back over the side to return to the beach and witness the transfer of the barrel. Shortly, with vital supplies stowed and the piculs of slugs safely in the captain's keep, *Fame* is made ready to sail.

Once underway, with Levula finally below the horizon, we set a course for north by west, leading through Bligh Passage. The bow skims the gentle rise-and-fall cadence of a cobalt sea, as we prepare to release Jacob Reilly into Poseidon's realm. A plank is placed on the gunnel. On it lies the white tarp bearing the form of the dead seaman. Crew gathers around. Recollections of the boy are invited by the captain, and a few recall his hard work and good nature. "There ain't nothing worse than losin' a mate," another adds. "That bunk don't ever fill up again." With my Bible, I offer a reading of the Twenty-third Psalm; Joshua recites the Lord's Prayer, as a handful join in. With the words, "We now consign thee to the sea," two of his mates raise one end of the plank and the body slips into the waves, slowly disappearing into the ocean's realm. In good time, after the shock of loss has passed—and as is the custom at sea—Reily's meager possessions will be distributed among the crew.

We steal a moment of silent contemplation, as all quietly consider how that could have been any one of us, given the perils of the journey. Then, as a single albatross drifts high above the masthead, we turn back to our tasks. Five-thousand miles of Pacific Ocean and China's coastline still lie ahead.

13. Doorway to the Celestial Kingdom

DAY 106- SEPTEMBER 19, 1819, THE GREAT CHINA SEA

THERE IS A common misunderstanding that the open sea is perpetually tumultuous. But it can also be a calming as one might discover sitting in a tranquil summer
meadow. For several days running, on *Fame*'s last leg, I awake early to absolute stillness. As howling night winds calm and dawn breaks on a distant, encircling horizon,
the ship is adrift over unfathomable depths of a vast, mirror-flat sea. An opalescent
dome surrounds us on all quarters—soft, melding hues of pink, yellow, pale blue and
magenta—as if confining everyone and everything within a massive, inverted iridescent glass bowl. There is no distinct horizon. The heavens and sea are as one, an
unbroken glaze of dream-like pastels stretching from the ship's starboard waterline,
in a continuous, an unbroken arc high overhead, then down to our opposite side.
Any forward progress (making *way*) is entirely due to ocean currents during these
peaceful morning hours. Invariably, the rising sun's warmth affects restive ocean
waters, stirring a fresh zephyr to fluster our slackened, dew-heavy sails. And with
that, droplets of fresh, cool water rains down from the spars and sails, taunting a
bare-chested, whooping crew.

DAY 110, SEPTEMBER 23, 1819

A RED-LETTER DAY! After a relatively uneventful last leg of this trouble-plagued
passage of 110 days from Gibraltar, I am happy to report that the mountains rising
around the port of Macao are at last sighted on the horizon. In just hours from now,
I will, finally, be able to prove my value to the partners in Providence, learning first-
hand what Canton and the temperamental tea markets have to offer me. I immediately
dash off a short letter to Mary, letting her know of my safe arrival; and to Carrington
& Butler, informing them of my eagerness to get to task. I am also hopeful to find a
bark making ready to return to the states, to carry these missives of mine in one of
their mail bags.

As we approach Macao Roads under reduced sail, this centuries-old Portuguese
settlement seems about to burst at the seams with intense color and activity. After
experiencing so many days of 'blue,' its dense clusters of baroque stucco buildings,
whitewashed spires and red tiled roofs hugging the hillsides are welcome sights, rising
and away from the curving, waterfront esplanade, *Praya Grande*. The bay is alive with a
virtual fleet of vessels, comprising various sizes and sail configurations. All are darting
about like so many wind-blown insects. A range of junks, lorchas, 'egg-boats' (taxis)
and sampans, under both oar and ribbed tan-bark sail, crisscross in frenzied activity.
To my eyes, yearning for signs of civilization after so many weeks at sea, this bustling
waterfront more closely resembles a sunny Mediterranean enclave, than a mundane
business destination on the far side of the world.

Following the commotion of *Fame*'s sails being flaked, furled and lines made fast,
Joshua joins me at the rail, surveying a scene he has known well in previous trips. "A fair

treat for the eyes, agreed, Sam?"

"Indeed, not what I expected, in spite of all I've heard."

After weeks spent in my narrow cabin, struggling to read, write and dress under a sputtering, swinging gimbaled oil lamp, the clear, warm overland air feels good against my face. My mind is rushing, though, through a long list of risks and opportunities before me, wondering if I'm up to the challenge.

As if reading my thoughts, Joshua says, "There's a hornet's nest of opportunity out there, and a possible fortune at the center of it, if you can reach in without being stung or fatally wounded by intrigue and back biting. Upriver a stretch, in Canton, is where you'll be tested. Macao'll become your retreat away from the madness at times. You'll need it."

"A few months to make my mark, then retreat here for the hot months, along with the rest of the Europeans, what I've heard."

"Way it works. Den of vipers, though, 'specially those English. Been here for years, built up their connections. Guard 'em careful, like. Watch your step. Trust no one. Don't let yourself be squeezed by the tax men. Make your own peace with the ones upriver you'll need...the hongs, I mean."

After a moment of silence and without looking at me, he surprisingly adds, "There are some fizzing English cheeks out there, many for the pinching. And 'follow-me-boys'—you know, those curls on bare shoulders. All depends on how you play it." Maybe he's speaking for himself, I'm guessing.

A bit off-put, I manage to reply, "...and a Latin one or two, as well, I would guess. Someone for everyone, but I've a new family at home, wife, son, another on the way when I left. There's work to be done, and I want to get home as soon as I can manage it... assuming I can survive here."

"Let me explain something to you, Sam," Joshua says, as we lean on the ship's rail, the glowing Macao skyline in the distance, "There's a big world over there, behind that pretty beach and different rules apply than back in Providence or Middletown. You'd best learn, and quickly. Power plays and power grabs the name of the game here. Fortunes made and lost overnight. Watch your purse, keep a careful eye on your ledgers; keep your friends close and your enemies closer. They'll turn on you for a few quid. The winners get the spoils—you've heard the term?"

"I've already got that figured out, I say. "Being supercargo's not easy. Lots of balls in the air. I figured out how to survive on those junkets to Europe. Brought home the goods, as it were."

"Listen to me, Sam, I've civilized a lot of cubs, supercargoes who were boys when they left Boston, or wherever. Taught them some manners, things they knew once, but forget when they've been on their own in the world. Macao and other parts here, like Canton, still hold onto old world ways. There's a better society here, once you're on land again. Proper society, like back home. Trick is...they got their own rules, own way a' doin' things. Chinese are damn polite, expect the same of us. But, keep a Chinese girl in Canton, good as a death sentence, and frowned upon by your fellows."

"In Macao, though, after so many years of foreigners, anything goes. Somebody you're likely to meet here...real English gentleman...got himself a pretty one, a Macao girl, with a pretty sister who he's been introducin' around. Then, there's a girl named 'Ayow,' fifteen if she's a day. Lives on a boat by the beach, prettier than both of 'em. She's still virtuous...refused an offer of 500 guinies to go with one of those 'gentlemen.' I suspect she'll relent before long. These kinds of things are looked upon by Europeans as amiable weaknesses...*overlooked* maybe's a better word. But, make no mistake, there's a lot of bastard children running around Macao."

"Sounds like a rat's nest to me. Better walk a fine line, I guess."

"Big difference, Sam. Here the Chinese don't like us one bit. *'Fangai*—foreign devils'—and all that. They'd as soon kill you as deal with you. Medieval Chinese justice is alive and well here: guilty till proven innocent, understand?"

"Yankee values..."

"Don't matter more than spit 'round here, 'less you wanna live in a bubble" Joshua interrupts. "Likely as not end up with a *dàopiàn*, a blade in the ribs, lying in some back alley. And there's lots of them dark corners in these towns."

"You're scaring the hell out of me, Joshua."

Raising his arm and gesturing upriver, he adds, "There's a vast empire up there, 'Middle Kingdom' they call it, *center of the world*, as they figure it; spreads all the way to Russia and India. Want nothing of what we've got. Beijing and the emperor's men have their hands in everything. This is the Land of Prying Eyes and Extended Palms. We're allowed to do our business here so long's we obey the rules, pay our way, not mix or mingle. But it happens. Get caught and you're gone...or worse, *dead* and gone. Just remember rule number one: 'money makes the world go 'round.' Here's no different— as you'll see soon enough."

"I'm here for the money, mine and my partners. Set my goals, keep my head down, head home as soon as possible," I say, as much to myself as the captain. Without diverting my gaze from the distant scene, I slowly nod. This is good advice, I know. And as I take it in, I'm silently questioning what I've gotten myself into.

"Too many men want more'n that. Many men got rich here after failing at other things back home. Here they got fine silks, wine, Western-type food stored up to the rafters, the good life...women too, if you're willin' to chance it. Disease, crime on those 'flower boats' in Canton harbor. Easy to come by if you're inclined."

We continue to survey the view of the city's rooftops at what is now mid-day. Lush green hills rise in the distance to meet mountainous skyline, extending as far as the eye can see to the south, in a series of gently undulating peaks. Atop the most prominent verdant hillside, one of many multi-storied temples in the surrounding landscape— with their characteristic repeating peaked roofs—protrudes into the sky. Small figures, women in sweeping Western garb, and men in topper and jackets can be spotted resting in the shade of *Gutta-perchas*, pines and Dove trees dotting the landscape. As a summer retreat for Western traders and agents like myself—required to leave the stifling tropical heat of Canton for several months each year—I can already picture myself roaming these very streets, balconies, and hillsides. At present, though, aboard a cargo vessel with myself as its supercargo, we're required to lay here until local authorities pay us that much-dreaded visit, when that first round of fees and *cumshah* come due.

14. Land of Fragrant Mountains

MACAO BAY IS SMOOTH as polished stone as I emerge from the dim confines of my quarters, into the blinding morning light. I wish to survey the city more carefully now, from this favored anchorage point a mile offshore. Through narrow, blinkered eyes, I assay a narrow thread of the crescent shaped, *Praya Grande* beach, cradling the harbor like a cupped hand. Behind it, row-upon-row of stucco buildings, swathed in the saturated amber light of sunrise, are arrayed in jagged rows on hillsides. While above, a range of peaked granite hills topped by fortresses frames the entire scene.

This narrow spit of land, Macao, consisting of just a few square kilometers protruding into the Pearl River estuary, became a Portuguese trading post in 1557, but only after those 'foreign intruders' demonstrated to the distraught locals that their powerful gunboats and a few well-placed volleys could effectively control marauding pirate bands. For centuries, up until then, these unwanted buccaneers had plagued Chinese shipping and trade to-and-from Hong Kong. Provisions allowing European interests to remain in this remote location—of a few scattered lightly populated islands—would serve to deter and protect the interests of all concerned: the Chinese could access Portuguese goods in a manner acceptable to the emperor, and the losses attributed to corsairs and their crews would be eliminated by a small group of foreigners, strictly confined to a small geographical area.

≈

I INTEND TO head into the city today, to meet several long-time residents—mostly English—who, over some years, have shaped the opportunity that I am now planning to be part of. Unbeknownst to me, Macao offers a lively social life, a fact I would only come to fully appreciate as this day wears on.

At breakfast in Joshua's quarters, I learned a pilot could only be secured to guide our vessel upriver after making such a request at the on-shore Customs House, and that no pilot and 'chop'—or tax man—would be available until tomorrow. So, the vessel will remain at anchorage for a while. Captain Rathbun orders a shore-gig to be lowered over the side, as a cadre of four men put their backs to the oars, with the assistance of a small handkerchief of sail on the short mast. We direct the small boat to the stone quay at the north end of the harbor, next to the Chinese Customs House. Once there, the crew is ordered to stand by for the captain's return. We climb the steep granite steps to the pier, where, upon spotting our progress toward shore, several locals had gathered to offer their sundries. Two gesture in the direction of a sedan, standing empty nearby, with door ajar, while others offer me miscellaneous edibles for purchase: plantains, oranges and a type of strong-smelling fishcake, apparently rolled in seaweed.

One stooped figure, a young woman in ragged dress, gestures me to follow, as she repeats, "*roomee, roomee, you get bed for night here. I know where, nicee for you, niceee sure, ya, ya.*" I raise my had to signify no—'*na, na,*' as I have come to learn, then proceed directly up the walkway to the main street where we split up. I head in the direction of the East India trade building, while the captain goes to plan for the next day's trip upriver.

Once at the company's offices, I meet a representative from the British firm of Jardine & Co, recently established here. He is to acquaint me with the residence I will share in Macao during summer's off-season and those temporary offices I'll soon occupy at the factories in Canton. Macao is the only location in China where Westerners and their families can live year-round. Only for the five months of the trading season—October through March—are merchants allowed to reside sixty-five miles up-river in Canton, during which time no women are permitted.

As I push forward up the steep incline, I'm surprised to find many beggars lining the narrow street. One in particular positions himself in the central thoroughfare, making passage nearly impossible. I call to him to "make way, sir," but with his back turned to me, he still shows no sign of movement. As I edge past him, he startles, turning to reveal deeply cataracted eyes and many missing teeth. He seems so alarmed by my proximity to him that I assume he is deaf, as well. Just as he begins to scream at me with a string of unintelligible expletives, a young man falls in beside me, taking me by the crook of the arm and spirits me away from the encounter. "G'day," he says, "You're new here." His comment seems framed more as a statement of fact than a question.

"Yes, Sam Russell, just arrived on *Fame*, from Providence, in the States," I answer. With a note of caution in my voice, I endeavor to keep the conversation going: "An Irishman, yes? What's your business here?"

"I work for the good Mister Jardine and was sent down ta fetch ya. I spotted the skiff lowerin' over the side of that fine bark with American colors flyin'. 'Flower flag' the locals call it, on account of them six-pointed stars. Thought I'd take a chance t'wer you, sir. Brian's the name, Brian Murphy, of Dublin, but a while ago, now, since comin' with the company," he offers with a broad smile and extended hand. "Want ta follow me, sir, fer the quickest way there."

As we walk a bit too briskly for my constitution—still unsteady after months confined on that sea-going gaol—I take in the scene around me. Over the centuries, Portugal had managed to claim this city as their own. Church spires and European-styled structures share space among local Chinese shops and residences along the narrow, steep streets. Western and Asian populations mix equally on the byways, as each goes about their respective business. As we walk further into the heart of the city, streets narrow and steepen, with short flights of stairs interspersed, connecting sections of roughly paved walkway. Buildings are stacked, one atop the other, yet each retains its own distinctive style. Whitewashed Portuguese churches, trading houses and merchants' shops stand side-by-side with simple gabled facades and elegant, breezy summer English-style residences.

We arrive at the East India Company offices, and my impression is of a building functioning as a business in name only. I had heard that a viceroy had yet to be appointed here by the Crown, and so, until that day arrives, this splendid location gets to serve—more so than in any official role—as a men's club and retreat. I'm led into a grand, sunlit space, enjoying stunning views of the distant bay and boating activity far below. Numerous tapered columns line the perimeter of the room, furnished with large round tables around which men are gathered in intense conversation and card playing.

No one seems to notice my arrival, as my guide, Brian Murphy, shows me to a spot beside windows with a vertiginous view of the busy streets and rooftops below. Once I'm seated, a Mandarin boy dressed in Western garb, but with the characteristic long, plaited queue down his back, brings me a cup of tea. Balanced on the saucer, a pair of sweet shortbread biscuits—a genuinely welcome treat after time spent so far from the comforts of home.

Across the room, I see Brian standing by a tall thin gentleman, gesturing in my direction. Soon, the Scotsman, William Jardine, is standing at my table. He is elegantly dressed in a dark green waistcoat and cream breeches, a starched collar and black cravat sit high on his neck, accentuating his stature. His intense blue eyes, the color of a Scottish bluebell, with a pronounced brow add to an impression of intelligence and ambition. His face is narrow, but well-proportioned, his burnished complexion a sign that he has spent some time under the splendid South China sun.

"Mr. Russell, I presume, welcome to our world," he says in a rich Scottish brogue, extending his hand and sitting across for me. "When I got word from our Indiaman, *Lady Hughes*, that you were en route, I wanted to take the time to welcome you and address any questions you might have. At some point, a pilot will take your vessel upriver, and you may find yourself engaged in Canton for a while. This could be our opportunity."

"Please, call me Sam," I say, adding, "Thank you for sending Brian to fetch me. I may have wandered a bit without his guidance. But I've seen a teeming city, a good sign, I would guess."

"No bother, at all," Jardine says, "You'll need a Brian of your own, sooner or later, and a good translator, and a lawyer, too, wouldn't hurt. I assume you're good with the ledger, business dealing, the lot, you know. I assume that's your bailiwick, at any rate."

"I'm here as an agent on behalf of some New York and Providence interests," I say, not wanting to give away too much. "I want to sell cotton, nankeen, burlap, mill goods, you know. Maybe some pig iron, otter furs, ginseng root, whatever the market will bear. Tea bales, porcelain, silks to send home. Specie to close the gap between what I broker and what I need to buy to satisfy my clients back east. You know very well how it works, My apologies for that rudimentary..."

"These are considerable objectives, Samuel," Jardine interrupts. "I wish you well and I'm here to offer my assistance as you get your feet on the ground. The Brits never shy away from a little competition. In my memory, the Company's always had a corner on the Chinese market."

"I'm hearing that the East India Company may lose their court battle back home to control this market. The rich are forever getting richer, as they say," I added with a smile, testing the waters of my competition.

"Maybe, yes, but the argument is that American adventurism in this part of the world is inevitable, sooner or later. Look at your presence here, for example," Jardine said. "You do business here and, let's face it, the demand by the Chinese for what the West has to offer only increases. That affords us, the Company, the chance to carve out the more profitable parts through our established distribution channels, while other demands are being met by the Americans, Swedes, Spanish, and the rest."

"What could be more profitable than mill goods for tea and silk? The market at home is only increasing," I add, laughing.

"Look, Sam, you seem a reasonable person to me. I might be able to help you think this thing through. Your ship is not going anywhere today. Come back tonight for a small gathering I've arranged. This is a festive city and we've learned to amuse ourselves in ways we can't up north. There will be charming female company here, and good food...and opportunity. There are connections I want you to make. I'll have Brian take you back to the quay so you can d'on your best 'bib and tuck.' See you at eight, sharp." And with that, Jardine stands, gesturing to the back of the room, "Brian..."

≈

ONCE BACK AT the waterfront, I decide to walk a short length of the beach, rather than immediately returning to the restrictions of my onboard cabin. I peruse the Bank of England and the Church of Saint Paul, Portugal's great 17th century Gothic "Mater Dei." As I turn the corner onto the harbor, just out of sight of the town, I spot a group of Chinese men and women—old and young, alike—sitting together facing the sea, legs dangling over a stone embankment. They appear at first, to be fishing, but as I draw near, I see they're conversing while enjoying the cool afternoon breeze off the bay. As I pass behind them, one-by-one they turn to catch a closeup glimpse of this *Fan-qui*. And with that, each gets up in turn, fleeing as quickly as possible, abject terror written on their faces. As I continue my way, the discomfort with my presence appears to spread, as more revelers quickly move away. By the time I reach the nearby quay, a once serene waterfront gathering of locals has been completely disrupted. The curious nature of that encounter, while not wholly unexpected—given my earlier conversation with Joshua—stays with me for some days afterward.

But that will not be my last unfortunate encounter before a day's sojourn ends.

≈

AS I'M UNABLE to hail *Fame*, I decide to hire one of the many livery boats that ply the harbor. Called *tankea*, or 'egg boats,' these strange-looking vessels more closely resemble a tub than a boat, being about eight feet long, with a beam almost equal to its length, a snub bow, flat bottom, and a gunwale about a half-foot above the water. Each has a rounded central housing, covered with straw matting, from which it may derive its name. Each is also lined with mats, kept very clean and operated, in this case, by two Chinese girls.

I hail one drawing near the pier. As I step into this conveyance, the crew places a stool for me mid-vessel, under the housing. They then move to both bow and stern, working determinedly at sculling, or swirling long oars in the water, to gain forward motion. Their dresses are made of blue nankeen. One has an extra piece turned over her head from behind, forming a hood. Their hair is not shaved, but divided and plaited down the back, with a scarlet string interwoven near the end. They are good-natured, pretty-looking women who smiled frequently, chatting incessantly with each other as they work. One of them seems to have taken great pains in adorning herself, having arranged some artificial flowers in her hair. As I sit close to her, trying to make myself understood, I inadvertently catch hold of her arm. This appears to give her great unease, as she immediately draws back, turning her eyes, with much anxiety, toward her companion, saying *"Na! na! Mandarin see? he squeegee mee! He squeegee mee! Mandarin see?!"*

It seems they are watched all the time, even when out on the water, and will be punished if they're detected doing anything improper. "Squeegee," as I will soon learn, means being sent to prison, and a sum of money extracted from them before they can be liberated. I try to calm her fears, asking as clearly as possible, why the Mandarins are always so strict. She answers with great expression, *"Na, na! When nightee time come, no man see. Now Mandarin see, squeegee me!"*

By this time, we have covered the short distance to *Fame*, and I hail crew to drop a ladder over the side. I'm relieved to see Joshua come to the rail, and with him, a Chinaman whom he identifies as a translator who will be accompanying us on the next day's trip upriver. I plead with the translator to explain that I mean no harm and can explain if she is confronted at a later time. This does little to calm the tension on board their tiny vessel. After much exchange of feverish dialogue between the two native speakers, the captain finally raises his hands in frustration, disappearing below deck. After a brief absence, he returns with a shiny silver coin—or more precisely, two halves of a Spanish *reale*—itself worth more than a day's work for the busiest "egg-boat" and its crew. This is passed down to the two women and does much to defuse the tension. With an assurance expressed through the translator—speaking for the captain—that any further issues should be brought immediately to him, the small taxi soon departs.

Much relieved, and with profuse apologies for my unintended breach of conduct, I retire to my quarters to prepare, along with the ship's captain and first, for the evening's gathering, and to faithfully record in my diary, the events about which you are now reading.

15. Portent of Grief

UPON MY LATER RETURN to East India Company offices that evening, the large room where I had met William Jardine has been completely transformed. The view toward the bay is now masked in darkness, allowing the windows to reflect into the room all the warm light thrown off by two large chandeliers, each bedecked with dozens of white candles and trailing white ribbons. Tables have been moved to the edges of the large room, freeing up space for dancing to the sounds of a small orchestra assembled on a distant dais. White linen draped over each table, with centerpieces of red, white, and blue flowers arranged artfully, are further illuminated by silver candelabras. Guests in elegant gowns and waistcoats are variously seated at the rounds or mingling and chatting idly in small groups. In our casual perusal of the room in search of our host, Captain Rathbun and I can make out several languages being spoken. This was truly an international gathering—and one, I would guess, happening with regularity.

When we finally locate our host, I make introductions. Jardine invites us to be seated at a table near the Portuguese representatives, their wives and other consulate executives. Before leaving us, Jardine raises his hand as fine sparkling white wine is brought to us. Then, he offers, "Sam, you must make it your priority to meet certain people tonight. Once you've settled in and gotten a taste of our fine English cuisine, I'll be certain to bring you around. For now, though, you must enjoy."

After a proper English dinner, served on fine Chinese porcelain—chops, mashed, sprouts and gravy, a fine Burgundy and rice pudding—I move away from the conversation at our table to gather my thoughts and quietly sip a settling glass of Portuguese Oporto, when I am approached by a stranger.

"I have been watching you all evening," the man says. "Myself, I do not indulge," glancing to the glass in my hand, "a dear shame as it looks to be giving you so much pleasure. My name is Jamsetjee Jejeebhoy, of Bombay, but for some years now, I've been engaged here in Macao with pursuits that interest me greatly." As he extends his hand, he adds, "My friends call me 'Walla,' which might be easier to remember, certainly easier for a Western ear." We laugh at his self-effacing humor, as I make a mental note about the ease with which he begins this conversation. "You are Samuel, from America, here to make you mark, I can only assume. I trust you have already made a good impression with the people here tonight—reason for congratulations." With that, he bows slightly, a gesture of deference to my initial efforts to make a good impression in this room full of strangers.

I remember thinking, 'this man is as smooth as oil on water.' But I'm intrigued by his exotic appearance and mock familiarity with me...as I'm slowly being drawn into the orbit of his style. With deeply pock-marked, olive-skinned cheeks, and sporting a drooping mustache, 'Walla'—a Parsi-Indian, attended this evening's event bedecked in long, heavily-brocaded, richly-colored robes, banded in tones of maroon, chocolate brown, and black. A white cotton tunic beneath, embroidered with silver serves as a collar, frames a deeply weathered face. A *topi*, or tall cap, also embellished with silver and gold threads, remains in place atop his head throughout the evening, as is the custom in his native India. He pulls two chairs close by, inviting me to sit. I do so; but his uninvited familiarity is, I confess, causing me increasing discomfort.

"Mr. Russell," he says, leaning in and speaking English with a richly-inflected Hindi accent, "*Uma Grande Festa*, as the Portuguese say, wouldn't you agree, Mr. Russell?"

"Yes, certainly," I reply, hesitantly.

He continues, "You are new here, and I take your measure of caution, as I hope we may become new friends here tonight, Mr. Russell. First, a question to you...if I might be so bold to ask?" He then hesitates, leaning back slightly to study me, lightly fingering a large silver mandala that hangs about his neck. He hesitates momentarily, determining if I might object to his familiarity in this very public place.

"Your question, sir? Without knowing its purpose, sir, and with all due respect to your apparent long-standing acquaintance with some others in this room, yet I'm afraid we're not yet well-enough acquainted to be considered friends. Your...purpose... for asking?" I say, hesitantly.

"Believe me, Mr. Russell, I have only your best interest at heart," Walla says. "I think you'll find that an association with me and my extensive resources can serve you well in the long run."

As I listen, my annoyance grows by the moment. Still, I answer with an eye to ending the conversation, if need be, "...Continue, sir," I say.

"Let me pose an answer to my own question...at the risk of seeming impertinent: You are here to sell goods, and in the process, make your competency. And, I assume you have many at home in America who would wish you well, but also desire your return, as soon as it is expedient to do so, yes?"

"Mr. Jejeebhoy...Walla...my patience is wearing thin. Is there something I should know, or I should be getting back to my group," I say, visibly frustrated, now. My intuition tells me he's deliberately bringing me to this point, to test my interest in whatever he has in mind.

"Mistar Russell...Samuel," he says, in a manner that draws out the sound of my name, "If I may, I have many business interests in Bombay, on the Arabian Sea," Walla continues. "I and my family have worked with the Portuguese and British for years and have much in common, especially when it comes to accumulating wealth. As an American here, now, and with your influence being added to that of Mr. Jardine and the Company, I am making you a confidential offer that might benefit us both to the greatest degree."

"My interests have been defined by my employer on the other side of the world..."

"Agreed, Samuel, and yet, if you come to them with an undeniable opportunity to propel their wealth—and yours, too—in the transaction of daily affairs here, do you think they would reject your first-hand observations and deny you both that chance?"

I've finally had enough of the vagaries of this conversation and stand to leave. "Mr. Jejeebhoy. Either come to the point, or this conversation will have to end."

Undeterred by my sudden and unexpected response, Walla nevertheless remains seated, calmly answering, "Very well, Samuel, here is my proposal to you: remain here in Canton for the next year, eagerly pursuing your dream of wealth and influence. One year from now, I will send a ship for you to bring you to Bombay, and to my estate. There, you'll have the opportunity to see what I am referring to, and if it pleases you, we can strike a business relationship that will produce the riches you so desire. If you are disappointed in any way, I will deliver you back to this place so that you may continue your modest pursuits. That being the case, I'll be, as they say in that great English game of cricket, 'run out.'"

With that, Walla stands, managing a broad, genuine smile, extending his hand to me, as a sign of an informal contractual agreement to meet again in a year—on his terms, not mine, at that time. I hesitate for a long minute, considering that I might never see him again, or that I can always decline if the offer were to ever seriously come to pass. Slowly, I extend my hand. "In a year, then, sir," I reply.

"In a year, then, Samuel" And with that, he turns, melting into the crowd.

As the evening wears on, and with more than a fair share of food and drink under our belts, Joshua and I decide to take our leave and return to the ship. With thanks to our host, Mr. Jardine, we wend our way down the darkened streets of Macao to the waterfront. Approaching the quay near midnight, *Fame* sits calmly at anchor in the near distance, backlit in the shimmering light of a half-moon sitting high in the eastern sky. This time there will be no need for one of the many 'egg-boats' that perpetually rock against the harbor breakwater. A night watch is stationed on deck, waiting for our signal. And with that, Joshua takes a deep breath and pipes a shrill, short three-blast call on a silver boson's whistle, tucked in his vest pocket. "I came prepared tonight. No more egg-boat rides for you.," he says with a smile. Soon, we can make out the gig being lowered over the side, and in short order, we're back on board for the night, making ready, at sunrise, for the next day's journey up the Pearl.

≈

BACK ON BOARD *Fame*, I stumble below deck, into the darkened confines of my cabin, where I drop the full weight of my body onto the bunk, anxious for a good night's rest. I am suddenly aware of a small object that had been placed there in my absence—a pale blue letter bearing a hand-scrawled note across its front, 'via *Allion*, New York, to Mr. S Russell, via *Fame*, Macao/Canton.' I stand to light my lantern, then carefully open the missive, my heart racing as I hope a note from Mary has finally caught up with me.

I read:

September 8, 1819
Dearest Samuel,

I can only hope that this correspondence arrives in your hands safely and within some weeks after I pen this sad news. There is no other way to express our profound grief, as I'm sure it will come to you as both shocking and tragic, to learn that your beautiful bride and love of your life, Mary, has unexpectedly passed on the 4th of this month. On her lips at the last moment was the question of your well-being and an affirmation of her love for you. We regret that you had to receive the news in this way, and that by the time you learn of this, many months will have already passed.

She appeared to give birth to your second son, John, with only the slightest intervention by the midwife in attendance, Annie Barlow. Doctor Joseph Barratt was also present, but as is his practice, not in the room at the moment John Augustus burst forth into the world. The difficulty arose when Annie had to reach in to clear the placenta from around the shoulders of the child. He was a perfect specimen of a child, placed on her breast within hours of arriving. Both seemed so content. Within days, though, my sister developed a high fever, with extreme abdominal pain. She bore up bravely under the condition for days, as we swabbed her body with cool compresses and kept her as comfortable as possible. Dr. Barratt bled her several times, but with little positive effect. The infection and fever, possibly caused by the mid-wife's actions, finally claimed Mary's life, and her countenance was finally serene.

She is surely in Heaven at last, looking down on you, George, John, and the others in our two families. I can assure you that your sons will receive all the loving attention we can provide and that they will be strong young men when, at last, you return to your Middletown home. Mary Osborne Russell was interred in the shade of a lofty oak at Vine Street Cemetery, where so many of your friends and colleagues came to pray for her on her journey of rest and salvation. She, and I will await your return, when you can finally offer your private prayers and expressions of longing for the woman you knew—and loved—only so briefly.

Mary is now with you in spirit, and I am certain she will be able to hear and cherish whatever you may desire to share with her in your most private moments. We wish you well in your endeavors and look forward to your rapid return to the arms of your family.
With regards and profound sympathy, Frances

A feeling of helplessness overwhelms me. With trembling hands, I drop the letter to my feet, unable to bear the weight of its message. My arms go limp, my color and breath leave me; only the rapid pounding of my heart is left to remind me that I still reside in this shell of a body. In my shock and disbelief, I retrieve the letter from the floor, reading the words repeatedly, barely able to comprehend their meaning. Mary, DEAD! How can that be? The reality of the message seems to float dreamlike, outside my consciousness. My Mary is *dead*?! Just twenty-three years old, so vibrant and beautiful. So devoted to me and yet so encouraging when it came time to choose this posting halfway around the world and the extended separation it would mean in our marriage. We loved so deeply, so completely.

"I'll save dinner for you," she would joyfully announce, when I departed the house for a trip to Hartford, or a carriage to Providence, or an inspection of a vessel in New London. We joked, we laughed. We made two sons together. The second child I will not see for years, yet...and my Mary, *never* again.

And then, I weep. I weep as I hadn't since I was a boy. Tomorrow was to be such an eventful day, one I have prepared for months. But, in this moment, I can't think about the future, not even the task awaiting me a few hours from now. I needed time...*time*... to consider this tragic news. Going home would be impossible at this point. It would take more than three months for the voyage, and Mary is already in her grave. What would be the point? I am a widower with two sons and a family preparing to do what's necessary until I can arrange to return home—a prospect involving one-to-two more years here, at best.

The *Andover* is set to sail to Boston on the morning tide tomorrow. I will write to Frances and express my profound sense of loss, along with my gratitude for what she is offering to undertake with the boys—all so that I may remain here to accomplish what needs to be done. I'm determined the letter will be in *Andover's* morning mail pouch.

I muster my strength and call on Joshua in his quarters to give him the news.

"I show him the letter, being at a loss for words. Then. "I have to take a few hours to gather my thoughts and plans."

"I am so sorry, Sam. I didn't know her, but you spoke of her so often. Was it the fever?"

"A fever that arose from birthing our second son, they believe. She suffered in the end. It pains me to think I wasn't there. My ambition sometimes gets in the way of thinking clearly. I should have been there for her, not here chasing dreams."

"You're *needed* here, too, Sam. There's nothing you could have done to change things."

"I could have held her hand, something that simple. So *simple* and it might have made a difference." I begin to tear up again, the wound to my heart still so raw. A moment of awkward silence follows as Joshua's sadness for me is apparent in his eyes, as they're affixed on mine.

After a seemingly interminable silence, "What can I do to help?"

"Time is of the essence. I don't want our plans to move upriver tomorrow to change, on my account. I'm going back to my berth to write to my sister-in-law, to offer whatever I can to soften this blow to all of us. Would you please send someone by my room later tonight to take a letter to the Andover, being certain they place it directly in the hands of the ship's master."

I retreat to my quarters, where I lie, my head down, only to fall into brief, addled sleep. In that semi-dream state, I regularly conjure an image of Mary visiting me at my bedside. This specter will repeat itself, time-and-time again, haunting me for weeks to come.

≈

IN MY DREAM, Mary stands on a hillside, draped in a long white robe, staring in my direction but oblivious of me. A stain of darkened blood covers her groin and her arms extend away from her sides, palms facing me, revealing stigmata-like wounds. A cold wind sweeps through her hair, crackling and rattling dry rushes around her as bare oak branches frame her pale countenance. I call her name, but my words are swept away in the gale.

My feet are immobilized, mired in thick, ankle-deep mud. Slowly Mary moves effortlessly across the landscape—an ancient graveyard with weathered headstones, like misshapen teeth, protruding unnaturally in every direction. Finally, she is swallowed by the darkness of an aperture cut into the side of a hill. The family name, 'Osborne,' is emblazoned in a stone marker above the chamber. A heavy metal door then slams shut behind her with a bone-chilling *shunk*, resounding out from that gloomy interior and across the valley behind me.

I am finally able to free myself and rush to the crypt's iron door, rusty and layered in coats of peeling black paint. A large bronze lock rattles on its hinge as I violently shake the door, clutching the bars on a small window, peering only into blackness. I call out for Mary many times, but it only echoes back from the deep, cavernous space beyond. She is gone and I am helpless beyond imagining.

Suddenly, in my incubus, I find myself *inside* the heavy metal door, glaring back out through the barred opening. The sepulchral breath of death is behind me now—not only that of Mary, but generations that have journeyed here before her, lying motionless behind row-after-row of neatly arrayed moldy gray marble markers embedded in a crumbling brick wall. Faint daylight slants through the small aperture and dusty, stale air in the crypt. It seeps around my panicked body, casting a distorted shadow of myself against the tombs. I scream for help, but to no avail... only to awaken suddenly with a start and find my clothes and pillow drenched in sweat.

I sit bolt upright, swinging my feet to the floor, cradling my face in trembling hands. I slowly rise and climb to the deck, bathed now in milk-yellow moonlight. Still hours till dawn and I've already spent a fraught-filled, endless night, at best. I inhale the briny night air and gather my thoughts. I search for my strength and resolve with a series of deep breaths, vowing to sit and write the letter to Frances. It will be one that surely marks the unexpected end to one phase of my life, signaling another, more uncertain course.

≈

September 15, 1819

My Dearest Frances

I am ill-equipped to put into words my response to your recent news of my sweet Mary's demise, now three months past; but indeed, must thank you for your expression of most heart-felt and sincere sentiment.

Our loving family that she so caringly fostered speaks to her love and trust in me, her humbled husband. And I am bereft not only with an indescribable grief at her loss but also for my absence in her time of need. Now regretting the selfish decision to pursue my vainglorious quest, I am out of my mind wishing only for one last caress of her silken cheek, and to be able to hold my sons firmly to my breast.

Knowing, gentle Frances, that my treasured sons, George and baby John, are well-loved and cared for by their dear aunt, I would ask that you consider carrying on as their mother would have, enabling my continued presence here in Canton, in order to procure means to ensure my family's utmost future security.

I must hasten to deliver this message by courier to the barque, Andover, now anchored in Macao. I have requested that it be in your hands as expeditiously as possible, by way of our offices in Providence, and personally delivered to you in Middletown.

I am yours truly, and forever in your debt,

With affection and gratitude, Samuel

16. Whampoa

SOUND SLEEP WAS A stranger to me for the remainder of that terrible night. At six the next morning, an insistent knock on my door jars me, and I roll into an upright position, feeling half- dead from overwhelming fatigue and grief. I wander into the galley where cook takes in my disheveled visage, offering me welcome coffee, a handful of dates and a fresh-baked biscuit with jam. Then, from a bucket of brackish river water sitting on deck for just such purposes, I throw a handful or two against my face, and I'm as ready as I'll ever be to meet the day.

The river pilot's vessel pulls alongside *Fame* just as the sun rises over the banks of the Pearl, its surface aglow in soft rose-pink morning light. The day promised to be warmer than usual, with early boat traffic already scattering in every direction. The day's task is to move our ship and cargo to the next anchorage—one more step in a series toward my objective, Canton. This protracted journey, as I would soon learn, is easier said than done.

Our pilot, A-kou, is a small, muscular man. His arms are deeply tanned and heavily tattooed. A small skull cap balances at the back of his head, revealing close-cropped graying hair; even so, he is of indeterminate age. With nervous, bird-like gestures, he moves to mid-ship, immediately kneeling on the deck to unroll a well-worn scroll. He carefully lays out a quill and ink set, then proceeds to carefully record specific details regarding our vessel. Captain Rathbun is familiar with this routine, carefully answering through our linguist, Arsee. He provides his name, the identifying features of the ship—name, length, girth, flag flown—type and amount of trade goods, specifying the number of crew and passengers on board, number of cannon ports and other armaments.

A-kou, speaking again through the linguist, makes it clear that, without real cargo to be offered for sale, we will not be allowed to move upriver from this point, assuming that without tangible goods to be made available to Chinese merchants, we're likely to only be 'smugglers or troublemakers.' This pilot is our river guide for the rest of the day, and will present these papers to authorities, along with his assurance that passage to the next station has occurred without incident. His role, apart from acting as river pilot, is to act as official eyes and ears, assuring authorities that proper fees—so-called cumshaw—can be properly calculated for all undisturbed goods accounted for on board.

The Pearl habitually silts up in unexpected places, forming sandbars that are shifting constantly. So, pilots earn their keep by knowing where those hazards are day-to-day and staking their reputations on delivering vessels though heavily fortified narrows called 'The Bogue,' twenty miles upriver. This day will cost us fifty dollars for the Macao pilot, and one dollar more for each of the sampan tow boats—dozens in all. I had heard these prices had risen steadily over recent decades, and with more than one-hundred-fifty ships arriving yearly now, these pilots can name their price. They're licensed by the local government, which helps curb the problem of price gouging known as the 'squeeze.' But in this case, a long-standing relationship between Captain Rathbun and A-kou helps keep the fee within reason.

"Keep your eyes and ears open from this point on," Joshua tells me, "If you're going to be doing business with the Chinese, you'll be repeating this process time-and-time again."

Fully freighted, we'll need twenty-one feet of water under our hull to clear obstacles lurking in this soup. We'll be towed through the Bogue by a small army—or should I say 'navy'— of sampans, outfitted with rows of oars and men willing to put their backs to the task of hauling a hundred-fifty-ton vessel against wind and currents, for hours at a time. Our pilot is in the lead sampan of a fleet numbering about forty craft, each tethered individually to our bow. A-kou employs a long bamboo pole to detect and avoid sandbars, barking orders to the oar masters, as we inch our way along, with a small boost from the incoming tide.

From our current anchorage just north of Lintin Island, the Pearl delta widens to some fifteen miles, meaning landmarks on both far-flung banks are best observed from the ship's crow's nest, thirty feet up the mast, and even then, through an eye glass. To gain this advantage, I request of Joshua that I'd like to head up to that vantage point.

"Have your way, Sam, but hang tight. Crew is used to those heights, but I'll not send one of 'em up there to rescue you if your courage turns to mush."

From my arial vantage point, I watch as we are slowly drawn through a strange, exotic landscape. The Pearl estuary is bounded by broad swaths of low-lying plains cast in brilliant shades of green and yellow. Under a thin haze, these neatly divided, terraced rice paddies and their irrigation channels sparkle in the mid-day sun. Scattered workers are silhouetted in the shimmering light, hunched over, calf-deep in water, pulling up fistfuls of fresh green shoots, then stacking them in baskets slug over a shoulder. Each wears a conical straw *kasa* as protection from the day's heat. These fields stretch for miles toward distant mountains, rising abruptly skyward in graduated row-upon-row—hazy gray-green leviathans fading into the distance.

The river itself is smooth as glass today, with barely a breeze to propel *Fame* upriver. Brightly colored sails of varying shapes and sizes drift by, becalmed by the same windless condition. A few helmsmen have taken to sculling their boats, swirling long oars off the stern to gain forward motion. Others just allow river currents to carry them along to some indeterminate destination.

I am struck, as an observer of this panoramic spectacle, that time—not just hours or days, but centuries, have ground to a standstill. I'm witness to scenes from an epoch where civilization's progress remains locked in ancient times. High overhead, a conspiracy of ravens circles slowly. From their perspective, we must appear like a massive, floating chariot, drawn in slow motion across a watery plain, by a phalanx of mythic multi-legged sea creatures. On the deck far below me, crew appear as miniature pieces on a game board, scurrying here and there to ensure that tow boats remain secure to tethers. Aloft, I can imagine being momentarily free of the dangers and challenges ahead. At this rare moment, I have become the raven.

～

WE MOVE SLOWLY northward, and the riverbanks close in like a funnel, becoming a defile whose walls rise dramatically out of the water. According to our charts, the river measures just a mile wide at this, its narrowest, with the entrance to this region of the Pearl, the *Bogue*, noted on charts as *Boca Tigris*, or 'Mouth of the Tiger.' The heights are marked by a series of ancient fortresses, conspicuously manned by men in military garb.

Now, back on deck, I say, "I'm feeling right now like I have a target on my back. Chinese brigades staring down from those perches, sizing us up." I confess to feeling unsettled for the first time since arriving at Macao Roads, three days ago.

"Oh, you mean 'French Folly' and 'Dutch Folly.' They aren't movin' against us." Joshua says mockingly. "Because, before long, we'll be greasing a few palms. That's how it works 'round here. We pay a lot a' salaries by comin' to these waters, includin' the emperor's army up there in those hills. Trust me, done this a few too many times ta' know, haulin' goods for the Brits...and the like."

The Chinese have cited several strategic fortifications along this section of the Pearl. These garrisons—six in all, located over just three miles—are designed to defend against pirates and invading forces. They've guarded this river gateway to Canton for centuries. From the deck of *Fame*, this heavily protected gauntlet along the length of the Bogue seems impregnable, indeed. But, on closer examination, these fortifications appear naïvely outdated to my eyes, a crucial flaw that could cost the Chinese dearly, if they were ever seriously challenged by more sophisticated Western naval forces.

After clearing the Bogue, in the final twelve miles to our anchorage at Whampoa Roads, the river widens only slightly, as the rocky inclines that had loomed over us, bristling with fortifications and cannon, recede from sight. For the first time since our anchorage in Macao, an expansive, confounding delta of small islands, streams, and tidal rivulets, comingled with verdant patches of cultivated rice fields, opens up around us. North of Whampoa, the river is too shallow and narrow to accommodate vessels of our size. Here, at Whampoa, though, a commercial ship like ours might linger for months, waiting for a profitable cargo to transport back to an American or European port, or when the Chinese winter trading season opens again.

As we approach Whampoa Roads, Joshua, Ryan and I stand together on the quarterdeck, observing the dozens of pilot sampans heaving off their lines, then scattering to the riverbanks.

"Step lively, men," Rathbun orders. "Set a double anchor at the bow, one at the stern to keep us aligned with that bank ta' port. No tellin' when we'll be on our way again." Several crew work the windlass to draw the ship toward the forward anchor, as the aft line is slacked, then tensioned and secured. This maneuver helps to maintain our relative fore-aft position in the tight lineup of vessels in the immediate area. Cleo casually surveys the scene, brushing against the binnacle pedestal, then settling near my feet, purring loudly in hopes of a scratch behind her ears.

Stepping to the rail and addressing me formally, as he always had before his men, Captain Rathbun announces, "Mr. Russell, see to those possessions of yours in that crib you'd be callin' home for th' last four months, 'n more, and I'll have you brought to shore, once your duties here're completed."

"I'm hoping to unburden the vessel soon. I'm as anxious to get ashore as you all," I add in a voice loud enough to be heard by crew, knowing they're anxious to be done, as well.

Joshua momentarily turns back to the crew working on deck. "Flake the resta' them lines on th' quarter deck. All of it. Gotta dry in the heat a while. If the sun lasts, we'll coil and stow tomorrow."

"Look, Sam, this is China," he says, a tone of earnestness in his voice. "You've gotta shake a few hands; be the diplomat. He'll never show his face in these parts, but the emperor is everywhere, and in everything you'll do, from now on. These taxes? Levies? Everybody knows some goes directly into his pocket up north in Beijing—the emperor's 'present,' they call it—some into the pocket of whatever hong you'll be workin' with. These guys, the Co-hongs, are the emperor's favorites, handpicked. They get nothin' for it, 'cept what they can squeeze out'a us."

As anchors settle into the mud on the river bottom, Joshua leans forward, shouting to the crew below, "Make sharp, now, men. Haul those line in an' flake 'em on deck to dry! We'll be usin' 'em again soon enough." Turning back to me, his dark brow furrowed, "This is where it gets dicey. Our length and beam, type a' cargo, all that'll go to figurin' what we lay out to these customs men further along, now we've reached the end of the line. This is where you take over, Sam."

"Been in this spot before, but never with so many layers. Supercargo's supposed to feel the pinch of a crafty customer once or twice, never like this."

"Soon's we get inspected, you'll take a report up river to customs. Ryan, here, will take you there. Pay the bill, be sure to get the chop on the paperwork, co'mon back and we can start to unload. Don't be afraid ta' bicker. They'll spot you as a newcomer. Push you ta' the limit. Stand your ground. They'll remember, repsect ya' goin' forward. Rest'll be up ta' you, here on..."

Sensing a shift in my connection to the ship and crew, I offer a kind of 'goodbye,' "Well, you got me here without a scratch. Cargo of English bunting, bolts of their finest roller-printed cotton, ballast stone from that quarry up north a' Boston, Brazilian teak to line some fancy room up north in Beijing... kept me and the rest dry, all the way from Providence. Good job, I'd say, not to mention that nasty run-in in the Fijis, Andreus and his band of thieves."

Without registering any positive emotion, this hardened New England seaman keeps his eyes fixed on the horizon, as he adds, "I'm deliverin' you to Canton, which I was tasked ta' do." You fill the belly of this ship with tea and what-have-yous, I'll restock the galley with the help of the comprador, and I'll be shoving as soon as possible.

'Agreed. Rest is up to me."

Joshua hesitates before offering one final bit of advice: "Based on what I've seen here, I'm a bit worried you're too wide-eyed about the world. Go make you mark and take care a' your backside. Once we're finally upriver, let's swap out this cargo for some choice tea for them ladies back home, good leaf ta' go with them sweetcakes they's always nibblin' on. I've got my usual shopping list and a few dollars from those fine women of Providence. Their havin' me look for some fine porcelain and silk wraps, bolts of silk in special colors, mind you, for those big windows of theirs. Protect their delicate constitutions from those cold winter winds blowin' up their skirts. Then'll be on my way, best sooner than later. Rather be at sea, than moldering in some Chinese backwater." He smiles at me, knowing I had to pretend not to be listening to his list of complaints.

Jokingly I reply, "You be sure to tell the company men back home this particular supercargo didn't spend too much time leaning over the rail when things got rough out there, in spite of your navigation skills; and that I'll put the spare pocket change they sent me here with to good use."

At anchorage here at Whampoa, I take note that on a few of the ships around us, upper spars and rigging have been removed to reduce weathering, hatches and gun ports are sealed, maintenance schedules have slowed to a crawl. With time on their hands, restless crews will be set loose to wander Canton's riverfront alleys and bars outside the city's old walls, drinking, fighting and seeking the company of 'flower girls,' when they think they can get away with it.

17. Departing *Fame*

ON THIS, THE last step of the journey, my cargo is broken up into components for transfer by smaller boats from the Whampoa anchorage to Respondentia Walk, a broad staging area separating the Thirteen Factories from the river, with a customs house at the eastern end. It is there where the next round of taxes will be levied, then 'factored' or inventoried by company men (hence the name, 'factories'), and finally warehoused. These steps, which can take weeks, occur under the watchful eyes of the tariff collectors—*hoppos*—and *hongs*, or Chinese agents for local businessmen, all with a keen, vested interest in what all transactions on the banks of the Pearl. It's there, at the center of the trading action, where I take up my responsibilities in one of the many buildings squeezed in along a three-hundred-yard long stretch of Western-occupied territory—the so-called 'Thirteen Factories.'

Later that afternoon, a barge pulls abeam *Fame*, and a small group of Chinese men, arrayed in silk and beads, climb aboard with several carefully wrapped bundles. Their presentation, made with great care and ceremony, consisted of several flasks of Chinese wine—*shamshoo*—two sacks of rice flour, and two sides of steer beef. *"We makee to for you. Here you bring us, we nicee, have from Hai Kwan Pu, makee contentee, yes?"*

Joshua turns to me to explain, "These are gifts being delivered from the *Hai Kwan Pu*, what we Western ear hears as '*hoppo*,' a sign of mutual respect and appreciation. They're hoping they make *me*, the captain, but especially *you* as supercargo, happy. Put you in good mood, yes?"

"Thank you," I say, offering a slight bow in the direction of the party of men. "Very contented, very contented."

Later, Joshua explains, "This happens every time we're in port. "'Gifts from the emperor,' s'posed ta' put us in a good mood dealin' with 'em later. I'll see to it the men'll get a ration of that rice wine. Likely I'll probably swap out the racks and flour with the comprador or tidewaiters for a few pounds a' th' good stuff. They can use it in better ways'n us. Anyway," he said smiling, "prob'bly couldn't get a fork or tooth inta' that bullock without a good three-day soak in some good Irish whiskey. Not a good use a' Dublin's best, though."

As I listened...watched, the political realities of doing business in Canton were becoming clear to me.

≈

AS SUPERCARGO, MY task is to see to it that all cargo is accounted for as it moves from the holds below, and to pay fairly assigned levies. Without oversight, we'd be taxed heavily, no doubt. My job, acting as agent for my clients back home, is to challenge any unnecessary or excessive levy. The linguist, Arsee, whom we picked up in Macao, is now a fixture on board. He'll work with a security agent to re-measure the boat—its length-times-beam calculation being the basis for our port fee. He then confirms that our cargo remains untouched since arriving in Macao and calculates the long list of other charges (including the emperor's 'present') to be collected and delivered to a waiting hoppo, stationed thirteen miles north, in Canton, itself, on the yet-narrowing banks of the Pearl.

Word of the contents on my vessel then passes along to one or more *hongs*, appointed by the emperor to personally take charge of the sale of our goods to merchants in Canton, or elsewhere. Direct sale by Westerners to Chinese merchants is strictly prohibited. Often, the *Hong*, sensing a profitable business opportunity, might, himself, become a buyer of selected goods. All fees are calculated and settled—linguist, comprador, pilot, hoppo, customs officers, and those due from merchants who are buying before goods can be transferred to shore.

Over the next several days, a fleet of shallow-draft barges, called lighters or chop boats, owned by Chinese merchants, will make several two-hour trips to the crowded wharfs, fifty-yards distant from the factory façades. The drop-off point for lighters is a row of low docks designated as Jackass Point. At the east end of the point, a granite stairway in the bulkhead leads up to ground level. Paperwork for goods unloaded there is reviewed and catalogued, or "factored" before being moved to warehouses—either those of the shipping company itself, or belonging to a hong, who might purchase the goods outright, or on behalf of one of his merchant clients.

"I'm going to follow the first load upriver," I say to Joshua. "There's hardly been anyone at the American office for the last couple of years, and I've got to keep an eye on this cargo until it's tucked away."

"Take A-kou with you. He'll help you find your hong. I'll get the jolly boat into the water. Wait for the tide to turn though. Might save an hour."

"Paperwork?"

"You're free to go up and down the river by yourself. No goods, just you and your small crew. Supers and masters can move about, doin' their business. Long's the goods stay put or move to and fro, official-like."

"What should I take with me, though?"

"Just our bill of lading with the hoppo chop. Makes you official when you get to Jackass Point. Merchants like you, bottom of the barrel as far as Mandarins're concerned. Low on the list of foreign devils, ya know, *gwai-lou*. All them fancy diplomats as such, gotta go to the south gate of the wall, present themselves...ask permission to come into the country. Then wait for word to go up the line, all the way to Beijing. Can take days...just waitin'. Called the Petition Gate 'cause of that little hitch. You...you just go to the customs house right there on Respondentia Walk with that bit a' paper. Says you're official and flush with the tax man, and you can go t' the factory office. No farther than that, though. Don't get any ideas 'bout wanderin.'"

I finally launch with Ryan, the ship's first, but not before saying goodbye to Joshua, who I will be engaging with on shore for brief periods, but under different circumstances. I also track down third mate, Haskell, and as many of the crew as I could find, reminding them of the hard time they handed me when I first boarded *Fame* in Providence, nearly four months ago.

We're itchin' t' get ashore and sample some a' what Canton has ta' offer but won't get shore leave 'til yer cargo be unloaded," says one.

"I get the hint, but you gotta dip a shoulder to make that happen. No good times till the heavy liftin's done."

"Mr. Russell," calls out another from a spar overhead, "Ya weren't the dead weight we thought ya'd be. Luck and a cold pint be with ya, sir," he says with a laugh.

"I'll take that as a compliment, I guess," I retort to the disembodied voice above.

Cleo executes a fine balancing act wherever the action unfolds, negotiating the narrow cap rail nearby. Crew are calling Morgan a 'lucky son-of-a-bitch' for heading ashore, as the jolly's lowered. No sooner are we in the water and underway by way of Fiddler's Reach, than a volley of cannon fire, five in unison, issue from the portals of *Fame*, a salute to my safe arrival. As it resounds off the nearby hills, I look back to see the ships ensign—our 21-stars and stripes the Chinese call the *'Flower Flag'*— being lowered to half-staff, then briskly raised again, a way of signaling farewell, and announcing to all neighboring vessels another safe passage for our American vessel.

18. Jackass Point

WITH FIRST MATE Morgan to accompany me, this is the final leg of my months'-long travail, just a ten-mile sail to my new enterprise. After so many months at sea, our first glimpse of the rolling landscape north of the Bogue, and, finally, the city skyline of Canton is breathtaking. Departing Whampoa anchorage, we raise a small flag on the jolly's masthead, The Russell Company's own blue diamond on a white field. These so-called 'flag boats' can travel the river freely, carrying ship's officers and super-cargoes, regularly moving between Whampoa and Canton. The one restriction: no cargo allowed.

We sail past the distant, nine-tiered Whampoa pagoda standing at a high point on *Pazhou* Island. It's one of many along our inland route, with an entire series of towers up and down the coast, and inland, too, Rathbun told me. With the last structure posi-tioned in line-of-sight to the next, fires can be lit atop each, progressing all the way to *Beijing*, to warn of invasion.

Traders anchor regularly here utilizing storage and tool sheds of bamboo and matting, called bankshalls, rented from local officials. Upper masts and spars—removed to prevent weathering—and other ships' supplies are stored here for the months'-long stay at Whampoa. For many sailors arriving here, the last deep-water anchorage on a long journey, the light of a setting sun behind this pagoda means the drinking lamp is finally lit. On a modest rise behind the tower is a small burial ground, done in the Western tradition, where the bodies of mariners who've died en route, or while in port—whether of disease, accident, or hard living—are buried. It's a sol-emn scene, rarely receiving even a glance by the men passing by, fearing a similar fate for themselves.

We sail along, with a generous push by a fair breeze and tide, as three women scull along a nearby bank in a small sampan. Their narrow vessel is heaped with oranges and bananas. They offer their goods for sale, while keeping up a remarkable pace at the helm—just two strong women at the oars. *"You wantshee fruit? All same plantain, all same orange."* They keep up this pace for several yards, as long as they believe they might make a sale. I direct Ryan to shiver the main, calling out, "Yes, I can!" allowing the women to get close enough to exchange a few pieces of fresh fruit for a handful of coppers—as we sail on.

We are not alone on the river. The Pearl is alive with activity against a backdrop of luminescent green rice paddies and cane fields, all splayed over broad plains extend-ing from the river's brackish highwater mark. Far beyond, ranks of conical, pale-blue mountains march off into the distance. Mandarin houseboats, lacquered and bedecked with fringe and potted palms; taxi-craft advertise with multi-colored streamers and brightly-painted lanterns; high-tilted junks whose demon-painted prows intending to ward off evil spirits, all move with determination under the blazing sun—all made more intense by a dizzying tumult of sunlight reflecting off the river's restless surface.

As we draw closer to Canton, the waterway becomes even more crowded, air pungent with the scent of city life: charcoal fires; rotting fish; tide-borne refuse, burning incense; human sweat. This crush of humanity only intensifies as we approach the break in the bulkhead—so-called Jackass Point—with its steps leading up to the broad, busy esplanade. Thousands of sampans are jammed together in the narrow margins where the Pearl meets the embankment. Rafted gunnel-to-gunnel, bow-to-stern—they become a floating city, a chaotic crush of men, women and children living in close quarters under ramshackle forests of bamboo canopies—offering no real protection from the elements, to say nothing of privacy or sanitation. Narrow courses of open water separate these clusters, allowing other vessels of every imaginable design and purpose to pass through these water-borne neighborhoods. These sampans constitute 'home' for generations-at-a-time, eking out their existence in any way possible.

Ryan and I tie off the boat at the foot of Jackass Point, climbing the steps onto the busy expanse of land separating the Pearl and its shoreline activity from the bleached-white, classical facades of the Factories. Hoping to remain unnoticed, we choose a less-crowded path than others along the bulkhead wall.

"Let's first head to the customs house and clear our paperwork," I say, just as a hail of refuse rains down from the direction of jumbled sampans along the river's edge. Shouts of *gwailou, gwailou*, and *Èmó!* rise up from the river. Fruit skins, small stones and even bilge water go airborne as we hunker down reflexively, hastening to the shelter of the customs house. Soon, others nearby join in, *Èmó!* Demon! Mothers hold up their children, gesturing, "*Kàn* (看), *kàn, gwailou, gwailou!* Look, look, Foreign Devils."

"I guess they don't think much of us," Ryan shouts over the din of the crowd, as we duck into the building. From a window, I see from the laughter and good-natured shoving going on outside, that this taunt is blood sport on their part, though not necessarily dangerous to us—a kind of gauntlet whenever men like us—especially unfamiliar faces—come ashore.

"I see my objective," I say to Ryan. "The American flag by that building over there is in front of our factory. You stay right here. That first barge of cargo is due any time. They'd planned to leave Whampoa soon after us. I'm going to dash through the crowd to that front door."

"Don't take this personal," Ryan says. "I've been here before and it's how it goes. Far as they're concerned, we're just more red-faced, big-nosed, hairy Englishmen to hate."

The boisterous scene attracts a group of seamen wandering toward the waterfront, fresh from the dives lining Hog Lane, one of several alleys that connect the Walk with Thirteen Factory Street, running behind the row of buildings. These dimly-lit haunts are notoriously dangerous and disorderly most nights—prone to street fights between rival crews, and visits by baton-armed police. During daylight hours, though, they offer sailors a chance to drink and gamble beyond the watchful eye of their commanders.

As a ramshackle group drifts and carouses closer to the customs house, one man stumbles out of the group, placing his sweaty, bearded face against a windowpane of the custom's house, cupping his hands to peer in. Clearly inebriated, with a dense East London accent, he slurs, "Moight there be soom a' dem foreign devil toipes hold up in heah?"

Sensing that the situation could escalate quickly, I step outside to pull the man away from the window and redirect him back to his mates.

Fixing his dim, blood-shot eyes on me, he squints, "Whash'a matt'a moight, you got'a problem?" He is weaving severely, his feet wide apart, his ship's uniform filthy and disheveled. He reeks of stale gin and old tobacco, his bloated, sanguine face distorted by confusion and seven drams of cheap swill too many.

As his friends congregate around him, I grip him by the shoulders and slowly turn him away from the building. "No problem, *yet*." I say. "But you're liable to make it worse."

He stumbles, but remains upright and undeterred. Ignoring my cautionary tone, he says, "When'd ya' ship in, moight?"

More local onlookers press forward behind the gang of drunken Englishmen, sensing a confrontation, only adding to the tension and confusion. Another blast of fetid tobacco and liquor-laden breath washes over my face, as the antagonist is now very close to me. To calm and distract, I answer in measured tones, "U.S., on *Fame*, out of Providence. Here to do business for the Americans up at that building. That's where I'm going" I pointed in the direction of the flagpole flying the stars and stripes, hoping to distract and diffuse the growing tension.

"Well, if yer goin', let's *go!*" he said, hooking his arm under my own. I quickly turn to Ryan, who's standing in the doorway, "Quick, hand me my ditty and wait here for the first chop boat. When it arrives, load the goods on warehouse carts and send a runner to let me know."

With that—and despite my protests—he and his bedraggled shipmates sweep me along in the direction of the American building—an unlikely and unruly procession— intimidating everyone within hearing distance, shoving some of whom had gathered clear of our path, stumbling over flimsy vegetable and fruit stands, all the while jeering at the mob as we chart a meandering course across the broad gravel and grass-patched fairway.

When, at last, my unlikely escorts and I reach the ground level of the factory building, I press my shoulder to the door and stumble in, only to be greeted by two Chinese watchmen retained to occupy the nearly empty building for the last several months.

"*You safee, mister, now? Na, na. Go way to here, now.*" Then, addressing the gathering outside, one of the watchmen, diminutive Wang-li, shouts over the ruckus, "*Shut up door, now. Vamos, go way, way, vamos, vamos.*" And with a repeated brush of his hand, he forces the door closed in the face of my would-be rescuers.

Having dragged my frayed ditty bag halfway around the world, I finally swing what remain of my worldly possessions onto the floor. Only then do I mumble, to no one in particular, "No wonder they hate us here."

19. A Walled-off Life

I CAREFULLY EXPLORE the nearly empty three-story structure called the American Factory, searching for any telltale evidence of the lives of the men who preceded me. This outpost on the other side of the world had been home to so many Americans since '88 when the U.S. first laid claim to the business opportunities they saw here. Notably, it was John Jacob Astor and his team who'd last occupied this space, when Astor believed that a fortune could be made in the China trade—specifically, opium. He eventually abandoned the effort, though, in favor of shipping and the slave trade, returning home to his native New York. I met with him there some years ago, seeing firsthand his command of New York City's busy waterfront. And while slavery was outlawed in that state some years earlier, he nevertheless managed his way around it, conducting business with his southern clients in the middle of North River Roads, on board any one of his company ships, remaining beyond the reach of the law.

Now, his legacy as a trader here in Canton, not a slaver, is mine to build on.

From the broad expanse of windows on the first floor, I can easily survey the range of activities taking place on the river. I readily identify our barge as it ties up, satisfied in knowing that Ryan is now at the customs house, handling its arrival. This affords me the opportunity to acquaint myself with my surroundings.

I climb to the third floor, where bedrooms were located. Each of the half-dozen rooms is long and narrow, very much like the building's overall footprint. The bed and bureau mean in design, matching the décor, monastic in its simplicity. The mattress, bare, stained and sagging, is held up by rope straps very much in need of replacement. Some rooms have multiple beds; but as I'm first in line, I'll claim this single. I suddenly pity the Chinese staff, who daily will be lugging water to the top floor for bathing, while balancing bed pans on the way back down.

From the rear window, facing north on the Old City of Canton, the vast dimensions of the city are clear. An ancient wall encompasses the original city, whose population numbers close to a million. Along its lower perimeter, a newer wall has been constructed to accommodate southward expansion toward the river. The multi-nation factory complex nearly backs up to this nearly thirty-foot high boundary. Only Thirteen Factory Street and a modest row of shops and residences lies between my rear door and a single, closely guarded gate leading into the old city. I will soon discover that the odor of charred fish and charcoal fires, the nightly baying of dogs, and the acrid smell of stagnant water in the gutters of busy streets below, together with the perpetual din of public commerce, will be a daily reality just below my bedroom window.

From my vantage point, I can make out neighborhoods consisting of a mix of red-tile roofed stucco buildings, and ramshackle abodes of wood and straw, woven together by a lacework of winding streets. These narrow thoroughfares are crowded at this late-day hour, as thousands crisscross under a shifting maze of street banners hung high over shops. Crumbling archways between buildings cast shadows on the action below, as fluttering laundry hung on sagging lines high overhead adds to a dizzying spectacle.

This beehive of activity fades into the distance, as the network of streets and alleys threads its way in and around homes, shops, and small factories, trailing to the north into the modest hills comprising Canton's outskirts. Thin lines of gray smoke rise from behind buildings and in open spaces, blending with the perpetual haze suspended over the city. On a nearby hilltop, the famous seven-story, Temple of the Six Banyan Trees. For centuries it has served as a landmark gathering point for the devout and curious. All of this is framed by the distant *Baiyun* mountain range, the so-called White Cloud Mountain, a dream-like towering visage, perpetually concealed in a veil of brilliant blue morning air.

Just as I turn to exit this warren of rooms, a single sheet of paper pinned to a panel at the head of the stairway catches my eye. With so little evidence around me of previous occupants, my curiosity is piqued. This single well-worn document, a harsh reminder of how welcome we are in China, reads as follows:

THE TEN REGULATIONS

1) No vessel of war is to enter the Pearl River on which Canton stands.

2) No arms are to be brought by Europeans into the factories of storage warehouses or any place where business is conducted.

3) The business season is to be considered September through March. Premeses are to be vacated and no business conducted April through August.

4) No wives or families are permitted in Canton and may only be visited in Macao.

5) All pilots, boatmen and agents working for the foreigners must be licensed.

6) No more than a fixed, agreed upon number of servants may be engaged by the foreigners.

7) Sedan chairs and boating for pleasure are forbidden. Visits to the city are prohibited. Outings to nearby Honan Island are permitted three (3) days a month, but visitors must limit their number to fewer than ten (10), returning home by dark, and not to engage in drunkeness or mix with the public.

8) All business must be carried on through local agents (Hong merchants) who will receive all complaints or petitions addressed to local government authorities.

9) No smuggling or credit is allowed.

10) All ships seeking to trade will anchor at Whampoa, thirteen miles to the south, where loading and unloading will take place.

AS I WALK down a flight to the level containing meeting rooms, dining hall, kitchen, and larder, I hear voices in the counting room, below me. Men are speaking excitedly in Mandarin. I recognize the voice of one of my watchmen, but not the other, higher pitched one. I quickly descend to see what the issue might be.

My watchman, Wang-li, is standing close to a tall, thin intruder, an elegantly dressed man whose hands are raised in a futile attempt to calm the situation. "*Na make come in, na, na,*" my man was saying, swinging wildly between pidgin and Cantonese, probably in the hopes that I would overhear and get wind of the situation. "*Bùyào dòng, Bùyào dòng, you no move, get me bossee man.*"

"What's the problem here?" I ask.

In clear English, the man turns to me, offering a quick smile, as if to communicate some good intention, saying, "*I here for Wu Bingjian, you call Howqua. He wait outside. Wish to talk you. No wish to enter, but you come me. Say ya, ya. Then talk, talk. Ya?*"

He gestures repeatedly toward the back door, leading out to Thirteen Factories Street, a bustling commercial street, but one rarely used by Westerners because of local rules. I nod toward Wang-li, to say I would follow, and it was alright. He follows behind, always my protector.

"I will come," I said.

Just outside the door bearing the sign, '美國館 'American Factory,' an elaborately lacquered sedan rests on the cobble pavement of the narrow, crowded street. Two bearers—one man in front, the other, behind—stand nonchalantly, smoking. In deep shade, under a fringed, domed roof, sits the legendary figure of hong, Wu Bingjian, better known to Westerners as Howqua. As I approach, he leans toward the glassless opening, to offer, "Nǐ hǎo." I reply with the same familiar greeting," Nǐ hǎo, Howqua." He seems pleased that I know of him, this same frail, aging figure who is the most powerful of the Co-hongs; a man whose alliances can ensure *my* own success and fortune.

The powerful agent, Howqua, has a delicate, feminine frailty about him—skeletal by Western standards. From the shadows of his plush sedan he speaks in barely audible tones: *"Have muchee good news,"* he says with a wan smile. *"Wu Bingjian bring good hand for you. Man-ta-le have come see you?"*

"Yes, the hoppo came and we paid what was due. Settled with hoppo," I say, nodding vigorously. "Do you want to come in?" I offer slowly, gesturing toward the door.

"Na, Na, time better wait. Good time you bringee piece chop me. Chop say fit for workee me. He no come see my. He sendee come one piece chop. He come to-mollo. He watchee you for goods."

Listening intently, but completely confused, I let out a sudden breath of exasperation, and turned to Howqua's linguist for an explanation. "Can you help me, here?"

"Howqua want you to know he seek to have subscription for you trade. Open doors for you quick, but must make good with hoppo first, all time. If trade for you, then hoppo come to Howqua for muchee dolla, if you no make good with hoppo first."

So, what is now becoming clearer is that Howqua wants to be my contact here in Canton, but any bills I leave unpaid as goods clear customs, he'll be responsible for.

"He watcha me two-lac dolla," Howqua blurts out. It seems he was following more of this conversation than he wants to let on.

Howqua leans into the conversation intently, as the linguist, frequently using hand gestures says, *"You pay Howqua 50,000 dolla for merchants he know. He partner now for you goods. No settle Hoppo, they come Howqua make good, na?"*

At this moment, I recall Joshua's advice. This must be the 'squeeze' he described. Hiding my astonishment, I calmly say, "He wants fifty-thousand dollars to move the goods I'm bringing in today? Without even knowing what I have?"

Seeing my shock, Howqua must sense this conversation is not going well. *"You pay he how muchee, how muchee? You pay he fitty, sikky thousand, so."*

I'm shaking my head vigorously at that point, partly out of anger, partly in disbelief that I'm being held up on the street by a man I hardly know. "Na, Na. Zàijiàn, Zàijiàn, goodbye!" I turn to walk away.

"S'pose he number one no contentee, my pay he one-lac."

I now sense I might be winning the argument. If 'two-lac' is fifty, then 'one-lac' must be half of that. His outburst clearly means he doesn't want me to walk away. There are too many other hongs I could be dealing with, and he knows that. "So Howqua wants twenty-five thousand to move all the inventory I'm off-loading right now?" I gesture in the direction of the river.

"Ya, ya," he says, understanding full-well my offer. *"He comee see my to-mollo. Make shake, you see Wu Bingjian make good for he."*

I take a step back, thinking, 'So, this is my trial by fire. I've only been in Canton for a few hours and already I'm in a high-stakes negotiation with one of the wealthiest men in the city, out to take *his* share from me, as well.'

Howqua, sensing a lull in the discussion, calls his linguist towards the window of the sedan, whispering something in his ear. His man then turns back to me. *"Howqua want to know, you have yāpiàn on ship?"*

"Opium! No, na, na!" I say sternly.

Without further comment, Howqua directs his men to lift the sedan, with his linguist trotting closely behind, they depart abruptly. From the darkness I hear a faint, lingering *"To-mollo."*

20. The Reception

I AM HARDLY settled into my accommodations by a few days, when I hear Wang-li's rapid footfalls on the stairs, later that same day. *"This comee for mistah. Must look, see what."*

He hands me a note in English from Howqua, who is wasting no time incorporating me into his complex life.

At Howqua's request, I'm invited to an event at his home on Honan Island the next night. I learn that his property lies just across the Pearl from the city. Honan has become the ideal retreat for the hongs, who have amassed their fortunes working in conjunction with Western agents and traders. Luxurious estate-after-estate front the narrow waterways fed by the Pearl. Opulent flower gardens, koi ponds shaded by carpets of lily pads and carefully manicured tropical plantings grace the landscape, each more elegant than the last. All of this is, yet a world away from my hollow footsteps, as I proceed to survey the factory's abandoned dining hall.

Once I arrive by water taxi, the following evening, I realize Howqua has planned this gathering in just such an Eden-like setting. I am led to a veranda designed in the Chinese style, a dozen tall, thin columns supporting a peaked, red-tiled roof overlooking a placid waterway. The songs of a pair of golden-caged magpies 鵲 (què), admired in China for their intelligence and guile, merge with a growing din of conversation. High overhead, cool breezes set palms and willow boughs in motion.

As is his habit, and to my surprise, Howqua flouts the usual restrictions on mixed company. Several young 'flowers' in the service of Zhao Feiyan, mistress of one of many 'flower boats' on the river, are present. Over time, he has observed with delight the eager attention paid by *fan-qui* to the presence of these women at his gatherings. With carefully-planned gestures like this—deliberately aimed at unspoken desires arising from our collective monasticism—his influence among the Westerners living and working in Canton, grows year-by-year. His guest list is selective—his first objective being to carefully control events during the evening. As a member of this select community, I can only assume he's also planning to introduce me, the newly-arrived American, to individuals who will play important roles in his—and my—future success. Key among them would be the merchants who'll buy my cargo, men whose agreements with Howqua are already clearly spelled out over years of dealing with the British and Dutch.

Soon after his guests have fully assembled, Howqua makes a dramatic entrance from a side room, trailed by two servant boys bearing trays heaped with food. They stand in shadow, unmoving. As he speaks, two of Zhao Feiyan's young women move to stand beside him, eyes directed toward the floor. *"You come here, English, Flower Flag Russell, some more, find muchee to be glad. Happy, so happy, you, me. Howqua makee nice you, comida e vinho, you see, so bené. So now, Púrén nánhái, how you say...helper boy, bring Xiā , hmmm...,"* Howqua hesitates in search of the English term for the delicacies on trays behind him, smiling as he rolls his eyes to the ceiling. Pursing his lips in deliberate exaggeration to mouth the word, he finally utters mirthfully: "Xiā...um...prawwwn, yah, yah, prawn." The group erupts in applause at his carefully staged performance. Bathed in this attention, Howqua grins broadly.

~

WHEN WE'RE FINALLY seated for dinner, Li-Mĭn, a young lawyer I am told, is to my right, and a merchant, Yamqua, is seated to my left—a traditional position of respect. Flower girls are scattered around the large table, strategically seated next to some of the most powerful agents and traders in Canton. Howqua's purpose is blatantly obvious, as I watch this powerful broker quietly play with the expectations of people in the gathering, maneuvering one after the other for favored position in the room.

A small army of servants serves dinner to those gathered in a high-ceilinged room. The space is lavishly swathed, with what seems miles of white undulating silk, gathered in a large knot high overhead, and swagging out in all directions to the perimeter of the room. Richly carved teak panels comprise the dining room walls, allowing summer breezes to flow, yet simultaneously affording a sense of privacy and intimacy. High-backed chairs set in a circle around a commodious table, accommodates nearly twenty guests—a mixture of Western and Eastern faces—all actively engaged in conversation. In a series of carefully orchestrated gestures by Howqua's household staff, quantities of European and Chinese wines and beautifully arranged dishes are placed before us, only to be cleared in time to make room for more exotic offerings.

I soon learn it is no accident, that I am casually introduced to Li-Mĭn that evening. As we engage in small talk around the table, I will soon discover this relationship is one that will serve me well during my time here. Handsome and articulate, this young man is of regal bearing, taller than the average man here on the street. His hair is oiled and combed back from his forehead, close-cropped on the sides in the Western style, accentuating his broad, tanned face. With flashes of bright, white teeth and intense black eyes. Li-Mĭn projects a level of energy and eagerness characteristic of most youth, but with a notable, focused intensity. He keeps a note pad at hand, consisting of notes he makes in both English and Chinese.

Venturing: "I'm Samuel Russell, new to the American Factory," I say, extending my hand.

"Yes, Mr. Russell, I know. I am glad to find myself seated with you. We welcome your arrival." With that, Li-Mĭn extends a hand, delicate, thin and white, but with a firm grip...in the well-practiced Western style.

I decide to ask about the note pad, "Are you making observations for later—perhaps a romance about your adventures in Canton?"

"No, sir, not the author, I'm afraid," he laughs. "These are my thoughts at any moment, to be taken up with some here in this room at a later time. My clients, you see."

"A barrister, officer of the court?" I ask.

"I boarded at English public schools when young, due to father's ambassadorial appointment in London. While there, I took an interest in Western law and read at Cambridge. After clerking briefly for the international courts connected to East India Trade, I returned to Canton, in the service of my country and its Western interests."

"A noble endeavor. It must keep you very busy with many of your clients here tonight, I would guess."

"Yes. But, tonight is different," he offered, much to my surprise.

"How is that, sir?"

"There is energy in the room as I have not seen before...change, perhaps. Greater matters at stake." He holds my gaze as he says this.

"If you mean by that, another trader in Canton, *my* arrival?"

"You bring new energy. Americans have knocked about here for some years, but with little effect. The English still have the corner...though less so, now."

"What advantages in this crowded market can a newly-arrived agent like me be hoping for?"

Li-Mïn withdraws slightly, a look of discomfort befalling his face. "I cannot answer in a straight-forward way. Or better, the answer to that must remain unspoken for now. Just let me say, I can be of help to you in ways you don't yet fully understand."

"Come now, sir, I can't be denied the facts of the matter! Is all of this just good will... or good business?" With that, I raise my hand to sweep the spectacle of the opulent room, filled with well-dressed men and women, all busily engaged.

"Let me just say that it is not the silk thread that binds us all together."

"You speak in riddles, sir," I say, my frustration rising. "I am a merchant, sir, here to sell my goods and buy others in return."

"And you have opportunity in this country. Our hopes are that you will become our next merchant of dreams, but only if you are willing to engage with the right men here. That door remains to be opened, but only by you, and you alone."

"You continue to speak in code, sir. But I take your meaning. People are dying in the streets and back rooms, the result of their 'dreams.' Let's be clear! It's *yāpián* we're discussing, Turkish 'mud,' no mistake, yes?"

Li-Mïn did not directly reply to my question. Instead, he drew closer: "There are many secrets in this room, those that fortunes are made of. I'm retained by many of the men here, sworn to guard their secrets. Fortune can be found below the surface in Canton, in alleys and rooms where confidences are kept and hardly ever shared. This is the harsh reality you must confront if you truly want to succeed here."

I sit for a moment in quiet contemplation, while I survey men meandering out onto the veranda with female companions, or into the gardens with others. I watch as other men cluster together with their hongs, engaging in good-natured banter. I watch as Howqua also silently observes all of this from an elevated position in the corner of the room, a glass of tea in hand, servant boy on the floor to one side; on the other, a flower girl kneeling at his delicate slippered feet, dutifully attending his every word and gesture.

My convictions are being tested at this moment. Inexplicably, a rush of memories overtakes me, recalling my Mary, missing from her bedside in her last hours, now laying cold beneath a carpet of snow. Happiness denied, my children without a mother, their father thousands of miles distant. My small New England town—a simple life there, so far removed from this place. Pangs of home sickness in my gut, regret, not for the first time. People, too many people waiting for me to come home, *counting* on me. For what? What's happening to me? Eyes closed, scenes of my childhood rush through my mind's eye: Seth sitting high on the wagon, reins in hand, 'Ca'mon boy, ain't got all day'; the heat of a summer's afternoon on the back of my neck; Pa, tall, smellin' like soap fresh from shavin', beside me as we walk through town. Random images...visions of *escape*.

After what seems an eternity, I open my eyes. Li-Mïn is still here, his black eyes fixed on me—patiently, expectantly. For him, given the scene I am now a part of, the choice seems inevitable. For me, I feel as though the once-solid ground is shifting under me. "Sorry," I say, "I had to take a moment." And then, I take the Faustian leap, abandoning long-held principles, as I hear myself ask, "Sworn to secrecy?"

"Safely kept with me," Li-Min answers quietly, as he glances sidelong at the activity in the room, letting me know that he's seeing the same scenes as I am being played out. "Trust is hard to find in this city. Solemn oaths and the rest fly out the window when fortune is involved."

I feel a sudden pain behind my eyes, as I consider the true nature of our conversation. But then, I extend my hand again, this time as a symbol of my intention to enter into an unspoken alliance with a man I hardly know. But one who assures me that he will serve my interests in ways I don't yet fully comprehend. He returns my gesture with a broad smile as he reaches up to run his fingers through his thick mop of black hair.

"Let's get started," he says, "Let me help with a conversation with that man to your left. That is Yanqua, a powerful merchant here, with contacts up and down the coast. You must become familiar with him."

As he stands from the table, I note again that Li-Min is tall and thin as a post. I think it a bit strange that he nervously fingers his collar and the lapel of his European waist-coat, as if not quite accustomed to their constraints. Earnest and engaging, though, I think in practical terms—tied to my own survival and success—that this young man might become an important resource for my new enterprise, especially given his solid working understanding of both Western and Chinese culture and juris prudence.

At Li-Min's urging, Yanqua then turns to speak with me. And, later that evening, following Howqua's event and the ensuing introductions, my new relationship with this ambitious young man, Li-Min, is soon to be officially launched.

21. Temple of the Six Banyans

JUST ONE WEEK later, Li-Min contacts me to request some of my time, 'in a professional capacity,' he is quick to add. I agree, and an acceptable time is set, before other demands of the day arise.

A blast of cool, early-morning air, laden with the unmistakable smell of rotting fish and camphor smoke, greets me as I open the back door onto Thirteen Factories Street. I stand at the threshold for an instant, glancing left, then right, considering the risk of my first few steps into this strange new world. Li-Min, my new solicitor, appears suddenly, standing before me, beaming. As he greets me with a modest bow, a small woman, hunched and hooded, moves slowly through the shadows behind him. She was swinging a short bamboo pole in tight circles, with a small, perforated brass lantern affixed at its end. As she moves from doorway-to-doorway, a faint trail of incense swirls from the lamp's pale orange glow, rising through her robes to hang suspended in the slant light of a new day. Li-Min reads my unspoken question as I glance over his shoulder.

"A shaman," Li-Min explains, tilting his head in her direction, "camphor smoke consecrates and purifies the houses and businesses along here. Maybe there was a death in one of those houses. It has cleansing properties against dark, unwanted energies, too."

I listen intently, eager to become more familiar with local customs, as I step down into this new world. Slanting morning light, its path traced by the smoke of unseen fires, funnels down between the buildings to form patchwork patterns on pavement beneath our feet. "Thank you for offering to do this," I say. "You're punctual—first light, and all that," adding, "off to where, today? My chance to see your city, I guess?"

"Not my city, really, but a good case for what you'll be dealing with," Li-Min says. "If we get an early start, it's best to see how things come to life around here."

This happens to be one of those rare occasions when so-called *gwai-lou* are allowed to leave the Western compounds to explore the streets of Canton, *inside* the old walls of the city. As a Westerner, I would never be permitted to do this on my own. Being in the company of a National—especially one as well-known in the city and with its people as Li-Min—makes this possible without being retained by authorities.

I sense that Li-Min is eager to expand his role with me and my company. He's been spending time at the American Factory recently, especially now as he sees my determination to grow the new business. A good lawyer—one knowledgeable in Chinese customs and laws—and read in jurisprudence at English university, as well—is a perfect match for my future needs *and* my curiosity. And, as a newcomer, I have no intention of going it alone outside the compound. Without a bi-lingual guide, there would be too many dangers for any Westerner.

We initially walk east, behind the well-worn stone-paved street behind the various hongs' offices, the blinding light of the morning sun causing me to shade my eyes with the broad brimmed hat I'm wearing to partially conceal my Western features. The cacophony of sounds—daily commerce and the usual crush of boating activity on the nearby Pearl—can be heard drifting up and over the rooftops of the factories.

There will be the usual gathering of locals along the river promenade, Respondentia Walk, with its now-familiar landing dock, Jackass Point. It's easily accessed from the Old City by walkways between the factory buildings: Hog Lane; Old and New China Streets. Once there, locals gather at water's edge—a motley mix of loungers, cobblers and peepshow men, fortune tellers, thimbleriggers and gamblers, soothsayers, peddlers and hawkers, sellers of tea and nuts, customs men and tars-on-shore-leave, the disillusioned and delusional—to say nothing of the occasional policeman, called in to clear a disruption, only to have another dispute quickly flair up.

Even early in the day, Li-Mĭn and I move determinedly against a disorderly flow of people, men heavily burdened with bundles and baskets, sacks and billets of firewood, baskets heaped with produce and cages filled to bursting with squawking chickens; all urgently crowding past each other. In the crush, I am nearly knocked over by a man balancing two large buckets of water tethered to a long pole balanced on his shoulder. I step off the street into a shop's doorway to catch my breath. Daylight now penetrates the gloom in the deepest reaches of these streets. Above shops and alleyways, innumerable banners of all sizes hang motionless above our heads, their colors faded by years of exposure to sun, wind, rain and city grime.

Observing me take in my surroundings, Li-Mĭn says, "You can buy whatever you could possibly ever need along this strip of shops and vendors. The sampan people come here early with scavenged goods—copper plating stripped from hulls of Yankee vessels at anchor; tin and homemade knives, brass buckles and buttons lifted in one deft gesture from drunken sailors; fish trapped in overnight nets down at the river; baskets and fish hooks crafted on board; stray dogs and caged chickens, fit for chops and stews; powders and elixirs of herbs, spices and ground up animal parts to cure diseases, aches and pains; and if you'll excuse my frankness, women and boys to service your every need...and of course, yāpiàn—in any quantity—especially if you're prepared to pay in silver."

"Where are all the working animals?" I ask. These men are just flesh and bone, thin as sticks. Can't they rely on horses and mules for some of this heavy work?"

"Only a rich man can afford to own a horse. That's a luxury out of reach for most over their lifetime," Li-Mĭn says. "Men do the work of animals here. They live on rice and a bit of meat each day and die young of diseases that might be easily cured elsewhere. In England, I saw doctors perform miracles with their new medicines and surgeries. Here, we rely on herbal cures and superstition to cure ills. By your standards, primitive maybe, but if you can believe, the body has powers to cure you haven't yet recognized in the West."

I observe the busy street scene around me, imagining the lives of these thousands of everyday Chinese whose survival depends on a subsistence income from discarded and abandoned artifacts—the debris of other people's lives becomes subsistence for untold more. I fall silent, forgetting for a moment that Li-Mĭn is standing close by, carefully studying me as I take in this alien new world. 'Determined to master all this,' is the only thought I have, as I stand motionless in a shop doorway on that March day in 1820.

≈

"WE'RE STILL OUTSIDE the city walls," Li-Mĭn finally says. "We should walk into the old part and head to high ground, to the temple and views of the city and long range down river."

Just inside the south gate, a dramatic scene is unfolding. A funeral is underway, public in every sense of the word. A large group gathers around a central point of activity. There, an empty pine coffin rests empty on a pedestal, its lid tilted against a crude wooden stand raised to waist level.

"Your largest export to our country has been something you can't tally in your counting rooms, or weigh on your scales...its Christianity," Li-Min says. "Western missionaries, mostly Jesuits, have strived for years to convert the heathen populations in places like China to believe in your Catholic Jesus, and with some success. This is a Christian burial rite you're seeing here. In most any other place or time, this would be a Buddhist rite, and the body would be dispatched very differently. We enshrine the memory of the ancestor, not the body. Our altar is at home, not in some faraway location. Cremation, not burial. We need the precious land to grow rice."

I stand and watch in amazement as a group of men labor to carefully enshroud the body, methodically wrapping all but the face in lengths of white cloth. The despairing widow and her children are gathered around the corpse, weeping and wailing, as they lean into the box to brush trembling hands over the ghost-white countenance of the deceased. The coffin is then slightly repositioned, as men carefully lift the body, lowering it into the rudimentary wooden box. Dozens swirl around the action, either to assist, or to get a better view of the proceedings.

"Such care is being taken," I say, "in spite of the confusion. Everyone's part of this. So different than back home. Seems more like a true celebration than a funeral."

"Death is a part of life here. Not unlike in your culture; but here we all participate. It helps the grieving process and reminds everybody in the community that we're only here for a while. Death is final, but only if you're forgotten by those who have cared about you. There's an invisible line between the living and dead in China, whether you're Christian or Buddhist. Ancestors always live on in the minds and hearts of the family."

Just as the coffin is being loaded onto a wagon for the short trip to the docks—and perhaps, on to a small village along the banks of the Pearl—another large procession rounds the corner. Leading the way is a phalanx of drummers, meting out a slow, rumbling but steady walking cadence. Behind them, a pair of servants carries massive fringed, brightly colored processional umbrellas, slowly swinging from rings atop long poles. Men wearing flowing silk banderoles follow, hoisting high banners displaying a family name and their particular social station. Then, two elaborate, enclosed sedans borne on shoulders by teams of four men in long white rob enter the square, in succession. Each is occupied be elaborately bedecked females. Their gaze is fixed forward, as they carefully chose to ignore events immediately surrounding them. Other drummers, umbrella bearers and, judging by the elaborately sheathed Dao swords at their side, armed bodyguards follow. The somber parade includes as many as thirty-to-forty participants.

Li-Min points out that each man in the procession wears a distinctive long-hair braid, denoting them as Manchu. "This means the procession carries two women of privileged birth, maybe on their way to a religious event, or to pay a ceremonial visit to an official from Beijing." Their intention is to pass unencumbered through the busy open market area filled at the moment with mourners. The procession is momentarily halted by the mourners' gathering; but the regular rhythmic beat of the drums signaled the entourage is apparently not prepared to delay for very long. "There might be trouble brewing here," Li-Min yells to me over the rising din of the crowd. "We should move on before things escalate."

The fevered pitch among the mourners grows as they focus intensively on the funeral bier's departure, with family and friends jostling to gain the best position behind the cortège to the river. The intensity of this movement momentarily overshadows the other procession nearby, as an increasingly frustrated group of the entitled class pushes to clear their way through this unanticipated gathering.

And, while I agree we had to leave, my eyes remain fixed on the scene, as these two diverse groups co-mingle into one impossibly chaotic, unruly mob, intermingling until it became impossible to distinguish one hostile group from the other.

"We need to leave *now!*" Li-Min shouts, as he grabs me by the arm, pulling me down a narrow alley. "Those armed men are moving to the front of the procession, and I suspect there'll be a clash." Unsurprisingly, as we duck into the shadows of the narrow street, shouts and screams rise from the scene behind us. We can make out the clang of metal, the thud of stones being thrown...or was it flesh against bone? It is hard to distinguish what may be going on, but a confrontation between the 'haves and have-nots' is unfolding just a few yards behind us. It would only be a matter of time before police arrive armed with whips and bamboo batons, with more blood and perhaps more funerals to follow.

≈

THE MELEE NOW left well behind, raising his eyes to a point in the distance, Li-Min says, "We've got some climbing to do." He points to a northern ridge. "Have you noticed that temple on the hill at the edge of the city? We're going there. It's important that you understand what it means to the Chinese people. I'm taking you to a sacred place, the 'Flowery Pagoda' or Temple of Six Banyan Trees (六榕寺), one of the highest points around here. There, you'll see beautiful gardens, our 'Laughing Buddha' and a great panorama of Canton and the Pearl River, which we call, *Zhu Jiang* (珠江)."

For the next ten minutes, we climb the steep, narrow streets of the Old City in silence. Red tile-roofed houses of stucco and timber are densely stacked like weathered stones against the sloping landscape. Dull gray-blue light flits and dodges at a steep angle through high, moister laden skies, but no rain falls. Children at play stop to stare at this unlikely pair trudging along the cobble streets. Further on a woman, scantily clad and wanton looking, beckons us closer as she slowly backs into a darkened doorway. Still, we walk on.

We pass very near the western gate, which, at this time of the day is open for caravans of camels and other beasts of burden from the surrounding countryside. Soldiers of the Emperor's army, clad only in loose-fitting blouses and pants called *ku*, sandals and leather helmets, stand nearby in small groups, armed only with short dao, belted and sheathed at the hip. They passively watch as countless travelers, merchants, drivers and farmers flood past the bronze doors.

"These gates mark the beginning of the trip westward, along the old Silk Road, "Li-Min point out. "For more than a thousand years, men have passed through these gates heading to places like Tibet, Kandahar and Constantinople to sell what they have," he adds, with a touch of irony in his voice. We stand for a minute, watching a long line of camels, swaying under the lumbering burden of goods lashed high on their backs. Their guttural mutterings and shrill calls of their drivers, greenstick whips in hand, fill the morning air. With equal determination, and in equal numbers, men stooped under the weight of great bundles file through the gate and into the city.

Slowly, as we gain altitude and distance from the conflict below, a profound stillness replaces the noise of the city. Those angry sounds of violent confrontation have faded; but the thought of any further death and destruction is very much on my mind. Li-Min seems little-phased by our encounter; but he may have only shown a brave face for my benefit. I can't escape the impression that he seemed inured of the experience of the conflict and confrontation between the funeral attendees and Mandarin procession. I wonder if it played a formative part in his experience as a young man in this seemingly tumultuous culture.

≈

HIGH ATOP THE HILL, the Temple of Six Banyan Trees stands nine stories tall amid placid gardens and pools of languorous jewel-toned koi and lily pads. The tranquility of this setting seems so contrary to the human disruption and cruelty witnessed earlier today. Built in 537 a.d., during the Liang Dynasty, the temple has been central to Cantonese culture for over a thousand years.

Li-Min and I move silently through throngs of pilgrims and worshipers in the gardens, and into the cool recesses of the main chamber. There, under a vaulted stone ceiling two massive, side-by-side golden Buddhas in sitting, cross-legged poses dominate the room. Positioned as they are in this dimly-lit space, their heavily bejeweled features glow with a life of their own, attracting sunlight from beyond the heavily carved teak doorway. In the Tianwang Hall a massive Laughing Buddha lies in repose, greeting us and the scores of others moving about at his feet.

We hesitate here for just enough time to acclimate our eyes to the darkest recesses of the room, before Li-Min gestures for me to follow. He moves with purpose to the back of the rise on which the Buddha figure sits. Pushing against a non-descript section of teak paneling, a heavy door slowly swings inward. He leads me down a curving set of well-worn stone stairs to a candlelit chamber, well below ground level. He moves with the confidence of one familiar with the temple's most remote features. He is confidently guiding me to a place that few will ever see, or even know of.

My eyes slowly acclimate to this dimly lit, richly adorned room. Heavily carved teak panels line the perimeter, revealing shadowy recesses trembling with projected patterns in the flickering light. Thick, richly colored carpets, portraying either dragons or sea creatures entwined in vines, conceal much of the stone floor. Torchieres filled with dozens of dripping candles illuminate a long-polished table of some exotic wood. High-back chairs, equally emblazoned with deep carvings surround that same table. To my surprise, I'm standing before a group of Chinese men, who are already seated in apparent anticipation of our arrival.

I lean and whisper to Li-Min, "Did you know about this?"

"If you're going to do business in this city," Li-Min whispers, "there're some people you'll need to know. These are the merchants who make up the Co-hong or *hangshang* (行商), appointed by the emperor to oversee trade with the west; and you're their foreign counterpart, *yanghang*, or foreign trader. Sit here, please, and I will introduce you. And then, as a whispered aside, he adds, "and remember, in their eyes, you are *Fan-qui*, a barbarian wanderer. You will need them to do business, and they *know* that." With that, he gestures to a large chair at the end of a long table. I study the faces around the table as I lower myself into the seat, seeking unspoken assurance from eye contact with Li-Min that there's no danger here. As Li-Min also sits, he places me to his left, a small detail which I recall from the Chinese tradition, affording me a place of honor in his estimation.

With that, a voice, high-pitched, thin and in pidgin English emanates from the far
end of the table, "*You comee here from land Flower Flag. Makee business with many. Some
ways good, some not. Fan-qui must know best way. Not makee mistake, yes? Can show way,
but listen, yes?*"

In response to what might have sounded threatening to Western ears, Li-Min rises
to speak, his hand gesturing as if to suggest restraint, at least until introductions can
be made. Speaking as an interpreter for the assembled group, he says, "Mr. Russell, as
an agent for the Americans here in Canton, understands there are important people he
should know. I've asked him here today, to show his respect for your status and importance by engaging with you in all he hopes to accomplish here."

As Li-Min motions in their direction, starting on the left side of the table, each hong
rises briefly, acknowledging me with a slight nod: In eloquent Mandarin, then English,
Li-Min offers: "this is Lamqua, known as *Kum Qua*, skilled as a negotiator and kind to
the many who know him" With that, a tall, heavy-set man in brown silk robes stands, a
hand placed against his chest to control the many strands of extravagant jade hanging
there. He gestures greeting with a nod. Li-Min continues, "Here we have Mouqua, the
distinguished and honorable Co-hong with much influence." He, too, slowly stands to
offer greeting, his prominent dark mustache and a bald pate are distinguishing features that will help me to remember him. "Then, there is Enqua at the far corner, known
for his brilliance and bright smile, to say nothing of his cunning." A ripple of laughter
allows a moment of levity in an otherwise somber room, as Enqua rises to pay respects.
I note a kind, engaging countenance on this man draped in layers of silk and precious
stones, whose great wealth would likely be the envy of any American back home.

Li-Min continues, "Please understand, Sam, that '-qua' means 'mister' in your language. At the far end of the table, the estimable Howqua, chief among the Co-hong
and the man whom you're already coming to know. You must get to know him, and he
will speak with confidence of your integrity. This man can clear the way for much that
you desire here." Howqua appears frailer and more insignificant from my perspective
than I remember from other settings—the street encounter behind the factory and the
reception at his home just days before. Strangely, he gives no indication that we have
met before, perhaps as not to disclose his previous efforts to reach out and engage me,
a business strategy his wishes to conceal from the other hongs.

Today, Howqua's small, balding head protrudes from the many folds of his elaborate robes. His leathery skin seems stretched-to-bursting over the prominent bones of
his face; his thin mouth barely visible above a wispy, graying goatee. His long fingers
nervously clutch the edges of his garments. Howqua's unfaltering gaze in my direction,
in response to being introduced in such a flattering way, clearly signals to me a man
accustomed to flattery. Li-Min is right, I think. Here is someone I must focus on and
enlist for my purposes.

An uncomfortable moment of silence follows before Howqua rises to speak: "*We
can do muchee for Yankee here. He know comee first see us before any else so no trouble visit.
Li-Min friend much here. You bring mud here, much silber, what else, no matter me. What of
it? No matter. Bigee ship, go far, come here again. Muchee can do for you. Yes?*"

I struggle to understand what Howqua is saying, surmising that this veiled warning
means something I'm already clear about: to work through the hongs as an essential
step in any success I might hope for. I decide then-and-there to make Howqua my principal contact, since every sign is that this hong is the most powerful man in the room.
And, with the groundwork laid for any future transactions with the Chinese clearly

spelled out, I thank the group with the customary *Xièxiè*, and move to rise from my seat. I must have looked confused as Li-Mĭn places a hand on my shoulder, urging me to stay. "The men's portion of the meeting is over, but there are two women I wish you to meet. You won't be sorry."

≈

WITH THAT, THE door opens, bringing with it a rush of cool air and faint scent of sandalwood. Two elegant, strikingly beautiful women enter the room, heads bowed, hands concealed in generous layers of multi-colored silk. Diminutive, yet commanding, their demeanor and striking appearance immediately becomes the focus of every man in the room. Even the opulence of the hongs pales by comparison. By contrast, my finest European waistcoat and vest, collar and cravat seem a poor example of refinement.

The level of activity around the table immediately increases, as the two women are followed by a cluster of female attendants, immediately setting to work preparing tea for all present. While they busy themselves with this carefully choreographed ritual of "taking tea," the two women seat themselves opposite the hongs, and to the right of Li-Mĭn and me. What had—moments before—been a gravely serious business affair, now takes on an air of levity and celebration. The broad smiles of the men at the table clearly indicate that these two women are well-known to all, but me.

Each woman is bedecked in jewel-toned silks: in one case, a brilliant jade green smock, heavily embroidered with a pale pink floral and bird design, wrapped and secured at the hip with black silk cording. Beneath that, and extending to the floor and hands, ivory brocade rustles as she moves. Small, severely pointed shoes of an iridescent red peek out from under her garments. The other, equally radiant, is adorned in a lapis blue robe, hanging in deep folds over an undergarment of pale yellow. Also, richly embroidered tendrils of jewel-toned green palm leaves wind their way across her shirts to waist level. Beads, flowers and hairpins dangle from elaborate, swept-up hair stylings called *liangbatou*, as well as around their necks and wrists. Heavily encrusted rings adorn nearly every slender finger, as they reach out to slowly run a single forefinger along the rim of teacups now being placed before Li-Mĭn and me, and the others at the table.

Low, indiscernible chatter fills the room until Li-Mĭn finally speaks. "Mr. Russell, may I present *Zhao Feiyan* and *Liang Dou*. They are business women who provide a very important service to the men here in Canton. Our hongs share an interest in their continued success, which is why they came to join us today. The flower boats occupying such a prominent place on the river are establishments ably run by our friends here. You should be aware of their common goals and support them when possible."

"Not personally, I would hope; but I understand how the world works...just not my world," I reply, trying hard not to be distracted in the presence of these beautiful women. The first, Zhao Feiyan, I immediately recall from Howqua's dinner party, where she was accompanied by several of her flower girls.

Howqua, silent yet observant, and sensing my mood as an uninitiated American, says, *"Silber comee many way, Yankee. You want, we want. You catchee wife at home, yes. So good. Many English here, day by day more. They want what Chinee woman have, Yes? Can do. Can do."*

And with that, he gestures emphatically in the direction of the two women. Not fully understanding, the women nevertheless smile demurely, sensing that the conversation is perhaps going in their favor.

Li-Mĭn looks pleadingly at me for some sign of comprehension, to which he adds for my benefit, alone, "These people have known each other for a lifetime. It all fits together in a big puzzle. It's best to think of the roles these women play as entertainers, with skills as poets, singers and musicians. For centuries, that has been their honored place in an otherwise restrictive society. It's best to support your men in whatever they choose to do, since it all benefits you in the long run. I think in English you say, 'turn a blind eye.' You don't judge the culture here, you flow with it if you want to succeed. Yes?"

"I want everyone on my side," I say sternly, being careful not to give my assent, but not wanting to appear contrary, either. "A fine line, yes, I understand."

With that, Howqua stands, as the other hongs quickly followed his lead. Li-Min and I then stands, signaling that the main purpose of the gathering—to acquaint me to the power structure in Canton—has been accomplished. Zhao and Laing slowly rise, as well, and with that, Zhao crosses behind her companion, raises a hand to her hair, removing a small white flower. Approaching Li-Min, she places her body close to his, her pale face now just inches from his chest.

As she draws closer, I can now make out Zhao and Laing's deeply lined and pocked completions. Here is the illusion of their success: they are well beyond the blossom of youth, having preserved an impression of beauty through a combination of careful grooming, and favor garnered by the powerful men who support them and the ideals they represent. Reaching up, and without comment, Madame Zhao places the flower behind his ear. Surprisingly, he is not the least bit put off by the gesture; in fact he appears to welcome the attention with a degree of familiarity suggesting they are well acquainted.

As Li-Min and I return to the light of day and the fresh smells of the temple garden, I turn to my companion, "This entire day was planned ahead just to lead me into that room for an education, yes?"

Li-Min has no comment, but leans down at that moment to place a single copper coin into the hand of a blind monk sitting on a garden wall. As we walk briskly away, he also spins with a flourish to hand that small white flower placed behind his ear earlier, to a pretty young girl on her way to daily prayer before the Laughing Buddha.

22. A Cautionary Tale

THE BLADE SO finely honed, so swiftly and expertly applied with a single sweeping gesture to the gut, Second Officer Ulysses Mulroy does not yet realize he is dying. He stares down, in disbelief, to see his bowels spilling onto the deck around him where he stands. Wide-eyed and gasping, he clutches the rail, attempting to catch his breath. It does not come. Sheet-white and trembling from blood loss, he soon sinks into a lifeless heap, only to be unceremoniously shoved overboard into the black waters of Canton harbor by his assassin. But not before a second swipe neatly severs the cord binding the victim's fat purse to his belt. The pouch is swept up from the deck, then quickly tossed to a female figure in the shadows somewhere nearby.

The night lights of the city sparkle and dance on the wavelets, rippling in ever-widening circles from the lifeless body now floating face down in the water. Moments later, crew onboard the flower boat—one of many vessels anchored in the bay—stoop low to hurl buckets of water across the deck over pools of blood and remnants of tissue, washing any trace of the slaughter overboard. By morning's light, the site of the murder shines clean and bright, as though nothing of consequence had ever happened on deck. Mulroy's only crime? He had mistakenly shown that very purse, thick in his palm with *"Yan-kee dolla"* to the prostitute he had been with. With a wink and nod to her companion, a slight man in black standing just outside her cabin door, Mulroy instantly sealed his own fate. The next day, his body is unceremoniously retrieved by police, the corpse having attracted notice as it thumped against dock pilings, as each harbor swell passed below the crowded pier-front marketplace.

I receive the news of the incident that same morning, as the dead sailor had been consigned to a charter vessel under the Russell & Company banner.

"What the hell? He didn't waste any time finding his way into that situation," I say, appalled that the old story could be happening to one of our own. Did the skipper release his men without the usual rundown? Get fall-down pissed on Hog Lane if you want but stay away from the fucking locals!"

"They all got it. Mulroy was there, as I understand it," my partner, Philip Ammidon explains. "I've been following the transfer of goods for two weeks, now. Worked with him on the details. Capable, hardworking, as I saw it."

"We can't let this travesty go unnoticed. The Chinese can't just walk away from this one. What do we know at this point? Have there been any arrests?"

"We're still putting the pieces together," Philip says.

"*Eustice* is down river, "I say. "Send word. Stop offloading for the time. Have Captain Emerson come here as soon as possible. Not only do we have to know the truth about what happened, but we must have a plan, since the locals will be concocting a story of their own. Otherwise, this won't end well."

Captain Emerson receives word later that day, while anchored at Whampoa. He orders a jolly lowered for a night passage to Canton—always risky in these narrow straits where thieves lie in wait in any of the shallow coves leading upriver. He decides,

instead, to depart at first light of day, and is sitting with me in the factory dining room
by mid-afternoon. The ship's third accompanies him, a man who knew Mulroy well,
back in Salem, and who was eager to attest to the man's character and motive. I ask
Li-Min to sit in with us, as well, believing that if the guilty assailant is found, a trial will
be demanded to protect the interests of my company. His understanding of the complex web of legal hurdles that have grown over the years regarding the complexities of
Chinese law involving Westerners will prove essential.

In that meeting, I take ample notes, which will serve to document the incident. A
report must be forwarded to my employer in Providence, the owner of the vessel in
Salem, and—for what it's worth—local Chinese authorities here in Canton, who have,
by now, surely generated their own version of the incident.

We gather in the factory's dining room. The testimony of Captain Alden Emerson
to me and other American authorities reads as follows:

'Mulroy arrived in China from Salem, Massachusetts, aboard the schooner,
Eustice, under my command, two weeks prior to the incident. Eustice had
completed an arduous five-month passage around the Cape. Morale for the crew
was boosted by provisioning stops along the way, in the protected Argentinean
port of Buenos Aires, before the rounding; and again on the lesser mid-Pacific
island of Honolulu, to take on barrels of sea cucumbers for eventual sale in Canton.
Warm tropic climes, and brief shore leave always serve to stoke the passions of a
ship's crew, but were left unattended in this case, due to the brevity of the layover.'

'While there as my junior deck officer, Mulroy was assigned to the task of
working with the local comprador to restock the ship's lard, consigning various
livestock to cages below decks and seeing to sundry repairs to spars and gear
damaged by storms during the southern passage. Unfortunately, he had little
time or opportunity to partake of the 'welcoming spirit' and generosity that this
remote Pacific port-of-call could offer.'

'So, when Eustice made landfall off China several weeks later, I'm sure it seemed
to Mulroy an eternity before the ship, heavy with a cargo of Canadian lumber,
bolts of New England cotton fabric, Northwest Pacific seal firs, sea cucumbers
and Maryland Ginseng root—essential for trade with the waiting Chinese
merchants—would finally clear customs and drop anchor in Whampoa Roads.'

'He stood at the ready, though, processing his vessel with customs officials,
arranging payment of the requisite import fees—the despised three-percent
Consoo tax on all imports, bribes to harbor officials, and a so-called tribute to the
Emperor. With that accomplished, and a steady flow of goods being off-loaded to
smaller vessels for the trips upriver to American warehouses in Canton. I gathered
the crew for their standard orientation to shore leave. I issued stern warnings
about contact with the locals—especially women. Finally, half the crew—
Mulroy among them—was piped ashore. Once they landed at Jackass Point, they
scattered like dried leaves into the dark alleys and notorious Western dives along
the waterfront, that district, as you know, operates in the shadowy recesses near
the factories, alive with multi-nationals, Asian culture...and an abundance of
free-flowing Western cash.'

Eustice's third officer Davey O'Hara, speaks up:

'If I may, I'd like to say some things 'bout that day, since he's dead an' all, an'
can't speak for hisself...'

'Ulysses and me was childhood buddies. Fathers both in the trades—
wheelwrights, carpenters in Salem. Never much on schoolin', but loved a good
adventure. With the harbor right there, an' all, just took to it...the sea and boats,
I mean. Lyss come from solid, ol' Massachusetts stock, even since before the war
with the Brits. We signed together a half-year ago, chance to be aboard one of them
sharp-looking company ships —pretty good pay and a chance to see some of the
world, particularly here, you know, China and these parts.'

'We landed together at the river point, there, where we're tied up now. He had
a big smile when any situation excited him, so we decided to break away from
the pack to find some dinner and excitement for ourselves. We cut up Old China
Street, I think, to Old Clothes Street...*outside* the wall, the city, ya'know, where we
weren't s'posed to go.'

'Anyway, we walk up that street with the funny name—till we got to a noodle
kitchen. There were a bunch. We just picked one called *Full Moon*. We just pointed
to the Chinese letters for what we wanted, not even knowing what we'd get. But,
after ship's rations for months, we really didn't care. The choice we made was a
good one: a bowl of steaming rice noodles with green and brown spinach-like
vegetables mixed in, all in some kind of a strange hotch-potch.'

'We didn't have no local money—*wén* they call it. Got square holes in it. Real
different. Anyway, we had none, so Lyss—I called him Lyss—shows the cook
some paper money from back home, hopin' it might work. Cook's eyes lit up and
he gets real excited. Couldn't 've been more than a couple of dollars, but he seems
real happy to get it. We was real happy and he was happy, and everybody was
leavin' us alone. Then he gave us somethin' called chopsticks—*Kuàizi*—cook said
and picked some up to show us how to use 'em. Real different from back home, for
sure, *jeeese.*'

'Anyway, we found an out-of-the-way bench to sit at, so we could eat in
peace. The problem was, Lyss began to attract attention 'cause of the way he was
dressed...you know, ship's duds. A big mistake I told him at the beginning. I just
wore my duffels, looked like a down-and-out, which was my whole point. But he
was decked out in his blues, a double row of gold buttons which he had sewed on
himself, white britches, and that damn tarpot of his with that damn *bright* red
bandanna tied 'round it. Take the damn hat off, I sez. Might as well send up a
flag lettin' everybody know we're here. Believe me, we started to attract a lot of
unwanted attention in that place.'

Li-Min, who had been listening intently from a distance, stepped forward to ask,
"How can you be sure which noodle shop you went to? They all look the same to
foreign eyes."

'We was foreign, for sure—*guówài* they called us, real mean-like. He also had
that drawstring purse in clear sight, laced to his rope belt. Tuck that in, I sez, you're
just askin' for it, sez I. Strangers started approaching us, wantin' to sell all kinds
of things we couldn't tell what they was—vials of strange white powder, skinny
plucked game hens, even mangy dogs! All spoke real fast in a way we couldn't
understand...no how, no way ta' heaven.'

'Lyss brushed 'em away with a wave of his free hand and a big smile. No, thanks,
no thanks, he'd say. Before leaving the street-side table, though, I seen him slip
them chop sticks into a breast pocket, a keepsake, ya' know. Like that, as they was

stamped with some Chinese characters along the edge of each stick, just like the name of the stall, *Full Moon Pantry* in English and local writin'...to bring sailors in, I'd guess, up there on a wooden sign over the doorway—bright red beads hangin' in strands at the door, made a racket when anybody walked through. I still got them crazy chop sticks of my own an' can bring 'em next time. Them noisy red bead curtains...recognize 'em anywhere if we can go back around.'

Li-Min, always the perpetual note taker, reminded himself to secure those chopsticks from O'Hara as soon as possible, and to inquire if the same was found on Mulroy's body.

'Lyss then took a simple map from his side pocket—one of the tars on board who'd been here 'fore penciled it out for him—and he asked the cook to point out a particular point on the waterfront. With that information, we managed a bit of the local talk, 'thank you,' *Xiè-xiè*, aimed in the direction of the kitchen crew. For a few Yankee pennies, we then purchased cups of Oolong tea and honey-glazed sweet rolls from a nearby cart vendor, and walked casual-like through the part of the city outside the wall. Then it started to get dark.

'Lyss, I sez, 'ought'n we be headin' back. Some shady types about.' But he was excited and kept walkin' toward the water. No, Davey, we're only gonna be here so many time again. Who knows. Let's see what's happenin' down by the river.'

'I had a feelin' he had somethin' special in mind for us, but I was nervous, rememberin' what the cap'n said, an' all.'

'We cut through Hog Lane as it got darker. Lots of tars there, some we knew, some Brits, other Americans, real crazy and noisy—but for Lyss, it was plain as day obvious, he was workin' his way to the harbor.'

Li-Min: "Did you talk to anybody you knew in the alley?"

'Oh, yah, lots. They's all makin' fun a' Lyss, cause he wouldn't stop for a pint 'r two, and they knew what he had in mind. He'd talked 'bout it on board comin' here, the pretty girls, an' all. They was on ta him.'

'I stuck with him, right down to the edge of the river. Even at night, there was lots of activity there—folks sellin' all manner of things, dried up ducks hangin' on hooks, live fish splashin' about, bundles of vegetables, piles of oranges and God knows what else. Watch your purse, sez I. I'll be gone in a flash down here, I says. Lyss's eyes're all lit up, like he's takin' it all in; but he never stops movin'.'

'When we finally make it to the river, Lyss gets even more excited. Look Davey, he says, those sampans look like a hive of swarming bees bouncing around on the waves. I figure they're so close packed I could step from one to another, right 'cross the river.'

'Course, I knew what he's thinkin': that place called the *Ivory Palace*, a 'flower boat' gleamin' in the moonlight and ridin' the waves just beyond them sampans. Even farther out, beyond the floatin' whore houses, lots a' masts, all shapes and sizes, junks mostly, made the Pearl look like the forest at night, back home where we come from as tykes, we'd pretend.'

'Lyss, we gotta get outta here, I says. But he kep starin' across the river at that flower boat.

'*Jeeze*, Davey, look at that, he says. Like something from a book when I was a kid, just floating out there like something out of a fairy tale, all bright and decked out, like for a wedding.'

'I could tell he was bein' drawn to that big ol' boat, right there after many months at sea, from other guys on board comin' here. It was so different from anythin' he knew back home. He kep' walkin' and walkin' right down to the edge of the river, regardless of what I had to say.'

Finally, we come to a bunch of flat-bottomed boats, call 'em egg-boats, some a' them water taxis. One in particular caught Lyss's eye, painted all bright colors...not like the others. Big dragon on the sprit, mean lookin', like get outta my way, an' all.'

'You're not getting' on that thing, are ya, Lyss? I ask, hopin' he'd say no. But he raises his hand and gives out a whistle, just like for the horses back home. Sure enough, over that fellow comes, scullin' like there's no tomorrow.'

Li-Min broke in, again. "You got close, Davey. Could you pick out the boat again? How about the taxi-man?"

'The boat for sure. Real bright, an' all. Oarsman...hmmm, maybe. He was real skinny, not just skinny, but like so skinny his ribs and shoulder bones was stickin' out right there under his skin. Dark, dark skin, almost Colored, an' all. I might be able to pick him out if we don't wait too long.'

'"You comee here, Go to beeg boats for fun," he says in the broken English. Sounded like English, anyway, and maybe some Portuguese. "I takee you. So nice ladee, many so nice ladee."'

'Lyss, I says, I ain't goin' with you. An' you shouldn't go either. Don't mean to leave you in a lurch, but this ain't for me. Too dangerous.'

'It was jus like I wasn't even there. "Thank you. Do I pay you to take me there?" he says to the boatman.'

'"No pay. Just come and you see nice ladee, so many nice ladee. Come, come."'

'I step back, ya have to unnerstand, ready to leave. Hope Lyss will follow my lead. The taxi man looks up at me from the dark part of the boat. "You sailor, sailor, you no comee. Nice ladee wait for you."'

'No, I says. But he kepp at me. Lyss jumps down onto the rocking boat and looks back at me once last time. The man reaches into his pocket and hands Lyss a small wooden token about the size of a checker game piece. He then tries to hand one up to me, too. Here, here, you takee, remember Juan-li. I turn it in my palm to see stampin' in both English and Chinese: 'Ivory Palace' 象牙宮 and another character 元利'

'The boatman is excited now, sayin', "Takee this one there. Tres by Juan-li to big ladee there." He then holds up three fingers and tap himself on his hollow chest. "Juan-li get yan-kee dollah' for buy. You takee this one there," he keeps insisting.'

'I take the token but raise my hands to let him know I wasn't going with them. He keeps swingin' his arms around, makin' pointin' gestures to the token, then himself, then the boat and the spot we was standin'. We start to make some sense of how it works. In a mixture of broken English and Portuguese, he's tellin' us his name is Juan-li, that the token is a way to let the people on the boat know he brought a customer there, and that if they have a total of three of his tokens—he kep' sayin' tres, tres—at the whore house, the madame would reward the boatman. He'd get paid out in American cash; a big deal for him in alley shops, I guess.'

'I signal back with a series of hand motions and nods, lettin' him know I understand, and put the token in m' pocket. I wave to Lyss, with a worried look on my face to ask him to change his mind. But, from the darkness down below, I hear him say, "You take me, now, Juan-li," as he points out into the harbor.'

'That's the last time I saw Lyss *alive.*'

And with that, O'Hara shakes his head repeatedly, as in disbelief, placing both hands over his face, repeating, *'Jeese, jeese!'*

Li-Min: "Do you still have that token?"

Turning back to Li-Min, he says, "Yep, sure do. Still in my pocket. I've no need of it."

≈

"WE'RE GOING TO have to do some quick work over the next few days to pull all of this together," Li-Min says. "We've got to gather the pieces, witnesses, evidence, time-tables, and so forth. With luck, the trail will lead to Mulroy's killer. Let me talk to the local authorities, to see where they stand on this matter. One dead American is no big deal in Chinese eyes. You'd see it the same if the tables were turned. We're going to have to push for a trial—where and under what arrangement I don't know yet."

I add, "Davey, if anybody connects you to this, you'll be in danger, too. I'll have one of my men take you back to *Eustice* at Whampoa tonight, where you'll have to stay. Do you *understand?* You're a key to helping us solve this, but you're no good to us or to your friend, Ulysses, if you're dead. Mulroy will be buried in the Western cemetery on Danes , but you can't be there."

Turning to Li-Min, I say, "Mulroy was one of my men. He shipped in on a *Russell* Company lease vessel. Anything you can do to move this along'll be helpful. I can arrange to have you paid for your time."

"No need right now, but we have to act fast. Let's map out a strategy and get busy pulling the facts together. This won't be easy. Lots of resistance from the locals. I'll go to Howqua. He can help open some doors. Let me take the lead; but I have some things you can do until we meet again, say, in two days. First step, Sam, put all of your notes about this into a document we can use to build our case."

23. On the Killer's Trail

OVER THE NEXT TWO days, Li-Mĭn visits all the stops along the meandering route that Mulroy and O'Hara had taken through the marketplace and alleys outside the old walls of the city. He finds the cook at Full Moon, who remembers the two sailors. The cook recalls the red bandanna, Hĕn hóng, 'very red,' much noticed, he says. He recalls that 'red bandanna' asked for directions to the waterfront, and that he drew himself a picture on a scrap of paper. He still had the bank note Mulroy used to pay for the food. 'Didn't know what to do with it,' he says. Li-Mĭn pulls a few wén from his pocket, more than enough to cover the cost of the food, in exchange for taking the bank note with him. The cook then points him in the direction where the two men went next that night.

After some trial and error, he locates the street vendor who sold them the sweet cake and tea. "Two English, yes, big red hat, big noses, too. Gave me coppers for drink. They went in direction of river."

Various sources also tell Li-Mĭn to focus on the waterfront sampans. The rumor is that someone from there is eager to convert American bank notes to wén. That search takes him to the warren of boats permanently secured to the bulkheads near the Western Factory complex. A steady stream of business transactions between Western ships, factory residents and their compradors for food and supplies suggests possible access to hard currency—silver specie and coppers. Li-Mĭn lets it be known along the banks of the Pearl that a reward in silver awaits anyone who can provide information about the death of the sailor, Mulroy. This leads to a possible break—someone living near the English factory has paper currency he wants to unload.

The pungent odor of cattle and sheep corralled in front of the English Factory tells him he's in the right place. Li-Mĭn moves from boat to boat, inquiring after the man 'who wants to change paper for silver.' This section of the riverfront is jammed with craft; but with any luck, he might locate that one person out of dozens in this cluster of boats willing to talk, sensing a quick profit from the handful of American bank notes still in his possession.

After several false attempts, he approaches an aging sampan tied near the river-bank. Scattered about the cockpit are randomly shaped pieces of scrap iron. Li-Mĭn speaks in hushed tones to the single figure at the stern. "I'm told you might have something of value. Something that might bring you good fortune? he says in local Cantonese dialect to this trader of scavenged metal. Tyshing is a small man, cloaked in a worn gray robe and tattered sandals; his shrunken figure and deeply wrinkled face making it difficult to know his age.

Tyshing must have inferred that this well-dressed stranger had something special to offer, as he eagerly invites Li-Mĭn to step aboard and sit with him under the cover of the rude bamboo arch he calls home.

Li-Mĭn gets right to the point, speaking affirmatively. "You have American paper money that you traded for wén, yes?

"Perhaps, Tyshing answers carefully, his eyes narrowed. "Many people come to me for many things. What would your interest in such matters be?"

"I am investigating the death of an American sailor, which I'm sure you've heard about. If you are in possession of American currency, I would like to see it. I can pay you well for it. Much more than you can likely exchange it for a few *wén* on the streets. Just as importantly, I would like to know the identity of the man who came to you with this money. It might be an important detail if we're to solve this murder."

Tyshing rises slowly, going to a dark corner of his small cabin, where he slides a small box out from underneath a low table. Turning to his interrogator as he holds the faded red box close to his chest, he says, "I may have what you need, but I must be assured that I will in no way be connected to this incident."

"I can't say that. I'm hoping to bring this case to trial, and you may be asked to tell what you know," Li-Mĭn says.

"I fear my life will be a short one, if that is the case. I think I have nothing for you, then." And with that, he gestures to return the box to its hiding place.

"Tyshing, you'll earn great favor with the new American who is now here. His needs services you can provide, with many ships and men coming to Canton. Mister Samuel Russell will be very grateful for the information you can give us, and will repay you with his business, I can assure you of that. His favor will be how you can purchase much-needed goods for his ships, and not depend on this, pointing to the piles of scrap on deck. As for the danger you say, if we can capture the man or men who did this, the message will be loud and clear that we are seeking justice. And you will be in no danger. Besides," Li-Mĭn adds for emphasis after a short pause, "I can pay you many times the value of whatever you have in that chest, for any useful information you give me."

Tyshing slowly turns back to the conversation, replacing the box in his lap. Removing a key from around his neck, he slowly works the lid open, holding up a stack of paper bank notes bearing American-style imprints. "These were brought to me by Fonqua, a man who works on the flower boat, *Ivory Palace*. He is there to provide security. I know him because he is a member of my clan and originally from my village. He came to me because he knows I deal frequently with the *gwailou*. He said this money was from the mistress, and that she wanted it changed to silver. But, I remember thinking that such a large amount would not find its way into Fonqua's hands. She would have handled it herself, perhaps through one of the hongs she knows so well."

Li-Mĭn takes the handful of bills from Tyshing. They bear the elaborate engraving of an American bank in Salem, Massachusetts, which would have issued these notes to the shipping company to pay their crew. Redeemable through any U.S. bank, this currency would have little value on foreign shores, except where an alert foreign businessman with American connections might see an opportunity for an unexpected cash windfall.

"There is twenty-two American dollars here, which would be a month's pay for you." Reaching into a purse hidden in the folds of his robe, Li-Mĭn says, "I would like to offer you a good *Gé yué de gōngzī*, 'six month's pay'—a silver coin worth fifty taels for each month. This, in exchange for these American dollars, and the assurance of your appearance before a magistrate if we go to trial. You also have my word that I will personally introduce you to Mister Russell, a powerful and well-respected man." With that, he reaches forward and drops the heavy silver pieces into the Tyshing's open palm.

As Tyshing closes his fingers around the bright treasure, his broad smile is evidence enough that an arrangement has been secured.

≈

LI-MÍN IS NOW accompanied by a local, armed police captain, Lei Zhou, showing up in civilian dress, as they await nightfall before heading to the riverfront. Lei, short, bull-necked, with a shaved head and heavy eyelids nearly obscuring piercing eyes, carries himself with the beleaguered mien and dogged determination of a career policeman. They're on the lookout for the same brightly painted, 'dragon' taxi and emaciated oars-man Davey O'Hara had described.

It's not long before that same eager oarsman is spotted sculling his highly deco-rated 'dragon' taxi out of the dim evening shadows to solicit us as potential customers. "*You comee here, Go to beeg boats for fun,*" he calls out. "*I takee you. So nice ladee, many so nice ladee.*" Delighted that our search yields the hoped-for result so quickly, I raise a hand to beckon the boat to shore. Once on board, Lei Zhou quickly moves to pin the boatman against the gunnel. A look of shock and surprise overtakes Juan-li's face as he falls backward.

"I do nothing wrong!" he calls out in Cantonese to the round Asian face loom-ing over him. "This man wants to talk to you," Zhou says to the hapless fellow, now sprawled across his seat.

"There's been a murder and, so far, it looks like you're the *shǎguē* at middle of this mess." Then, turning to Li-Mín, he says in Mandarin, "I think we've got his attention. This so-called '*fool*' should tell us what we want to know."

Li-Min moves closer to the fear-struck man. "Look, Juan-li. you took a sailor out to *Ivory Palace* the other night, an American sailor, dressed in uniform, red cloth on his hat. A friend with him refused to go. Do you remember them?"

"How do you know my name?...I don't know, I don't know. I take many men every night. I don't think so."

"Let me refresh your memory. These two men came to the river. One wanted to go, the other said no. Both men took one of your tokens. One went with you—the one with the red striped hat—the other did not. One *never came back*, the other came to me with one of your tokens, telling me all about you. Does *that* refresh your memory?"

Juan-li's wandering eyes finally lock onto the determined face of his interrogator. "You mean that fancy sailor boy, very eager to see flower ladies. Two nights ago. Yè wǎn, you know, at night time. Moon light. Can see him clearly."

"When you got to the boat, who met him at the ladder? Think clearly, now, who?"

"Man in black, dark up there. Can't make out."

"Think! You're there all the time. You know these people. *Who* met him at the ladder?"

"I think...I think...it Fonqua." Hands raised over his face, Juan-li cringes now as he spits out the man's name. "I be in big trouble, big, big trouble now," as though that bit of information somehow seals his fate with unnamed people behind the nefarious scene.

"Very well, Juan-li. That's what we need," Lei Zhou says. "Play it straight with us and you'll be fine. Now get up and take us to the boat, and don't let on when we get there, or I'll pull your permit and you'll never work this harbor again."

The taxi then proceeds across the darkened harbor, stopping abeam the flower boat, *Ivory Palace*. The abundant flower pots arrayed on the garishly painted deck was designed to attract attention from shore. The scene looks grotesquely out of place, given the act of violence that had allegedly taken place here. As the taxi approaches the ladder leading up to the main deck, I reach out to stabilize the boat so we can both climb up to meet the man in the shadows on deck. I watch carefully as the taxi departs, being certain that Juan-li hasn't signaled the crew in any way.

"Welcome, gentlemen," our greeter says in near perfect English. "I am Fonqua and I be your host tonight. Introduce you to some Canton's most beautiful women. I'm sure you find perfect companion during visit here."

With that, Lei Zhou presents his police credentials and demands that we be taken to talk to the madame in charge of the bevy of colorfully-dressed women who—not fully understanding what was transpiring—have already begun to pose near the doors of their individual cabins.

Fonqua is smooth and unflappable at that moment, and with no visible sign of surprise or alarm, bows in agreement and with a gesture of his left hand, directs us forward to a large stateroom which once—in all probability—had been a captain's quarters.

Once seated in the ornate room, Lei wastes no time providing the madame with the reason for our visit. He speaks in Cantonese: "Madame Shi, we are investigating the murder of Ulysses Mulroy, an American, who was believed to be on this vessel two nights ago when he lost his life by violent assault. We have reason to believe you and your people were complicit in that incident."

Immediately tensing up, Madame Shi relies, "I know nothing about this matter. I am only responsible for my ladies and men who come to seek their company. I have certainly seen no such incident. How could this unfortunate event occur when we keep a well-run business here?"

"Madame Shi, we have evidence that ties the unfortunate Mulroy to this location, and after being dropped off here, was never seen alive again. I can't divulge much about our efforts, but I can assure you if this goes to trial, you and your group of security men and your ladies will all be implicated," Lei says.

Li-Min leans forward into the conversation, attempting to change the tone with a softer, pleading tone: "Madame Shi, do you understand that this murder will be solved, with or without your cooperation. We would be grateful for any information you may have, which in the end, can only reflect positively in any future legal action against you or your people."

"Gentlemen, I only say that my people bear no guilt in this unfortunate matter. Now, if you will excuse me, I have clients I must attend to."

"We understand, Madame Shi. We will take our leave; but one last question."

"One more, but please make it brief."

"We were greeted by your man, Fungua," Li-Min asks. "Do you know if he was on the job two nights ago, at about ten?"

"I will inquire and be sure to be back to you with that information," Madame Shi says, dismissively, as she stands to signal the meeting is at an end.

On the taxi ride back to shore, Captain Lei stares out at the lights of the city. After a long exhale, he says, "I think we've done a good job of learning what we can. We've traced Mulroy's activities until the trail goes cold. This case needs a break before we can decide how and where to try it. You know the Chinese authorities have no interest in this matter. Any evidence we have must be iron-clad to capture their attention."

Li-Min says, "I'll go to Howqua tomorrow. If anybody's capable of rattling some cages, he'll be the man to do so. An American bench should try this, but without the Chinese authorities willing to back up any finding, this effort might become a massive waste of time. At first light, I'll meet with Mr. Russell and bring him up to date on our efforts. I'm sure he'll want to be part of that discussion with Howqua."

≈

AS THE DAYS tick by, and with no leads and little evidence to be found on site, the incident rapidly fades from public memory and attention. Life becomes routine again, if by routine one means the jammed waterfront markets, busy hong trading offices and regular procession of visitors to the brothels at the *Ivory Palace* and other flower boats permanently moored on the Pearl.

As hunger and curiosity gnaw at his insides, taxi-man, Juan-li, finally decides to use the bonus money given to him on the night of the incident and spend it on a lavish meal at one of the many kitchens in the alleys off Old China Street. Before tending his taxi for the night, he proceeds to Full Moon Pantry, where the head cook knows Juan-li and his many brothers well. Cook will certainly be impressed with the *Yan-kee dolla* Juan-li will hand him, and the wonderful meal of boiled fish, vegetables, and rice he'll prepare—one fit for the emperor, himself. He stands anxiously near the pantry door, salivating as he imagines the meal he is about to enjoy, one that would far exceed anything he had been able to afford for longer than he can remember.

With the heaping dish finally laid on the counter in front of him, he places the American bank note into the extended hand of the stall owner, who stares at it in disbelief. Not delaying even long enough to hear Juan-li's effusive expressions of gratitude, the cook is through the kitchen and out the back door, where he sends a runner to immediately fetch the police captain who had recently paid him a visit.

Within moments, as Juan-li sits curbside enjoying the first few bites of his newly-acquired feast, excitement builds just one street away. Soon, the hapless, startled Juan-li is pulled to his feet by Captain Lei, as a pair of uniformed police stand nearby. In the confusion, his meal tumbles to the pavement, only to be crushed underfoot by the curious crowd quickly gathering around the scene.

Gripping Juan-li by the collar of his loose-fitting shirt, Zhou demands, "Where did you get this money?"

Startled by this unexpected intrusion, Juan-li blurts out, "It was payment for my work with the big lady on the *Ivory Palace*," he answers in Cantonese, "I swear that is true. My bonus for good job. I bring clients to boat, she pay me. She happy, she pay me."

"How long have you had this money?"

"Two days, maybe three. Let me think. Yes, it was four, *four* nights ago." Juan-li knows the answer well, in fact...four...just long enough, he hoped, to let the shock of the murder wear off, so he won't be implicated. That strategy is proving wrong at this moment.

"Did you take this from the American man when he was dead or alive?" Zhou pressed.

"Neither, neither, I swear! Big Lady give me money late at night. She like the job I do for her. Yes, yes, don't you see?"

"We'll look into your story," Lei says. Right now, you're under arrest on suspicion of murder. Zhou then gestures toward the officers gripping Juan-li's arms. Soon he's manacled and roughly led away, over the jeers and objections of a gathering crowd. His ill-fated destination? 'It won't be one that offers him a heaping plate of freshly-prepared fish and rice,' Lei thinks, amused at the prospect.

≈

I'VE BARELY NODDED off for the night when I'm disturbed by a brisk knock on the bedroom door.

"*Misser Russell, man here to see you,*" Wang-li calls out, breathlessly. "*You know, Li-Min, Li-Min say comee now.*"

Feet on the floor, I grab for my same-day's breeches, pulling on a soiled shirt as I rush to the factory's back door. "Break in the case, big break," Li-Min says, excitedly. "The taximan, Juan-li, shows up at the Full Moon with Mulroy's cash, looking to buy a feast for himself. Cook remembers and sends word to Captain Lei. He and his men pin the poor guy down for an answer. Says it came from Madame Shi...bonus money. Let's go rattle her cage a bit, see what comes of it." His body visibly animated, his eyes afire, he asks, "Are you ready?"

As I rush to pull on shoes and jacket, I ask, "Where's the taxi driver at this point? We don't want anything to happen to him. Anyone who speaks up at this point is going to be at risk. Who knows..."

"He's in custody," Li-Min interrupts. "Thinks he's under arrest for murder. Lei will keep him tucked away for a while, but we don't have all kinds of time."

With this new break in the case of the murder of Second Officer Ulysses Mulroy, Li-Min, Captain Lei and I return to the riverfront, this time employing an official gig and two oarsmen ordered in place by Lei's department to take us out to the Ivory Palace. "Shi will be surprised to see us again, so soon," he says to Li-Min, who repeats it to me in English. We all chuckle with satisfaction at the idea.

Abeam the vessel, we rap on the high tumbledown to alert someone...anyone...to let them know we're coming aboard; but don't wait to be greeted as we climb the gangway. Surprise is of the essence at this moment. We intend to catch Madame Shi off-guard in the hopes of extracting new information or some semblance of confession.

A man in a black robe trails behind us, as we move hurriedly down the deck. He repeatedly demands to know the reason for our visit. While not immediately evident, a brief glint in moonlight makes it clear he has a knife at the ready in one hand, should it be necessary to quell a dangerous situation.

A loud knock on the madame's door and we burst in. She is already moving to some dark corner of the room, having heard the loud shouts coming from just outside.

Speaking in Cantonese, Captain Lei says, "Madame Shi, we have new evidence that points to your role in this murder. There is no doubt for us now."

She remains cool, in spite of Zhou's accusatory tone. "That is not possible."

"I can say that one of your men has shown up in the city with funds used by the victim while on board here," Zhou says firmly, holding his hapless subject in his gaze. "Does that change your answer at all?"

Madame Shi hesitates, then expels a long breath. She turns away, as if to take a moment alone to weigh the risks involved in her next reply.

"I have many men working here," she says, haltingly.

Sensing a shift in her attitude, Li-Min steps closer to say, "Yes, but only one murderer, and he likely brought his find to you, otherwise, he would be quickly dealt with. Madame Shi, you can cooperate at this very moment and the courts will be lenient with you. You're not the one who wielded the knife, nor is it likely you ordered the killing; but you are part of the puzzle and your choice not to help us at this moment only deepens your guilt in the matter."

After another long moment, "Can I be assured that I and my business will remain secure?"

Zhou says, "If it happened the way we suspect, it is very likely you will remain free to run your business, but you must tell us now what you know."

Madame Shi sits down heavily, her hand taking a swipe at her brow. "Fonqua came to me that night with the man's purse in hand. He claimed he found it on deck; but it, and his hands were covered in blood. I was very displeased when he told me he had to defend himself against a drunken sailor, resulting in an altercation with a knife." Shi became visibly agitated at this point in her story, as tears began to run down her cheeks. "I did not believe him, of course. But I was panicked. I ordered Fonqua and the other men that night to clean the deck of any trace of the incident. Fonqua then told me the body had been dumped into the river. When the taxi-man, Juan-li, came to me for his night's bonus, I gave him some of the Yankee dollars. He was very excited, but had no idea of the circumstances. The taxi man is innocent."

"Is Fonqua working security tonight," Lei asks?

"Yes, all night."

"Madame Shi, he is now the principle suspect in this murder," Li-Min says. "He'll be arrested. But, I must caution, if you alert him in *any* way, or we do not find him here when we return, you will be charged with conspiracy to murder and be held equally liable in the eyes of the law. Both Western and Chinese law apply equally, here. Do you understand?"

"One more question," Lei asks, "do you still have any of Mulroy's dollars in your possession?"

Shi slowly stands, as her eyes dart in the direction of a cabinet against a far wall. She walks slowly to the piece, pulls a key from her sleeve and opens a door. There is the bloody purse, with the few remaining bank notes inside, also stained black with traces of blood. She slowly hands the evidence to Captain Lei, with a look of resignation on her face.

"We *will* be back," Lei says, perfunctorily, as he and Li-Min hasten to the door and then onto the waiting boat.

24. Mandarin Justice

FONQUA IS ARRESTED by a team of officers who hasten to return to *Ivory Palace* at midnight. A look of surprise and disbelief wash over his demeanor, indications that he received no advanced warning.

The trial takes place just a week later, but not until high-level negotiations have taken place between me, Li-Min, as Russel Company counsel and Chinese authorities. The suggestion that—once again—a Chinese national would be tried in an 'English' court for the death of a mere *gwailou*—foreign devil—aroused not only anger, but suspicion of Western motives in Canton.

Finally, it's agreed that the case will be heard by two Mandarin district magistrates, together with senior counsel from the American company of James & Thomas Perkins, representing Western legal proceedure. All will sit in judgment of the defendant, Fonqua, but without benefit of counsel, in the Chinese legal tradition. It is agreed they will hear evidence, including all witnesses brought into the court proceedings, presented by Li-Min, representing American interests. In the end—since there will be no jury—judgment will be meted out by the magistrates—and by these, alone—but only after the merits of the case are fully aired. Court records are kept in English and Mandarin, to be available for review during the sentencing phase.

≈

THE HEAT OF the day only serves to accentuate the restlessness and pent-up rage of the crowds gathering outside the municipal court building. Li-Min and I enter through a rear door, avoiding a confrontation with the growing mob. Moments after we are seated near the front of the court, Fonqua is led in, his arms bound uncomfortably behind his back at wrists and elbows. Shoulders hunched, strands of black hair hang in his eyes, as he draws a narrow bead on the judges. He rages uncontrollably at the bench and his circumstances, refusing to be seated.

"Sit down!" One Chinese magistrate demands, or I'll have you gagged."

Fonqua continues to writhe, resisting every effort to place him in the single, straight-back wooden chair at the center of the proceedings. Again, he screeches at the two magistrates, "*Fangai, Fangai.*"

"I will have you gagged if this continues," rages the American judge. The Chinese magistate repeats the threat in a more modulated tone, causing the accused to finally desist and be seated.

This is a trial, but not in any sense of American law as I understand it. It is more a hearing, and not in the least a balanced trial. In accordance with the standards of the Chinese court, Fonqua is not allowed representation or to offer his own defense. I and my Western counterparts had to agree to this one-sided system of justice before any explication of the matter could take place. And, given the tensions that have historically existed between Western and Eastern cultures, this is the way it had to be.

Examination and cross-examination of witnesses: including Captain Lei, who details the condition of the body, and the fact that chop sticks and a map to the river were found in the victim's pockets. The key witness, Davey O'Hara, spends hours on the stand, relating his story. Under questioning, the cook at Full Moon recalls the two men who provided the bank note, including Davey O'Hara, now sitting in the second row. Juan-li, the boatman, Madame Shi, and some of her escorts and the two guards ordered to clean the deck of the spilled blood also relate their part in the events of that night. As accomplices to the crime, all except Fonqua are granted immunity, in order to speed the trial along.

Over the course of several hours' testimony, a more complete story of the events of the evening Ulysses Mulroy died, unfolds:

Second Officer Mulroy jumps into the rocking boat, as Juan-li sculls him by means of a long starboard-mounted oar to a waiting gangway suspended beside the *Ivory Palace*. As they approach, Juan-li repeatedly salaams in the direction of his passenger, appearing to express effusive gratitude with many low-bowing gestures, right palm to forehead. His actions and his broken English cause Mulroy to turn repeatedly in the boatman's direction, fixing his American features and red bandana in the boatman's memory.

Within minutes, Mulroy steps on deck, greeted by Fonqua who immediately leads him to an interior space with a gathering of beautifully adorned women in native dress. They're all seated in a large, circular room, each inviting him in serviceable English to consider what they might be able to offer for his pleasure. Instinctively, he makes his choice—a dark-haired beauty in a long, high-collared brocade cheongsam, calling herself, Lotus Blossom, *Jiāng huā*, in halting English. They soon find their way into one of many windowless cabins on the promenade deck. A small man, dressed in loose-fitting gray clothes and cap, stands inconspicuously near the door. He appears not to notice their arrival, as he leans against the rail, drawing smoke from a small clay pipe, casually blowing it into the moonless night air.

The door closes and Mulroy and his lady are finally alone. For the next few moments, he realizes a long-held dream, momentarily elevated to a level of pleasure he had been imagining for months. All too soon, though, he reveals his canvas purse, fattened by a role of recently issued banknotes, to pay his companion. Her eyes alight on it as she watches. She offers a final embrace goodbye, and ushers him to the cabin door. A subtle gesture to her companion at the rail, and Mulroy's destiny is, at that moment, forever sealed.

The fatal signal is passed along from man-to-man on deck, until Fonqua appears from out of the shadows, moving closer to Mulroy as he works his way to the gangplank. Sensing motion behind him, the hapless man turns to see Fonqua lunging, a long blade in hand. His last memory is a pool of blood blooming on the deck as his vision and will slowly dissipate.

Once the evidence had been heard, as detailed above, the Chinese magisrates and American counsel, together with an interpreter, adjourn to chambers to consider the bench verdict. Nearing day's end, after a period of just two hours, they return with their decision. Fonqua is sentenced to death by stangulation, to be carried out in the public square the very next day. The defendant, continuing to struggle against his restraints, is remanded to Canton's police department holding cells until final arrangements can be made. The defiant Fonqua is quickly led away but not before turning briefly to cast a pleading eye toward Madame Shi.

In the morning, as they arrive to transport Honqua to the execution post by the river, police find him quite dead, hanging from a noose strung over the high central beam of his cell. Captain Lei Zhou is immediately summoned. He walks slowing around the body, looking for any clues that might help to explain the latest in this complex case. At Lei's direction, Honqua's body is cut down and removed for cremation. A close examination of the rope in question shows it to be thick hemp line, heavily abraded and flexible from frequent use. It is of the sort he observed on deck when boarding *Ivory Palace* nights before. The only reasonable conclusion: Madame Shi had one of her black-cloaked men slip behind the gaol and drop the length of line through the barred window, allowing Fonqua an honorable suicide—*jigai* (自害).

25. Aboard the Opium Schooner, *Aberdeen*

Having once taken service aboard the Indiamen, Aberdeen, at Calcutta, Packed with
Chests of Opium and Bound for Canton & How I came in the Service of one American,
Samuel Russell & his company.
  ~Lindsay Andrews—My Story

IN THE COURSE of a wandering and adventurous life, I find myself one morning, sitting on a stone seat, at the gate of the British Consulate at Calcutta. It's early in the year 1821, and there was at the time much talk about expanding opportunity for young men in the China trade. And, as such, I am patiently waiting for the consulate to open its portals, that I might see if there are any notifications for me in that respect. After some time, a gentleman in the garb of a sea captain comes towards me, eyeing me steadily and seemingly taking my measure.

As soon as he arrives within speaking distance, he accosts me with a polite "Good morning, sir."

"Good morning," I reply, raising my hat.

"Waiting for the Consulate to open, I suppose," he says.

"Yes, sir."

"Excuse me," he continues, "but might I ask if you are a seafaring man?"

"Oh, yes," I reply, I have been well trained to the sea. I suppose I have been in all kinds of ships belonging to almost every nation under the sun. As for my capabilities, I leave that to my superiors to judge upon." Much of this is an exaggeration, but I am taking his measure in return.

"Well," he observes, "I am in want of some men and officers. Would you care about joining our service?"

"What service is it?" I ask.

"The opium trade, and there's the vessel," he says, pointing towards a moderately sized, trim-looking schooner lying at anchor in the river not far from where we are standing. She looks a perfect beauty as she lay there, with her boarding nettings triced up all round her, and her guns run out and shining in the rays of the sun, so brightly are they polished. Her booms are also swung out for the various boats to hang on to, for there is more room in the river then, than there is now. I doubt much if the increased traffic would admit of vessels having boat booms swung out nowadays. I had heard a good deal about this opium trade, one way and another. Some condemned it, while others laughed at their conscientious scruples. I am young and eager for adventures out of the ordinary way of a seafaring life, so I reply to my questioner that I have no objections to joining him, but only if pay and other conditions are satisfactory.

"Well," he says, "You are a bold young man, indeed. I'm Captain Gulliver, the schooner is the *Aberdeen*, designed by the Englishman, Ephraim White, the celebrated yacht builder, and constructed right here in Calcutta in '14. She is nearly solid mahogany, and costs as much as would build a good oak ship of ten times her size. I'll give you the post of third officer, depending of course on your proven abilities," as he names a rate-of-pay that would make the mouth of a chief officer water, nowadays.

"You can join to-night or to-morrow morning, and if during the day you can pick up any European seamen, you can bring them with you. Their pay will be forty dollars-a-month, or five more if they are the right sort. And something in it for you, as well. We carry a large crew, so the work is light, though it might be attended with some danger. There is no stint of food, and everything of the best."

"Very good, sir," I say, not fully believing my good luck. "I accept your offer, and as soon as I have been inside the Consulate, to have a look at the letter-rack, I will go round to the boarding-houses and see if there are any men to be had, and then I will come on board."

"By-the-bye," asks the Captain, "what is your name?"

"Lindsay Andrews, sir," I reply.

"Scotsman?" he suggests.

"Yes, sir," I happily assent.

"Mr. Andrews," says the Captain, "You have the great good fortune to be dealing with another Scotsman, after a fashion, since the owner of my vessel is a Scots, as well—Mr. James Matheson, of Edinburgh. I may as well tell you we are in the opium trade just now. We are running the large quantities from here to Canton on behalf of those who are favorable to opening up of that country to further intercourse and trade. You will be engaged in some curious transactions with the Chinese, but not much real danger."

Captain Gulliver now wishes me 'good morning,' and we both enter the consulate together; he to confer with British East India Trading Company Consul on Chinese affairs, and I to overhaul the letters which lay scattered about on a table in an ante-room, for all comers to handle, and the unscrupulous ones to do as they like with. There were none for me, and although disappointed at first, the feeling soon wears off, and I proceed to fulfil the behests of Captain Gulliver.

≈

I AM STAYING in the house of a respectable Indiaman within the city of *Kolkata*, known in the West as Calcutta. I am just a few streets away from *Aberdeen's* anchorage on the Hooghly River; I therefore go first to my lodging, informing my host of my engagement, settle my score, and get a boatman engaged to come for my belongings in the afternoon.

I then wend my way to English Town and Dutch Town, so termed from the presence of the consulates of those two nations. Not far from the consulates are several boarding-houses, where seamen generally are to be found when out of employment. At this period I am writing of, men are scarce, a good many finding work on the luggers, flat bottomed, relocated English fishing boats used up the river, as well as in the English gunboats, which are still in their infancy, here, needing the skill and intelligence of Europeans. Pay is high on the gunboats as well as on the luggers, and the excitement intense to the wild spirits who crave for life out of the common everyday jog-trot.

My search in English and Dutch Town for able seamen proves unsuccessful. I therefore hasten to the river, and having hired a wherry, row across to the opposite bank. Nearly abreast of the English consulate on the further side, stands a pretty large and commodious house, built somewhat in the American style. The house is walled in and stands in large grounds. Beneath the house's sloping roofs and expansive walls, the owner has extended the walls outward some fifteen or twenty feeet landward, limited

only by sloping roofs. Covering a breadth of fifteen or twenty feet of ground are vegetable and flower gardens of the American type. The establishment goes by the name,
Rob Allen's American Boarding-house. Here are often to be found seamen of every
kind and of every country—deserters from the English, American, and other navies,
and from the various merchant vessels frequenting the Port of Shanghai and Macao.

It has always been easy to get a passage on a bark from Macao, and Rob Allen's
always open to receive the straggler, whomever he might be.

≈

THIS IS HOW it works: Rob's emissaries take some men out of one ship to-night, and
then to-morrow supply that same ship with the men who had been longest on his
hands; Rob receiving a good *quid pro quo* on the transaction. However, Rob is not a hard
boarding-master for any ol' 'Jack' who might show up at his door, whatever insult or
injury he might have leveled at the the captain and owners. When once our 'Jack' gets
landed in Rob's house, he was safe; no captain ever will be able to secure a return of
a deserter from that place. Whether it's that the house is on ground well away from
the towns, or the fear of force-against-force, I know not, but Rob's house is carefully
avoided by consuls, officers, and captains, alike. I have been in Rob's house before, and
so was not entirely a stranger when I again walked in; although Rob was a little stiff at
my not taking up my abode there instead of inside the city.

My reason for seeking out Rob, is that he's known in the business of crewing out
a vessel as a 'crimp.' Crimps what's known to do is 'rob from Peter to pay Paul,' as the
Bible says. That is, he'll take his head fee from one captain to fill out a manifest, by con-
niving with the men aboard another to jump ship for promises of better grub, lighter
duty, a less harsh captain, what have you. All this while stuffing them with vittles and
hard cider at his place. Enough of that witbeer will get 'em every time,' he's tells me.

So, Rob is the first man I want to meet with, as I enter this, his castle. "Good morning, Mr. Allen," I say.

"Good morning, Andrews," Rob replies, not unpleasantly, adding: "What has sent
you over the water today?"

"Well, Mr. Allen, I have come over after some of your men, if you can let me have any.
I have just shipped as third mate of that opium schooner lying in the stream, abreast of
your front door, and the captain has commissioned me to find some men for her if I can.
So here I am; and will you have a drink before we begin business?"

Rob is smiling all over his face now at my intelligence, and I could easily suppose he
had a few boarders to be got rid of. The bartender is soon found, and two sherry cobblers adorn the bar. I then tell Rob the conditions of pay and service.

"Well," says Rob, "it is not a bad offer, and I can let you have a dozen or more, not
but what I might make a little more by hanging out and getting runs for them in the
tea schooners. They're getting more plentiful and runs are high now. I get the half of
it, while I'll only get a month's advance for your men. You'll be coming back here again,
perhaps?" he queries.

"Oh, yes," I reply, not knowing what is true or not. "We're to run between here and
Canton for some time, I believe."

"All right, then, Andrews, I'll let you have as many as I can, and perhaps another
time the captain may favor me again."

"I dare say, if all turns out right, the captain and I will be only too glad to be
served by you."

"The men are just going to dinner now; while I am carving, I will have a talk with them; although some of them will have to go without much talking, being rather fond of no work, and a good game of billiards with plenty of good grub into the bargain."

≈

AS SOON AS their dinner is over, Rob called me into the room where the men are assembled. After introducing me as the officer in quest of hands for a particular service, he named eighteen of them as willing to join. A motley crowd they are, of all nationalities in Europe, and one or two hailing from Uncle Sam's territory. Some of then, as Rob afterwards told me, had been chased out of California, having made the place too hot for themselves, even amongst such a rough class as the hustlers so commonly found in those regions. Still, hustlers have a code of honor, which it seems some of my future shipmates might be unable to live up to. Others of them had been soldiering in the Russian Imperial army, under General Yermolov, against Napoleon, and tiring of camp life, wished for a taste of the briny again.

The younger and more respectable-looking of this varied lot are those who had deserted from some down-east Yankee vessel, or perhaps from some hard-worked and half-starved English vessel. The food in merchant vessels of these days is none of the best, and the captains have more unlimited power for evil than in those days of conscription and floggings. There has also been a good deal of remedial legislation on behalf of shipmates in recent years. Desertion was then the only remedy crewmen had for a tyrannical master or mate or hungry ship; and if he were not a married man, or had not a good balance for the time he had served, or surmised that the captain or mate could, by some trick, deprive him of this balance, then he never took a second thought to jump ship; but when Rob Allen's emissaries broaches the subject, and laudes the high pay and good grub to be had for the taking, he eagerly jumps at the chance for freedom.

Sailors in a forecastle—for the crew's bunks are always forward-most on ships—are generally very true to their shipmates, be they right or wrong; and when Rob's boat arrives at midnight, under the bow of a competitors ship, to take away perhaps half-a-dozen out of a ship's company of twenty or thirty, all are 'blind,' even to the watchman, while the transfer is being made. Next morning when the boatswain turns the hands to, he finds himself six short. He will, of course, report it to the chief officer, who then comes forward, and if he is one of the bullying sort will threaten all sorts of disagreeable things to be done in the future if he were not told that things have changed when it comes to laying hands on the delinquents. Then, if the captain is on board, he'll come and have a try, only to find that there was no information to be had. No one saw them go, not even the watchman, who, as he says, was aft for an hour, between eleven and twelve, watching a suspicious dugger near the stern.

Now engaged with me to add to the list of crewmen, Rob makes a visit to the one hotel on the Dutch side, where most captains meet ; he comes across the captain, and soon they are both carousing in a friendly way together, for is not Rob to supply him with some men on the morrow? Rob suggests to the captain that his chief officer had better go over then and there, to pick his men. The captain agrees to this, and gives Rob a note for the mate, telling him what to do. Rob, armed with the note, is received on board, when all visitors are excluded. On his way to the ship, he has seen his own men and prepared his plan. Rob and the chief officer leave the ship, a gentlemanly looking man steps on board and tells the second officer he has come at the captain's request to sign some men on his articles. The second mate takes him into the cabin, while the gentlemanly man engages the officer in an amusing conversation.

While this is passing in the cabin, a boat glides quietly under the bow. One of Rob's runners is in the forecastle amongst the newly released men. Very few words are spoken; the captain has threatened to make them pay the cost of substitutes for not informing on their absent shipmates. The iron on their wrists has entered their soul. Rob's runner is hailed as a savior. In half an hour all are safely landed, clothes and all— nothing left but chests too old to be worth anything but for firewood. After waiting an hour with the second mate, and no men turning up, the gentlemanly young man says he will have to go, and requests the second mate to tell the captain that he will call first thing in the morning.

≈

THE GENTLEMANLY YOUNG man gone, the second mate takes a stroll forward to see that all is right. Alarmed at the dead quietness, he peers into the forecastle; seeing no one about, he enters and, to his amazement, he finds the place deserted of all its living inmates. Flabbergasted at the sight of the empty place, he knows not what to do; only he and the steward are left in the ship. He walks aft and takes counsel with the steward. The first question that arises is, what will the captain say? Neither of these two have been long in the ship — only the passage up from Hong Kong, from whence she came in ballast to load for New York. They do not like the ship or the captain.

The only way out of the difficulty they can see is to follow those who have gone. A ship's pinnace is lowered, and in a very short space of time they are seated in it with their effects, rowing feverishly to English Town, where Fat Jacks boarding-house receives them. Fat Jack, like Rob Allen, has many places to put a sailor in till his ship has sailed away. Half an hour after their silent leave-taking, the chief mate returns, and finds very soon, from the absence of his junior officer and steward, that he is sole monarch of the vessel beneath his feet. He takes the precaution of locking every door on board, then climbs down into a tethered shore gig. He takes the risk of leaving the vessel to watch herself, hurries on shore, runs rather than walks to the hotel, finds the captain, and in very few words acquaints him with what has taken place on board.

The captain swears loudly and deeply, "Rob Allen has done it," he says.

The mate says, "No, sir, I was with Rob at your request, to see the new hands."

They are powerless, for it is now ten o'clock. There is nothing for it but for both to return on board and watch their deserted vessel.

Morning comes on apace. At ten o'clock the captain is at his consulate. A peon is sent to search for his men; the peon does not go far—only to an opium den in Dutch Town. Fat Jack is on the lookout, too. But, upon returning to his mansion, he finds none but Lugger hands who are known to him by sight. For some reason or other the peon takes little interest in the search, and never ventures over the water to Rob Allen's, but close on one o'clock finds his way back to the consulate and the now very irate captain. He reports his non-success, and tells them he has been all over the place. Whether the consul believes him or not, we cannot say.

The consul is a merchant trader and has his private business to attend to; he cannot waste all his time over this captain, and he may also think the captain somewhat to blame, although not thinking aloud. He advises the captain to ship another crew, and get away to sea as soon as he gets them on board, and not stand the risk of losing a second lot. The captain, smothering his rage, is forced to coincide with this view. From the hotel he sends for Rob Allen. Rob agrees with him for an entire crew instead of the six men originally picked out by the mate. The captain gets all his clearance papers that afternoon; next morning Rob Allen brings him his crew, receives from the captain his head-money in hard Mexican dollars, and takes his leave.

The anchor is hove up, and the ship, with her new seafarers, and for weal or woe, sails away to the wide and trackless ocean. The story of this typical case of desertion was related to me by Rob while I was having lunch, after the parade of the men who were to be on board of my new cruiser next morning, to submit themselves for inspection by the captain and my superior officers whom I had not yet seen. Lunch finished, I shake hands with Rob and proceed to the city for my traps, and then to finally board.

26. Underway, At Last

ARRIVING ABOARD THE *Aberdeen*, I introduce myself to the first and second officer as their new junior. Captain Gulliver having been on board during the day, has
acquainted them with my appointment, and also tells them of the errand in search of
men he had sent me on. After shaking hands with my new shipmates, who receive me
very cordially, I am eagerly questioned by both whether I had been successful in finding any men. I tell them the result of my expedition to English and Dutch Town and its
non-success, which makes them pull rather a long face. When I tell them of Rob Allen's
promise of eighteen men in the morning, they were highly pleased.

It seems that they had been previously manned with Malays as seamen, carrying
also a staff of Europeans as quartermaster, boatswains, and gunners. The Malays could
not stand the intense cold of winter, therefore they had come to the conclusion to dispense with them. In the service on which she was now employed they could rub along
with these eighteen until we get down to Canton, when we could complete whatever
complement will be required.

After I've given all my information, and disposed of my traps in my cabin, I go on
deck to have a look round at my new floating home. I find her the perfect model of a fast
cruiser, everything in perfect order, and clean as a new pin. She is armed with four eigh-
teen-pounders of a side; a long eighteen on the forecastle, and a sixty-eight-pounder
amidships —these two last being pivot guns. She measures somewhat about two
hundred tons, and is strong and faithfully built, at a great cost for her size. Her main
boom is one hundred and ten feet long, so that her mainsail is a swinger, and in need of
some handling. The second officer, Mr. Nealance, who has accompanied me round, and
explains all that seems new to me, also tells me that underneath the nicely floored hold
I notice—on looking down the hatchway—there are nearly two hundred tons of iron
kentledge as stationary ballast.

Their cargo, he says, rarely occupies much space; sometimes it's caskets of dollars,
and sometimes from a hundred-to-two hundred chests of opium. The accommodation
for captain, officers, and crew is excellent, although, looking at her from the outside,
you can wonder how they had contrived to make so much room. My brother officers
seem all that is desirable. The first, Mr. Jule, is a medium-sized, thick-set Scotsman,
every inch a sailor; the second officer, Mr. Nealance, is a typical Englishman, tall and
finely proportioned, a thorough seaman, and full of dry humor; while Mr. Jule is rather
given to be serious and sedate, although at all times courteous and agreeable. They are
each enamored of their vessel, the captain, and the service in which they are engaged.

I am soon made to feel one of them; and when I awake and turn to my duty in
the morning, I almost feel as if I've been on board for some time. Washing down and
gun-cleaning is got over by eight bells, when all hands (excepting two armed sentries
and an officer) go to breakfast. At nine a.m. Captain Gulliver arrived alongside, and
is received at the gang-way by the chief officer. After several minutes' conversation
with the chief officer, he turns, and saluting Mr. Nealance, wishes him a pleasant good

morning. He then advances towards me, and answering my salutation, says, in a pleasant manner, "Welcome on board the *Aberdeen*, Mr. Andrews. I hope we shall have many a pleasant trip together."

"Thank you, sir," I reply; "I will endeavor to prove worthy of your appointment."

"Did you succeed in getting any men yesterday?" he asks.

"Yes, sir. I got the promise of eighteen or more from Allen's boarding-house over the water; and there he is with two full luggers come alongside on the port side."

"Good ! We shall soon see if they are the right sort for us. I dare say, coming from Allen's over the water, they will do; they are generally a dare-devil lot."

Rob Allen arrives alongside, telling the chief officer who he is, and is admitted on board, his crowd following at his heels. Rob wishes the captain good morning in his politest manner, and from the looks which passes between them, one could see it was not the first time they had dealt with each other. The Captain beckoning the chief officer turns with him and Rob, and walks forward to have a look at the men. After scanning them closely, the Captain askes them if they are all willing to join. He also tells them that sometimes they might be engaged in what to some might appear a dangerous service. In spite, all reply in the affirmative. The chief officer then brings a form of agreement on deck, which is read over to them. Each man signs his name or his mark, and the shipping business is concluded. Rob Allen receives an order on the agent for a goodly sum of *reales*, and departs well satisfied with his morning's work. The new recruits proceed to the forecastle, where they dispose of their belongings, and before dinner all are, in a manner, conversant with the general routine of the ship.

It is not my present purpose to write of the work we perform for the several weeks traversing the Indian Ocean for our destination in the China Sea. Suffice to say we have a steady following seasonal southwester, and a knife-like cut of the bow, which favors our passage in open waters. But, I write to relate what I term a cruise on an opium schooner, and some description of our destination. We carry no fewer than 300 chests of opium with the intention of trading with the natives residing in the region of the Pearl River. I will therefore pass over the ensuing period of five months, and transport myself and reader to the wide mouth of the Pearl River, guarded to the west by bustling Macao, and to the east, some forty miles distant, by a remote fishing village, Hong Kong.

≈

IT IS THERE, on the docks of Macao, that I have yet another providential conversation, and how I soon found myself in the service of another opium trader. I had no sooner made the leap from skiff to dock, when I'm approached by a stranger, asking for space allowance, as his ship's tender is about to arrive at the crowded pier. "Make way, son, if you would kindly slide your vessel to the right. We'll need twenty feet or so to tie up that small craft approaching, there."

"Yes sir, of course. You be from here?" I ask through a broad smile, as I lean to re-secure my lines.

"Some part of each year, mostly up river, though, in Canton. That ship that just dropped anchor, yours with the 'Jack' flying?"

"Yes sir, *Aberdeen*, under Captain Gulliver, fresh in from Calcutta. I'm third officer on board, here to track the customs agent. I be Lindsay...Lindsay Andrews, hailing from Edinburgh and perhaps not likely to see kith-or-kin for a while with this life I've chosen." And with that, I extend my hand.

"Sam Russell, with a small company trading here. I'm in the factories, up in Canton, but come down river to meet my ships and clear paperwork. Let me ask, how old are you, son?"

"One and twenty, sir. Not seen my mum and sis for nearly a year now. Sea's made a man a' me, reckon that!"

As his vessel's skiff arrives, we both help tie it off; then Mr. Russell waves his ship's crew off, allowing us more time, the reason for which would only soon become clear. "And you've made third on your first voyage. You must have impressed someone?"

Yes, sir, a Mr. Matheson I'm told—fellow Scot and in the employ of the British East India Company. I'm not so much talented, as lucky. His man pressed me with the offer and a few quid back in Calcutta.

Mr. Russell's eyes suddenly light up and he moves closer, as if to speak in confidence. It's hardly necessary, given the general state of chaos on the docks and streets all 'round us. But there it is. "Do you remain in their employ, now that you've made landfall here?"

"That is not clear, sir. I have yet to hear my ratings from the captain. All has been so busy...why?" I was sensing that good fortune might visit me again...two lightning bolts in the space of a year.

"Lindsay, is it? Let me say that I'm impressed with your ambition and I can use a good man in my company," he says. "As long as you have no clear obligation to Matheson hence, can we agree that you'll come to work for me here? I will match or better your wage and give you some additional responsibilities on the docks and warehouses. Do fine by me and there's room to move up...perhaps a position as first on a vessel heading over to the states. New horizons, and all that."

Mr. Russell's eagerness to hire me on the spot...here on the docks at Macao, strikes me as curious, and so I ask, "Sir, you hardly know me...is this a position that carries some risk I'm not aware of?"

"No, no, not that. You haven't been here long to know, but you will soon enough. See, son, you're one of Matheson's men. Lots of competition. If you'd come with any other credential, I may have passed you up; but a Matheson man! Anything I can do to improve my edge at the expense of my competitor—and Mister James Matheson and his compatriot, Mister Jardine, in particular—I'll certainly consider."

Mr. Russell impresses me as extremely driven, highly competitive and prepared to succeed at any cost. I agree to accept his offer of service, believing that my fate and future accomplishments will tie to men like this—men with great ambition and a desire to win the game at any cost. At that moment, and at whatever cost to my youthful ambitions, I chose to join the fray and enter the employ of this man, Samuel Russell and his growing Russell & Company.

BOOK IV
YĀPIÀN

27. Uma Grande Festa

THE AUSTERE OFFICES of the American Factory, together with prohibitions denying Westerners access to the streets of Canton, add up to months of social deprivation, in spite of my staff's affability and our shared workload. In the many months since learning of Mary's death, I have turned my grief and sadness to my ledgers and journals, hoping to find solace in columns of figures and accounts of goods successfully sold. These preoccupations do little to assuage my guilt and despair, but help to pass the winter days' dim light and weeks of confinement. I've been assured in correspondence from Frances that the children are well-cared for and that George's education is moving apace. This news is comforting, as I slowly accustom myself to the fact that Mary is no longer of this earth.

As is our regular spring ritual, our business activities are required to move south for several months to offices in Macao. Our accommodations there are modest, with sleeping quarters and dining facilities adjacent to the cramped location of our factoring desks and records. But, we trade cooling China Sea breezes and access to the entire city for the oppressive heat of Canton, pinned as it is, in an estuary at the head of Pearl, between languid back waters and the natural boundary of nearby peaks.

The move to Macao carries with it the anticipation of an invigorated social schedule. I am delighted, therefore, to receive an invitation from the expansive, luxuriously appointed British East India Company to a gathering on Friday evening, next. I share the news with my associate, Philip Ammidon and my young assistant, Lindsay Andrews. And while Philip usually eschews such occasions, I believe it will be good for spirits and morale to be out among others in the world. Lindsay is particularly intrigued, as he'd stories of the many young daughters of factory personnel who opportune themselves of this sublime summer retreat to spend family time with their fathers.

"Honor bright, Mr. Russell," Lindsay blurts out when hearing of the plan. "I'll be on best behavior," he smiles, 'specially in the company of those fizzing young ladies. I'll wear a fresh pair of sit-upons, an' all, for the chance to be in the company of those bright-eyed follow-me-lads."

Given that my two affable companions agree to accompany me to the occasion, with an emphatic swing of my fist through the air, I announce, "then, let's accept their invitation," to a demurring nod from Philip and whoops of agreement from my young Mr. Andrews.

≈

THE LARGE ROOM where I had once met with Mr. William Jardine has been completely transformed. The view toward the bay is now masked in darkness, allowing the windows to mirror back into the room all the warm light thrown by two large chandeliers overhead, each bedecked with dozens of white candles. Tables have been moved to the edges of the expanse, allowing space for dancing to the sounds of a small orchestra assembled on a dais at the far end. White linen is draped over each table, with centerpieces of artfully arranged red, white, and blue flowers, further illuminated by candles on each. Guests in elegant gowns and waistcoats sit here-and-there at the rounds or mingle and chat idly in small groups. In our casual perusal of the room in search of our host, Philip. Lindsay and I can make out several languages being spoken. This is truly an international gathering—and one, I would guess, occurring often.

When, we at last locate our host, I make introductions. Jardine invites us to sit at a table with the Portuguese representatives, their wives and consul executives. Before leaving us, Jardine signals and stems of sparkling white wine are brought to us. Then, he offers, "Sam, you must make it your priority to meet certain people tonight. Once you've settled in and gotten a taste of our fine English cuisine, I'll be certain to bring you around. For now, though, you enjoy yourself."

It has been months since I've been in the company of women, and their presence— their bare shoulders and creamy flesh, their scented hair, the sparkle in their eyes, their ease of movement on the dance floor—only serves to remind me how I miss these reminders of home, so many thousands of miles away. I am constantly reminded, as I reflect on my life in Canton, how welcoming female presence is in everyday conversation. And given the prohibitions against mixing with the Chinese female population under any circumstance, I doubly enjoy the pleasure of intermingling with the opposite sex in these circumstances.

In particular, the daughters and young charges of the merchant and political classes are always called upon to attend these *fetes*. They are there to represent their families and countries, bolstering the profile and reputation of those commercial men and government officials for the few months each summer when all are reunited here in Macao. Owing to his ocean-going life, Mr. Ammidon has remained a confirmed bachelor. In situations like this, it is his nature to hang back, a bit. But, our young Mr. Andrews is always ready to charm. He spends a great deal of time this evening conversing with these ladies, as they gather 'round to hear tales of the high seas and exotic ports. Young and foolish, this bevy of flighty, youthful girls hang on his every word—much to his delight.

As I survey the gathering, I observe one woman who appears to be taking little notice of Lindsay's hijinks. She is standing slightly apart from the rest, disengaged and slowly surveying the rest of the room. Despite my best intention otherwise, I find myself thunderstruck by her beauty. An off-the-shoulder gown of fawn gray silk, adorned with crystal beading frames her arms and neck, bronzed and radiant in soft candle light. Her slender neck is adorned with a black velvet choker, a small cameo affixed at the throat. Long hair, the color of midnight sky, is pulled up in a chignon, with small, spiraling wisps left to trail down along her temples. High cheek bones frame distinctive almond-shaped, blue-green eyes beneath delicately arched brows. Her nose is petite and decidedly non-European, positioned as it is, above a pair of pursed lips the color of claret wine. She is standing just feet from me, her movements imperceptible, except for her eyes, keenly scanning the crowd. Her stature and studied gaze speak volumes to me: here is an intelligent, opportunistic mind at work, taking measure of the powerful and powerless, alike, assembled in the room tonight.

I find myself fascinated by this woman—so distinctively different from the rest of her female companions. Her name, I am to learn, is Isabella Calebro—'Belle' to her friends—here on leave from her classical studies at the church convent of São Vicente de Fora, in Lisbon. She is the daughter of the serving vice-governor of the Portuguese consulate, here in Macao. Later, I was to confess to Joshua my infatuation. As I describe

it to him, two features of this young woman intrigue me: the first is her choice to mentally separate herself for a period of time from the din of that party in order to carefully scrutinize human behavior; and secondly, her distinctive physical features, clearly
suggesting a 'union' of East and West—not unexpected, I presume, when two cultures
interact so closely.

≈

ISABELLE, OF COURSE, is not alone at this event; she is accompanied by a bevy of
young women, all of whom hover near their table. A matronly figure carefully attends
the group, also engaging with friends seated nearby. This, I can assume, is her mother.
Diminutive, yet erect in her carriage, her Asian roots are clearly evident in her features.
Her dark eyes are wide set with the palpebral slant characteristic of this native population. Her raven hair, graying at the temples, sweeps up into an arrangement held
in place by a jeweled comb. Her gown, made of billowing yards of cream-white satin
shimmers in the candlelight, its left sleeve adorned high on the shoulder with a single
pink rose crafted of silk brocade.

While I study the entire scene carefully, I hope, nevertheless, for a moment when
I might approach this alluring young lady—"Belle"—separate from the group, in
hopes of an introduction and brief exchange. As 'mother' turns in her chair to speak
with another guest more earnestly, I take my chance, circling around to approach the
table from behind. Ever observant, Belle turns, seeing me approach from across the
crowded room.

"You are a curious man," she says to me. "Why are you struggling so to advance this
when the other side is free and clear?"

"My desire to meet you, Miss, is my only excuse...and perhaps to sidestep your
mother's ever-vigilant gaze, if I may be totally honest," I say.

Belle laughs at my fumbling honesty, and the wisdom I show in correctly assessing
the situation.

"Now you've taken such great pains to arrive here, sir, may I ask who, are you then?"
she remarks, bemused.

"I am Sam Russell, agent for U.S. companies, assigned to Canton. We Americans
don't know how to celebrate like this. I must say, I'm quite amazed."

"It helps pass the time when we are far from home," Belle confesses. "But, since
you've troubled yourself, thus far, I will gladly introduce myself. I am Isabella Calebro."
She extends a delicately gloved hand, adding, "I am here for the summer with my family
and friends to visit my father."

I take her hand in mine, and unclear what to do next, bring it to my mouth and
briefly kiss its perfumed back, in the European style. "I must seem foolish to you, with
these old-fashioned gestures," I say.

"Not at all. You are quite charming in that old fashioned way, Mr. Russell," Belle
replies, half mockingly.

I nervously shift from one foot to another, as a moment of awkward silence becomes
an eternity. Finally, grasping at straws, I respond, "I am here with some of my people
and we must leave soon, but I had to let you know I was admiring you from a distance, and that..."

"My mother has been observing us for a while now" Belle interrupts. "She will have
questions for me later. It may be best if you are not as memorable to her, as I seem to be
to you. Thank you for your kind words, Mr. Russell. But, we should say goodbye now."

"I hope to see you again when we might have more time to talk," I say, fumbling for words, "and please, and call me Sam."

"Perhaps, Mr. Sam. But, for now, you must go."

I barely remember traversing the room to join my colleagues after that brief encounter. I do recall her arresting gaze, however, and the instant when I swept a stem of champagne from a passing tray, toasting my own boldness, as I realized what I had just done. 'Isabella Calebro, Isabella Calebro'...the lyric to a beautiful song.

≈

HAVING MANAGED TO engage with Belle, however briefly, it was more difficult to focus on seemingly trivial events taking place in room. I communicate my success to my compatriots, as I continue to superficially mingle, Belle's every word is foremost in my mind. I could not know then that it would be months before I would see her again, and only then would Lady Fortune's wheel be spinning in my favor.

It was not long after my encounter that I concluded we had more than a fair share of food and drink under our belts, as Philip, Lindsay and I take our leave to return to quarters. With thanks to our host, Mr. Jardine, we stumble through the darkened streets to our offices. As we climb the steps, we take a moment to admire the late night vista. Among many other nearby Western vessels poised off Praia Grande, our brigantine, Brilliant, recently arrived from Providence, sits calmly at anchor in the distance, backlit in the shimmering light of a half-moon high in the eastern sky. In our questionable state of sobriety, we find ourselves lingering over the scene on this warm summer night, reluctant to head up to our confining chambers.

"I have a Brilliant idea," I posit. "What if we spend the night on Brilliant's deck, under this vast expanse of stars?" I raise an unsteady hand toward the heavens, nearly losing my balance in the process. "It's our ship, after all, and we've got business aboard in the morning. What say, fellahs?"

There is general agreement, as a night spent in our overheated rooms, compared to blankets and bolster on Brilliant's deck; the latter wins the day.

"I'm a tad pished," Lindsay announces, as though we weren't all in the same state. Think I've found m' wobbly sea legs again, unfortunately."

"Blinkered or not, I'm not favoring that bunk of mine on the third floor tonight," Philip adds.

"There'll be no need for all that jockeying to and from on one of those damn egg-boats at the breakwater," I say. "A night watchman's always on deck." With that, I reveal a boson's whistle from my vest pocket and with a deep inhale, pipe a shrill three-blast call, the universal signal for 'come get me.' That, and some vigorous waving, and soon we can make out the gig being lowered over the side. In short order, we're on board, provisioned for the night's stay on the balmy deck, and ready, with sunrise and some black coffee, to resume the business at hand.

28. Shadow Dance

I FULLY EXPECTED the day would soon-enough arrive when one of Walla's Indiamen would arrive in the Pearl River to make good on his offer to deliver me to Bombay, and his enterprise. During the intervening year, I worked diligently to lay the foundation for my business in Canton. Then, I receive word in May of 1822, that an eight-gun bark schooner, *Shadow*, under command of its master, Augustus Heard, has cast anchor at Macao and is now at my disposal. Since my first-and-only encounter with Jamsetji Jejeebhoy—*Walla*—at the East India offices, I have sought to learn more about the man and his involvement with Jardine & Company. The tale is a complex one, requiring more time and space than I and this journal might allow. But suffice to say, over the decades the British did much to capture and control opium production, particularly in eastern India, surrounding Calcutta and Bengal. They have forced numerous independent states in that region to become subservient to English market forces, and their profit motives. Certain powerful Indian lords—including my new-found benefactor—have positioned themselves to be on the side of the East India Company, profiting immensely from those British alliances along the way.

In a word, the source of Walla's fortune is opium. It had captured the fevered imagination of all involved: the production forces in India, the marketers and brokers seeking rapid fortunes from its transport and sale; and the smugglers working in coordination with those entities who increasingly preyed on a hapless Chinese population, caught in a web of dependence. My initial reluctance to take this journey signified a decision to join forces with others who have chosen to profit from this plague on civilization. Am I strong enough to resist? Or do I subjugate myself to the allure of riches and a life devoted to calculated deception and delinquency? What do I owe my new family, their mother now deceased, the boys living without their father? What do I owe *myself*? Can I survive and prosper in a setting where my successful counterparts were engaged in transporting and selling a drug which remained legal, but for generations has been declared by that nation's emperors as deleterious, if not fatal, to all in its grip?

I must confess to another conversation I had a year ago, while in attendance at William Jardine's East India Company offices, in Macao. I only came to recognize later how pivotal it was in deciding the course of my future efforts, while here in Canton.

At that time, I happened to have been seated next to William Jardines's associate, another Englishman by the name of Charles Magniac. At first, I chatted casually with this stout, bulldog of a man, whose rough manners reminded me of some seamen's company I'd kept. Nevertheless, as we casually converse, I learn his father was a goldsmith who exported clocks and watches to China. In order to keep an eye on his business interests there, his father dispatched him to Canton, where he went into partnership with one, Daniel Beale, an experienced China merchant, forming Beale, Magniac & Co. some years ago.

I share a bit of my own history and my intent to develop my business here as an agent for American goods in an expanding Chinese market. "With America expanding so rapidly as a nation, I believe in the future of our manufacturing interests, here," I say, enthusiastically.

"You will pardon my frankness, sir, but you are naïve, Magniac said, briskly. "And I would suggest you may want to seek your fortune elsewhere if this is your plan."

I'm flabbergasted, and momentarily rendered speechless, my water glass frozen halfway to my lips. "Your reasoning...sir?" I say, not quite believing his temerity in this otherwise casual setting.

"Listen, Mr. Russell. Your time here will be limited. This is a dangerous country and we are not well-liked by our hosts. In fact, we are distrusted, taken advantage of and despised by all we deal with, each day. Your own adopted American, John Jacob Astor, has been doing business here for years now. He considers these people menials or curiosities. The Chinese are faceless to ambitious men like that. Like him, you must decide how to gain the advantage on behalf of your clients, your family and yourself. There are many others at the factories in Canton doing just that."

"I met Mr. Astor in New York very recently and he never mentioned it. It's furs for him, I believe," I say defensively.

"Of course, that's what he's wanting you to think. Men never discuss this dirty little secret. Listen," he continues, moving nearer to me and speaking in *soto voce*, "The Brits enjoy a monopoly here, but that *can't* last. Too many others are agitating Parliament to open up markets for them. There's a Scots-born seaman, an ambitious fellow, John Reid, a partner over at Cox & Beale; he's discovered a way to circumvent the East India Company's monopoly. He took out an Austrian citizenship and was appointment Chinese Consul to the Emperor of Austria, of all damn things! He now has diplomatic residence rights, so's he no longer needs the Company's permission to trade in Canton. Clever, eh? Other men quickly followed his example. My brother, Hollingworth, is looking to become Prussian Vice-Consul under *me*, so he can come and help out, 'cause we're growing so damn fast."

"All very interesting, Mr. Magniac, but not above board, I will say. I like to think I run an honorable business. It's what got me here to begin with." I reply.

"I'm trying to help you out here, My Russell," he shot back. "You're still new. Got high-minded plans. But, you want to stay around for a while, right? Listen, the Turks have opium, lots of it. Pretty good quality...not as good as that high-priced Bengal *Patna*, though. Bring your boatloads of cotton, other bric-a-brac there. Those Ottomans will buy all you've got. No silver, perfectly good and safe... just a credit from a Constantine bank...honored by the Brits once you get to Bengal. They control everything there, even the banks. Use that credit voucher to buy the best you can afford and ship it here. The Manchu will buy it, as much as you've got, all day. They come from up and down the coast. They'll bring specie, so much you won't know where to put it for safe keeping... I've seen it myself. They're bringing silver on board in exchange, sometimes in bars, sometimes Mexican dollars, even antique ware—vases of silver and gold; in fact, so long's it's precious metal, it went on the scale against the opium, considered as good as cash.

"This sounds very risky," I say. "I like my head right where it is, attached to my shoulders. Besides, Beijing's been issuing warnings and bans about this for decades... rath of God and the emperor and all of that."

"Makes no difference," Magniac says, "Qing regime and their 'Celestial 'prince's been getting weaker every year, ever since we arrived to bollox things up. Besides, the Company doesn't carry the opium itself, 'cause of them bans. We farm it out to 'country traders,' maybe local men like you, licensed by us to bring the goods here from India. Those boats sail into Lintin Island, transfer the chests to receiving ships, called go-downs, anchored there for months on end. The opium is sold to local villagers who show up in droves, all hours of the day and night, keen to traffic this so-called, 'noxious drug' to their friends and neighbors. No worse than alcohol, back home, I'd say. Believe me, keep the right people in your pocket, 'tax men' they call themselves, hongs, the rest, and they leave you alone.

"And why do you want to help me?" I ask, a note of skepticism in my voice.

"Because, Mr. Russell," Magniac says earnestly, "the Brits have a corner in the market and their sending fortunes home to London banks on their Indiamen; and the Americans—you, Mr. Russell—are here to stake a claim in the Chinese market where there's more 'en enough to go around. Finally, Mr. Russell, I have a minor share of the profits going to the others with Jardine." He hesitates, as though to share some great confidence... "You might remember your new friend, Charles Magniac, when you find your pot o' gold." And, with that, Magniac places his hand on my shoulder and gives me a wink.

≈

IN THE END I decide, now that a year has passed, to make the journey on the vessel *Shadow*, discovering for myself the source of wealth beyond imagining, and the place that has cast a spell on so many men of reason.

I travel the sixty miles from Canton to Macao with a hired crew in a small forty-footer I had purchased for just such occasions, finding the schooner *Shadow* at anchor, a half-mile north of Lintin Island. Her inbound cargo, two-hundred chests of opium, has been transferred to one of Jardine's go-down vessel, one of those floating de-masted warehouses serving as a staging point for the sale of smaller quantities of opium to local runners.

There will be no return cargo in the usual sense, since the orders accompanying this delivery consist of just one cargo—myself—to be safely delivered into the hands of my brief former acquaintance, Jamsetji Jejeebhoy. After meeting the ship's master, Captain Augustus Heard, and principles, I settle in for what was to be a 4,000-mile, 24 to 30-day journey, plying the waters of the South China Sea, to Singapore for re-provisioning, then northwestward, via the Malacca Strait and the protected waters of the Malaysian Archipelago, then across the Arabian Sea, to finally arrive at India's west coast, and Bombay's teeming harbor. Unlike past ocean passages, I explain to Captain Heard that I am determined to play a more active role in daily onboard activities, insisting that my place on *Shadow* not be one of mere 'cargo.'

Unfortunately, we lie at anchor in Lintin bay for a protracted period. The weather continues in the same unsettled state for eight days—sultry, with drizzling rain, varied with heavy thunder-squalls, an altogether very uncomfortable and aggravating state for crew and officers alike, who wish to be underway. At length, on the eighth day of our enforced idleness, Captain Heard finally orders to weigh and proceed. The weather has cleared, but there is a lack of anything like a breeze to blow away the sultriness of the almost dead calm that prevails. We will rely on an ebbing tide and a cadre of pilot vessels to tow us to open waters.

We unmoor, heave short to one anchor, set lower mains, then weigh and proceed from the crowded Lintin anchorage, round the west end of the island. We crawl slowly along towards the mouth of the Pearl with the little breath of air there is. Pilots are cast off in open waters. We hope for a freshening breeze once we entered the South China. When we got fairly into those deeper seas, it remains a dead calm, as we scarcely move.

Augustus immediately orders the sweeps to be manned. All these vessels are supplied with long heavy oars, about forty feet long. In calm weather, when threatened by pirates, or in the near vicinity of land, these sweeps are run out of the gunports and manned with six men each. The ship makes way at some three-or-four knots with perfect ease. With the sweeps run out and manned, we glide through Macao Narrows and out into open water. After pulling to a good offing of about ten miles, the sweeps are stowed, and the guns which had been run in out of the way are again secured.

We do not lay long becalmed, for as the heat of the sun subsides, a light and gentle breeze springs up from the landward side. All sail is trimmed to catch the breeze, and by sunset we're soon rattling along at ten knots, the wind almost abeam and everything pulling to perfection. When the log is hove at eight p.m., we're making twelve knots. The wind being off the land, the sea is comparatively smooth, so we have every advantage of trim, wind, and sea, as well as canvas that holds every capful of wind that comes along. The night is beautiful, all that could be desired; not a cloud in the sky, nothing but the clear blue above studded with its innumerable stars and shining distant worlds.

My watch, which I am eager to provide, began at eight bells, so I go on deck to relieve Mr. Jule, who remarks on the pleasantness of the night, and that we should fetch the first waypoint, the Paracel Islands, on the port side in a day and a half if the breeze holds out. I accompany the chief officer as he takes charge of the deck. Anxious to do my part in a journey with me as the principal cargo, he gives me a hasty course in helmsmanship, and watches over me for a good while. He also advises me to give an occasional look at the barometer should any change in the weather occur.

With him always nearby, my confidence at the wheel only grows as the hours pass. Nothing arrests my attention until nearly two hours later, when the wind all at once changes from a steady breeze, becoming gusty. Dark-looking clouds are forming ahead, and although I am wishful, like any man in my position might, to carry on till the end of the watch, I feel I must look at the barometer. I'm spelled at the helm by First Mate Lightner, then jump down into the fore-cabin, where the barometer hangs. To my astonishment it has fallen more than one inch since I noted it at four bells. I immediately call out to Captain Heard, resting in his quarters, informing him of the state of the weather and the fall in the glass.

Augustus is already on his feet, having sensed a change in the action of the vessel from his location below deck. He follows me on deck in his nightclothes, and after taking a good look round, and noting the change in the steadiness of the wind, says to the first, "Mr. Lightner, keep her away three points more off the land; call all hands on deck; send a quartermaster to call the second officer, and tell them to look sharp. Take the watch forward, Mr. Jule. Take the topgallant-sail in; then send the yard on deck," he shouts to crew, already in the rigging overhead.

"Aye, sir," is the reply, and we were all soon busy with flapping sails.

The officers, with all hands, are soon on deck. I can hear Captain Heard's stentorian voice issuing orders in a firm and rapid manner.

"Mr. Nealance," I hear him shout, for the wind is now rapidly increasing with noisy gusts, "clew the gaff-topsail up; boatswain's mate, lay aloft with eight hands and secure it. Mr. Jule, lay forward and take that square-sail in. Nealance, have you got that gaff-topsail clewed up?"

"Aye, sir," replies Nealance.

"Lower away the mainsail, then, with the rest of your hands, and get it made fast," Heard shouts above the din of the fast-coming storm which we've encountered.

"Jule and Lightner," he calls out," haul all the jibs down, leaving the stay-foresail up." With the jibs down, the next order is to clew the topsail up. We manage to clew it up, but before the men reach the yard it's flying away in pieces a yard or two in size, as if bound for some nautical rag-store.

The boatswain's mate and his eight hands are unable to secure the gaff-topsail. "We might lose it yet, Nealance explains, when he comes down with his men, bearing signs of a severe scuffle. "It filled like a balloon and went clean out of their hands. The danger's that there's twenty-eight-feet yard on its head. The flapping about left several marks on those who tried to secure it," he alerts the captain.

They're more fortunate with the gallant-sail; the sail is not very large, and, when once secured to the yard, is soon on deck; the men being often drilled in sending this yard up and down, it all comes easy to them. In two hours, we're down to the stay-foresail and half the fore-trysail, the lower half having taken leave as it split in the lowering. We're in a typhoon now and no mistake; you couldn't hear anyone speak close to you unless he yelled at the top of his voice. The scene is the wildest imaginable. *Shadow* is flying along in the darkness, under two rags of sails, and when squalls were on her, she lay down with her hatches in the water.

≈

AFTER WE'D DONE all we could in terms of making fast and securing whatever was necessary, the officers find their way aft to where the captain stood conning the ship, still in his night-dress, no one having had leisure to dress.

As we close up to the captain, he says: "Well, gentlemen, we're in for it now; this is going to be a swinger. Jump down, Mr. Jule, and let me know what the barometer says." Mr. Jule soon returns to report 27.80 millibars.

"By George!" says the captain, " that's very near as low as the *Swatow* one of last year, which we rode out when all those ships went on shore.

"Mr. Nealance had told me of that typhoon of last year. They rode it out in *Shadow*, riding on one chain with another one hundred and fifty fathoms out, with a second anchor backed on it at sixty fathoms. They had to cut her masts away; but they hung the wreckage astern of them, and four days afterwards they had the masts in again, much shorter, of course, but were enabled to fetch Bombay in three days under double-reefed sails, where they docked and refitted.

It is difficult to portray the awful scene in which we're madly scudding. As the captain says (after he remarked about the lowness of the barometer then, and the one they rode out at *Swatow* the previous year), there's nothing for it now but scud, scud, scud. *Shadow* seems to make the best weather scudding, for when she broaches to, she lies with her crosstrees almost in the water, making it impossible to stand anywhere on the deck.

The sea did not rise much, for it was actually one mass of seething foam. The wind howled through the cordage with a noise like thunder; the wind and rain came along in solid spiral columns, tearing everything before them. Two boats in the weather davits were blown up against the shoulders of the davits, and smashed themselves to pieces. The lee boats had gone, tearing away the davits from the side of the strongly-made *Shadow*.

At four a.m. Mr. Jule is again sent by the captain to note the barometer; he's not long in bringing his report. No one seemed to care to be off the deck, except their staff of Chinese schroffs, stewards, and cooks, who lay on the floor of the cabin in a miserable plight indeed.

Mr. Jule reported the barometer at 27.50. They claim they had never seen it so low in their years at sea. Captain Heard takes it calmly, however, and if he ever thought of the vicinity of the land, and the circular course we're making, he had the good sense to keep it to himself, and not damp the spirits of those around him with miserable forebodings of any other danger.

Catching me by the sleeve, he yells into my ear when I got close enough to him: "Mr. Russell, do you think you can act steward for the nonce, and go and find some cheese and bread, and pass them forward to the crew, and serve out a stiff glass of grog all round? If you can't manage the grog, send them some bottled ale."

"Yes, sir, I will make every effort," I reply, and made for the companion, with a couple of quartermasters. We manage to get down to the storeroom, and after no little trouble succeed in getting the wherewithal to make up a snack, deliver it and see it washed down. The crew appreciates the meal, I have no doubt, having had four hours' hard and trying work in a howling tempest, whose raindrops hit like hailstones.

The crew having been attended to, the officers go down also—one by one—and have some slight refreshment, which helps revive us, and preparing us for what was to come.

Daylight has not yet dawned upon us, and the darkness adds a wild intensity to the typhoon; nothing can be seen ahead or astern ten yards from the ship, only the white and seething foam, in which we're enveloped, as in a shroud. The noise of the wind crashes heavier than the roar of a battery of heavy artillery when the squalls are upon her. I myself stand at the wheel with the quartermaster for an hour; in that time, we've scudded under a deluge of seawater, three times round the compass.

At length, day begins to break, but one can almost have wished for the darkness again, for in the darkness we can only surmise a good deal of the awful majesty of the storm we're in. With daylight, we see more of the power of the devastating force of this wild cyclonic gale. Ropes have broken by force of the wind, and are streaming to leeward from both masts, as from a deserted vessel. To climb aloft is impossible; the wind blows so hard on to the rigging, that crew cannot back their feet out of the rat-lines to step upwards, so the streaming pennants must be left as they are. Our four lee guns worked loose with the power of the seething water in which they were awash, their breechings chafed through, and they had washed overboard during the night, as a result.

At ten a.m. the barometer has dropped further, to 27.30. Captain Heard then orders the carpenter and his mate to be stationed, one at each mast, with their sharpest axe; a hand at each weather-shroud and backstay with sharp knife and boat-axe. Should the squalls, which are now coming in more rapid succession, overpower *Shadow*, it's his intention to cut her masts away, being the only chance of saving the hull. This he explains to the officers and me, as he proceeds to station the men.

The squalls, which at six a.m. had come about every quarter of an hour, and at eight a.m. about every ten minutes, as also at ten a.m. about every five minutes, are now upon us in fierce and rapid succession, seemingly one long, dismal howl. About eleven it seemed to culminate in one wild burst, as if all the windows of the heavens had opened. Over went *Shadow* with her cross-trees in the water, flat on her broadside. The captain, through his trumpet, shouted "Cut!" But before a stroke had been given, with his next breath came " Hold on all!"

In a moment, like the lightning flash, the scene is changed. *Shadow* is again upright on even keel, the wind gone, the rain suddenly ceasing. We can see two or three miles ahead and astern. The turmoil of a sea has suddenly left us, as we lay becalmed, bereft of motion, listing about in this jumble of a sea.

Augustus is carefully scanning the surrounding horizon. The barometer shows but little change; the sea now running in every direction the compass could point; not a breath of air stirs; while a dense misty cloud hung all round at about two miles off on either side, ahead and astern also.

After the lapse of a quarter of an hour, Captain Heard gives orders for a new fore-staysail and inner jib to be bent forthwith. Mr. Jule and I go forward, and soon have the sails out of the locker and lent our hands at work bending them. The men are nimble, glad to be out of the throes of such a devastating and tempestuous scene afflicting us for the last twelve hours.

Although busy with the sails, I often glance in the direction of the quarter-deck, where Captain Heard stands, anxiously surveying the weather.

In about half an hour the crew and I had the staysail and jib bent and set. Officer Nealance reports to the captain that the sails are bent and new sheets rove. Mr. Jule again comes forward, and they're ordered to get up a new topsail and bend it also. Soon, the topsail has been brought on deck, with the sail's rope secured around it. As they're in the act of swaying it off the deck, I hear the captain, in loud stentorian tones, shout: " Hold on that topsail; all hands to their stations, and secure that hatch again."

≈

THE WORDS WERE scarcely out of his mouth, when, with a loud and deafening roar, that can only be heard to be really known or described, the full furry of the typhoon was again upon us.

Over went *Shadow* on her beam-ends.

"Stand by your axes," shouts the captain through his trumpet, "but don't cut till I give the order."

This time, the fury of the storm strikes us on the starboard beam, the new fore-staysail and jib taking their departure with a report like that of a heavy gun, the sheets having parted with the first sudden jerk.

The fore-trysail, from the close-reef band up and with the throat lashed down, is all that's on her now, and seems quite enough, even with so much iron kentledge, or brick ballast, in her bottom.

The wind having caught us on the starboard side, we're on the same tack as before, and the same lee rail lay buried in the seething foam. As every fierce gust rushes upon her, *Shadow* goes over again, till her starboard broadside is in a horizontal position. Had the kentledge not been perfectly secured, no doubt she would have gone right over; but the kentledge being secured as if it were a portion of the structure of the vessel, saved her from capsizing.

I find my way to the quarter-deck with the other officers, and as I look in the binnacle, I observe she's heading N.W., and the wind is about S. and on the port quarter. She's tearing through the water like a racehorse, and the captain orders the helmsman to keep her N.W. and make a good course.

After half an hour's hard fight with this second round of the storm, I notice the captain's hard and anxious look relaxing slightly, a slight smile lighting up his features.

Turning round to the officers, who are ranged behind him hanging on to the weather-rail, Captain Heard says: "I think we are all right now; the time between the squalls is increasing, and I rather imagine that last one was not quite so fierce as the one before. Go down and take a look at the barometer, Mr. Jule," he adds.

"Ay, ay, sir," said Jule, hastily making his way below, for I think we're all getting anxious for his report. He soon arrives back on deck, his face beaming with pleasure, to report the barometer had risen to 27.60. This good news relieves all within hearing.

After the next squall passes, Captain Heard turns to Mr. Jule, and says: "Keep a good look-out for her now, while I go and get a change into drier garments. Keep her N.E., and let her come more easterly when the squalls are not on her. You can also let each watch go below and shift themselves, and then set the watch. Lightner," he said, turning to the first, "go and beat up those cooks and stewards, and tell them I expect something to eat in an hour's time, as well as all hands. We don't want a heavy spread, but something in the rough that will fill a sixteen hours' vacuum."

The captain dives below, and only then do the officers congratulate themselves—and me as a willing, but unskilled 'crew,' on our escape through the calm center of a wild and tempestuous hurricane.

Shadow was now tearing through the water at twelve knots. Every mile greeted as good news, for the typhoon is progressing southwestward, and we're soon enabled to bring her up to WNW, about as high as the captain wishes to come. Eventually we're out of all danger and able to wear ship and proceed on our course to Amoy.

By three p.m. we have all dined after a fashion; but what is more to the purpose, we have all changed from wet to dry clothing, and feel again, as Mr. Jule describes it, "as comfortable as a pug in a lady's lap." At six p.m. the weather eases so much as to allow for setting the topsail, which, with jibs and staysail, and a new fore-trysail bent, we are well underway. I'm happy to report there were plenty of hands, including my own, making the work light and easy.

As a fierce orange ball sinks below the western rim of the sea, the atmosphere is clear enough for us to make out the land on the starboard beam, about eighteen miles distant.

We've scudded north-westerly about forty miles since the calm center has passed us, and since going on our course of N.W. about another forty miles, so that when we were madly scudding round the center in the morning, we were never much more than twelve miles from the land. We had escaped a great danger and were thankful we had kept clear of the hard and rocky shore.

The next morning we're running along the coast under all sail, with a pleasant and refreshing breeze from SSW. At sunset of the second day after the typhoon we are safely moored in the harbor of Bombay, with two anchors, a cable's length astern from our own receiving ship. The boarding ladders are secured out of reach, and armed sentries, with one officer, keep watch over Shadow, on the lookout for the daring and exceedingly cunning thieves who infest this busy harbor.

29. Bombay Mud

INCREMENTALLY, OVER THE last two centuries, the British East India Company has wrested control of the nation of India from its inhabitants, themselves. By the time of my visit in '22, the harbor of this West Indian province's capital city is so densely packed with European ship's masts and spars that it resembles a forest. As we drop anchor and await customs officers to board, I feel as though I could walk to shore just by stepping from deck-to-deck. A series of signal flags hoisted on *Shadow*'s mizzen spar marks our arrival for Jaamsetji Jeejeebhoy's men, waiting on shore to transfer me from the docks to his offices. The schedule beyond this moment is uncertain but I hope to find comfortable quarters and a respite before setting out to witness Walla's opium production for myself.

My arrival in late October promises a sweltering hot month in Western India. I step from the skiff to the bulkhead ladder, hoisting myself up to the broad quay, shading my eyes from the *Brilliant* sun. After weeks on board a rocking ship, my sea legs read solid ground as an illusion, as I momentarily weave like a drunken sailor. Soon enough I gather my composure, scanning the busy harbor front scene. Hundreds of bales of bound raw cotton, resembling massive rolls of bandage, are stacked in high rows along the pier's edge, as dozens of men, bare-chested, with knee-length *dhoti*, haul overstuffed sacks of fresh-picked cotton bolls down long ramps to waiting barges. These goods are bound for England, where modern factories will convert then into woven goods and brightly dyed and printed fabrics, only to be returned here and sold back to Indian merchants.

A four-horse cabriolet pulls into the congested waterfront area, its driver signaling me with a broad wave. I take a few wobbly steps and throw my duffle in. Then, to my surprise, I am beckoned into the open carriage to join 'Walla,' Jamsetji Jeejeebhoy, himself.

"Thank you for coming to meet me. I ordinarily require much less in the way of welcome."

"You are my guest of honor for the time you are here, and I hope to make the most of it," he says. "We will proceed to my guest house and you will have your dinner. Then, you must rest after your arduous journey. Tomorrow we'll talk some more, as I have much to show you."

As we drive, I recall when we first met at the dinner in Macao. He is stouter than I remember; a broad-faced man with snowy mutton chops set against mahogany-brown skin. Instead of more formal garb, though, he's now heavily adorned in a loose-fitting turquoise silk kurta over white linen, ankle-length pajamas. A rich-looking gold brocade scarf, requiring constant adjustment, is artfully draped over his right shoulder. A massive gold medallion hangs around his neck; gold pointed slippers and a tall black turban complete his appearance. Prosperity and charm are clearly the messages he intends to project during my visit.

Two black-clad liverymen sit high, reins in hand, urging the team onward through this crush of humanity. The drivers bark orders at passersby who only reluctantly give way, as we edge through the apparent chaos at the docks. The crowds here are mostly locals, convening at the nearby fish market. As I would learn, this is peak time at the bustling market. Fresh trawls of saucer-shaped pomfret, iridescent yellow dolphin fish and massive tuna lie stunned and wide-eyed in pungent seawater. Women rush by our carriage with baskets of glistening fish balanced on their heads. "These are the *Koli* women, their role here in Bombay dating back centuries," Walla explains. "Like you, they're agents for the fishermen, bartering with the mongers for the best price. They make a small fee for whatever they can then sell."

The dust-clad, open carriage rushes through the streets at frightening speed, as my senses are overwhelmed by the sounds, smells—and colors--of Bombay. A generalized din arises from the mass of humanity moving in every direction—the pervasive sound of a crowd in what appears a perpetual state of disorder. A panoply of pungent smells overwhelms my nostrils in rapid succession: first repugnant; then sweet and aromatic; then vile and other-worldly. European dress has no home in this steaming tropical city, as vast undulating crowds pass by, draped in every brilliant color known to nature: fluorescing oranges, yellows and greens, saturated, radiant blues, and purples, mixed with the humblest grays, browns and faded blacks. Class and station in society are determined at the moment of birth; a destiny pre-ordained by Brahma, codified by laws of man, and reinforced by rituals as ancient as time, itself.

Along the way, my host points out the newest building constructed in the Western style—all part of East India Company's expanding influence in a growing city. Waving his arm in a broad circle over his head, he says, "This used to be a cluster of swampy islands before the English. They control much of the business here now, and pay the government in Delhi handsomely for the opportunity. We both gain from this alliance. Otherwise, this would be nothing more than a poor fishing village."

"Cotton, fish, what else? I ask.

"Wealth beyond imagining, my friend, as you shall soon see. All because of men like me. In Hindi, we are merely the *Vaishyas*, or traders, created from the thighs of Brahma, the Hindu God of creation. But, unlike your culture, in Hindu society we occupy a place well below priests and princes, even though they create no wealth for our nation."

I'm thinking: 'This is a city of wealth, but also one of poverty beyond belief.' To my right, crumbling hovels stand in seemingly endless dust-filled rows, home to thousands of menial workers and outcasts. Their dilapidated dwellings border this busy thoroughfare just opposite the elegant, high-walled estates of the economically privileged. There seems to be no middle ground between riches and abject privation...a living, breathing dichotomy.

I point toward this scene, but before I can frame a question, Jeejeebhoy says, "These are the lowest castes among us—*Shudras* and *Dalits* or untouchables—created from the feet of Brahma.

"The poor are everywhere," I say, as we pass a row of street barbers, fruit and chai sellers, papaya hawkers and enfeebled beggars entreating passing strangers. Also, an array of wandering animals—cows, goats, and dogs—intermingle with pedestrian, wagon and carriage traffic in every direction.

"But, what of the cattle and sheep wandering the streets? It all seems so haphazard."

"The cow is sacred, and a part of city life." Walla smiles broadly at my question. "They are members of our family and are allowed to roam as they wish. To strike a cow—*gaay*, in our language—brings severe punishment, even prison if one is killed out of neglect. You must always take care and be on the alert. We do not eat the *gaay*. It is part of our religion."

"And the poor?"

"In India, you are born to a class, from the highest to the lowliest. There you remain for life. Very different from the West. Here, the poor are a fact of life, and there is little to be done about them. Nevertheless, they can serve our ambitions...but you have too many questions. We are here at your quarters. I'll have the men show you to your rooms, and I will call on you in the morning. Prepare for a journey of several hours. We shall be heading into the countryside."

And with that, Jeejeebhoy bids me a good night.

30. The Beautiful Lie

I AWAKE AT first light with the sound of the *Azaan*, the soulful call-to-prayer, echoing through the streets from the minaret of a nearby mosque. The cleric's song drifts through my open bedroom windows, floating on the summer breeze, mixing with the cacophony of sounds already floating up from the busy street beyond the gardens.

The tangle of blooms and branches below my windows is a riot of color to the eye. Hot pink bougainvillea overtop and cascade down walls, threading their way along sides of buildings. Ginger blossoms and jasmine bushes abound, their scent riding heavy on humid morning air. Countless birds, likely the Indian cuckoo, koel and dove—unseen from my vantage point—unabashedly contribute their songs and calls to my tranquil bedroom surroundings.

I enjoy a breakfast of steaming crepe-like *dosas*, a hot stew consisting of potato, greens and cashews, the cook calls *saagu*, fluffy discs of fresh-baked naan and minty chai. No sooner have I finished than there's a knock on my door, as one of the black-clad drivers comes to call. "*Aapakee gaadee, sar*, you carry-age sir," he says in broken English, gesturing toward the street. I step out into another scorching day, as Walla eagerly waves from the seat of a smaller transport than yesterday's. "My new britzka carriage," he says, "new from England. *Aao-aao*, Come-come, sit beside," as he pats the seat. "This folding top will cover you from the day's heat."

"We are going north today, into the cool mountains where you will be more comfortable. You will find the district of Asangaon to your liking."

We soon reach the outskirts of Bombay, as dense city life slowly gives way to broad, flat farmlands. Rice and cotton fields stretch for as far as we can see, interrupted only by distant hills, bathed in a dense, moisture-laden, golden-green haze.

"The mountains offer an ideal climate for growing poppy...rich soil, sunny days, cool nights," Walla says. "And the poor are scattered there, in need of work, income. The acres you will see need tending. The first step requires patience...labor intensive...lots of time to get the most out of any crop.

"You pay them to work their land, then?"

"No, I pay them to work *my* land. You will see I own this land. I purchased it from the government. These farmers happen to live on it...have for generations. They tend my crop, I pay them for their work. Allow them to remain and grow what they wish for their own purposes...feed their own, sell the rest at market. No matter to me."

"These people are indentured to you, then, men women, children, all working for you? They have no choice but to accept your price."

"My price is fair," he says, turning away from me, apparently annoyed that I don't readily concede his point. Turning back, he patiently recounts, as if for my benefit, "I am Parsi, my ancestors fled Persia to avoid persecution at the hands of Muslim invaders. I am the orphan son of a weaver, taken by pirates on my way here. We Parsi are self-made ...beginning with nothing but what we could carry. I have no pity for the downtrodden. Are you not here to make a difference in your *own* life, even at the expense of all else?"

"I'm a businessman, like you, but I hope to make my competency through legitimate means."

"Mister Russell, I think the expression you Americans have is, 'you speak from two sides of your mouth.' When we met in Macao, I offered you an opportunity to see a way to rapid fortune. You did *not* say no. In fact, you endured the perils of a long and dangerous sea voyage, and the oppressive heat of an Indian summer to satisfy your curiosity. What I am about to show you is how riches are made. *My* choices were made of necessity. And I would submit, sir, so too are yours."

I sit in silence. I realize my die had been cast the moment I decided to board *Shadow* in Macao. There was no turning back at that point. I have to face the reality that my ambitions run deeper than my principles. I confess I am drawn to this place. Am I setting aside moral values and all that my father stood for in my childhood, in the interest of wealth? My very presence here in the sweltering fields of a country halfway around the world from home attests to my unbridled ambition...to my desire to succeed at any expense.

≈

WHEN AT LAST, we arrive at our first farm, I am stunned by what I behold. Infinitely vast carpets of blood-red poppy blossoms spread like a blanket across the valley floor. Cloud-draped jungle peaks surround us on all sides. Small villages, consisting of a few rush-roofed, timber homes dot the landscape. Narrow dirt roads cling to steep ridges, weaving between fields and tying one small settlement to another. Dozens of figures, little more than specks of white against an ocean of crimson, can be made out, stooped and working the crop of *Papaver somniferum*, a deceptively beautiful flower with the Latin word for 'sleep' buried within its name.

Our carriage pulls up beside one of the fields. Jeejeebhoy calls out to a foreman nearby and we dismount to walk to him. Walla stoops to pluck, then gently cups a hardened seed pod in his hand. With a mock cutting gesture, he then says to the man, "*use dikhao*, show him...show how it is done."

The workman leans to steady the walnut-sized globe in his own palm, running a knife vertically in a few deft strokes along its sides. Slowly, a white latex sap oozes from the cuts.

"Once the petals have fallen, this is done hundreds of times a day throughout the field," Walla explains. "We wait a day or two and come back to scrape the sap from the pods. It will harden slightly in the sun. This is gathered and brought to the processing house...a step that I will soon show you."

"The amount seems so small," I say.

"Many kilos leave this field each week, but the final product is a concentration. I can see you are intrigued. *Aao, aao*, come, come, you shall see. Our factory is nearby." And with that, we re-mount the carriage.

"This field is one of dozens I control. And there are many more just like it throughout the region, owned by other men," he explains as we ride a short distance to the warehouse. "But the quality of opium it produces, *Patna*, doesn't bring the highest price...better than Turkish, but not the highest. For this, we must travel too far in the time we have together. But, later, I will explain how you and I can profit from yet another growing region farther to the east of here."

The large, open-sided production 'mixing room' stands in an open field, under the direct rays of the brutal Indian sun. A fence surrounds the building, carefully guarded by a dozen or more of Jeejeebhoy's men. In the cool, breezy recesses of the building, dozens more scantily clad men are consolidating and processing the milky sap, shaping it into balls just slightly larger than the palm of my hand. These were then weighed, wrapped in cotton gauze and tied off with cord.

"Trays of these balls are then carried over to towers of racks like the ones along this corridor, where they are set out to dry. This will take some weeks, but storage intensifies the chemicals, making the *afeem* the powerful substance it is."

"These men, are they being paid by you?"

"They are compensated in many ways, yes. These are men from many nearby villages—Nirmal Nagar, Armarsh Nagar; farther reaches, too, into the villages above the clouds, Hanuman Mandir, Walshet, places where men still live as they did a thousand years ago. I bring them into modern times.

"These men are bone-thin, their faces drawn, emotionless. It seems hundreds work here."

"They are given enough to live, a place to sleep, a few *rupes* to send home to families. They chew the *mawseed*, you know, the poppy seed, which I make available to them. They shape the *afeem* balls with their hands, releasing small amounts into their systems over the course of each day. They *have* no troubles, *make* no troubles. It is better for them than walking behind an oxen and plow all day, yes? And still, more they come. *Aao, aao*, see here is where we make our chests. See, ten kilos to a chest, thousands go from here each year, and more with each passing year."

"There are millions of dollars' worth here..."

"Mister Jardine agrees to buy all I produce. The chests travel by caravan to Calcutta on the east coast, and to Bombay by wagon. My men secure the routes. The camels are driven east by Multanis, with hundreds of years doing this. Very reliable, although I also pay them well."

"I know William Jardine. You are under contract to provide *afeem*, as you call it, to him alone. In fact, these fields are really obligated to him and the Company because they receive all you produce; and you are paid well for your trouble. Why bring me here to see all of this?"

"This, I will explain. But, the day is late. Let us retire to my country home and dine. All will become clear," Walla says, begging my patience and indulgence for just a few more hours.

~

JAMSETJI JEEJEEBHOY'S PALATIAL home sits atop a vertiginous ridge, its high, creamy-white marble walls and domed turrets aglow in a late afternoon sun. Jagged cliffs drop into a mist-drenched precipice just yards from formal, English-inspired gardens extending off the rear of the house. Tall gently-arched, Persian-styled windows add a touch of elegance and airiness. The shrill calls of a choir of tropical birds and chatter of acrobatic bonnet macaques, unseen in a nearby tree line, fill the incandescent air. Together with an ornate, recessed portico facing the large circular drive, the overall effect is one of serene prosperity.

Upon our arrival, the doors swing open at the hands of attendant staff. Sunlight glints off expanses of polished pink marble floors extending in an unbroken line to a rear balcony. Through the far windows, a low, dense mix of Jujube, Banyan and palm trees blanket the valley, the canopy pulsing with staccato insect sounds quavering in the fading heat of day. Beyond an expansive balcony, a cloud-capped mountain range extends far into the distance.

Jeejeebhoy walks ahead of me, leading me into a high-ceiling, domed great room. We sit in large, over-stuffed chairs surrounded by richly appointed teak furnishings. Countless paintings, massive carved ivory tusks, and intricately carved statuary are on display. Tall vases of fresh, exotic flowers are placed strategically around the room. At the perimeter of the space, finely fretted marble panels filter sunlight into abstract patterns on the floor. As we settle in, the soft tinkling melody of a distant wind chime gently marks time.

"As a Rastafari, I do not drink, but, if you wish, I have some of Mister Jardine's finest scotch whisky to offer."

"I think I'm ready," I say, settling into my large chair and gesturing with a broad sweep of my arm at the magnificent setting around me.

Shortly, a tall, elegantly dressed woman approaches me, balancing a silver tray with a crystal glass containing a splash of whisky. She wears a jewel-toned *salwar-kameez* with a long stole draped across her throat and streaming down her back, a small red bhindi gracing her brow. She's olive-skinned doe-eyed, with long, dark hair drawn back in a braid resting on her shoulders. A stack of silver bangles on her slender wrists shift and jangle as she reaches down to serve me.

"Mistar Russell, this is Chavvi. She will be here to attend your every need while you are my guest, tonight. She is accomplished at English and will follow your direction."

With that, I slightly nod as a gesture of 'Halloo.' Practiced in her every gesture, she turns and with a small curtsy to acknowledge me, smiles briefly, then departs to direct dinner preparations.

≈

DINNER IS SERVED on the piazza, cooled now by a gentle evening breeze. On an expanse of crisp white linen, dishes of fine Chinese porcelain sit on golden chargers, with gold flatware and crystal glasses to complete the setting. Candles are positioned at random along the length of the table, protected from the wind by hurricane shades. Just feet away, a cadre of kitchen staff in starched white attire stand attentively, ready to serve. The entire scene sparkles against an evening sky, marked by an array of slowly fading bands of butter yellow, pink and tangerine light drifting above the distant mountain range.

At the table opposite me for the evening meal—a vegetarian offering—is Jeejeebhoy's accountant, Nimish Singh, a rotund, hirsute man with a tangled salt-and-pepper beard, a man so essential to his complex business operation, I assume, that his attendance is required. A charming man, he chooses to say little; but I have the impression he is actively sizing me up as a future 'partner' for whatever his employer has in mind.

And, to my surprise and delight, the elegantly poised Chavvi is seated next to me. Hints of jasmine and honeysuckle tease my senses as she leans toward me, lifting the napkin from my plate and handing it to me with a modest smile. My hand brushes hers as I respond to the gesture. I can feel my face flushing at the unwarranted attention I'm receiving.

She claps twice briskly, directing our attention to the dinner, as servants converge on the table. With silent gestures and glancing eye movements, staff place one elegant dish after another before us. Apparently for my benefit alone, she points out a feast of onion and garlic-rich corn *kadai*, steaming on porcelain platters; a stew of steamed vegetables, apricots, and cashews on a bed of golden saffron rice; lentils and parsley in sour cream; steaming *roti*; and, later, lemon cheesecake for dessert. By late evening, I have also indulged in several glasses of a fine French wine—also courtesy of Willian Jardine's long-standing relationship with my host, from a seemingly inexhaustible wine vault.

By dinner's end, and with a snifter of pre-revolution French brandy in hand, Walla, Singh and I adjourn to the great room to discuss—I assume—the principal reason for my invitation here.

"We have new fields opening up, as I said earlier. Malwa is a remote district in the central mountain regions," Walla explains. "I have every expectation that the quality will be far superior to what we have been harvesting to date. This is not the Persian, *Kem fa t'ou*, Indian Patna or Benares kind. Better quality means higher price at auction, and increased demand in the marketplace."

"But you are contracted to East India Company, with Jardine and Company, yes?"

"Yes, but only for existing fields. These Malwa fields are far removed, and can be developed without their knowledge...at least for a while. By then, the market will be secured. We need a trustworthy agent in Canton who can represent our shared interests."

"And that would be...?"

"You, sir, *you*, if I may be so bold. You have a stake in the market. You are not yet fully established, so your loyalties are still open, and you have the backing in the U.S. to bring ships to our shores to transport large quantities of *afeem* into the Pearl, undetected.

"You say *undetected*, but the Company's Indiamen and their agents are everywhere."

"But, therein lies the weakness—and the opportunity for you and me to prosper. The British have looked to one particular procedure for years. They've always relied on Indians, like me, to move *afeem* to Turkish and Indian ports, where they can be auctioned off to British buyers. The Company acquires the *afeem* using credits available to them through London banks. The auction house is paid by the bank. These lines also allow them, in return, to buy English goods, like fabrics. It is all very clean. No silver changes hands.

"So now the opium sits at port—Bombay, Calcutta, Bengal—and British interests own it outright. How do you fit in?"

"I'm a trusted partner in those transactions, because of my own good reputation, built up over time. I transport the product on my own ships to Lintin Bay, where I sell directly out of my hold to runners and pirates who pull alongside. They take no time to even tie up to our vessel, quickly transacting, then disappearing into the landscape with none the wiser. Jardine and any others connected with the Company, and I, then share in the profits. They take profit because of their British-backed banking power; I for the willingness to take the risk once in Chinese waters.

"But why do you need me in this scheme?"

"Because I am too well-known to them—and you, Mistar Russell, are as yet the big *unknown*. The British are not yet aware of the Malwa fields and the quality they can yield. I *control* these fields, or much of them. My close colleagues own the others. I compensate the growers who live on the land directly. I am all they know, and remain beholding to. No auction house is needed. Your ships can journey to Karachi to sell your American cotton goods. Then with an empty hold and specie in your locker, take on my *afeem*, to depart to Lintin for quick sale directly from your deck. The word will quickly spread regarding the quality of your offering, and the price you fetch will soon bear this out. And my British partners will be none the wiser."

"How long do you think *that* charade can last?"

"Not forever, Mistar Russell, but long enough for us both to prosper. I must continue with the British for as long as possible; but I'm not bound to them. Nor am I bound to you. But you are here now, as am I..."

"You can turn on me just as quickly, then? How will I know that this arrangement might...?"

"Sir, the bond between us is what we need at this moment. Your doubt resides in your Western notion of *permanence*. The Buddha teaches that when Life asked Death: '*Why do people love me and hate you? Death replied: Because you are a beautiful lie and I am a painful truth.*'"

"Very sensible, I guess, but business can't be that fluid and succeed in the long run."

"We can live the beautiful lie while it lasts, Mistar Russell; but we both know it cannot last. So, fill your holds in Karachi with Malwa *afeem*, bought and paid for by me, and we share in the greater profits when you sell to the Chinese from the deck of your vessels in the Pearl River. Do you understand? Do you agree?"

Along with the effects of my alcohol consumption over the course of the evening, my head swims with the possibilities Jeejeebhoy is offering me. This arrangement alone could be all I will need to achieve my financial goal—my competency—and be back in Connecticut sooner than expected. I remain silent for what seems an eternity, until finally saying, "I would like until the morning to decide."

"Of course, sir, this is an important decision for your future in Canton. I will see you then, in the morning for *subah ka naashta*, what you Englishmen call '*brrrek*-fast,' and the ride back to Bombay.

≈

IT IS WELL after midnight when I stumble down the hallway to my bedroom. My door is slightly ajar, a fact I briefly consider curious—though my reasoning is clouded by drink. A gibbous moon and host of planets hang suspended in a star-studded, black velvet sky, entangled in the branches of a nearby tree, animating shadows on my carpeted floor. The sounds of *kriket* fill the perfumed night air, as Chavvi lies, soon to be discovered, naked in my bed.

31. Conflagration

AT DAWN, I awake alone amidst heaps of blankets and pillows now littering the floor—a jumbled reminder of my night's adventure. A single ivory hair comb lies beneath my outstretched arm, while the faint aroma of jasmine lingers on the sheets. Prying myself into an upright position, I stumble to the washstand, and with a few handfuls of cold water dashed against my face, I'm ready as I will ever be for the new day, and the long journey home.

As the intoxicating veil of sleep slowly lifts, Jeejeebhoy's offer returns to me. It's appealing, though it strains the moral principles that have always guided my life. Here I am, in a distant land, surrounded by opulence. *My* dilemma is that the reward for following Walla's lead will have me abandoning my principles in the name of fortune; I'll have a secret agreement, a clandestine source that relies on vast numbers of opium-dependent, indentured workers—little more than slave labor. Back in Canton, I owe the British nothing in the way of loyalty. They have been, after all, making their own arrangements. My men and my partners back in the U.S. will have to know of my decision. If I choose to go this route, I'll be compelled to let them know.

Throughout it all, I remain a man of unshakable faith and principle, or so I believe. Maybe all those convictions are just so much bullshit. My faith in myself is being strained to the limit. I stand for a long while, head bowed, taking short breaths as my hands grip the washstand counter. I cannot bring myself to view my own haggard countenance in the mirror, just inches away. I feel I need another sign before I can finally decide.

≈

RICH AROMAS COMING from the kitchen finally draw me in the direction of the great room. Shavvi had promised I would partake of a classic Indian *subah ka naashta* before I left: *idlis*, steamed rice-dough pancakes, with dips and chutneys, as well as spiced potatoes. But first, my host is awaiting me on the balcony, speaking earnestly to his man, Singh. He greets me warmly as I step into the bright light of day, the omnipresent Singh moving into the shadowy recesses of the house. I mentally note that the beautiful Shavvi is nowhere to be seen.

"Did you rest well?" Walla asks, somewhat whimsically.

"As well as can be expected, thank you. You're a wonderful host."

"I'm always ready to share what I have. It is a mark of Indian hospitality." And with that he bows slightly in my direction, as if to say, 'you're welcome.' "But," he adds, "I'm afraid I have some grave news for you. Word was received during the night from one of my vessels just arriving yesterday in Bombay. You may wish to be seated," gesturing to the room where we met in the previous evening.

"No, thank you. What is it, please?"

"Mistar Sam, several days ago your factory buildings burned to the ground. A small fire began in the crowded neighborhood behind the factories, spreading quickly with the winds, and entire compound was lost. Efforts by local fire brigades came too little...too late."

"Are you sure they're all *gone*? How about my men? Are they safe? Has everything been lost?" As the news washes over me, I can feel my face going pale. My knees weaken, a surge of acid rising in my throat—last night's poor choices returning to punish me.

"I am sorry you had to learn in this way. The Chinese are not accustomed to such large wooden building. They build with rushes and bamboo, easily replaced. This was beyond them to help. As we discussed, now you will be returning to a new start...a new life for you, yes?"

The news pierces me like an arrow, deflating my resolve in ways I can't explain. I was more than two years into my efforts to build a company and all of that will be gone when I return home. "Was anyone hurt, do you know?"

"The fire rose up at night, and burned for two days, but with no loss of life that I know of. But, I can't speak to the facts.

"In fact, knowing you were here, your men sent a sealed letter. It is stored safely away from unwelcomed eyes and I'll bring it to you now." And with that, Walla goes down the hallway to his study, returning with a packet addressed to me. I excuse myself and return to my room to learn what I can about the disaster. Suddenly, my appetite for breakfast is lost, as I read:

NOVEMBER 10, 1822

For the Attention Only, Mr. Samuel Russell

This is to inform you of the loss of the American Factory in a conflagration that consumed all the buildings here, along the waterfront row of the many nations, on the 1st and 2nd of this month. It is believed the fire began in a cluster of wood frame houses on the west side of the Old City. Flames moved quickly, driven by seasonal winds, engulfing other neighborhoods, before sparks descended on factory structures. Efforts to contain the flames were in vain. The alarm quickly passed through the dormitories in the various buildings. Your men had just a few minutes to rush down to the counting room and secure as many documents as they could reasonably carry out to the safety of Respondentia Walk.

By then, hundreds of residents and the merely curious gathered in various craft on the safety of the river. Winds continued to fan the flames, engulfing all but a few facades of the remaining structures along the waterfront. Billowing smoke rose high enough to shroud the full moon, which, together with the bright glow of the fire itself, lit up the entire harbor area. It was reported that melted silver specie, stored there, ran in a thin river for nearly two miles.

We are all safe and well, busying ourselves with the task of salvaging and restoring existing files, letters, and ledgers, reconstructing our lost documents and journals to the best of our memory, while assuring our clients, Co-hongs, merchants, and vessels at anchor at Whampoa, that we are prepared to conduct business, more-or-less as usual.

Be assured that we are protecting your interests here and, as all other agents and nations shared a similar plight, we are at no singular disadvantage. The British—long-standing in the region, have options to conduct their affairs out of their Macao facilities. I have taken the liberty to contact our Hong, Howqua, who generously arranged for us to continue the work of Russell & Co. out of leased facilities nearby. Re-construction will begin as soon as is practicable.

Ba assured, also, that to the extent possible, all will be in order upon your return, which we hope and expect will be expedited upon receipt of this unfortunate news.

With sincere regards, as I remain in your service, Philip

≈

I RETURN TO the great room, my host, and Mister Singh. Looks of grave concern are etched on their faces. "Based on my letter, I should plan to leave sooner than planned."

"Samuel, I have arranged for one of my ships to take you back to Canton. You may leave on the tide tomorrow if you wish. They are loading presently and will be ready as you direct."

"Thank you. I believe I need to return as soon as possible. Much needs my attention."

"But first, sir," as he motions toward the table, "I must insist you enjoy this wonderful repast. I know you Americans cannot tolerate going without your 'brrek-fest.' So, join us now please. Shavvi has prepared something beautiful for us."

Following breakfast, and knowing the plan for returning to Canton, I find time for quiet contemplation in the idyllic estate gardens, and in my room, updating my journal with the notes seen here. My host must have sensed my need for solitude because I saw little of him, Singh, Shavvi, or the household staff for most of the day. My dilemma: a major setback in Canton, with all records and ledgers possibly lost. My time and effort wasted—lost to the flames. Any chance of returning to America delayed by years, perhaps. With these delays, I will be lucky to come out alive.

And yet, I have earned the trust...no *trust* is not a word that seems to apply on this side of the world...confidence, then. I've earned the confidence of this powerful Indian. Should I throw it all away, knowing that I'm returning to the ashes of my convictions, the ruins of a plan that I rode high, above the corruption that perpetually surrounds me there?

I confess to a weakening of my spirit, a temptation to succumb to a tide carrying me inexorably toward a dangerous shore. What did John Astor cite me in his study that day?... *'There's nothing wrong with fortune, as long as you can turn a portion of it for the public good.'* John Locke's words in that slim volume sitting on my shelf...at the factory... no wait! Now GONE with the rest!

My boys back home, my reputation in town, my future hangs on this moment. Why did I agree to come here, to make the journey, if not to consent to whatever I find here? Can I ever realize Locke's words—'the public good'—without myself first doing well? What is *good* in a world where evil, things like slavery, addiction, drunkenness, tobacco, rule human desire? My desire? What *do* I desire? My choice, my choices, my actions, where is my heart in all of this? I cannot know at this moment, my pen poised motionless above this page.

≈

LATER, WE SIT without any further discussion of the proposal, while I attempt to clear my mind, enjoying dinner, wine and a lively performance of local music and impromptu dance by household staff, who seem delighted to show off their culture and traditions to an appreciative foreigner. It is, I confess, a pleasant distraction, with the hint of jasmine once again in the air as I enter my room at nightfall. So, too are the warm hands on my back and shoulders, as I listen to the door close softly behind me.

The next day, my host, Mister Singh, Shavvi and I travel back to Bombay and the harbor, where *Alliance*, and Captain Dhruv Amin await me. I exit the carriage, swinging my duffle to the ground. I turn to shake Jeejeebhoy's hand, and with solid eye contact, I say determinedly, "You have a deal."

"I had hoped you would agree," he says. "You will be home in less than four weeks, *eeshvar kee krpa ho*, 'God willing,' and with a favorable westerly at your back. I will need two months to have my first shipment harvested, processed and taken by caravan from Malwa Province to Karachi. Please plan to have your vessel there by mid-January. I will send further instruction to you at your offices in Canton, or wherever you may be."

Once aboard, I stow gear below. I move slowly, disconcerted by the notion that I allowed the riches and indulgences of Walla's life style to seduce me into a disastrous decision. Perhaps that was his intention. All of that, plus the timing of the factory fire and the unknown that I'll be returning to, propel me to make this choice. It is one I will have to live with, remembering Locke's words and hoping they will be ones I can honor.

In the privacy of my cabin, I open my journal once again. A bright pink bougainvillea blossom falls onto the table from between its pages. On the inside cover, I find an added inscription beneath my name and year. It was penned in indigo, and written with a flourish:

सुरक्षति यात्रा

Safe Journey

~Shavvi~

32. Reconstruction

TWENTY-FIVE DAYS LATER, I return to Macao from Bombay on *Alliance*. I calculate the Factory fires have laid waste to nearly three-years' work. Having made this same trip up the Pearl dozens of times in my stay, I'm not prepared for the actual degree of devastation. From our Whampoa anchorage, telltale traces of smoke still waft skyward over Canton, ten miles to the north. Faint gray-brown veils drift slowly up from the river's edge, suspended above nearby rain-soaked hills. As we approach the scene by skiff, lush citrus groves, running in neat, verdant rows up from Pearl's banks, hang heavy with oranges and limes; the eternal walls of the city, stained with age and darkened by the last downpour, then come into view; river traffic, never changing, still darts and churns frenetically in all directions, just yards from what had once been the center of my world.

When we finally tie up at Jackass Point, I ascend the stone steps to find a vast expanse of smoldering black lumber, heaps of rubble where walls and roofs once stood. From left to right, ruins extend from one end of the complex to the other. The inferno has spared nothing except three intact, white-washed, and columned facades, aglow in intermittent afternoon light breaking through storm clouds, making a mockery of the tragic event.

After securing the skiff, the ship's first, Anshu Anand, walks up beside me, as I stare in disbelief.

"Mistar Sam, theese is *kathin...how you say...*difficult for you, *Haan*, y-yes, *Haan?*"

"*Haan*, Anshu, very *kathin*," I say slowly, unable to take my eyes off the colossal pile of rubble. I survey the remaining superstructure, looking for some familiar sign of what was once the American Factory. The flag poles of nations remain standing on the lawns in front of the wreckage, and so, by elimination, I was able to pick out what remains of my offices.

"My captain, he saw big fire from Whampoa. Want you to know when we returned Bombay. Find your people, ask to bring letter to you. Sad, sad. But, you make right, *Haan?*

"*Haan*, Anshu, *Haan*, I'll make right. I'll go to find my people now, Anshu. You can tell your captain thank you... *dhanyavaad...*and also, *dhanyavaad* to *mistar* Jeejeebhoy. But before you ship out, I'll have a letter for you to take to him. The hoppo, over there in that building,"

pointing to the customs house shed, "will tell you where to find me."

"*Haan*, Mistar Sam, you make right."

Over the next few hours, I search for my company men, and Howqua, as well, to develop a plan for carrying on business. I climb the crooked steps of the old stone building at the east end of the dock, spared from the flames, except for roof tiles singed black by the heat. The old bones of the building—shadows of cracked ribs and struts, worm-eaten beams, and spanners—bend and sag from age beneath time-worn plaster walls. A wobbling banister, worked smooth and blackened by countless hands, guides me on a steep stairwell to a second floor, where I'm greeted by whoops and huzzahs, as the men from several nations, now working together there have already spotted me crossing the yard through an open window.

For the next several months—key months in our trading season—we turn our attention to survival and recovery, putting into place temporary procedures and systems while construction of a new factory complex continues apace. Our new offices and dormitory will not be complete before the summer season will force us to relocate our operation south to Macao, once again.

But the urgent matter of dispatching a ship to Karachi weighs on me. I'm able to commandeer one of our recently-arrived Providence vessels, a twelve-gunner, the *Grafton*, lying at anchor at Whampoa, and redirect Captain Wm. McGee to reserve a portion of our U.S. cargo for trade once he arrives in India. He will find the market there less crowded than here, and favorable prices can be had, as a result. He's to deliver written instructions from me to Jeejeebhoy's people, who will expect him, proceeding to load the shipment of Malwa opium waiting for him.

He's under strict orders to notify me immediately upon his return to Lintin, when I will have made necessary arrangements with Howqua to dispense the goods through the usual channels.

From the beginning of my assignment as an agent in '19, I had been invited by my partners in Providence to pursue whatever line of trade I thought most profitable for all involved. The reality on the ground in Canton over the last several years was that both British (East India Trade., through Wm. Jardine) and certain Americans (the 'Boston Concerns': Thomas Perkins; J.P. Sturgis and John Cushing; and the New Yorker, John Jacob Astor) have promoted and developed trade in Persian and Turkish opium, with considerable profit accruing to their companies. I had turned a blind eye to this activity, allowing some marginal involvement in opium trade from those same regions since arriving, but always careful to bury it deep in my manifest, making no direct reference to it in my ledgers, and never relying on it as my principal source of revenue. In this way, I believed—mistakenly so—that I had clean hands.

These self-imposed controls in my own thoughts and actions are owed, in part, to the strict prohibition placed on the import and use of the drug by the emperor and his minions. '*This is poisoning our people,*' he had said in numerous communiques to regional governors. His proclaimed restrictions were of limited value, given the great distance to the seat of the Celestial Kingdom in Beijing, and the vigorous black market with resulting graft finding its way to even the lowest levels of harbor authorities, on the length and breadth of the Pearl, and beyond.

Certain Mandarin authorities have searched random vessels in Macao and Whampoa, promptly expelling those ships bearing *yāpiàn* without benefit of unloading their cargoes. Those hongs thought to be associated with those ships and their opium contraband have also been publicly reprimanded. These punitive actions, however, appear to be limited to Western agents and their ships who were unwilling to make the appropriate payments to authorities. For those hongs whose reputations appear severely threatened by reprimand, though, are soon back at work. The general impression is that the emperor's threats ring hollow once you move two feet beyond the Forbidden City's palace walls.

After my determinative meeting in Bombay with Jeejeebhoy and given strained conditions with locals following the destruction of the factory buildings, together with the growing demand for opium in the Chinese market, I decide to act decisively. In fact, my employers had always been clear that my actions while in China should be free and independent, determined by what I perceive to be best for the company.

I therefore wrote the following to my Providence partners:

DECEMBER 20, 1822

Sirs:

There is not an article of Merchandise that we would recommend your sending at present, so completely stocked is the Market & so depressed in value. Opium is the only article which of late can be said to have a profit. I have notified our Hong, Howqua, of my intention to import a significant quantity of the drug from reliable, but secreted Indian sources, and expect that market forces for these high-quality goods will command nothing less than 1500$ per picul, which for purposes of definition, is understood locally to be "as much as a man can carry on a shoulder-pole". Quantities of 100-125 of these chests will be arriving at Lin-tin Island in late January-to-early February 1823, subject to immediate transfer onto our go-down and expedited sale.

This action is not without its risks, however. On September of last year, the Chinese accused a Sicilian sailor, one Francis Terranovia, aboard the American ship 'Emily,' (out of Baltimore, under Captain Wm. Cowpland), of killing a Chinese fruit vendor by knocking her off her sampan with an olive jar. The vessel had been anchored at Whampoa, selling the ship's opium in regulated quantities, much to the satisfaction and benefit of local authorities. After the alleged murder incident, the captain was advised to pay the usual bribes to local officials, in the hopes that they might be placated. Captain Cowpland refused.

He made the additional mistake of allowing the Chinese to try the hapless sailor on board the 'Emily,' where he was found guilty and strangulated just days later. Few British or Americans attempted to prevent the action for fear that their trade would be stopped. Later, as a result of the incident, opium was 'found' aboard the "Emily, and once again the embittered Chinese authorities unleashed edicts upon the foreign nationals at Canton, denouncing their illegal trade, "which flows and poisons the land."

I am determined to meet our objectives as I remain in your service,

~ Samuel Russell

≈

IN ADDITION TO my choice to engage more aggressively in the opium trade, I have made another important decision. With the arrival of the '23 summer season, I am returning to Macao with every intention of re-engaging with Isabella, making my intentions clear to her father that I wish a more serious relationship with her. In her long winter's absence at school and mine in India and Canton, my feelings of affection have blossomed into genuine desire—even love. I have no right to expect she might reciprocate those feelings, given the time and distance that constantly plagues our relationship. But, I feel compelled to pursue her and, at the very least, express my truest emotions and have any lingering doubts and fears addressed by all parties, once and for all.

33. Reunion

AS GOOD FORTUNE would have it, Isabella Anna Calebro, re-appears serendipitously early in the summer season of '23. As previously noted, each year all factory men are required to live in Macao for the summer months. It is there I have occasion to attend a memorial service at the Church of Saint Paul, a beautiful Gothic cathedral standing in the shadow of the Fortaleza do Monte. A service is being held to honor the memory of the recently passed governor of the city—one of many felled in this season of fever. Pomp and ceremony always attend the death of a member of the Portuguese ruling class. This service offers all the usual pageantry, with the rich and powerful of the city gathering to pay respects. I attend less out of a personal interest in the deceased, than reasons of curiosity and to shelter away in the cathedral's cool stony recesses on yet, another sultry summer day.

From the street below, I glance up at the towering structure atop a small hill, its intricate 17th century façade carved by exiled Japanese Christians and local craftsmen, under the direction of an Italian Jesuit, Carlo Spinola. He and dozens of other long-forgotten Jesuits now lie in crypts beneath this vaulted space.

I climb dozens of steps leading to the church's massive, heavily carved doors. As I ascend, a blazing morning sun at my back casts my shadow across the broad stairway in a shifting zig-zag pattern. A carved dove, with outspread wings hovers on the edifice overhead, as if inviting me to press on. Along the way, statues of saints stand in silent vigil, witness to the thousands of Western and Chinese Christians who have made this same pilgrimage. I stop to catch my breath beside one statue, a portrayal of the Blessed Virgin stepping on a seven-headed hydra. The Chinese inscription below describes, 'The Holy Mother tramples the heads of the dragon'—an artful blending of Catholic and Oriental themes.

Once in the darkened sanctuary, I hesitate momentarily at the rear, letting my eyes adapt, as distant, resonant strains of organ music wash over my senses. I slowly discern dozens of people gathered in orderly rows close to the altar. I slowly find my way to an empty pew near the back of the crowd. The altar and its ornate trappings are aglow with candlelight. Shafts of rainbow-hued light stream from a row of high-placed, stained-glass windows, angling through the voluminous space in a haze of incense and candle smoke, to illuminate the center isle of the sanctuary. In the apse, a small army of white-robed clergy slowly move through elaborate rituals of devotion and remembrance.

I can hardly imagine a life devoted to faith and mystical indulgence such as I'm seeing here. It seems so far removed from the life I know: harsh realities of business profit and loss; debits and credits; unsold goods rotting in warehouses; men and cargo lost at sea without a trace. These thoughts and others wash over me as I sit alone, disconnected from the proceedings. Only slowly am I aware that, just inches away from where I sit, is the very young woman whose raven hair and brown shoulders captured my heart at the East India Company reception so many months ago. She's sitting with the same friends who had accompanied her back then; but today, the group is silent and attentive.

I am struck by my good fortune. Here I've come for a solemn occasion as all my desires come flooding back, just as though no time at all had passed. I am suddenly overcome by feelings of shame and panic. I am a widowed man with a deceased wife lying in her grave, children awaiting their father's return, and a world of responsibilities here in Canton. What right do I have to harbor feelings toward this total stranger? Young, beautiful, naive, optimistic for her future—I feel self-loathing for my impulse to want to be with this woman, and immediately get up to leave the ceremony.

Sensing movement behind her as I stand, Isabella turns and, recognizing me, smiles in my direction. Her eyes hold me for a brief instant, as I nod back. My heart leaps from my chest, my breath catching in my throat. I smile in return, but shuffle to the aisle and rush to the back of the church.

I step out into the day, but I'm not yet ready to have my legs carry me down that flight of steps. So I find myself dropping onto a narrow stretch of wall leading away from the massive doors. There I sit for some length of time. I want to have a word with her—but, what to say? I'm unclear—but determined to do so. If my professed intentions are to remain true, she might exit these doors soon and I *must* find some way to engage her.

While I wait, I pick up a stick, absent-mindedly tapping out a rhythm against the wall. Then, I became more aware of the grass beneath my feet. Life is teeming beneath those blades: armies of insects moving with determination over a gargantuan landscape; a moth navigates the serrated edge of a single leaf, legs and feelers probing the air; a thrush on a distant stump explores the rotting bark for grubs; a cricket scratches out a ragged tune to protest the day's heat. I consider: are nature's wonders, played out in this nearly invisible world beneath my feet, a metaphor for my life? Am I blind to life's true meaning? Have I ever allowed any of this beauty to matter to me, with my eyes so habitually locked on my ledger pages? And yet, here I remain, with all these doubts, not fully able to explain this to myself.

Yet, I wait.

As the doors of the cathedral swing open, a blast of cool, incense-laden air engulfs me. I lift my head to see a cluster of people emerge from the ceremony, but Isabella and her friends are not among them. All are engaged, in many languages of the factories and the city of Macao. They take no notice of me, as I sit well below eye-level and off to the side. Perhaps she left by a side entrance? From my vantage point, I scan the streets below me to see any sign of her black hair and white-lace shawl.

When the plaza in front of the church is nearly cleared, she finally emerges, surrounded by her friends, apparently joyous to be freed from the solemnity of the event. I stand and nervously face in the direction of the small group, hoping to be noticed. Her attention diverted, she suddenly quiets and separates from her friends, approaching me.

"Olá," she says, cautiously. Her light blue linen dress, bedecked with swirling floral patterns of creamy silk embroidery, hugs her waist. Where it flares to meet the ground, the tips of patent leather shoes peek out from beneath the hem.

"Hello," signaling I'm prepared to have this conversation in English. "I am happy to see you again," I say, somewhat inanely. "Do you remember me?"

"Yes, I remember, from the dinner months ago. You were the new American. Very nervous then, I think."

"I've settled in, I hope. Have my feet under me, hopefully."

"That is a funny expression. Where else would your feet be."

"I mean...I mean, I'm settled in. Understand more about things...I mean..."

Sensing my discomfort, Isabella changes the subject. "My father insists that I make an appearance at these things," she says, taking her piercing blue-green eyes off me to gaze out at the panoramic view of the city and harbor.

It's a beautiful vantage point. My first time here," I stammer.

"I come each week for services, but I never get tired of it. The light is always changing."

First with my hands in my pockets, then out, then in again, I fumble for something to say. "Are you going to be with your friends, or may I ask if you would like to walk in the church gardens for a spell?" I ask, my hands again at my side.

"I will speak with my friends, but I think, yes. But for just a minute. I will send them on their way. But they will wait for me around the corner."

As we slowly walk the formal meditation gardens, I find myself studying the curve of her neck, the soft angle of her chin, the gentle slope of her eyes, and lips as she forms her next thought. She finally says, "I dream about my farm back home in València. It is beautiful rolling countryside, with horses and wine and the city of Lisbon close by. This is beautiful, too. But I miss my country sometimes. How about you?"

"I am here long enough, now, that I forget much of what I left behind. I was young when I arrived here, with a young family and business back home. My wife died in my absence and here I am, unable to move in the foreseeable future. I make the most of what is in front of me." As I speak, feelings I haven't had in so long wash over me. Isabella smells of orange blossom and ginger, the small locket suspended by a golden chain around her neck coming to rest just below that hollow spot at the throat, rising and falling with each breath. Her arm brushes mine, and I yearn to take her hand. My heart quickens once more.

We sit on a bench near a small fountain. The sky behind her is the color of oyster shells, the air around us infused with a soft mist carried up from the harbor. A summer zephyr stirs the boughs of trees overhead; her face now perfectly framed by a grove of palms in the distance. "What do you hope to find here in Macao when you come each year?"

"I come because my father wishes me to be here. I stay busy and pretend to be interested in his work with the government, but I want something more in my life...a purpose of my own."

"Could you ever imagine...?"

And with that, our concentration is broken by two Jesuit novices deeply engaged I conversation nearby. Both are dressed in the hooded robes of their order, entering the garden from a back door of the church. They're speaking Portuguese and appear to be arguing. They take no notice of us, sitting the shadows near the fountain.

Though not meaning to, we clearly hear their interchange. Isabella tips her head to decipher what is being said. After a few minutes, her face lights up. Turning to me to, she says "They're fighting over a *woman*. One feels he has a claim to her. The other warns against any action to violate his vows. They are novices, studying to become priests. They are free to leave the order at any time to resume their civilian life. One wishes the other to stay." As she speaks, her face brightens. She is thoroughly enjoying this real-life drama, played out just yards from where we sit.

As they slowly wander back toward the church sacristy, I say, "This is an affair of the heart for them, then—Christ or a woman?"

"Yes, you might say, the heart for one of the young men, the head for the other," at which point she laughs softly at her own insight. And with that, she turns her gaze back to me and I feel the world suddenly brimming to overflow in the dazzling light of this summer afternoon.

"Isabella, there is a battle raging between my head and heart, as well. But I should say no more."

Then, more abruptly than I had intended, I blurt out, "May I ask to accompany you back to your father's residence? And, if it's not too forward, I would hope to see you again."

"Yes, you may accompany me, but not to my home. It would be too daring on your part to arrive on my father's doorstep without proper introduction. He believes in the Old World way. Please walk with me to the road and I will fetch a sedan to take me home with my friends. He will be expecting me to be with them. I broke a rule to spend this time with you and 'order must be restored in the universe,'" she says, tucking her chin toward her slender throat, pantomiming her father's basso voice and stern countenance. And with that, she laughs again.

"And to my second question...?"

"Yes, you may call on me. But you must wait until the twenty-third, just ten days away. There's a gathering at the Portuguese consulate, hosted by my father. Please come at seven. But you must promise me to be on best behavior." She smiles again, then leans forward, briefly touching my hand and placing a kiss on my cheek. "Shall we go, then?"

At that instant, the rest of the world, my company, my endeavors, my plans and dreams, my worldview, becomes merely two-dimensional—as flat as numbers on a page. Isabella's intelligence, poise, beauty, and not least her dancing eyes, will occupy the entirety of my thoughts and hopes from that moment, until we can meet again.

34. Thieves in Broad Daylight

THE RECEIVING VESSEL, or so-called 'go-down,' has swung at anchor for so many months in this one location in the protective lee of Lin-tin Island, known as the 'Solitary Nail,' due to its isolated position in the bay. Long tendrils of yellow-green kelp hang from the hull, fluttering just below the water's surface in shifting light and tides. Razor-sharp colonies of barnacles and zebra clams cake the submerged copper sheathing to such an extent that the vessel wouldn't be seaworthy again, without a hauling and thorough refit. As a floating warehouse, and with no immediate prospects as a seaworthy enterprise, the mizzen boom has been lowered and lashed to her gunnel, topmasts removed, sails stripped and doused, ports, skylights and scups sealed, turnbuckles, clews, sheets, and ratlines tied off or stripped to minimize windage.

Below decks, space usually set aside for most of the crew's quarters have been converted to secure, locked storage for valuables, like specie and valuable goods brought in trade, as well as chests of opium—or 'mud'—as it's referred to by those who regularly deal it. The central hatch now leads to a space below deck, arrayed with tables and chairs, allowing business to be transacted comfortably.

On one day in September of 1823, with thousands-of-dollars in specie under lock and key, and fresh stores of Malwa 'mud' bagged in small quantities and ready for sale as soon as crab boats and other local buyers began to arrive abeam the vessel, crew presence had been stepped up. Armed with pistols and scabbards, no fewer than fifteen men are assigned on board in support of Russell & Company. Clerks, too, are on board, to record sales and document weights and measures for each transaction. As later reported to me, the day's sales went briskly, and without incident—except for one flare-up that should have signaled future difficulties.

My lead security man, Lindsay Andrews, stands watch on deck at sunrise, just as several crab-boats and scrambling dragons are spotted to the east, making haste under oar and sail for the ladders dropped alongside the go-down. These are the Chinese smugglers and 'country traders,' prepared to buy small quantities of mud for cash and other considerations directly off the deck of my receiving ship. They're expert at avoiding the custom's patrols with clever disguises and bribes before running back to shore, disappearing into small creek and villages, where parcels are broken up even further and sold all over the countryside.

Noticeably different on this day, a large man-of-war junk is among the array of vessels profiled against the horizon. Closer inspection through the ship's eye piece shows it flying an official-looking commodore's flag. The crew on the go-down have hardly prepared for what might be a troublesome encounter with Chinese authorities, when the junk soon pulls alongside, shivers its main, goes into irons and quickly drops a scow into the water. As the smaller vessel approaches, Andrews notices a figure wearing a small yellow button atop his hat, an official sign of Manchu high office. He is seated comfortably in an armchair under a large, embroidered umbrella, smoking a long pipe. He is surrounded by an entourage of staff, oarsmen, servants standing beside him with fans and several security guards in grass cloth robes and conical rattan hats, tied with the ubiquitous red silk cord.

"Who is this person, and why is he here on a government junk?" Andrews apprehensively asks of a company man with more experience on the river than he.

"He is the official in charge of Heang-shan, a small town in the river estuary northwest of here, in the center of the Inner Passage, leading up to Canton," is the reply. Lots of isolated fishing outposts tucked in there, under his control. His job is tax collector and enforcer for the courts, like a police captain and mayor rolled into one."

"But what prompts his visit today?" Andrews asks, a hint of concern in his voice.

"There might be some new buyers in that fleet of crabs and dragons lingering out there. Quite alright. In fact, his approval might be necessary before they can get involved. Hard to know. These formalities may be necessary before new agents can take delivery. That's probably the purpose of his visit."

Noticing that the flotilla of smaller sampans surrounding the junk are holding back, as if in deference to the larger vessel and its passenger, Andrews decides to proceed. He reluctantly posts himself by the gangway, as it is lowered onto the deck of the arriving scow. He watches this official's minions coordinate, ensuring his safety and balance as he struggles to maintain dignity in the boarding process. Once accomplished, Mister Andrews gets a clearer picture of the man he will be dealing with. Just a few inches north of five-feet tall, balding beneath his tasseled cap, and with a sparse goatee and long curved nails protruding from the ends of skeletal fingers, this unlikely, enfeebled authority figure is nevertheless clad in layers of richly colored silks, crossed at the chest and bound at the waist with a bright-red silk girdle. He appears even more weighed down by the strands of jade and onyx beads around his neck.

He stares forward without comment, leaning on a crooked, gold-crowned walking stick. His translator finally steps forward to speak for him, "This is His Excellency, Zhang Wei, The Auspicious One (张伟 吉祥之人). He is gracing your presence today for he wishes to discuss a matter of importance and conduct a business." With that, he briskly steps back to rejoin the half-circle of much taller men looming behind their leader. And while his entourage stands with military stiffness, glaring blankly at a fixed point in the distance, Zhang Wei nods ever so slightly, emitting a faint grunt, as if to say, 'Can we proceed now?'

With that, Andrews and the other Russell Company men, along with Zheng Wei and his shroff, or treasurer, acting the role of translator, are escorted to the cabin below, seated, then offered a glass of wine and choice of cigars. The ship's security crew and a few of the guest's bodyguards remain on deck, the groups standing some distance apart, quietly taking a measure of the other.

After a polite interval and an exchange of low-key, dignified courtesies below deck, Zhang Wei's narrow face suddenly darkens as he speaks, asking through his translator, "His Excellency wishes to understand why yāpiàn is being sold to the people of his village without his knowledge or consent? Men from other places on the river come in the night to extract life blood from the poorest of us, only to vanish before the sun rises."

Andrews inhales deeply at this unexpected challenge, recognizing for a moment that much might hinge on his answer. "Sir, there are many today, more than in years' past, who wish to share in the business of yāpián that the English and others have brought to these shores. There are no controls, once our ships reach these shores, and men like those still waiting out there on the river, board. There is no way to know what they will do with their supply, sir."

Knowing that everybody here understands there was little he could do beyond the narrow confines of his ship, Andrews is certain to intone his response with a note of authority—but, a false one at best. He senses from the start, that this pompous man with an exaggerated view of his control over sales, is attempting to exercise his authority, but for what purpose is still unclear.

Zheng Wei responds, now visibly agitated, "You say the English, but Flower Flag men are also much a part of this abomination. You seek to profit but have little care for our welfare. Any privilege granted for supplies delivered must be secured by application, and that authority resides with His Excellency." The shroff gestures toward his master, as if in consent. "And as soon as they are delivered you are to desist from engaging with others. No loitering is permitted by Imperial Decree."

Andrews knows Zheng Wei is bluffing now, since so many royal decrees have come from on high over the years, but they make little difference in the growing volume of opium finding its way into the countryside. But, he decides to play along. Shooting a quick knowing glance in the direction of his companion, and knowing he is playing a dangerous game of cat and mouse, Andrews says, "Perhaps your eminence could offer some guidance, so our transactions here could proceed without incident, and with the assurance of protection that only someone in your position of influence might be able to provide. I assume your demands are backed by authorities in Beijing." He then drops his eyes to the table, as though allowing time for his counterpart to consider the possibilities.

With that, Zheng Wei stands and reaches down to his boot, removing and unscrolling a document which he hands to his translator, who reads in a grave voice:

"*True copy of the Imperial edict, dated Tao-Kuang, 12th year. 6th moon, 4th sun. As the port of Canton is the only one at which the foreign barbarians are permitted to trade, at no account can they be allowed to wander and visit other places in the Middle Kingdom. His Majesty however, being ever that his compassion be made manifest ever to the least deserving, cannot deny to such are in distress that they may be forced to linger in other ports open to supplying them with succor and sustenance allowing them to continue their voyage. When accordingly supplied, they must not linger, but put to sea again immediately. Respect this.*"

With that, the document is again folded, and returned to Zheng Wei, who slips it back into his boot. On a pre-arranged signal, and unbeknownst to those meeting below deck, the rest of Zheng Wei's enforcers climb the boarding ladder, dramatically changing the balance of power in opposition to the ship's crew. This threatening action by Zhang Wei's men means he and his translator remain with Andrews and Russell clerks at the table below deck, negotiating his demands, and are yet unaware of events overhead.

≈

"LET ME BE frank," Zhang Wei says, as he gestures to his shroff to approach the table, "and get to the business at hand. How many chests of foreign mud do you have remaining on hand?"

Allowing no surprise to show on his face, Andrews says, "That is *our* concern, sir. Are you here to procure for yourself?"

As the question is being posed, the scroff reaches beneath his robe to release a sagging cloth sack. He pulls at the opening and tips it toward the Americans seated opposite. Out spills dozens of Spanish silver dollars, specie flashing in the dim light, as the trove clatters on the table. "There is 5,000 here. What will that secure me; and more importantly, how can I be assured that the villages above the entrance to the West River estuary can be mine, and mine alone."

Andrews hesitates, never breaking eye contact with this shrewd negotiator. "I can offer you two piculs of the finest Indian regional Malwa. You will not be disappointed." And with that, he unfolds a sheet of paper to reveal a scatter of white crystalline powder. He pushes it across the table, inviting Zhang Wei to touch a wetted finger to the sample. Zhanq Wei hesitates briefly, then drags a long nail through the 'mud' and spills it onto his tongue.

"This is pure, yes. It will do. But a mere one-and-twenty kilos—not even two chests—is barely enough to meet the needs of my people for more than a few days. I must be assured of greater quantities...and to the exclusion of all others to the west of here."

Tension is mounting across the table. Mister Andrews considers that this is a man who is not used to hearing *no* for an answer. 'Our reputation as insolent barbarians can't be helped along by this encounter,' he thinks. "Sir, I can offer you this much, and more where it comes from, but I cannot assure you that you can have the west delta region for your own. That, I have no control over." His voice is now stern, as he leans into the conversation from his side of the table.

Zhang Wei suddenly stands, clearly insulted by the unexpected direction the conversation is taking. He gestures with a snap of his fingers, as his translator moves to the ladder, issuing a stern command to his crew, waiting above deck. Suddenly, four armed men descend into the room below, most leaping down through the open space, pistols, and scabbards in hand. It all happens too suddenly for Andrews and the other company man to secure the loaded pistols hidden in a compartment under the table.

The Russell company men are being held at gun point while overhead, the deck resonates with the sound of men's cries and open combat, as the rest of Zhang Wei's men rush the ship's outnumbered crew, attacking, wounding and quickly overpowering them with fists, short blades hidden in their belts, and lengths of chain and ropes snatched from the deck.

The silver that lay on the table is quickly scooped up and re-bagged by the translator, as Zhang Wei orders one of his men to kick down the cabin door behind which the chests of opium are stored. One powerful kick by a booted bodyguard, and several chests of Malwa and fine quality kong pan are handed up, to be loaded onto the scow. It would later be estimated that 50,000 dollars in inventory, or approximately twenty chests were taken at that time.

Before leaving, Zhang Wei turns his attention back to Andrews, and speaking through his translator, smugly announces, "If you are thinking of reporting this, let me remind you that the authorities in this region are in my debt and I have their allegiance for many more years than you have lived. Years before the Flower Flag came to lay claim on this nation, I enjoyed the support of my people. Any actions will only rebound against your interests. I have an army of men I can call upon at any time. Next time, perhaps, you will see it my way."

As he speaks, two men descend to the lower deck to bind Andrews and his associates to their chairs. And with that, they are gone.

35. Pursuit (Tree of Heaven)

WITHIN MINUTES OF Zhang Wei's departure, two crewmen rush below. They report that several men lay injured on deck, one likely has bled to death from a knife wound to the gut. Even worse, Zhang Wei took two men hostage at gun point. "Tell your man this is our insurance that you won't pursue us."

When Andrews and the others are finally untied, they rush topside. Zhang Wei's junk and many of the other sampan that had been nearby, sensing trouble in the air, have fled the scene. Douglas, the lead clerk, sees to the wounded as best he can; then kneels to see that linguist, T'ung-shih, lying in a pool of blackened blood, is dead. Andrews immediately orders a skiff lowered to go into Macao to retrieve a doctor to attend the wounded. "And go directly to Covenant House, too, where Mr. Russell is boarding, and tell him what has happened. Bring him here, as well. "Go, go!" Then, the next logical question: "Did anyone see which way Zhang Wei's junk sailed?" Andrews asks.

Many attempt to answer at once: "Yes, north, and then we watched as the masthead trailed off to the west. This is piracy, sir. We can't let this stand! Not this time. Too much of this is goin' on now, but never for us, and in broad daylight, too."

"Never mind that, right now. Who's missing here? Who did they take?" Andrews asks.

Again, all the men, highly agitated now, relay a confusing jumble of accounts. Andrews raises his hands to quiet the group, asking one man, the comprador, Tyshing, who is familiar with the Chinese men in the group, to speak.

Tyshing steps forward: "*We see Liú Mǐn go, Wāng Gāng go. Muchee medrosó...fright, you know...for they. Cry out, na, na! Tie up, tie up. 'then vamos de barco,' then, big man say... so, to boat they go.*"

"Look," says Andrews, we'll go after them. He warned us not to, but we've got the hongs on our side, and the hoppo, and the revenue men at Whampoa...too many to count. And Mr. Russell will be here shortly. He came down today to inspect this shipment, and you can bet we'll put a plan together. Who's game to go after these bastards?"

Though some were still suffering from their wounds and assaults, a loud *Huzzah!* Clenched fists then rise in unison.

Andrews directs the men to put T'ung-shih's body in an empty sail bag and stow it below; then, to wash the deck with buckets of sea water and scrub it clean. He orders the men with injuries to go to mess and await the physician. He then goes below with Douglas and Tyshing to begin planning, while awaiting my arrival. In the hours that pass, little sleep is had. Tension and shock following the theft run high; anger, thoughts of revenge and concern for the lives of the two kidnapped crew, also on everyone's mind.

Andrews then flags a passing Chinese maritime patrol, one of the many who regularly police the bay to report the incident, to request two tidewaiters be dispatched for the overnight hours. These sampans and crews-of-one routinely hire out, tying up to the stern of Western vessel to keep watch for any unusual over-night activity in the vicinity of the ship. An alert would consist of three sharp knocks on the hull to awaken those below. These night watchmen serve as an early-warning system, being more-or-less effective as a force against greater numbers of pirates or other intruders.

≈

I'M IN MY room at Covenant House in Macao when the knock comes. Once I'm told of the incident, I gather my things and send a runner to fetch the house physician at East India House. I hurry to the quay, where we all meet up to row out to the warehouse ship. Andrews had been busy, doubling the watch on deck. His reasoning is sound. "The word will spread that we've been hit by a band of thieves. We'll be like a wounded animal in the forest. The incident might invite more—pirates and the like—to try their hand," he says.

"Good thinking," I say. "My cutter Minerva is still tied up at the bulkhead from my trip down from the factory. I can ready her by daybreak. What's our weapons' count on board?"

"Three muskets, three side arms, enough powder and blades to go around. I think we've got lots who want to sign on for this junket," Andrews says. "Let me show you the plan." And with that, he unrolls the chart of Macao Narrows and the lower part of the Pearl on the table.

"Based on what crew saw, we suspect he headed back to the vicinity of Heang-shan, over here in the Inner Passage," Andrews says, his finger sweeping the short distance to the west of our current position. "Heang-shan is the largest settlement in a warren of creeks and villages there, offering the best chance to blend into the landscape. We should save some time and go the shortest distance to here," pointing to a small island sitting close to the west shore of the bay. "There's good anchorage there, called Cumsing Moon. We approach the town over land from the east. If Zhang Wei is expecting us at all, he'll figure it'll be by the Inner Passage, the water side...a two day sail." With that, he traces a route southwest, around the tip of Macao Roads, then north along an estuary marked on the chart as 'West River.'

"We'd have a welcoming party that way, for sure," I agree. "I don't care as much about getting the stock back, as I do about pulling those two men out of there, alive. Unlikely he's still holding onto the chests, but if some are still intact, that would be a bonus for us. How soon can we leave?"

Andrews hesitates momentarily. "We hadn't planned on you coming with us."

"I wouldn't miss this for anything," I say. "I'll head back and change clothes, update the staff and pull alongside in a few hours. Let's plan to drop anchor at Cumsing Moon at sunrise. Have your men ready here by three."

≈

AT DAWN THE next day, the twenty-five-foot cutter, Minerva, slips silently into the sheltered anchorage of Cumsing Moon Bay under a tangerine-rimmed sky threaded with strips of purple and gray clouds resting near the eastern horizon. Pinned to an azure dome overhead, the last of the night's stars and planets have yet to fade. A steady, chilled air courses from the distant blue peaks beyond Macao, as my men—twelve, including me—lower ourselves into a pair of skiffs we had towed, quickly rowing ashore. Over their objections, two men're left to guard the vessel in our absence.

Our goal: to trek the five-mile, marshland route to the small village of Heang-shan, a cluster of stilted bamboo shacks and rude stucco buildings balanced on the rim of the Inner Passage's tidal flats. This remote settlement was constructed decades earlier to serve as a permanent settlement for the governor-general's bureaucrats and salarymen. His focus is imposing order—and taxes—on a scattered population of impoverished farmers and fishermen and their families, living in the vicinity. Thousands eke out a living from the many surrounding acres of planting fields, sparse orchards, and tidal estuaries, supplying the markets and tables of nearby Canton.

There, we hope to locate and surprise Zhang Wei and his band of thieves, subdue the likely violent response we may provoke, retrieve our captive crew and—hopefully—some, if not all the chests of opium. And to accomplish all of this without further injury or loss of life on either side—a tall order.

The skiffs are hauled up on the beach above the tide line. Mr. Andrews, I and the rest of the team gain the ground afforded by a low-lying dune, surveying a vast tract of characterless flatland, mile-upon mile of swampy, reed-clogged fields. Here and there, in the distance, a quilted landscape of yellowing and bright-green swaths of vegetable fields are evidence of human effort. This broad matrix is divided into checkerboard patterns by stands of tall rushes—frayed black-topped grassy crowns swaying in morning breezes. Poverty had laid waste the economy, to say nothing of thousands of lives in communities subsisting over centuries on these destitute, low-lying lands. Every typhoon blowing through this region floods fields and streets with brackish seawater, sweeping human, animal, and vegetable life away, inundating and poisoning the soil and condemning it to paltry rice harvests for years to come.

Before stepping off into the wetlands, a handheld compass reading of 290° is our only means of determining that we're heading in the direction of the outskirts of Heang-shan. With that confirmation, Andrews leads the us away from the beach, tentatively probing his footing with a long stick, as I and the rest of our small army walked single file into the first of many obstacles—a dense tangle of undergrowth marking the sandy rim boundary of the bay. The morning sun, still low on the horizon, casts long shadows as we slowly probe our way forward, weapons and other gear strapped high on our backs, keeping it secure and dry.

Some four hours later, and much exhausted, we find a small patch of high ground—just a few feet above the surrounding fields—to hastily consume a lunch of cold meats, cheeses, and dried fruit. Water is carefully allocated, since we didn't know when we can replenish our scant supply...or where. In the near distance, the low profile of some manmade structures protrudes above the scrub brush. This, and a small group of women, stooped over tending their crops in a distant field, also means we're closing in on the village. With this settlement as our objective, we decide to hold another impromptu strategy meeting.

"Check your flints and primes, men, and maintain your weapons low and close at hand now. And be certain to keep an eye out for anyone approaching our flank," Andrews warns. "Those women over there seem little concerned with our presence, here in the middle of nowhere...a good sign. And stay in single file. From a distance, we'll look a lot less threatening if the far-off profile resembles a single man."

"Let me be clear," I add, "I don't want any more loss of life. Stick together, no heroics. I mean it. Our objective is the retrieval of our two men and the stolen goods. An eye-for-an-eye at this point will only mean more trouble. Is that clear?"

All nodded in agreement, a mumbled mix of "Yes, Sir," and "Aye," rippling through our rag-tag squad. It's also agreed that we should wait until darkness to get as close to the village as possible without giving away our number. Our target: a stand of dense *chouchun* (臭椿), 'Tree of Heaven,' rising behind the largest of the stucco buildings. A fast-growing, foul smelling variety of this particular tree—sumac—has already found its way into American landscapes, brought home by sailors; so we all recognize our objective. Its distinctive profile against the night sky allows us to get close enough to pinpoint our next objective in near darkness.

We crouch in the reeds, waiting for failing light to move closer. We pass the time with recitations of sea shanties and stories of wives and sweethearts waiting at home, in near-whispered tones. A 'tot' of rum had been pocketed by at least one of the men before leaving, and it's agreed that we all take a 'wee nip' before heading out...screwing up our courage with that small dose of the 'Windward Isles' under our belts. It's also agreed—more so at my insistence than for any other reason—that I be the one to leave the stand of trees to infiltrate and scout the village in search of our men and Zhang Wei. I will reconnoiter with the team, reporting back where stores are kept, and possible locations for our other target—the kidnapped crewmen.

≈

AS DUSK APPROACHES, we begin to move toward the copse of *chouchan*, where the team will remain hidden in the understory until I can give report. My hopes of finding Zhang Wei on the streets, or even in the official building, where he was likely to conduct his business, is low; but there may be some hint of a thick-walled bankshall, perhaps with barred windows or padlocked door, where the stolen chests will likely be kept.

The streets are largely deserted, since women are not allowed out after dark, and most men having returned to their homes for supper and an early night in bed, perhaps. I cut between two stone and masonry buildings leading to the main street. I'm seeking a route allowing me to move directly, one way or the other, in search of our likely target. Across from me, a row of fragile straw and mat shanties stands facing the river, backlit against a silver-gray evening sky. They are high above ground level in an unlikely configuration of bamboo poles and fragile cross-pieces, vulnerable, yet easily replaceable in the face of storms or rushing tide. Dim, flickering candlelight is visible through open windows, certain signs of life inside. Heading down, I move quickly and stealthily along the facades of a block of more permanent building, toward what appears to be a village square or marketplace.

What I find there shocks and appalls me. I stand, disbelieving and paralyzed with fear, as I observe the scene across the open plaza. There, in front of what appears to be an open, straw-roofed pavilion—a village meeting place, I'd guess—are two bamboo spikes, about ten-feet tall, with the decapitated heads of my crew, Mǐn and Gāng, mounted high and in full view. Their contorted faces are the color of bleached paper, their eyes pinched closed, mouths agape, their hair an unrecognizable pitch-black tangled mess hanging across their brows. At the foot of these twin horrors, their headless bodies that lie side-by-side on straw mats, are blue and bloated from the day's heat. Some yards away, two scrawny dogs that had been sniffing and skulking about the carcasses, scatter as they catch sight of me.

The contents of my stomach churn, as I turn away to recover my senses. It's clear these two men had been sacrificed out of pure spite and frustration, by a man who simply didn't get his way the previous day. They were made a spectacle of because of their association with *me* and my enterprise. Then, the color in my face rises, as my rage builds at this man, and his unwarranted act of vengeance. My anger turns to determination, as I stand in the deserted square, trying to decide our next move.

There was nothing I could then do for these two men, except to honor their memories later and trace their families in Canton. For now, I return to the staging area to rejoin the group. The report of my findings has them all equally horrified by Zhang Wei's barbarism.

"There is no one building that I could see which could be a secure storehouse or armory," I report. "I think that building there, the largest and most official-looking, with the flag pole out front, must be his headquarters and office. I'll bet that's where the chests are being kept."

"Should we break in?" Andrews asks. Many of the men chime in, in unison, "Yah. Let's go. Hand the bastard a lesson he won't forget."

"No, I say, *no*," raising my hand to signal I need a moment to explain. "Given that Min and Gāng are dead, I don't give a damn about a few chests of mud. We can more than make up for this loss in future months. I think we need another plan, one that will wreak havoc in the village without harm to the undeserving people here, cost Zhang Wei his booty, and still allow us to return to the boat, unscathed."

≈

MOMENTS LATER, AS my men huddle at the edge of Heang-shan, a flint is struck to stone, setting alight a thin line of gun powder that hisses and pops in a meandering line across the stony soil behind Zhang Wei's building. A thin trail of smoke, smelling of sulfur rises into the still night air. Assured that the trail of flame will continue, uninterrupted, Andrews, the other men and I proceed quickly toward the tall grass at the edge of the open fields behind the village. Moments later, as the flame reaches the back entrance of this, the largest building in town, the door—soaked with what remains of our rum—ignites, The flame then follows the freshly-poured alcohol trail under the door and onto the straw matting covering the carefully varnished, spotless mahogany floors leading to Zhang Wei's private offices and study.

A bright light fills the interior of his office space, then rises higher to envelop the curtains, desks, document files containing his appointment by the governor-general in Canton, then the walls and roof of the building. Cases of firecrackers and skyrockets stored away for future festivals, are ignited by flames, filling the night air with rapid fire pops and hisses, sending dozens of multi-colored, phosphorescent arcs zig-zagging skyward. These loud bursts rouse village men from sleep, as dozens of silhouetted forms scramble helplessly in every direction before the conflagration consumes the entire building.

Within minutes, the heat and flames turn twelve well-hidden chests of opium to ash, before consuming Zhang Wei's cache of copper coins used to pay locals for their labor. Next, his secret trove of millions in Spanish silver dollars, more silver and gold taels accumulated over years and hidden high in the rafters, turn to liquid. They flow like quicksilver into the void far below, scattering and disappearing into the smoldering sands and ash that will be the remains of the building, tomorrow. The white-hot flames blossom into the night sky, as glowing embers swirl skyward, mingling with the stars. The inferno illuminates distant fields, some two miles away. My men and I then move stealthily through the tall grasses, our well-trodden path lit by the fire's glow, retracing our steps back to *Minerva*.

36. The Concert

WHILE I HAVE had much to occupy me of late, Belle's kiss in the gardens of Saint Paul's lingers in my imagination for the endless days that I count—and count again—until the reception at the Portuguese consulate. As that event draws closer, I decide I won't attend alone, believing that my singular presence will arouse too much suspicion on the part of my imaginary foe—Isabella's redoubtable father. I coerce two members of my staff, young, attractive, well-enough groomed and socially acceptable young men, Captain Rathbun and Philip Ammidon to accompany me. A quick dispatch to the consulate, and their names are added to the list of invitees. They confess to being more than a little curious about my most recent infatuation, the young Portuguese woman I so often describe as the one with the 'dancing eyes.'

One companion, the estimable, recently-arrived, Joshua Rathbun, master of E. Carrington & Co.'s vessel, *Fame*, appears for the evening's event in ship's dress uniform, all brass and buckles on a field of blue and buff. A notable scar on his left cheek, a faint aura of tobacco and signature battle-weary appearance combine like a nectar and will, no doubt, attract any number of Isabella's female friends like bees to honey, desiring to hear tale-upon-tale of high seas' adventure. The other, Philip Ammidon, an able, blue-eyed intellectual with sound Boston breeding, will once again hold his own when conversations turned erudite, leaving me—as planned—with an unobstructed field around Isabella and the opportunity to make an unschooled, yet persuasive, impression on Portuguese Deputy Consul-General Amando Santiago de Sintra Calebro.

Early evening shadows slant across high privacy walls of exclusive homes and down narrow Macao streets as we make our way from our residence to the consulate. The building, a two-story, columned structure in the European style, is aglow with lights, enlivened by clustered silhouettes of small groups engaged in earnest conversation, just inside a row of street-level windows. At the main doors, stand a group of men, carefully examining engraved invitations, as more guests slowly work their way up a short flight to the gala. I reach into my vest pocket to retrieve our own invitations, turning as I do to notice the moon-lit sands of crescent-shaped *Praya Grande* beach, far below us, extending like a glistening jambiya blade against the harbor's blackened waters.

Soon, we've become part of the noisy celebration. Rathbun and Ammidon immediately make for a center island table, arrayed with a presentation of breads, cheeses, fruit and other epicurean delights. "*Iguarias, senhor*, you know," another guest offers, observing a perplexed look on Philp's face, "'delicacies' like tartare, mushroom, squid, caviar, carpaccio, samosa. The Portuguese, they're very big on seafood, yes?" And, even while in conversation with those around, my men nevertheless make a point of stacking their small plates to overflowing with some of these exotics. I note Rathbun, our irrepressible sea captain, wistfully eyeing the sideboard, with an impressive selection of decanted brandies and wine carafes. But, to my delight—at least for the moment— propriety and restraint appear to have won out over impulse. My eager companions continue to satisfy their bottomless appetites, though, as a dozen impeccably uniformed men—Chinese kitchen staff, mostly—circulate through the crowd with silver trays heavy with mysterious canapé, tall stems of Champagne and various wines.

I casually sidle up to Ammidon to remind him, "Try not to embarrass me. You're acting like you haven't eaten in a week. Remember why you're here, to watch out for my interests. Yes?" I add in mock seriousness.

Mouth full, his hand and glass extended for a refill, answers without looking at me, "Yes, tops on my list. How about that table full of women?"

Rather than sating my appetite, though, I have other objectives in mind. I gain the high ground in the room—a small stage at the side of the room—casually scanning the crowd for a glimpse of Isabella— 'Belle.' But, neither she, nor her friends are anywhere to be seen. My next target, her father. Standing near a door leading to a darkened room of some kind, stands a tall figure, a scarlet sash angled across his chest bearing a large baroque medallion. His bright blue-green eyes offer some hint that my assumption is correct. He's surrounded by other men, engaging in earnest conversation. My impression, if he is to be my target for the evening, is that of a man of elegant appearance, both influential and austere—a formidable admixture of traits for which I'd have to gather my confidence, to engage him with any pretense of equal footing.

Soon enough, a uniformed maître d' circulates through the crowd, ceremoniously striking a small chime, "*por favor fique sentado, fique sentado*, please be seated, be seated, *por favor.*" We are assigned to large, round tables, and I find myself next to an English woman, large-framed, amiable, with a layered, heavily perfumed bouffant. "I trust the goose will be as well-prepared as last time," she says, speaking to no one in particular, while placing a napkin in her lap.

"I am Sam Russell, American, here in Canton, of late," I say, above the din in the room, while nodding in her direction. "An elegant evening, I believe."

Turning her attention to me at last, she says, "Yes, we have had many here. But you might consider this the last for a while, with the consul being called home soon."

From over my shoulder, soup is being slowly ladled into a shallow dish before me, as the full meaning of what she has just said washes over me like a cold bath. "Consul leaving? Leaving Macao?"

"Why, yes. King John IV has, of late, returned from Brazil, restored to the throne. Senhor Calebro has been recalled to negotiate peace with the French and Spanish, and to drive the radicals out of Lisbon. It's a large and rather important task he'll be undertaking."

"But when did this all happen?" I ask.

"Just days ago. This was to be his annual event, but now it's a farewell, I'm afraid. Very sad for all of us to see him and his family depart on such short notice."

The room now spinning around me, I feel faint. The elegant meal ahead suddenly has no appeal. The mix of voices in the room recedes, reverberating off the walls like meaningless gibberish. I long to find Belle and speak with her about this turn-of-events...her feelings about leaving...about *me.*

As the main course is being served, I excuse myself and go to a table near the stage where the Calebro family is gathered. The consul's chair is empty, but that same refined Asian woman I identified as Belle's mother months ago is sitting at the center of it all. The rest of the table is filled out with younger men and boys, and a single young woman with similar Asian features and refined manners to suggest it might be another Calebro off-spring, a sister, junior to Belle, perhaps.

"Excuse me, madam, *com licença*," I say, trying my best to maintain my composure, "your pardon, please, but, is Isabella here this evening? She had extended this invitation to me for tonight, and I would love to be able to speak with her."

Madame Calebro partially turns in her seat to consider me carefully before speaking. "And you are?"

"I am Sam Russell, of the American factory, in Canton. Your daughter and I have met and spoken on a number of occasions, and she wished to have me here tonight to meet her father and you, I believe."

"Indeed!" she blurts. Madame Calebro seemed unimpressed by her daughter's impetuous invitations, or guests, but nevertheless, turns away from me after a moment's hesitation, beckoning a man from the side of the room. He leans down as she speaks to him *soto voce*. She then dispatches him with a whisk of her hand, as he disappears around the corner.

As I stand there, waiting for some word, I survey the room for my companions, spotting Rathbun at a far table, chatting amiably with a female guest. I catch his eye and rush to his seat. "Bad news, Calebro's shipping out soon, going back to Lisbon to work for the king. He'll be announcing it tonight, I think. It's the talk at my table already, 'throws a good party,' and all that. Belle's here somewhere and I'm hoping to locate her so we can talk.

"Shit, *shit*," he whispers, so's not to be heard. "Idn't that a barnacle'n the hull 'a yur plans, Sammy, m'boy."

"Listen, when this is over, you fellows head back without me, no matter what. I've got to try and meet with Belle...find out from her what the hell's happening." And without waiting for a response, I return to the vicinity of the Calebro table.

After countless minutes, the messenger is back with information. Madame Calebro turns back to me. "*Sehnor* Russell, Isabella is in practice, now. She'll be out soon to be with us all. Soon her father will tell us what she can do. You watch, listen. Soon, she will be here for us." And with that dismissive update, she attends to her dinner, plunging a knife and fork into a fat shank of beef sitting on her plate.

≈

WHILE THE ENTIRE room is animated with talk, raucous laughter and the ringing of crystal wine glasses, I serve out my time on my personal island of gloom, awaiting Belle's appearance for the evening, and attempting to understand what the delay might be.

Finally, after a light dessert of rice pudding and cream, *Sehnor* Calebro s appears suddenly from his office, taking his place on stage to a round of applause. As he speaks, offering gratuitous, bi-lingual 'thank yous' and 'welcomes' around the room, men scurry behind him, undraping a beautifully-lacquered pianoforte, setting up two additional chairs, a 'cello on its own stand and additional music rests with sheet music. Then they carefully shift and align it, at the careful direction of *Sehnor* Calebro, as a hushed, expectant audience awaits.

"As many of you already know, and perhaps some have not yet heard, I have been recalled to my capital to undertake another mission for our government. Events demand this, and it is with great sadness I must say goodbye to this city, and this beautiful land which has been my home for the last five years. But, my family, my farm, my country...and most of all, my horses, have missed me." And with that, a ripple of laughter passes through the room. I listen with a grieving heart though, recognizing that my plans, however fanciful they might have been, may end here, tonight.

And still, no Isabella to resolve the sadness sitting like a stone squarely on my chest, a shallow, irregular breath is all I can manage at the moment.

Raising his arms to request silence, *Sehnor* Calebro continues: "The concert planned for tonight was intended to merely entertain my honored guests, but with the recent news, I am sad to say it must also serve as a farewell performance. Here, tonight, are my daughter Isabella Anna, her brother and a friend of many years, all of whom have been working tirelessly to prepare a musical sampling for you. Come forward children, and take your places, please."

And with that, Belle steps from her father's sanctuary. Beaming as she strides into the large room, her black hair pulled back, sapphire eyes made all-the-more brilliant from the deep azure satin dress of her dress. She takes her place a at the pianoforte, aligning herself for eye contact with her fellow performers. She's accompanied by a young woman whom I recognize from that day at the church. They sit motionless on stage—Belle, her friend with a silver transverse flute, and her brother with the 'cello poised between his knees—as we await further comments from our host.

I watch as Belle takes up position, scanning the room; and when she makes eye contact with me, offering a broad smile. I nod imperceptibly in her direction from two table away, establishing without a spoken word that I hope to speak privately before the night is over. Her recognition of my presence at the dinner helps assuage my concerns but does little to staunch my sadness regarding what seems—barring a miracle—to be the inevitable course of future events.

"*Meus amigos*, my friends, tonight, we are in the company of royalty. Perhaps not directly, but in spirit. Tonight, I dedicate the work you are about to hear to our recently re-crowned king, John IV, as he once again assumes his rightful claim to the throne of Portugal. But, tonight also, we might imagine ourselves in the company of the recently departed George III of England, and his consort, Queen Charlotte, for whom this delightfully joyful piece was written in 1765, by six-year-old, Wolfgang Mozart. In his dedication, he wrote to the queen: *'Full of pride and joy at daring to offer a homage to You... It is said that everything should be allowed to Genius; I owe mine the happiness of pleasing You, and I forgive it its caprices. Deign, Madame, to receive my poor gifts.'*

"And so, my dear friends, I offer these 'poor gifts' to you as an *obrigado*—a thank you—six brief sonatas whose genius becomes more evident over time, but especially at the hands of my lovely princess, Isabella, and the other members of her trio, Angelina and Pablo. *Por favor aproveite*, please enjoy."

≈

FOLLOWING DINNER AND the splendid concert in which Belle radiated both beauty and skill, I linger outside as inconspicuously as possible. My colleagues have already left. I wait at the base of the stairs in front of the building. Dozens of guests are flooding from the door, bidding goodbyes and mounting carriages cued up on the steep street leading to the consulate. I know our meeting would be frowned upon by Belle's father; and, especially, her disapproving mother, who had dealt with me so dismissively earlier this evening. If this encounter is to work, it will have to be clandestine, a state of affairs we have grown quite accustomed to.

Suddenly, I feel a tug on my sleeve from behind, as Belle appears from out of the darkness beside the building to deliver a hurried, frenetic message. Her eyes are darting wildly. "I must meet and talk with you as soon as possible, she says. "We must find a time and place." And with that, her father appears at the door, engaging with departing guests, while also surveying the crowds gathered on the street below.

"I must go. He expects me to be in his office, waiting. I will get word to you, somehow. You are at the American guest house, yes?"

But, before I could answer, she is gone.

37. Masquerade

DURING THE LONG summer recesses, our days in Macao are spent managing the details of the business to every extent possible. Orders still need to be processed; lines of credit managed; ledgers maintained; Chinese staff, like linguists, hoppos and household help paid; provisions ordered through compradors and warehoused for both inbound and outbound vessels scheduled to arrive once the winter season resumes each October.

In this, the summer of '23, I confess to being in love to a point of distraction. Images of Belle intrude when I least expect: as I hunch over my ledgers, a vision of that soft line of dark hair at her neckline I studied while sitting behind her in the church, loom in my memory; as I lie in bed at night, the scent of her lips while in the garden, as she lightly kisses me on the cheek, play out over-and-over again; as I survey the latest cargo in the warehouse, the intense concentration in her eyes that night at the consulate, as she so masterfully performs before her father's friends; and later that night, the hurried tug on my sleeve in the street, and the urgency in her voice weighs so heavily on my heart in the endless days that follow.

The many ups and downs of our limited time together, is made more urgent by the news of her imminent departure for Lisbon with her family. It means the prospects of a proposal of marriage and a life together here in China, becomes more remote by the day. But I remain hopeful. At thirty-four, my prospects have improved greatly since my arrival four years ago. My company has grown, and I can imagine bringing my sons, George and John, to create a new life together here, as others have done. I can now afford to establish a household here in Macao, a well-appointed Western-styled home offering comfort and security for a new family—one that can only grow.

It's the nature of this business while on summer recess in Macao, that accommodations for factory personnel are modest. Whether here, or in Canton, our comforts are few and lifestyle sacrifices, many. Our dormitory rooms in the Macao American guest house are spare, at best—a simple bed, wash station and small desk, bounded by plaster walls scarred by years of neglect. A single slender window offers a view of the narrow alley behind the building, but only as far as the weather-beaten exterior of my occasionally raucous neighbor. At times, I would have given my life for a small touch of green, or a bird's song just outside the confines of my narrow room.

We are gathered in the dining room on one late summer day—I and my staff—to discuss matters relating to pressures from Howqua and the other hongs to increase payments to them considering higher opium demand and the resulting increase in price we could now expect. The attention of our comprador, Tyshing, sitting at the far end of the room, is distracted by a persistent knocking on the front door, one flight below. With a nod, I direct him to investigate, since unscheduled visitors to our building often mean either new business opportunity, or trouble in the streets.

"Meesta Sam, two boy here. Want Meesta Sam, no more, but you, Comee see two boy, yes?"

"What do they want, Tyshing. Did they say?"

"*Na, na, no say. Much laugh, juss Meesta Sam. Ask juss Meesta Sam. Comee, por favor.*"

I leave the meeting to go down to the front door, where I encounter two very unconvincing 'young men' dressed in ill-fitting school uniforms—short white nankeen jackets trimmed in blue and knee-length breeches, with loosely-knotted satin ties completing the conceit. As I stand in the doorway, looking down at this apparition, two beaming countenances stare back up at me from under squat, black toppers, pulled down to the ears and stuffed somewhat unconvincingly with heaps of dark brown and black tresses.

"Can we please come in, before we are spotted by someone we might know?" Belle pleads. "Two 'boys' on the streets of Macao must be careful who we talk to."

I step back, disbelieving the complexity of this charade, urging them to come off the street immediately. "What are you two up to? What is this?"

"Maria and I were bored with our day and decided to come and see you. Maria dared me that we should wear our brother's clothes and walk the streets of the city unaccompanied. Our father would be furious if he found out. Please say nothing, *por favor.*"

"Of course not. Come away from the door and sit with me in the front room." And with that, the over-sized shoes they sported slapped noisily on the hardwood floors. "These Buffo outfits actually got you out of the house and here across town without arousing any suspicions?"

"Some people looked curious but say nothing. We think they did not know what to think."

"I'm going to call for a sedan to take you home. You can't stay here."

"No, Sam, we will walk home to my friend's house where our things are, the same way we got here. But I must first talk to you about so many important things that are happening right now,"

Belle pleads, a look of concern and sadness replacing the mirth I always saw in her eyes.

"What is it, Belle? Why have you taken this chance to come here?"

"I will explain later today. I've told my mother I wish to go to confession before I leave. I will go with my friends who know to leave me there with you...in the garden, as before, yes? Can you meet me there after vespers? We must talk."

I am once again transfixed, as I reach out to lightly touch the golden-hued warmth of her chin, her blue-green eyes the color of glacial ice, round and pleading, as long strands of hair work their way out from under her hat, tumbling beside her cheeks now flushed with urgency. I answer, "Yes. Belle, I will be there, of course, I'll be there," even as I sense the prospects of a private meeting with her father asking for her hand fading from view, my hopes shrouded like a ship's masts in fog.

As they pull their disguises together and slip back onto the street, the realization that my dream of a life with Isabella is not to be overwhelms me again. Culture, distance, Old World traditions, iron-clad family values, all conspire to keep me from having this woman in ways that have fed my imagination and hopes during these months in Macao.

I return to my meeting, as matters of finance and logistics soon overshadow the small matter of my aching heart.

≈

AT THE APPOINTED time, I traverse the streets of Macao in fading light, as though to my own grave. I find the spot in the garden, the same we first met months ago. Distant organ music emanates from behind the church's ornate stone facade and backlit stained-glass windows. A single thrush somewhere up in the trees repeatedly sounds a hopeful eventide song in the fading summer light.

Faint conversations drift from the front of the church, as vespers let out. After a few minutes, Belle appears from around the corner, looking resplendent in an ivory satin dress, her hair resting on her shoulders in banks of dark curls. She's wearing that same black satin ribbon around her slender neck, a small cameo attached at the throat. She's alone, although I know her friends must be waiting just out of sight.

She sits close beside me. Through the layers of her dress, I feel the warmth of her hip against mine. "Sam, I must tell you something sad, something I have known for days, but have been struggling to accept in my heart."

"Before you do, let me confess that in the few times we have managed to be together, even across a crowded room, I have discovered the deepest affection for you. I can think of none other. From the first..."

"I, too, have found my thoughts drifting toward our time together," she says, taking my hand in hers and turning to look at me directly, her face just inches away. "I find myself wondering what you might be doing at any moment...how you are spending your time here in Macao. But, it cannot be. I..."

I place my fingertips to her lips and slowly lean forward to kiss her gently. My eyes are closed. I sense her motion toward me as she raises her lips to return my gesture, a surge of energy rising from my chest galvanizing my mouth. The garden scene feels unhinged, spinning in an orbit around the bench where we sit. She tastes as I imagined, sweet, warm, her mouth infused with faint traces of mint, honey, salt. As our mouths separate, I blurt out, "I must confess I am in love with you." I stumble awkwardly into my next pronouncement. "I had hoped to speak to your father..."

At that moment, she pressed a single slender finger to my mouth, keeping me, in turn, from what I so wanted to say next. Her eyes well with tears. Her lips, always so disposed to self-confidence and joy, are trembling. "That's just it, Sam, my father has pledged me to another. A man I have never met...well, once or twice as a child, but not since we have grown. He has explained that once we return home, plans are to proceed for us to marry."

Crestfallen, but not entirely surprised by this news, I say, "Can you say no? Can you refuse?"

"Not if I want the love and approval of my father, and my mother who is so hopeful about the future of her children. Women in my culture, my sisters and I, we need an assurance for our futures. It all ties to a man, having a man at the right time in our lives. My father believes this is my time."

"What do you know about this man, anything?"

"He is wealthy, this much I know, because my father would have it no other way. An estate owner of many generations, with horses and farmlands, and political influence. I'm sure he is a gentleman, and he will treat me well. Beyond that, I have no idea what the future will bring."

"Belle," I plead, "stay here with me. I, too, can give you all those things. I am earning well enough right now and will return soon to America, and a future I can build for us, if not here, then there...land, horses if you wish, a beautiful house with staff and gardens..."

She kisses me again through her tears, gently around the mouth, on my eyelids. I feel her hand resting on the back of my head. She says nothing for the longest moment.

Finally: "I would have everything but my family, which is the world to me. They would never speak to me again. I would become an outcast. I cannot lose their love, or their support. Sam, I must do as I am told."

"You *are* my world, Belle, I have no other."

"You must be strong, and help me to accept what has to be,' Belle pleads. "We must say goodbye tonight. We must say farewell and remember each other and this place... this garden, the love I found in our time together. You saw wonderful strength in me and admired me for that. I saw your goodness and integrity and adored you for those qualities. We had this brief time together, and nothing can erase it, yes?"

I place my hands around her waist and draw her close to me. Her breath is heavy on my neck, as I lean over to place another kiss on her mouth. She opens hers to my gesture and we sit, unmoving in the silence of the garden, our very essence fused for that brief moment, until she leans away, tears streaming down her face. I reach into my jacket to retrieve a handkerchief, which I offer to wipe her tears. She studies it through the blur, noticing that it contained a small monogram on one corner. She manages a small smile, as she asks, "'SR' is this so you remember it's yours?"

We manage a faint laugh together, as I say, "Yes, Belle, I don't let anybody else use my handkerchiefs, until now. You should be honored," I say, extending the moment of levity.

"Thank you," she says, as she pretends to demur. And with that, she extends the fingers of her right hand to remove a ring, no more than a simple band of gold, one that had been on her hand since we first met. "And I don't let anybody wear my jewelry, until now. I want you to keep this for me, should we ever meet again." She then takes my hand in hers and places the band on the pinky finger of my outstretched hand, where it stops at the first knuckle.

"I'll treasure this always, my dearest Belle," I say, tears brimming in my own eyes.

A call from her friends around the corner, whose patience had finally run short, and Belle slowly stands. She calls out in response, then turns back to where I sit. "Goodbye, my dear friend. I will never forget this summer, my last in Macao, and everything you have come to mean to me. May we both find love and affection in our futures." And with that, she slowly turns and is gone into the darkness to join the others, her arms akimbo as she gently lifts the hem of her dress to carefully navigate the uneven stone walkway.

IN THE DAYS following our last meeting, I long to see Belle again, knowing full well the impossibility. Her small gold ring becomes an inseparable part of me. When it's not on my smallest finger, I sequester it in my pocket, so my men will not think me the sentimental fool. At night, as I lie sleepless, I hold it in my mouth, shifting it with my tongue between the roof and cheek as I might a hard candy, to draw any small essence—any lingering sweetness—of the women embodied in this small token of her affection for me. It's a talisman I long to make a part of my own body, calling upon it to do the impossible: salve my gut-wrench of loss and longing.

Eventually, though, as I learn to accept her inevitable departure, this keepsake finding its way into a carved ivory box on my bureau, one gifted to me by Howqua, himself. In the years that follow, whenever I go to that box to retrieve collar stays or cufflinks, my eye invariably goes to that petite band, and Belle's radiant visage instantly reappears, just as though she is standing there before me.

38. Humiliation

"*ZHEN, WHERE ARE* the *xié* (鞋) I am to wear today?"

Greatly agitated, my emperor, Minning calls out impatiently to me, as I am nowhere in sight. After so many years together, I sometimes feel that he treats me as he would one of his many consorts—necessary, but burdensome. Hearing his frustration, I rush to his side in the garden, sweeping the ceremonial embroidered shoes he is searching for from the table near his dressing room as I go.

"Here, Excellency, I have them here for you. You will be looking very well on such an important day."

"I can't be so easily placated, Zhengrui, with a full day's schedule such as this." Minning glances at the gleaming sundial strategically placed in the center of the palace garden—the only one in the kingdom—as only the emperor is allowed to precisely know the hour and minute of the day. "The hour of the rabbit. The sun is barely over the horizon and already I'm in need of a dyspeptic. He hesitates, gripping his abdomen while hunched over in some distress. "Have my physician bring the usual preparation of papaya and ginseng. I will see him in my quarters...and have the acupuncturist come, as well. We still have time."

Taking advantage of this unexpected time, I retrieve my confidential diary, to write:

'These have been difficult times for Minning, the Daoguang Emperor. He has often confided that he feels disparagement and ridicule emanating from his father's grave, as generations of Qing-era ancestors look on. In this, just the fifth year of his rule, our nation is in disarray. The empire is plagued by famine and rebellion—one brought on by the other, in a seemingly endless cycle, together with my emperor's ill-conceived notions of far-flung military escapades. As a result, the national treasury is nearly empty. I must exercise caution in the expression of my opinions, for if the sentiments expressed here were ever to become known, I would certainly be invited to accept the velvet rope.'

'On this particular day he is to celebrate the day of birth of his stepmother, named the Empress Dowager Gongci after she personally selected him to ascend to the Celestial Throne in the Year of the Dragon (1820), following his father, Jaiqing's death. Two of her own sons were passed over in the process, as she announced her decision even before an official edict could even be issued. This has placed tremendous pressure on Minning in the ensuing years—attempting to live up to this powerful woman's expectations. Today, there will be the annual formal greeting between mother and son, followed by a ceremony honoring her. All of this is to take place before the sun is highest, followed by other, more serious matters of state.'

"Zhen, we must go," Minning commands, suddenly appearing in the doorway of my quarters. I hastily roll up my manuscript, appearing to casually set it aside, until I can conceal it later; but only after I attend to the emperor, who will soon proceed to his stepmother's traditional residence in the Forbidden City's Palace of Longevity and Health.

Minning is resplendent in his formal court regalia, his modest stature all but obscured by layers of brilliant yellow and crimson silks, gold embroidered sashes and head gear towering above his diminutive face. It consists of a large black and red silk *guanmao*, topped by a ruby ball and a string of pearls cascading from its peak. Beneath the layers of silk flowing to the ground, Minning's narrow feet protrude, revealing the much sought-after *xié* he sought earlier today.

Minning trundles through the endless hallways of the grand palace, greatly impeded by his ceremonial garb; I beside him, reciting aloud the schedule for the next few hours. "First, you are to go to the Hall of Central Harmony, where you will read a memorial for the Empress Dowager, wishing her well. I have that document here for you. You will then proceed alone to her quarters, where your presence will be announced. Then, and only then, do you enter. Remember to kowtow before her, out of respect for her essential role in your life—the only place and time you are expected to.

"Each year I do the same, yet each year her diffidence toward me is more pronounced," Minning complains to me.

"Excellency, she is getting on in years—forty-nine and widowed—with little to do now except perform her ceremonial role and attend to matters of her own staff's devotion to her every need. Bring kindness and understanding into the room with you, in the knowledge that in a short while this part of the day will be over and you can return to matters of state. There are many who wish to be in your presence later today, and you must preserve your energy and thoughts for decisions yet to be made," I explain.

Moments later, the massive teak doors of the dowager's chamber swing open and my dear emperor, supreme ruler of the known and unknown world, lumbers into the darkened abyss, tremulous at the prospect of having to confront his mother alone, as the doors imperceptibly close behind him.

Soon, after some fraction of an hour, they emerge together, the Empress Dowager Gongci appearing equally regaled in ceremonial layers of heavily embroidered blue and crimson silk robes. Scenes of writhing dragons in gold silk, undulate through mythic gardens of jewel-toned emeralds and sapphires and Imperial yellow vines on her broad skirts and sleeves. Black silk trim at her hemline, forearms and neckline are accentuated by a short, black-trimmed cape lined in red and gold silk patterning. A long string of pearls hangs around her neck. A bejeweled *guanmao* topped by a woven tower of pearls and threaded with gold complete her regal appearance.

Together, the move with difficulty for the weight of their clothing. As attendants are not allowed to touch either, they are cumbersome mounting nearby sedans. They then depart to the west Gate of Eternal Health, where they slowly disembark. Carrying a memorial plaque in his hands, the emperor and his mother are accompanied by an entourage of nobles and high-ranking officials. After the emperor delivers his message and birthday gifts, the retinue jointly presents Empress Dowager Gongci with a court scepter, before heading back to their residences.

For Minning, a man who, over the years, has grown contemptuous of affairs of court, this day of official responsibilities is not nearly at an end. Still, he breathes a sigh of relief, and his mood brightens as he recognizes this agonizing annual ritual is, at least, finally over.

≋

IT IS NOW *zhōngwǔ* (中午), noon by the sun, when my emperor enjoys his mid-day repast: a dish of salmon with an orange glaze and slivered almonds from his very own summer retreat; a bowl of sweetened rice with raisins and a pot of steeped Oolong. With the obligatory first taste taken always by the server, he then consumes the meal slowly, but methodically, each bite an exercise in Zen mindfulness.

His schedule always allows for a brief retreat to his quarters from the cares of the world, where he will rest for a portion of an hour. As is my daily responsibility, I awaken him and assist with preparation for this afternoon's event, for which hundreds have already assembled in the massive courtyard facing the Hall of Supreme Harmony, and its prominent elevated terrace. The purpose for today's gathering is to address the national crisis of famine and hardship plaguing the countryside. Those regional magistrates—ten in all—whom the emperor concludes have played a negligent role in this current state-of-affairs, have been summoned to account for their behavior. Minning harbors the belief that a public display of his dissatisfaction will go some distance to assuage the rumor that he bears responsibility for the wide-spread problem.

I step outside into the brilliant November sun, in advance of the emperor's appearance, assessing the mood of the assembly and ascertaining whether all the parties in question are in place. Phalanges of palace troops comprise dozens of well-ordered columns, extending as far back as the gates leading to the courtyard. Each is outfitted for the event in combat uniforms of their function: black for archers; red for spearmen; and green for mounted troops. Another section consists of Lama monks, distinguished by their oversized bright yellow head gear and maroon robes. At the base of the terrace, twenty armed security guards form a human barrier between the gathered crowd and the emperor, ensuring no access to His Excellency, by anyone who might mean him harm. Each has pledged his life to protect the life and well-being of the Celestial Ruler.

At the base of the long ramp leading up to the terrace, three members of the Royal court, judicial magistrates of the highest rank are seated facing an opposing line of ten regional authorities—those who have been called to account for the current crisis. They stand, heads bowed, each separated by ten chi (尺) from the next. Forced to wear nondescript dull white pajamas, they stand out in this resplendent, colorful gathering, already looking like the deservedly accused. Behind them, local peasants gather, clustering together, fear and uncertainty revealed in the agitated crowd. They have been called here today to offer testimony regarding the hardships and suffering they have endured in recent months, due to the acute shortages of food in the countryside.

I turn to the doors leading out onto the terrace to inform the emperor of the situation just beyond. He sits in quiet contemplation.

"Are you ready, Excellency?" I ask.

Eyes cast to the floor, Minning asks, "I am never ready for moments like this. Have the judges been informed as to my bidding in this matter?"

"I have spoken to them days ago regarding the gravity of the situation. They are aware but will let the facts speak for themselves. Many are watching. There is enough blame to go around, I fear," I say.

After a long delay, Minning reluctantly gets to his feet, slowly moving to the elaborate chair-of-state he'll occupy during these public proceedings. Once seated, he is borne out into daylight by four men in identical blue robes. I walk close behind. And, with his appearance before the crowd, all those standing immediately drop to the ground and kowtow. Even the judicial authorities turn to respond to this rare appearance by the emperor before his people. Following this mandatory gesture, the assembled mass remains seated, while stirrings of excitement and anticipation are audible. Once the emperor raises his right hand ever so slightly, the judges take the signal to begin the trial.

THE CHIEF JUDICIAL magistrate calls for a reading of the charges against the ten accused. A clerk of the court steps forward:

"China's population is growing. Today, there are believed to be 450 million of our people living on the land and in the cities. The result is arable land shortages that prevent the raising of more crops, famine, and impoverishment among the rural population. Heavy taxes, rising prices and the actions of greedy local officials further worsens the farmer's situation. Their selfish concerns mean that landowners, secret societies, and military strongmen can move in to take over local affairs. Rebellion, lawlessness and foreign exploitation in the form of an infestation of debilitating yāpiàn continue to plague those who live beyond the immediate protection of the emperor and government agencies established to maintain the rule of law."

"Frontiers won through military conflicts—particularly in the west and southwest— are teeming with refugees demanding food, clothing, and shelter, but without the means to do for themselves. The emperor has ordered new irrigation systems to be built, new kinds of seed to be planted, and closer inspection of agriculture goods traded at the regional level, to insure that expanded needs are being addressed. Regional authorities have done little or nothing to promote these new ideas. Higher demands on farmland have only depleted the soil, added to erosion, contributing to a labor surplus in many parts of the country."

Thus far, into the high court's presentation of the case, my emperor does not sense the finger of blame being pointed at him. I know it to be true that Minning cares little for these matters, but there are those around him that do. To admonish those closest to him and Beijing's administrative machinery will run the risk of calling attention to his own failings; so best to push blame out into the countryside...to these ten magistrates from regions were they are responsible for hundreds-of-thousands of countrymen, and their crisis, is most acute.

"It is going well, I believe. Is there anything I can instruct the magistrates to be doing at this point, Excellency?" I say, leaning into Minning's ear.

"Yes, get to the testimony. These peasants are doing us no good standing there."

I descend the long ramp to attract the attention of the chief magistrate. He nods, immediately beckoning the first group of farmers from the Shanxi region to come forward. The man chosen to speak for the group, trembling with fear, casts an eye in the direction of his local magistrate, a man he might be well acquainted with and fears, now standing a short distance away, head bowed. He bravely steps forward, speaking in tremulous tones to the three judges:

"For a time, the sufferers could borrow from one another, but this soon came to an end. We were forced to kill our ploughing oxen, pawn our farm implements, coverlets and clothes just to eat. We have given up on any thoughts for the future, resorted to selling our furniture and other household items...then finally our fields, for a mere song, till at last no purchaser could be found."

With that, he places his straw hat back on his head, stepping back into the small group. Another reluctant witness—a woman—is called forward:

"The burning sun is in the sky and the locusts cover the parched ground after eating our crops. There is no green grass in the fields and no fuel remaining to cook our food. We strip off tree bark and boil it to make it edible. We dig up grass roots for food. We catch rats, spread nets for small birds or grind wheat stalks into powder, or knead the dry grasses into cakes. There is no more food left to feed the men working our fields."

And yet another, an elderly-appearing man from Henan, probably much younger that he appears, recounts heart-rending story with a determined voice:

"Our old and weak find it hard to continue living. The young, solitary, and feeble are not able to move about. Many wait for death in their houses, stripped of everything. The cold winds pierce through to their bones. We have no rice to cook, the cravings of hunger only grow more painful. There is no pathway to heaven, no door for us to enter the earth. Our plans are exhausted. To die is better than to live. Many hang themselves from beams, or throw themselves into the rivers. These scenes are common."

Finally, a young woman from SHaanxi province bravely steps forward, seemingly emboldened by those who have gone before. Bone thin and wearing soiled, tattered clothing, her voice in nevertheless strong:

"These are the horrors of famine. My sister gave birth to her child in the open air, in a dirt field that had long since stopped giving us food for our table. In that strange place, with death and disease all around her, my starving sister breathed her last from exhaustion. Her child took a few feeble breaths, wailed and died, as well. Few babies survive in the time of famine, and where are we to find the swaddling clothes, food and money to keep them alive?"

Throughout the witness statements, the three judges sat impassively. With the last witness, and without comment, they adjourn to walk the short distance to a door inset beneath the long ramp, where a chamber created for such official deliberations, awaits.

Awaiting the verdict, Manning leans to me, "Those stories are a good reason to see justice done. I hope the judges were listening carefully."

"I'm sure, Excellency. Guilty verdicts may make these peasants feel better for the moment, but it doesn't alleviate the ongoing problems. Please let me convene our counsel in the next few days and discuss strategies to improve the lot of these people. Perhaps greater capital presence in the outlying areas, more grain and seed from our warehouses delivered to the provinces, greater policing of local authorities and their actions. Taxation of the wealthy and elite military classes might bolster our coffers and allow more to be done in the long run. In the meantime, thousands are dying."

Minning appears to only partially hear what I am saying, as he scans the assembled group to measure their reaction to the proceedings. Soldiers and monks sit passively, while the ten accused show every sign of fatigue while they remain standing for the duration of the trial. One man, from the province represented by the young woman, has collapsed to the ground during her story, but palace security step forward to lift him back to his feet.

Finally, as the sun nears the rim of the western palace wall, the judges return. They pass their verdict to a security guard who climbs the long stone ramp, handing the folded sheet to me. I, in turn, hand it to Minning, who studies it carefully. All eyes are on him as he eventually raises his head to nod assent in the direction of the judicial panel. As the three judges stand, members of the palace guard move forward, taking up positions—one behind each of the accused—and shoving them forward to within a few chǐ of the chief magistrate. He reads from a prepared statement:

"It is the opinion of this court, having heard the evidence and testimony of the witnesses, that you shall each be returned to your provincial posts by military guard, to wear the cangue for a period of thirty days. You will be yoked of both head and hands, manacled at your side and unable to reach your mouths. You may wander your village at will, relying on the good nature of those you have allowed to experience similar privation, for your very own food and water. Given your ability to survive, at the end of the full moon's cycle, such restraints will be removed, and you will resume your normal duties. The lessons learned may prove to be a guide for future action, fully accounting for the desires of the esteemed Daoguang Emperor on behalf of his people."

Minning immediately sends me down the ramp to express gratitude to the magistrates for their attention and fair judgment. But, before I can return to the terrace, the emperor has directed his men to carry him inside, out of the brisk evening air. Once I enter the great hall, my emperor is nowhere to be seen. A secretary, standing nearby approaches me to say that the emperor wishes to see me in his chambers.

I proceed to his private quarters, where he is stands, looking out the window at one of his favorite garden spots. Upon my entering he turns, my diary scrolls in his hand.

"Zhengrui, I see that you have are finding time to be critical of your emperor."

I go pale as I realize my failure to return my diary to its hiding place. I attempt to stutter an apology, but Minning calmly interrupts, "I will have this document destroyed. In fact, I will do it myself. I can trust no one else with this information. But I want you to know that if this continues and I learn of it, I will have your head."

39. Ithiel's Vision

BY '25, MY INTENTION to devote myself to task for a period here in China, then returning home for a respite, allowing others to manage the company has long passed. My business in Canton is as secure as it will ever be. The original plan was to switch off with my partner every two years—allowing for some relief from the distance and pressures. I have little confidence, with market forces and demand constantly shifting, that Philip Ammidon can manage on his own. He has made it clear to me that his future tenure in Canton is limited, as he longs to return to home and hearth.

I am moved by the same impulses but have managed to place the success of my business above matters of the heart, at least until now. I still ache at the thought of losing 'Belle,' but with passing time, it is clearer to me that my hopes for that relationship were little more than a youthful dream. Still, with increasing frequency, I find myself, yearning for the familiarity of home, and contact with kith and kin, just as any man would. I have two sons who haven't yet come to know me, and a community of friends and family who have lived entire lives since I was last in their company.

I caution myself that, as an agent, I bear much of the risk of faltering prices in volatile Chinese markets. Yes, commissions will vary, but...the very essence of my business hinges on an inventory of ships, goods acquired on borrowed money, which may sit unsold in warehouses for periods of time. And, with the confidence of my ability to weather those storms, improved financial security, and a growing reputation among hongs—Howqua, in particular—I find myself, with increased frequency, envisioning my life back in Middletown, once I can finally return there for good.

In recent months, I find myself dreaming of a beautiful home on an elm-shaded street in Middletown, where I and my boys can prosper and grow close. Correspondence from home suggest that the family home, our 'Old Mansion House,' is much in need of repair. My aging mother and sisters, Julia and Lucy, to say nothing of Frances and the two boys, deserve better. Of late I've set to work to accomplish the dream so clear in my mind's eye.

Still half-a-world away, I've allowed myself to escape into my plans for a new house, a modest one, yet one I can now afford to build. I've been sketching and calculating wildly in my Canton office bedroom each night. I often recall the generous and tender Frances, sister of my departed wife, Mary, protecting and guiding my three children in my absence. Increasingly, I contemplate her as a wife and companion in this undertaking. I dream of once again being part of a community—the one I had left behind when still just a boy. The places I've been, horrors I've witnessed, choices I've made, grieve me so profoundly. I fear I may never again rediscover that boy who once roamed the hills and dusty roads of Middletown.

≈

EVENTUALLY, THOUGH, I arrive in New York on the bark, *Sea Ranger*, in the winter of '26. There, I meet briefly with my old acquaintance John Astor, to consummate a Canton trade to occur during my absence. I then proceed by carriage to Middletown, where I receive a warm greeting by family.

In the few months I will be able to remain in Middletown before returning to Canton with new contractual obligations, I will arrange for the purchase of land and the construction of a new house of some configuration, based on my rough drawings and notes. I am aware of a spirit of expansion now gripping the nation, a new trend since I was last here. It invites speculation and a renewed sense of optimism regarding the American experiment. So, any return on my part must be triumphant, befitting my accomplishments, and reflecting well on my family and our prominent place in the Middletown community.

Several plots of land were presented to me, the most favorable in terms of location and convenience to town, is that on the corner of High Street and Old Meriden Road, newly named, 'Washington' Street, after our first president. Negotiations would remain ongoing for this, and other choice parcels, unable to be consummated prior to my upcoming departure to Canton as soon as spring weather was anticipated to arrive.

I have a series of meetings with a trusted local man, Samuel Hubbard, a friend whose family has lived in the town for generations. He has agreed to superintend the planning and construction of the new house. I provide him with a series of specifications to be included in the finished structure, such as window size, interior trim, kitchen location (in the rear, two story), and other details. What remains, however, is the guiding hand of an architect, who can formulate the final design based on my broad-brush requirements. But, just as important, I have other matters to attend to.

≈

I MUST ADMIT to myself that my affection for Frances has deepened in my absence. It's unclear to me whether my heart is moved by a sense of obligation for all she's done in my absence, or whether I truly desire her intimate companionship. Within days of my arrival, we visit her family plot where Mary is buried. I am moved to tears as I stand before the humble spot containing her remains. Frances sees my grief, taking my arm, tears streaming down her face, as well. At that moment, as a light dusting of snow swirls around the frozen cemetery grounds, we are of one heart in our sadness over the loss of one so young, so beautiful, so important—however briefly—in my life.

I rattle around the old house, feeling displaced and vaguely anxious. I feel out of place here, now, unable to come to terms with this, my old, abandoned life. The power and authority I command on the other side of the world is like a foreign language to my family here, as I remain an untested man in their eyes.

Winter winds howl outside the cracked windows and sagging roof of the homestead of my youth. I am still lying in my childhood bed on that New Year's morning, awake for some time, hunkered down against steely winter light, cutting a pale-yellow swath through trails of airborne dust drifting beyond the foot of my bed. An urgent knock on the door and an instant later, it's thrown open. My sister, Julia, stands there, speechless, arms in a self-embrace against the cold, her jaw shuttering, more from fear than the chill. Finally, she blurts out, "Come quickly, John is on the kitchen floor and it's bad this time."

I rush to don a day jacket and slippers, flying down the stairs to the scene—one repeated several times in recent months, and yet, always shocking and upsetting to witness again. John, my second-born—a boy of five—lies writhing on the hard wooden floor, head thrown back, arms and legs twisted, fingers and toes contorted like dysfunctional claws, eyes rolled back, mouth rimmed with white spittle. Frances is kneeling beside him, having thrown a small blanket over his chest, stroking his sweat-drenched brow with a damp cloth. She glances up at me with a look of helplessness and despair. "This is the third time in as many days," she says anxiously. "This is all I know how to do, Sam, I'm sorry."

I stand helplessly over the figure of my child, writhing on the floor, as my sister, along with Frances, attempt the near-impossible task of comforting John. "This will pass in a few minutes," I say, my words ringing hollow considering the scene before us. "Has the doctor been summoned?"

No, Frances says, "he's been here many times before this, or it passes before he can arrive. But his advice is always the same—care and comfort, hands away from the mouth, cool compresses. Nothing else for it.

As we speak, the convulsions began to ease. John shows signs he's returning to us. "Let me carry him to his bed, He'll be more comfortable there, I say, feeling like I wanted to offer some gesture—anything that might help—at that moment.

Later, Frances and I are in the front room, each emotionally drained by the morning's event.

With a note of ferocity in her voice, she says, "It's what killed Mary, you know, this sickly child in her womb, all kinds of poison being passed into her blood."

"That's ridiculous, Frances" I snap back. "It was the ague and not his doing and I won't allow that nonsense to be said in this house."

"It's not normal you know, bright and cheerful one minute, choking and squirm-ing the next. Nobody'll play with him. Teachers says 'no' to havin' him in any school in town. I agreed to be a mother to these boys while you were away, but this takes a toll on me...too much to contend with at sometimes. And you, half ay 'round the world, not carin'.'"

"I do care, Frances. I'm doing what I have to do right now. It won't last forever. The end will in in sight, soon enough. Then I can come home and be a father again. I feel terrible about this, you know."

"What can be done about it, Samuel? How can we fix this...this old leaky house, these boys in need of a father, John with this condition doctors sayin' there's no cure for it. Hartford, Boston, New York hospitals, no answers except 'hold him till it passes.' And me with a full plate of responsibilities and nothing to look forward to except more of the same."

I have no answers. I'm speechless at that moment. I storm out of the room, heading to the carriage barn, where I saddle up a horse and ride to the river. I had a 'thinkin' place' as a kid, up at the elbow near the edge of town where the Connecticut curves east, before coursing south again after a bit. Years earlier, I had discovered a flat rock amid a jumble of rocks and driftwood carried there by floods—a secret place where I could watch the ships and people coming and going. It was out of sight, which I liked. That day was bitter cold, but I paid no mind. I go there again, like no time at all had passed, because I had some 'thinkin'' to do.

It's afternoon, near dusk, before I ride back to the house and put the horse. I stride back into the house, finding Frances tending household records at my father's old desk. I walk up behind her, placing my hands on her shoulders. She rises slowly, turning now to face me. "Frances, I'm sorry. I expect the world from you and give you so little in the way of support."

With that, I reach for her small, pale hand, placing a brotherly kiss on the forehead.

Her skin was cool to my touch. She raises her face to look squarely at me, her eyes brimming with tears. I can't say what moved me at the moment, but I find myself placing my lips however tentatively on hers. She pulls away in surprise, but never lets go of my hand. "I'm doing what I can to keep kith and kin together,' she pleads through her tears. "All I'm asking is for your support and understanding."

"I believe you and value you in my life beyond imagining," I reply in a whisper. "In my heart-of-hearts, I believe we can find happiness together."

Before the week is out, on a brilliant, blue February day in 1827, Frances and I are married in the Mansion's front room, before friends and family, presided over by Heman Bangs, preacher of the First Methodist Episcopal Church, here in town.

≈

SAM HUBBARD'S ACTIVITIES on my behalf continued apace in the next few months. I 'took him at his word' that he can be relied upon to guide the construction process and watch out for unnecessary expenditures and abuses that often accompany projects such as this. In exchange, I offer him some insights on the woolen and cotton trade, something he had taken a passing interest in. It would be the case that, through a series of letters conveyed by our vessels sailing between New York and Canton after my departure, that Sam had, in fact secured that two-acre piece of land I so admired, that belonging to Mr. Dana, along 'Paradise Row,' on the corner of Washington and High Streets, for $2500. With that early success, I requested a modest structure in the Greek Revival manner, much in favor at that time.

Believing that my design could be accomplished "simply by the addition of a mason and carpenter," Sam wisely proceeded to select Ithiel Town as my architect. A local man, his accomplishments in Boston, New Haven, and elsewhere had established him as someone who could best represent my vision. I had mistakenly believed that my highly detailed drawings, design specifications (inside and out), as well as a model provided to him through long distance communication would be enough to guide that 'master builder' through to completion. My assumption proved naïve. It would take the combined vision of Ithiel Town and renowned builders, Hoadley & Curtis to complete my new home, but Frances and the designers insisted on a design more in keeping with my stature and accomplishments, a neoclassical masterpiece.

Over the next several months, and with the support of a tireless Frances, the project moves toward completion in '27-'28, pricing out at slightly more that I had hoped to spend—a total of $11,000, when all was nearly said and done. Most significantly, Ithiel Town added a front portico, utilizing a set of six massive Acropolis-styled columns salvaged from the failed New Haven Eagle Bank, and hauled by oxcart to the building site. Their incorporation into the design necessitated an additional cost to the finished property of $1000. In my absence, and at Town's insistence, legal entanglements with Hoadley Curtis over original estimates for completion are being fought out in court.

When I learn of this, I later write to Sam Hubbard from China, making it clear that the building project, which I had originally believed I could control from Canton, proved impractical. I am quite pleased with reports of the beauty and simplicity of the finished home and will gracefully acquiesce to the additional costs. In the same letter to Mr. Hubbard, I express my approval for any additional expenses relating to the house on High Street, writing:

March 31, 1830

"...It was my intention to have left this Country this winter but owing to events which occurred here in August last, I had an additional burden placed on my shoulders and at the same time lost a valuable assistant in our business and consequently was obliged entirely to abandon the idea of returning home this year, much to my regret.

I do hope, if my life is spared, to have the pleasure and satisfaction of seeing you next spring, when I will in person express my acknowledgements of the many obligations, I feel myself under to you in which Mrs. R will heartily join me.

40. A Peruvian Uprising

DURING THE LONG DAYS of my passage back to China in the winter of '27-8, aboard *Integrity*, under the command of Captain Orvis Slater, the prospect of returning to the culture of rampant corruption and graft, the seething rage against the *gwai-lou* festering in every interaction, the unrelenting surge of men, women, and heaped carts on narrow streets each day, the abject poverty at every turn, weighs heavily on my spirit. I lie for hours in the confines of my cramped quarters, or restively pace the deck in heaving seas, unable to shake the recurring vision of countless back-alley opium dens, the torpid bodies of men and women sprawled in darkened rooms, with no one to account for the wasted days and years tallied up; millions, their minds numbed, lives eaten away by *yápiàn*. They come to me in fevered dreams—an extramundane world of walking dead.

When I awake in the abysmal blackness, our ship plunging through midnight seas, their lingering images cry out with every creak and groan of the ship's beams, just inches above my sweat-drenched brow. Have I betrayed myself, my family, my God, by allowing this abomination to occur on my watch? My youthful passion to do what was right, just, honorable, in the way my father might have, now lost to ambition, greed, expediency. As I grow increasingly hobbled by guilt, self-loathing seems to follow me each day, until I can no longer lift my head from the pillow.

Finally, as my delirium progresses to headaches and vomiting, my condition comes to the attention of Jean-Paul Boulanger, the ship's surgeon. A caramel-skinned mulatto, of Haitian birth, I had learned from Captain Slater he is the offspring of a White sea captain from Baltimore, and a freed household slave. Fit and hazel-eyed, with waves of gray-flecked, mahogany hair swept away from his broad face, his instincts for humorous limericks and skills as a fiddle-player have enlivened the doldrums for crew and officers, alike. A skilled physician, his instincts had been honed while in medical training at Baltimore during the British invasion and burning of that place in '14. A hero of that encounter, his modest style never permits a mention of the lives he saved on the streets of the city, during that notorious assault.

"A man of many talents I hear, sir," I say, struggling to lift my feverish body to an elbow in my confined quarters.

"Thank you," he answers, with a vague hint of an unidentifiable accent influenced by his island upbringing. "Oh, you must mean my performances. But I'm no entertainer, Mister Russell. Nor do I aspire to be a musician. First and foremost, I'm a diagnostician. A bawdy joke or two at mess is sure to rouse the men's laughter—a chance to quickly survey rotting teeth and gums for bleeding, a sure sign of scurvy. And I scrape that violin of mine to encourage a round dance or two on deck—good for inspiriting the crew and a chance to move those muscles when doldrums slack the sails for days-on-end. Always a method to my madness, don't you see."

"You deceive us all in beneficial ways...*that* I see."

A quick shift in mood, as he turns his attention to me, a note of seriousness in his voice, "Mr. Russell, I am of the opinion that you've contracted malaria somewhere on our route along the South American coast. "Those long walks of yours on deck at night, that miasmic night air has felled many a good man."

After consultation with Captain Slater, we agree that treatment at a Spanish-run dispensary in Callao, Peru, will be in order. Just 150-nautical miles to our east, we can be there in two-to-three days with a fair westerly. There, according to Jean-Paul, a local medicinal has proven successful treating the ague. In the interim, I'm being treated with liquids, compresses and bleeding, all of which do little to reduce my discomfort.

≈

SEEMINGLY ENDLESS DAYS and nights are spent in delirious sleep, as contorted images of Howqua, nameless Chinese faces, scenes of Canton, even spectral images of Isabella and Mary swirl about in my fevered dreams. Sometime later—maybe days—I slowly awake in a clinic, an occupant of one of many beds aligned in two neat rows against the walls of a narrow, sunlit ward. Individuals who appear to be nurses and attendants move about with determination. As my eyes clear, I can make out several other men in the unit, in various states of convalescence. No one takes any particular notice of me. As my head clears and I gain my orientation, I attempt to sit upright on the side of my bed. Across the distance, a young woman in a starched white apron—a nun in an elaborate wimple—rushes over to coax me back to a reclining position.

*Senior, deberías estar descansando...*you must rest, si?

Where am I, señorita. What's this place?...*qué?* I say in halting Spanish.

"This is Hospital Santa Rosa and I am Sister Amelda. I will call the doctor to come to you. He can explain all to you. But you must stay. *Descansa, comprende?*" She adds, sternly.

Within minutes, I can make out the figure of Mr. Boulanger, in consultation with staff at the doorway. He is taller than the others in the group, holding their attention with a series of animated gestures directed toward a clinical file of some kind. He is still in ship's uniform, cutting an impressive figure with the civilian women in the room.

"Thanks for coming so quickly," I say.

"I've been waiting for you to come around. We almost lost you two nights ago, you know. Fever almost took you, Sam."

"How long have I been here?"

"Five days. We sailed into Callao Harbor on the 12th, and today is the 17th. You needed to be here. I couldn't accomplish what I wanted as long as we were at sea."

"And what was that? What could be done here that we couldn't do aboard?"

"It's called the *Chincona* tree. Goes by lots of other names but grows local in this part of the world. The Spanish missionaries found that fever and the 'shakes' could be treated with the powder from the bark of this tree. That was two hundred years ago. It's also been called the fever tree bark, or Jesuit's bark. Back in '20, a couple of French chemists figured out how to separate out the active ingredient in the bark to make a medicine for general use...called it quinine. Very effective with malaria."

"So, that's what you needed to get me here for?"

"Yes. We can dissolve it in water, but in your case, wine. You were delirious, but always drank it all," he joked.

My color and strength slowly return, and within a few days I feel fit enough to travel again. During that time, Jean-Paul and I talk at length about his training, his Caribbean roots, and his interest in seeing the world from the pitching deck of a ship.

"My father supplied the slave owners in Haiti with American goods from the holds of his ships for many years," he explains. "A non-violent man, through-and-through, he slowly came to understand the sin of slavery, though. Once he fell in love with my mother, he quit the sea and dedicated his years to serving the freed Blacks who lived marginally in and around Port-au-Prince with homespun forms of medical aid. He read voraciously on the subject, scraping together whatever he could for a makeshift clinic. The Whites wanted nothing to do with him—a reputation he wore as a badge of honor. When I came of age, my father enlisted the favor of some wealthy men he worked for back home in Baltimore, sending me off to Maryland to apprentice with a doctor. He wanted, more than anything, to have me continue his work, but with proper training. I guess you could say I learned a lot, very quickly."

"Abolitionists were pretty important to me as a lad," I say. "My father, in his time, caused no little bit of mischief with the slavers in Connecticut. We relied on an alliance of men with the same commitment to emancipation for safe haven to the few we could save.

"As soon as I could, I came back to Haiti to attend the locals. My father had died of Yellow fever in my absence. My mother wanted more for me than to be part of that poverty. I stayed, though, until her death, working with the poor. So, here I am, ten years-or-more later, lending my services to another poor, undeserving lot," he adds, clearly referencing me as he leaned forward with another of his good-natured smiles.

"We share a bond, then," I say quietly, "witnessing a kind of plague on civilization, slavery, I mean," as we sit rocking on the porch of the small dispensary, observing diving pelicans and mewing gulls, slowly circling above the distant harbor.

After minutes, Jean-Paul adds, "There's no medicine for it, though—none I've yet to see."

≈

BY THE TWENTY-FIFTH of November, in '27, I'm ready to get back to sea. During countless hours of idle time, I've written at length to Frances, generally describing my passage, but choosing not to mention my close brush with death. My correspondence is deliberately optimistic, as I have many questions about the final stages of construction of the Middletown house and the progress of her pregnancy. At least a half-dozen letters, tied together with course twine will hopefully be dispatched to any American vessel we encounter heading westward to New York or New England, along the well-traveled Pacific route from the Far East. Under the best of circumstances, and with the good fortune of a friendly vessel siting, I can only hope they will ultimately arrive in her hands within two or three months.

Jean-Paul Boulanger comes to the hospital, to oversee my discharge. We walk together—I still on shaky legs—to the waterfront and docking area, located on a narrow peninsula extending south from the city of Callao, proper. We're overdue to depart, as *Integrity* recently began on-loading additional provisions, awaiting my recovery, for the last leg across the Pacific.

At the mouth of the bay leading up to the city stands a massive, drum-shaped fortress, *Real Filipe*, built in a previous century to defend against pirates. As we head down the hill to the harbor, we notice a slender thread of gray smoke rising from behind its thick walls. It strikes us as strange, given that the embattlement has been largely dormant for decades.

We stop to ask a port official: "What's going on over there, do you know?"

Si, señors, a slave revolt. Some of them from a boat here to deliver to the mines in the mountains ask for trouble. They will not want to go. *Muy malo,* very bad.

We soon meet our ship's second, Mr. Stevenson, on the docks. He explains, "A slave, name of Shodreny, rallied sixty captives of the six hundred on board at one a'clock, overtook their guards and fled from their cells to the empty fort. They're threatenin' mass death—suicide f' the lot-of-'em—'less they get $100,000 and two ships to carry 'em home."

"Where's home?" I ask.

"No damn idea, but they're crazier than coots if they think *that's* gonna happen."

Jean-Paul shoots me a knowing look, studying my face for any reaction. Old emotions from my emancipation days rise up, like no time at all had passed. I suspect similar feelings of indignation toward treatment of these men happening for him, as well. "Who's talking to them?" I ask.

"Nobody, near as I can tell. The Brits have a ship-of-the-line in the bay, a big man-o'-war, third rate, on the way to somewhere. The governor asked for help. Lob a few rounds into their lap might change a mind or two, is the attitude."

"*That's* it? Cut them down?" I say, amazed at the brutality of the possible response from one of our own men.

"I dunno know and care less. There's the slaver captain, right there, jawin' with the guy's takin' possession of his trouble makin' property, near as I can tell, "Stevenson adds. "Why don'cha go ask?"

A quarter mile away, on the grounds of the municipal building and jail, a small group of men stand in animated conversation, windblown under a tropic sun, gesturing between both the English war ship in the harbor and the fort. Jean-Paul and I approach and introduce ourselves. "We're anchored nearby and intend to leave soon. Can you tell us if there is any present danger while we're preparing," I ask?

As we soon learn, among the group is Commander Sir Humphrey Fleming Senhouse, of the ship, HMS *Blenheim,* a third-rate 74-gunner deployed to protect English shipping in the Pacific, now sitting at anchor in the harbor; the captain of the bark slaver, *Elizabeth,* Jacob Dunmoore, out of Mauritania; and the foreman of the Andes-based tin mine, a Peruvian named Eduardo, who protests, "Those *bastardos* want for trouble," he complains. "My boss don't want *no hay problema. Mucho dinero* to buy these and no problem. Get to work soon, get to work for me soon, yes?"

While the locals squabble, Commander Senhouse, his face flushed red in the excessive heat, tall in his bedecked dress blues, gold epaulets and fringed bicorne, stands apart from the rest, surveying the scene. "Sir, do you have a plan, yet?" I ask.

And with that, while ignoring my query, he looks toward his distant vessel and briskly raises one hand high. Moments later a plume of blue smoke appears on the ship's upper gun deck, the report reaching us a second or two later. Then, a splash in the water beneath the walls of the fortress. A stand of gulls on a nearby dune startle, taking wing to circle overhead, protesting loudly.

"By way of a reply to your question, that is a warning shot, Mr. Russell. *That* is what I intend to do, alert them to the fact that these men mean business."

After several minutes, and with no overt reply from inside the bastion—no flag, no movement at the door to the keep—the commander again raises his hand sharply. A second report reaches our ears, just as an incendiary ball clips the battlement, the explosion sending stone shards and burning Sulphur raining down into the sea and interior reaches of the stronghold.

"No, stop, stop, you don't understand," says Captain Dunmoore. "Any losses here come out of my pocket. I get clipped if any of 'em doesn't get delivered. I kepp most of 'em alive all the way 'cross the Atlantic, not to have 'em end up dead here on the door-step. Just scare 'em, for chrissake, don't *kill* 'em!"

Commander Senhouse stares impassively at the slaver, as though his actions and any loss of life are of no concern. "You asked for my assistance," he says disparagingly. "So here we are. What would you have me do next, sir?"

Jean-Paul steps forward from the back of the group at that point, "Might I suggest something... a negotiation? Please allow neutral parties to approach the men and assess their position. As a physician, along with being foreigners in this part of the world, Mr. Russell, and I might be able to help them see reason."

$$\approx$$

SILENCE BEFALLS THE group. Condescension is written on the commander's face, as he sees the group begin to embrace an alternative to his violent proscription to the crisis, particularly coming from this well-spoken man of color. Dunmoore then says, "If you're willing to have a go, things can't get much worse." Eduardo, the mine fore-man, obviously in despair of the situation as it currently stood, agrees with a slight nod. Commander Senhouse considers the proposal in silence and with a dismissive flick of his hand aimed in our direction, signaling nonverbally, "Go then, you fools."

Jean-Paul and I walk the half mile to the bridge over the *Real Filipe* Fortress moat, until we stand before a narrow bronze door leading to the interior courtyard. We pound loudly on the door, as Jean-Paul calls out, "I am a doctor, and I'm here with a friend. We would like to enter and help if we can?"

No reply.

He repeats, adding, "We have no weapons. I am doctor, *doc*-tor. We're here to help resolve the problem...your demands...your current situation. You have no food, no water, injuries, perhaps. How long can you last?"

No reply, only the screech of gulls riding the updrafts overhead in the pale blue sky.

Only after a passage of time measured by our slow breaths, as we each held our ears to the massive door, do we first detect any movement from the other side.

Finally, we then detect the sounds of a bolt works tumbling and a crossbar being drawn to one side—a low groan of metal-against-metal. As the door slowly opens, we're greeted by a towering figure, an African man—with blue-black toned skin, tattooed along both long arms, with a long, tendinous neck—standing alone, red-rimmed eyes narrowed, fearful but intent on assessing this sudden change in his sit-uation. He appears weary, unwashed, his ragged blouse torn, breeches grayed with age and poor treatment, barefoot. A small, soiled white cap is tipped to the back of his head, tight black curls protruding to frame a haggard, but determined countenance. His black eyes, fire-lit, though, are intensely focused on us: our every movement...our questionable intent.

Our hands remain in plain sight, assuring the absence of weapons. We gesture our wish to enter the confines of the fort. "I am Samuel, this is Jean-Paul. We come in peace. I attempted the only word I knew from that part of the world, *his* world...Africa. *Salam*, I utter, my hand raised, palms toward our man.

He seems startled, taken aback. Here is a Black man, standing beside me, dressed in Western clothes, and free to move as he pleases, without restriction. The leader's eyes register confusion, then apparent relief. He backs away slightly, gesturing with an outstretched hand to enter. "*As-salaam 'alykumas*," his eyes soften and alert body language eases slightly. "*Hal 'ant 'akhi*, he asks haltingly, assaying this other Black face, "Are you my brother?"

"*Ahlan*, hello. Yes, I have been where you are, have seen firsthand the pain you have known," Jean-Paul says softly, as they briefly embrace. "May we please come in?" he gestures. Jean-Paul's words are not so much understood, as sensed by the rebel leader, as we slowly work our way into the bastion.

"My brother, yes, '*akhi*, '*akhi*," he repeats, hand over his heart, as he ushers us into an open, cobbled courtyard. Some fifty men and ten women are gathered there. The area is strewn with the rubble and rock fragments of the recent fusillade. Two men and a female lie on makeshift stretchers, made from abandoned bunks and bedding scavenged from nearby barracks. They're bleeding and bruised, but conscious. The remaining stand nearby, watching us intently—guardedly—ready to respond to any unexpected move on our part.

"I am Shodreny," he says, haltingly. "No English much. *Nurid alhuriya, huriya*. We...want...freedom," he said, urgency in his voice. "Return our place, *Afriqiaan, eabr albahr...from across the sea, huriya, huriya, freedom, freedom!*"

Jean-Paul and I listen carefully. Jean-Paul can't take his eyes off the three injured figures lying nearby. "He's speaking Arabic to me," he says. "I've heard it spoken in Haiti...central West African coast, like Dunmoore said back there. Most likely Mohammedans. These are not tribal jungle people. Elegant, educated, God fearing... *Jeesus!*" he blurts out, voicing his disgust and frustration at the reality of the situation. "I am doctor, *doc-tor, tabib*," he says pleadingly, his hand patting his chest to signify body function, I guess. "Can I look at the injuries of your people?" And with that, he gestures in the direction of the cots on the ground.

It works, and with that Shodreny steps back, gesturing toward the wounded. In turn, as Jean-Paul walks toward the litters, Shondreny's people clear the immediate area, straining to see what this *tabib* will do next.

After some time with each victim, he returns to me. "There are some superficial flesh wounds and burns here. Nothing we can't address easily at the clinic. I have an idea. A negotiation that might break the log jam and see an end to this. Not ideal, but our choices are limited."

After explaining the plan to me, we again approach Shodreny, appealing to him in a series of fractured English phrases and hand gestures to bring the siege to an end, with no loss of life. We explain that the Whites don't want to see killing, but they will absolutely *not* allow escape under the terms set by the group.

With time and his reluctant ascent, we leave the fortress, conveying the terms of surrender to the group standing on the quay.

An hour later, we supervise the transfer by cart of the four injured individuals from the fort to the hospital. Each victim, plus Shodreny as their titular leader, is 'allowed' to be accompanied by a 'spouse', in order, as we describe it, to assist with care and speed recovery. Then, all will rejoin the others holed up in the fort for the long trip to the tin mine. In exchange, their leader agrees to surrender, with the assurance that he won't be punished for his recent actions. We let him know that "each member of his group is valuable to the Whites, and that any loss of life would be considered a bad thing."

This compromise makes Jean-Paul and me sick at heart. We recognize we can't stem the tide of slavery but might be capable of diverting one small tributary. We also understand the reality of the situation—the revolt we've inadvertently sailed into—knowing that any further resistance on the part of this group of these African captives will result in the inevitable, untimely slaughter of many in the group. The tin mine foreman will not and cannot let insubordination and revolt stand. After all, White pride and profit are at stake.

≈

AT THE HOSPITAL, Jean-Paul consults with the nurses to direct the treatment plan, and instruct that he will regularly be checking on his patients. "These 'husband and wives' should be well-cared for, to be fed and housed until their discharge becomes possible in a few days." He thanks the nuns profusely for their cooperation on this important matter.

In the meantime, I busy myself at the warehouse by the docks, preparing our list of goods and supplies needed for the next, last leg of our journey. Inspired by my father's story of long ago, I particularly request potatoes, a good source of nutrition for our crew, and a novelty once we reach China, I explain. Each large burlap bag is clearly stenciled, 'potato' on one side, 'patata' in Spanish, on the other. These are now standing by, dockside, along with other supplies ready to be loaded in time for departure on a proper tide and wind.

Two days later, the captain indicates that weather and tide are right for departure. Jean-Paul and I then put our plan into action. I ready three horse-drawn carts to carry 'goods' to the ship. Jean-Paul goes immediately to the hospital to prepare his 'patients' for discharge. Overhead, mounds of cumulus clouds scud across the Peruvian sky as we transport supplies to dockside to provision the hold. As the sacks of potatoes make their way to the harbor, space in the stock room is readied to receive the cargo.

Once aboard and well out of sight below, Jean-Paul's 'patients' are released and directed to the deepest hold of the ship. Then, a surprise we had not expected. Shodreny emerges from the darkness to say he cannot in good conscience leave his people. Even at the risk of his own life, he tells us he must return to his people. With his island experience and scant understanding of native tongues, Jean-Paul listens intently, and with numerous hand gestures, turns to us to interpret as best he can.

"That will be very risky," I say.

"The risk is to my people if I am not there to speak for them. I must return."

Jean-Paul and I see the courage and determination in Shodreny's eyes. We glance to shore. On the distant chase, Dunmoore, Admiral Senhouse and the others are still gathered.

Standing with Shodreny in the confines of the lower deck, I point through a portlight at the shore. "If we return you across open water, our plan will become obvious to those men. What would you have us do? Think of the ones below."

"Bring me by small boat closer...over there," he points to the north side of the harbor behind the seawall. "I go over side and swim ashore. I wait there until you are gone, I walk up to waiting men, wet and tired, say I escape to be with my people. No harm comes to you, and to ones you take with."

"This could mean your life, slavery, even death," Jean-Paul says.

"I have no life away from my people," says Shodreny, as he gazes anxiously back at the fortress.

We are dumbstruck by this man's bravery, and only after a moment of precious time—given our impending departure—does Captain Slater order a skiff lowered on the starboard beam, the side of the ship facing away from the harbor. We offer our earnest best and assurances that those below will be well-treated, as the crew takes up oars. Assuming our every action is being watched through a scope, Shodreny lies low in the skiff, covered with a blanket.

A half hour passes when the skiff finally returns, our man delivered to the beach and whatever fate awaits him.

≈

OUR DEPARTURE DELAYED past noon, we finally weigh anchor on an ebb tide and are nearly out of sight of Callao within the hour. Our bow dips and rises again, throwing aside wave-after-wave of crystalline, sapphire seas on our westward trek. Below decks, with equilibrium restored, Jean-Paul attends his patients, our three wounded Africans and their three unrelated companions, now able to move about freely, enjoying clean bunks and warm broth. Our plan: to deliver these six souls to the Jesuit ministry on the Hawaiian chain, and bid they care for them until an eastbound vessel can safely carry them back east, to our colleagues in New York or Boston, and on to safety in Canada or another secure haven.

Shodreny walks the length of the inner harbor and quay to finally reveal himself to his captors, relaying a story of his harrowing escape to rejoin his people. He is immediately shackled and told to appear at the gates of the fort and proclaim the revolt at an end. Wet, bedraggled and apparently defeated, Shodreny agrees to do as instructed.

But before the slave captain, Dunmoore, and tin mine foreman, Eduardo, can account for the six missing pieces of 'property,' *Integrity* is well on its way over the horizon. We later receive word that they had implored Commander Senhouse to give chase in his fast-moving man-o'-war, *HMS Blenheim*. He apparently dismisses their pleas with a brusque, "This is *not* my problem, of no official concern to the Crown...I was distrusting of those Yankees from the start."

And, after a grumbling assent from the group, he adds, "I have another piece of advice, based on my long experience with these people. Agreement, be damned to hell, you should immediately hang that leader of theirs in front of them all. After this close call, he'll be nothing but trouble from here on."

41. Homecoming

IT'S A BONE-CHILLING JANUARY day in '28, when we once again clear Macao Roads, the treacherous, reef-strewn gateway from the South China Sea into the protected waters of the Pearl River. And, except for my perilous brush with death in a South American hospital and a risky engagement with a slave revolt, at least I can claim it was an uneventful sea voyage from Boston.

Heavy sheets of cold, gray rain sweep down from looming fissures overhead, slanting across the Pearl's broad estuary. The deluge obscures the Macao skyline and, to the east, blankets the distant, low-slung archipelago beyond Lintin Island.

Despite misgivings, constantly bedeviling me on my return journey, my eighteen months away has done much to restore my energy and commitment to the task awaiting me in Canton—securing the company's future with new partners and expanded contracts as a free agent, integrating new employees from the states into their routines and building good will among the hongs and other officials. All this, essential to keep goods—including growing inventories of Indian Malwa *afeem*—flowing smoothly into the Chinese marketplace.

Lindsay Andrews, the young Scot whom I'd hired on the docks more than two years ago, has proven indispensable as my assistant. His understanding of the vagaries and dangers of the job are equal to that of men twice his age and experience. He gigs over in rough bay chop from the Company go-down to apprise me of events since our last written correspondence. As I had expected, he is invaluable to the operation, managing the warehousing and transfers from arriving vessels, negotiating tariffs and *cumshaw*, all the while dealing shrewdly with inveigling shroffs and their proverbial 'squeeze' at tariff time, without significant loss or conflict.

Ascending the ship's rope ladder, red-faced, with his untamed red locks escaping the rim of his Monmouth cap, Andrews breathlessly extends a hand from beneath his dripping oiled slicker, "G'day, Mr. Russell. Safe journey, I'm bettin'?"

"No more than the usual lumps and bumps rounding the Horn. Southern climes a good deal more forgiving this season of the year. Dreadful Nor'easter and coastal flooding back home, but alive and well, happy to report. News?"

"In 'your absence, much's transpired along the waterfront. Gardens been planted and fences erected in front of several buildings. The Brits and you Americans been cordonin' off land 'tween you and the river for private use...you know, where the Chinamen's been gatherin' and sellin' each day. Been needin' more turf for themselves close by to th' factories. Safety and such what's the factory men been plannin'. Recent upturn in violence and protests against Westerners right under 'your windows!"

"News came to me while I was back home of assassinations and public executions, according to some captains returning stateside. True, yes?"

"You bet! Town's getting' rough, especial for you flower-flag folk. We all look th' same to them, though. Don't matter—Yorkshire or New York, sailor or company man. You put yur life on th' line to go about unaccompanied. Took place right down by the river at that floggin' post. Takin' to chokin' off a few poor blokes before cheerin' crowds, Claimin' they'ers Jiàndié...you know, spies."

"What's got these folks so on edge since I left?"

"Mud's got 'em all agitated, is what. Them that want it versus them that don't want 'em to have such. We're shippin' in those quality goods now. Malwa's comin' in bigger 'n bigger volume, drivin' up demand. Locals and provincials under pressure to stop the flow. Big game of chess on the streets, down th' river especially, where we're movin' most of those chests comin' in, everything sold piecemeal before ever reachin' shore. Everybody's got their hand out. Near impossible t' control."

I hesitate for a moment, then say, "Look, Lindsay, you find a man at the warehouse to take over your job there. Now I'm back, and with the stakes increasing, I want you in the counting room to help keep the lid on things. It's only going to heat up."

A broad smile greets my offer. "Yessir. Be there tomorrow, once I can find an able body in the lot-of-'em who can count and tally rightly to the ledger's bottom line." Then, after a short hesitation, he turns back to say, "Ya' know I'm tellin' tales out a' school, and all, but thought you'd want to know: the men're plannin' a bit of a cèilidh for you, in light of the new wife, and such."

"Thanks for the warning, Lindsay. I hate surprises." Even as I speak these words, I feel the recent delirium of my fraught ocean voyage fade, as I am obligated to wave aside self-doubt in favor the welcoming enthusiasm of my staff and the complex tasks required to manage this opportunity successfully. For myself, and the many men whose livelihoods depending on me, survival in this hostile world must brook no second thoughts.

≈

SOME WEEKS LATER, after a busy schedule on my return, a reception is finally held near the American factory in recognition of my marriage to Frances, while back in Middletown. My company and the growing Christian community in Canton also wanted to recognize the arrival of several missionaries from England and the United States. When I'd first arrived in Canton in '19, so too, did a gentleman, David Washington Cincinnatus Olyphant, a fellow New Englander, acting as agent for the Thomas H. Smith Company. He was seen as a staid, deeply-devout Christian man, who limited his business dealings to Northwest American seal furs, in exchange for tea, silks and porcelain—what we thought of in the pre-opium days as the 'old' China trade of the last century.

Owing to his conservative Christian roots, as well as my ongoing interest in honoring my Protestant upbringing—as I'm now so far from home—he and I soon joined forces with the Scottish missionary, Robert Morrison. This alliance, outside of our business interests, resulted in a long-term effort to expand Protestant missionary endeavors in the Far East—those willing to live under crude, even dangerous circumstances. Olyphant even went so far as to offer any and all missionaries free passage on his company's ship, Roman, and free lodgings in Canton. As a result, a chosen individual, Elijah Coleman Bridgman, became the first of many American Protestant Christian missionaries sponsored by our group, here in China.

Olyphant additionally allows the physician and missionary, Peter Parker, to use one of his warehouses as a hospital, in his words, "so that patients can come and go without annoying locals by passing through their hongs or excite the observations of natives by being seen to resort to a foreigner's house, therefore rendering it most suitable for the purpose."

An uneasy truce exists between Chinese authorities and our Christian missionary's efforts in Canton and in surrounding countryside. Jesuits have resided in the shadow of the Forbidden City for nearly a century, without major incident. Their proximity to the center of power, however, allows the emperor to keep the Catholic Church and its papal emissaries on a short leash, severely limiting their contact with locals and constraining their travel. With increasing American presence in this region, there is greater pressure by church authorities—particularly Protestant sects—to convert the vast, 'unwashed' population of 'heathens' residing on this, the 'other side of the world.'

We once believed that Christian conversion would incline the population to be more amenable, given Western presence and influence, thereby opening the door for increased trade. Much of this zeal, however, arose from a stateside movement called, 'The Great Awakening,' which required adopting the One True God, as a central article of faith. It was considered an essential individual step toward redemption from original sin, in an increasingly callous, industrialized world. I personally witnessed the quickening effects of this movement on ordinary people in recent months back home in Middletown.

Because of growing local animosities, our efforts to preach and educate must move forward cautiously. So, while any recognition of my marriage is cause for celebration, our gathering calls for a need to exercise restraint while among our Cantonese neighbors. As a result, our gathering is relocated to the modest residences of the missionary brotherhood, a converted dormitory and humble kitchen at the back of the Thomas Smith Company warehouse. Lights are dimmed and conversation muted. Crumbling walls, uneven floorboards and dusty rafters will be certain to allay suspicion of a fête for anyone walking behind the building on Thirteen Factory Street.

"Let people know I'll be running a bit late," I say to Lindsay, who understands my demanding schedule. I had just arrived at the factory residence from our warehouse to freshen myself and change my collar and tie. "Give me about a half hour and ask Olyphant to hold his comments until I arrive, please."

≈

FEELING A NEW man, at dusk I briskly walk the quarter mile to the Smith warehouse along the narrowed Respondentia—newly planted gardens and fences to my left, the riverbank to my right. I keep my head lowered to avoid accidental eye contact, appearing in every way to be on an errand of some urgency. Local merchants and boatmen are busy in their stalls and sampans, thankfully take little notice of me.

My eyes refocus as I enter the missionary's cramped quarters. A dozen cassock-cloaked men stand in small groups, engaged in earnest conversation. Olyphant and my partner, Philip Ammidon stand together, signaling me with a raised hand when I arrive. Most faces in the room are already familiar to me: the postulants, Addison, the lover of Psalms; Quinn, who hopes to form a children's choir; Downing, dark-browed and serious about salvation. But a tall figure, his back toward me, towers above the rest; two young men, smooth faces turned upward, are in thrall to his comments.

A vague sense of unease settles in my gut as I draw closer. I move to within range of the discussion: his face is mostly obscured by a broad-brimmed, black hat and shoulder-length, gray-streaked hair; a skeletal frame barely supports an oversized dark shirt and frayed breeches; shoulders hunch forward as if to disguise his notable height, and a voice—*that* voice—lugubrious and hypnotic. Where do I know this man from, and what is he doing here?

"...was invited here to be part of this exciting effort to bring Christ to the masses, an inducement I could not refuse. My people, my flock felled by disease and perpetual conflict, became impossible to inspire. My health, after all, was at stake," I overhear him say.

That voice, haunting and strangely familiar. I circle 'round the group for a clearer look.

"...resisting temptation...the man by the docks when I arrived...'show me some ladies, all the same foot, so so, all same weery little can do,' the man said to me in a high-pitched voice, all the while holding his finger and thumb about three inches apart. Bound feet is what he meant, I gathered. What a strange custom among these people. So in need of salvation," he continues.

The long, drawn face is ashen, with reptilian skin and a prominent nose running like a blade between dark ophidian eyes. An oversized silver cross hangs about his neck, conspicuously framed against a faded black shirt. Suddenly I realize it's Father Andreus, the missionary from Nevula, in the Fiji chain. Here is the very same man who so brutally repressed the locals—events I witnessed to my lasting horror.

He glances in my direction, a lingering, probing stare, but reveals no sign of recognition. He is much too pre-occupied, holding this small group of young neophytes under his spell with endless magniloquent pronouncements. Again, turning his attention back to the young men, he says, "...they explained there is a better class of women long acquainted with the captains and officers, and that I should come aboard once I am settled for a chat and some fine Oolong tea."

It has been more than six years ago, now, and I would have only been only an insignificant player—behind the captain and his crew—in the tragedy that had played out on the beach that day—murder and mayhem in the face of his effort to control everything and everyone around him. Then, he appears to slowly scrutinize me, again. Perhaps he was aware on my unwavering eyes, locked on his countenance.

"You look familiar. Should I know you?" he asks, extending his hand toward me. "I am Father Andreus, of the Methodist mission, here to lend my voice to the effort." He extends a long, thin hand, his grasp cold, dry and frail in mine."

The mere sight of him and his unctuous manner fill me with anger. "Samuel Russell, sir," I respond coolly. "We met in your village years ago, along with Captain Rathbun. Perhaps you recall the dead boy on the beach, a spear in his back? The terrifying night he spent in the jungle until being set upon by men directed by you?"

What little color he has drains from the man's face, the already-dull light in his eyes fading as he finally makes the connection. "Most unfortunate, Mr. Russell," he says dispassionately. "You never got to witness my consternation over that unfortunate matter. I reprimanded my people sternly after your vessel's hasty departure. But, that is behind us now, ancient history, as it were...yes?"

"I think not, sir," I respond, as I feel an old rage rising in me like molten lava. "You are here as an invited guest of Mr. Olyphant, who is certainly unaware of past events. I will say nothing to him tonight, as it's my evening to celebrate good fortune. But to be honest, I'm circumspect of your intentions, and I'll be watching your actions here in Canton carefully."

Ignoring my stern tone, he adds with a viperous smile, "I have deigned to take up my responsibilities in the nearby village of Tung-kun, where a small mission church has been constructed in your absence. These two young men, here, will be working with me to offer prayers and guidance in our Christian ways to the villagers."

"Perhaps so, Andreus, or whatever your name is. But just be certain, that I'll have an eagle eye trained on you. *All* reports of impropriety will come directly to me. I'll be speaking to Mr. Olyphant tomorrow about all of this. A warning: walk the straight and narrow, sir."

≈

THAT CONVERSATION OCCURRED in April of '29. Andreus was, in fact, dispatched to our mission home in Tung-kun, just a few miles south and east of Canton. It was a single day's journey to his location. After discussing my Pacific Island experience with Mr. Olyphant, we decide not to immediately assign theology students to his station. While in the process of moving our offices to Macao for the summer months, we learn of a series of incidents involving our 'Father Andreus.'

After some inquiries were made via letter back home, I'm informed by letter from John Astor, that our 'Father Andreus' is, in fact, a notorious flim-flam man, Nathan Riley Burgess, who'd narrowly escaped the hangman's noose for theft and attempted murder in the Northwest Territories, some years before. He managed to stow away on a China-bound, Astor fur trading vessel. He jumped ship during a stop for repairs at Fiji's Nevula, where he apparently convinced the locals, who were enamored of Westerners, that he could function as their spiritual leader, while also adding his voice and business skill—together with the reclusive, 'Driff'— to any number of passing vessels dropping anchor in Nevula's picturesque bay. Our vessel was just one of many they took advantage of.

Apparently, his reportedly insatiable appetite in local boys *and* young females did not fare as well here in China, as it might have with the island people of the Pacific. We learn, to our shock and dismay in July of that year, that his body is discovered one morning, bound to a lemon tree, strangled to death, with his genitalia cut away and stuffed into his mouth. And, as if intended to be a message for all espousing the redemptive power of the Holy Word, a Bible in Chinese translation is laid at his feet, opened to the passage:

"Be not deceived; God is not mocked: for whatsoever a man soweth, that shall he also reap."

~Galatians 6:7-8

42. Scapegoat

THE MORNING SUN-SHING was to be garroted in the public square began without any apparent sign of trouble. The sun was suspended bright and hot above the harbor that October day in 1830, while unbeknownst to me, my 'outside man'—one of many on the company payroll to run errands between warehouse and local merchants—is under arrest and soon to pay with his life for his role as a Western 'spy.' A designated intermediary and occasional translator for the Americans, Sun-shing made the mistake of frequenting foreign bars and being seen in the company of whores on the narrow streets of Hog Lane last night. Just this once, he had neglected to proceed directly to his contact to deliver a discrete packet of *yāpiàn*, then return to the usual meeting point with payment.

Instead, he delayed and a pair of Cantonese gendarmes, recently instructed to look for signs of opium trafficking, detained the poor man for the simple act of loitering. What they found in his pocket, though, was enough to have him immediately arrested. Sun-shing's behavior had not been unlike his other sorties into the city's better neighborhoods, when he diverted from his assigned task to linger in the dimly lit doorways of the brothels, making small talk with the loose women, *Jìnū*, some of whom he had known since childhood. But, of late, he'd been earmarked because of his conspicuous connection to my company, widely suspected of trafficking in Indian 'mud.'

Sun-shing's arrest is surely meant to send a powerful message, since increasingly, regional authorities are pressuring locals to crack down on opium use at all levels in Cantonese society. It would be a harbinger of things to come, a sign that the narrow line between opportunity and profit I have walked of for years, is being increasingly challenged.

Within moments of arriving at my office, I am appalled to learn of the incident and the current danger posed to my valued employee. I drop my coat and paperwork on a nearby table, rushing down a hallway to find my linguist and burser, *Acook*.

"Did Sun-shing return with the receipts of our sale last night," I ask?

"No, sir. We have no record. But package given him to take, and we learn it no arrive," Acook says, a look of alarm in his eyes.

Even as we speak, a small group of men leave their desks to gather behind me, anxious to understand what is unfolding. I say, "We have to find him. This is an audacity. Everyone knows our people and they have never been harassed. I'm well-known and trusted by these people. We must know the meaning of this. I'll go to the Prefect's office and demand his freedom."

Andrews asks, "Why now? Why after all this time would the gendarme take an interest in a minor company employee?"

They're out to display a no tolerance attitude...no mercy," I say. "The governor's newly appointed chief enforcer has to demonstrate his authority and new-found power by making an example of a low-level minion of an American company like ours. I've got to track down the people doing this." And with that, I'm out the back door onto

Thirteen Factory Street, to the west end of the busy alley, heading the police station located on Puantiqua Street. The nocturnal rabble and drunken sailors wandering the bars on Hog Lane often have the misfortune of spending more than one night in this particular police substation's gaol.

Entering the building, I find no one to detain me, so I head down a hallway. Soon, I find the prefect's open door. I remind myself to show restraint, as any sign of anger will yield me little or no information. As expected, my meeting with the prefect is perfunctory and distressing, as I hurry back to my offices with the latest update on Sunshing's case.

"The threat is a planned execution scheduled to take place without trial or even public hearing on the circumstances of Sun-shing's arrest, I explain to my men. "It will be nothing more than a highly visible, deliberate murder, carried out beneath the thirteen flags of various factories...designed to send a signal."

Over the course of the morning, business matters are set aside to develop a strategy to save Sun-shing's life, if possible. I've sent for Li-Mĭn, hoping his stature in the eyes of local authorities and his bi-lingual skills will facilitate a less-than-deadly solution to this crisis. When he finally arrives, his assessment of the situation is not encouraging: "Sam, authorities have been pushed to a breaking point. They're looking for blood revenge, a way to make the 'flower flag' people pay for what's been going on in the neighborhoods, at every level of society."

"Sun-shing has had nothing to do with any of that, except what we've ask him to do. He's just an employee. Why not come after me?"

"They may, at some point. But, right now, they just want to do something to hurt your effort, warn other Westerners and find a way to please the governor, who wants action of some kind, any kind."

As the morning wears on, our small group strategizes, sitting before large, south-facing windows, overlooking newly fenced-in factory building lawns bordering Respondentia Walk. The formal gardens stand out in stark contrast to the disarrayed lines of sampans stacked against the riverbank, just beyond. Farther out, the sun-drenched Pearl is alive with its usual boating activity.

Time passes with no clear solution, except, perhaps, to have Li-Mĭn serve as an envoy to local authorities, on the chance of arousing sympathy for our hapless Sunshing. But, as this prospect is weighed, a large, flat wooden cart is being wheeled down Old China Street into view. It is being slowly pushed and guided by a phalanx of uniformed men, finally coming to rest just beyond the fencing at the river's edge. The spot is in clear view of all those now gathering on the factories' large pediment-capped porticos and verandahs.

Protruding from the center of the cart is a well-worn, cross-shaped post, measuring about two meters in height, by two meters on the horizontal. And while it may resemble a Christian symbol to most Western eyes, to this growing crowd of townspeople congregating nearby, this is a timeless symbol with a sinister purpose—protracted death meted out at the hands of provincial authorities.

While tensions on the riverbank build moment-by-moment, a small group of company men decide to step into harms' way, feeling obliged to leave the building in support of Sun-shing. Out of desperation, they are driven by a belief that sheer numbers—a *force de guerre*—might compel authorities to respond and set the prisoner free. Among the small group of company agents are Lindsay Andrews and writer, Asha Gardner, a trio of my security men and Arsee, the interpreter.

By the time they reach ground level, the crowd gathers in an ever-widening circle around the cart and the uniformed officers. The mob has grown to a point where passage along the broad river front embankment is nearly impossible. The scene incenses me, because tensions between traders and government officials can erupt any minute into a needless violence; but also, that my valuable man, Sun-shing, is being scapegoated to die in such a public way.

With Andrews and the others hemmed in by the unruly dock-front mob, the shouts and jeers slowly abate in response to the resonant sound of a distant drum. Its regular *thrump-thrump-thrump* sets the cadence for a procession, working its way through the crowd, which slowly gives way. Two men enter the execution area first, their colorful banners raised high above the heads of those assembled. Each fringed flag bears a dragon symbol, that of the Qing emperor. They are intended to mark this event as one ordered by the provincial court, itself. Following are two robed figures— drummers—holding large heavily decorated instruments, suspended vertically by rope sashes, beating out the relentless cadence with a single, padded drumstick. Next come four gendarmes, identically garbed in blue shifts, baggy pants, and ankle height leather sandals. On broad belts, each carries an assortment of knives and clubs, tucked close to the body. Between them, our own Sun-shing stumbles forward, head lowered.

I stare in disbelief at Sun-shing's appearance. His hands are bound behind, as he struggles to keep pace with his guards. "This is like a parade, or celebration," I say to Li-Min. "It looks like he's been beaten. He's all bruised. His shirt is badly torn and covered with what looks like dried blood."

I am now so angry I can hardly control my emotions. "Let's head down there," I say to Li-Min. We've got to find a way to interrupt this circus."

Once we find our group, I say, "There are clear signs of torture here. Sun-shing has been abused by police. Arsee, come here please. I want you to go there to where all those uniformed men are, and tell whoever is in charge to come see me immediately. Explain that this man is my employee, and he has done nothing wrong. This spectacle must stop at once. No...wait. Just bring the main man to me and I will explain."

Sun-shing appears glassy-eyed and semi-conscious, seemingly unaware of the angry crowd surrounding him, and any of the familiar faces of his fellow company men, nearby. He stares fixedly at the ground, a passive player in the scene. Around his neck a roughly lettered placard has been placed. It hangs askew, entwined in his tattered clothing, but is legible: Pàntú - Xié'è de xíngdòng zhě (叛徒-邪恶的行动者).

Arsee returns all too soon. "The sergeant in charge...there, the tallest of the group. He will not speak to you. Sun-Shing wears a sign calling him a traitor and Chinese evil doer. The sergeant say you are like him, you a I-chien, a 'foreign devil' like Sun-shing. I am sorry. He will not come to talk with you."

Soon, Sun-shing is thrust forward to stand before the jeering crowd. They mock him with gestures and loud cries; yet he remains standing, unmoved by their taunts. The Tall One takes him roughly by the arm and shoves him, nearly tripping, onto the cart, where he is turned, and his wrists are quickly bound to the horizontal beam. A ligature is draped over his head and that part of the vertical post jutting above his limp body.

≈

THE ROUTINE IS familiar to the crowd. They've witnessed this kind of execution many time—convicted felons, political enemies, some friends, or neighbors who have affronted the ruling class or their sycophants—all marched unceremoniously to *teen tsze ma taou,* 'The Execution Ground,' and to a cross-like structure like this, only to be slowly strangled by a thin cord around the neck, looped through a short rod and slowly twisted ever tighter from behind. Under the restricting effects of the ligature, the victim's face first turns red, then purple as he struggles to breathe. Soon, his eyes bulge in a gruesome parody of a theater mask, as spittle drips from a quivering chin. Bowels and bladder then loosen, filling the air around the victim with a stench, discoloring the trousers and ground around his bare feet. Fingertips tremble, then convulse into fists, before going limp. Toes curl upward, then peddle the air, as if escape might be possible. Lower extremities then go flaccid, as well. Death arrives slowly, but without the dignity of the head slumping to the chest. Tension on the neck means death is only marked by the absence of flailing. When the executioner releases his grip on the cord, only then does the body of the deceased collapse, the long ordeal of dying finally at an end.

And only then—after witnessing the gruesome spectacle for what seems like endless moments in hushed silence—does the assembled crowd burst into cheers.

With Sun-shing due a similar fate, those company men and I who intervened before it escalated, protest loudly from the margins of the crowd. Enraged, I lead our uproar, fists raised. My men add volume to the call for justice. Others in the crowd notice the unexpected disruption, seeing it as an opportunity to protest their own past treatment at the hands of the gendarmerie. *Zhèngyì* they shout...Justice! *Wúgū* ...Innocent! Like fans cheering opposing teams on a field of play, excitement grows as the mass of protesters moves closer to the cart and the police assembled around it. *Zhèngyì...Wúgū!* The uniformed men's stance is at first defensive, as they grip the hilts of their batons and collectively face outward toward the threat. *Zhèngyì...Wúgū!* But, as anger mounts body language changes, with the possibility of bodily injury of their own numbers at the hands of the agitated mob, growing by the minute.

The Tall One raises his hands, as if to quell the excitement, but to little effect. My men take advantage of the upheaval to move toward *Sun-shing,* hoping to at least make eye contact and let him know they're there to stop the execution. Finally, a daring young man steps out of the crowd, mounting the cart. He seems unafraid of the police—perhaps because he has had too many run-ins with them to fear their motives, or because of some personal connection to the victim that makes the risk worthwhile.

Unsheathing a small knife from his belt, he cuts the cord holding the sign and tosses it to the ground. Then, reaching up and with two more quick strokes, he manages to cut *Sun-shing* free. The accused's arms drop as though lifeless, only to have them thrown, dangling, over the shoulder of his rescuer. After a few paces the young man stops, lowering *Sun-shing* to the ground, leading him off, half-walking, half dragging him through the densely packed, cheering mob. The police have lost interest in their victim, as their concern now turns to their own safety in the face of a violent mob. Within moments, *Sun-shing* and his rescuer have exited the scene down a side alley, leaving the executioner's cart standing empty.

As the crowd slowly disperses, my men and I sense that immediate threat has passed, as we congratulate ourselves for an outcome that could otherwise have gone tragically wrong.

"Where do you think Sun-shing will be taken from here?" I ask.

Arsee in the first to respond. "He will probably go to his brother's house to heal his wounds and become strong again. We spoke up for him. That was good. Others from his clan and his village north of here saw our courage and spoke up, too. They were there in the crowd. Here, we are clan and family first. The imperial palace rules over us all, but in matters of life and death, we live and die for each other first. The Celestial Empire can have what's left."

"When he is stronger, have him come to see me, Arsee. I want to thank him for his courage, but not until I admonish him for being in the wrong place at the wrong time. These are dangerous times we're living in. For now, we have our own form of *zhèngyì*— justice. But the stakes may be changing, and we have to consider new ways to get the job done. Opportunity is one thing, danger of major proportion to us and those we rely on, makes a very different story."

≈

A FEW STRAGGLERS remain after the embankment area clears. Members of Sunshing's clan immediately close in with hammers and jack saws to make quick work of dismantling the cart and its ominous scaffolding. Moments later, lengths of timber and shards of lumber float aimlessly in the harbor. Residents on a nearby sampan, employing long paddles to move pieces of the growing debris field to within reach, gather them up to use as fuel in their evening fire.

43. A Crucial Visit

ON THE MORNING OF MONDAY, October 12, 1831, I'm paid a visit by Howqua, the most important hong merchant and founder and head of the E-wo hong (怡和) and leader of the Canton Co-hong. In the years I've known him, his accumulated fortune has made him one of the wealthiest men in the world; his influence with authorities far-reaching, and the protection he can offer against threats to the fragile arrangements within the country cannot be overestimated. Howqua is my lynchpin in the ongoing relationship with the range of merchants, traders and petty agents that carry out trade negotiations with my people on every front.

And so, when Howqua requested to meet with me, my offices accepted immediately. I asked Li-Min to be there, as well. He readily agrees, given how essential he had become to my daily operations with Chinese authorities.

At the appointed hour, Howqua arrives by sedan, accompanied by a retinue of body-guards and assistants—enough to fill a small room. Today, his multi-layered wardrobe flows as he walks, draped by a chángshān, or knee-length tunic, made of the finest silks, richly embroidered, and trimmed with fur. His black leather shoes are pointed at the toes like the bows of small boats. His only other adornment is a long, double-strand jade necklace arranged in colors of verdigris and coral. I'm experiencing a vague sense of trepidation about this unexpected request, as I bow slightly and offer tea, which he modestly accepts. I ask that it be brought to the expansive second floor conferencing room, which offers an unobstructed view of the boat-filled harbor, through the arched portico windows.

With ceremonial greetings and pleasantries concluded, Howqua, Li-Min and I are finally alone. Howqua's English remains fractured. He leans over to ask Li-Min to speak as his interpreter, given the nature of his concerns. "There is renewed and growing concern at the palace in Beijing and among the highest ranking here in Kwantung Province regarding the flow of opium into the countryside," Howqua relates through Li-Min. "Our police are arresting opium-dealing men in the provinces, and seizing their property, too. Invariably they turn out to be Kwantung men, or know somebody who travels here regularly. My sources are telling me that so much yāpiàn is flowing into the villages that overall health and production is failing to meet standards."

"We're only responding to demand, and there seems to be no limit..." I reply, only to be cut short.

"My pardons, please...perhaps," says Howqua, "but there are persistent rumors that the limited measures taken against the rising influx of trade is only salutary. Too many local officials are benefiting directly from the transactions in their provinces. I don't think the Governor-General can ever be successful in putting down the trend, but there may soon be assigned a special commissioner whose task it will be to greatly interfere with the flow of opium from Lintin Island, through Canton, and then into the provinces. While Canton's factories appear on the surface to have no direct role, they are a well-known steppingstone along the way."

"Howqua, you've be good and fair to deal with over the years. You're a friend of every agent who works here. To sleep in the lion's den means to assume some risk, which is what we've all undertaken to do. Our fate and fortunes depend on it," I reply.

"I am here to tell you that the pressure will continue to mount," Howqua says. "I must caution you, as my trusted client. The number of chests coming into the river each month only grows. My colleague and advisor to the governor, Pao Shih-ch'en recently cautioned me that he has been questioned in detail about how the situation in Canton should be handled. He points out that possible British seizure of Singapore could represent a serious threat to China. The Europeans could have a naval presence there and flood the countryside in that region with opium from that new location."

"It's only a matter of time, then," I say, my concerns growing by the minute, "before our arrangements and relationships will be threatened to a point where we're at serious risk of arrest?"

"Expulsion, more likely, for the Europeans and Americans, but the men left behind would be labeled *pàntú*, 'traitors,' and their lives surely threatened," Howqua says, gravely. "Take the case of your English colleague, William Jardine. He's well known as a foreign ringleader in this trade—with a reputation as a particularly unscrupulous merchant. His wealth is apparent to everyone; but he keeps authorities at arms-length by dealing with them 'gently,' as he puts it. Governor-General Teng was ordered by His Majesty to investigate his case and expel him. Jardine learned of this, and on the pretext of reviewing his records prior to departure, recently slipped away to Macao. From there, he's planning to take a ship to England, in the event they come in search of him at Macao. It's understood the Chinese navy would be ineffectual against a British vessel, so, like him, you must act with impunity."

"Thank you for coming to me with this information," I say, placing the palms of both hands on the table and rising, signaling the end of the meeting. "I'll speak to my people and the others I deal with, encouraging them to exercise caution. But I'm afraid we've awakened that lion I spoke of earlier, and controlling his appetite will be difficult, at best."

Howqua extends his hand to shake mine, Western style. 'An asset to all the agents in the factories, this clever man knows how to manage his relationships' I think, as I walk him to his sedan and waiting entourage. He's come to warn me that the complex relationship he enjoys with his Chinese counterparts—in the dark art of matching high-profile sellers with vast numbers of anonymous buyers in which he has been so complicit—might soon shrivel and die, exposed to the relentless light of day by men anxious to do the bidding of the emperor and his minions. I'm left with the following questions: if all of this is about to collapse, what will become of Howqua and his fortune...and what will become of me?

I return to my desk to hurriedly attend to several matters, calling Andrews in to alert him to the message delivered by Howqua, and warn him to use caution in all outside dealings. I then proceed through the fenced-in factory garden, passing under its high gateway to Respondentia Walk, leading to the river. There, a boat will take me on the ebb tide, for the eight-hour, two-part journey down river to Macao, where tomorrow I'm to meet with James Gulliver, captain of the *Hercules*, newly arrived from Bombay, and anchored off Lintin Island. In its hold: a million dollars' worth of Malwa opium, which I have every intention of selling to an ever-growing contingent of buyers.

44. Chasing the Dragon

ON A SPRING DAY IN '32, the aptly named Pearl and surrounding landscape has never been more appealing. A relentless April sun hangs low and heavy in the eastern sky, a mantle of amber light cascading down hillsides, flooding the harbor below. The river just beyond the bank of windows shimmers in ribbons of silver and saffron in the still morning air. Countless junks, sails hanging lifeless on slender spars, await the usual rising breeze to shake off the night's dew. Heaped against the Pearl's river banks, warrens of sampans slowly jostle on the currents, as generations of gōng (工.)—artisans and craftsmen, tinkers and thieves—'river people,' have already begun to stir, preparing to move goods and trinkets to shoreline stalls for sale, or to serve on any one of dozens of flat-bottomed wherries, slowly sculling the floating neighborhoods in search of itinerant crew to fish the river in these early hours.

I stand at the far end of the counting room, motionless in the early morning shadows. I observe my men, as I often have, hunched over desks, shuffling stacks of records, the shuffle of abacus beads a regular sound in a busy office. Time is marked by the slow tock...tock of the works in the cherry-wrought, tall case clock, and slow progression of sunlight and shadows cast over the hunched backs of my men. The angled rays, highlighted by a fine airborne cloud of dust, creep across the highly polished floor, and hovers as refracted rainbow shards on the ceiling, momentarily captured by stacks of crystal glassware on nearby shelves. My sense of time seems suspended at this moment, as though this scene might last forever.

In the twelve years I have lived in Canton and summered in Macao, to the south, I have mastered the art of the contract, won the loyalty of Europeans and Chinese, alike, and amassed a fortune for myself along the way—my so-called 'competency.' But the increasing violence and strained relations with my Chinese hosts has made it most difficult to conduct business. The bonds of trust, I can plainly see, are near a breaking point. And so too, it seems more apparent to me each day, that this world I have created by dint of pure conviction and determination, has become a fragile one, as well.

I had not slept well in recent days. Pangs of conscience seem to afflict me with greater frequency, now. I miss my family dearly and have increased concerns for my own safety and for my men. One fragile moment, years ago, I expressed to my partners back home that I 'feared I might never escape this place.' I have immersed myself in my appointed task, as I am wont to do, and my long-ago fear is probably grounded in the idea that I might get so caught up in my own ambition, that I might die here before allowing myself permission to go home.

My gut is now tied in knots much of the time, particularly on those occasions when I must leave the confines of the factory compound, where we all live and work. Increasingly, I've had to mingle with the locals along the broad Respondentia Walk leading to the custom house pier. I also travel with greater trepidation through the open waters of the Pearl to meet newly arrived vessels from India or the States, anchored at Lintin or Whampoa. Guilt—and *fear*—continue to gnaw at me with increased frequency in ways I can no longer ignore.

OF LATE, I have taken the unusual step of carrying a small, single-shot percussion pistol in my jacket pocket—a late invention by one, Joshua Deringer, of Philadelphia. I acquired it at the insistence of a ship's master hailing from that same port, who promised he could easily replace it with another. While only good for a few yards, the piece fit nicely into the palm of my hand and for that very reason has been *nekenamed* "peanut" by others. I knew that in a mêlée, discharging the gun would be of little value, but the noise and smoke alone might allow me time to escape further harm.

Standing at the edge of the busy room, I mindlessly pat my right pocket, assured that I've remembered to move 'peanut' to my new waistcoat today. Another reason for my recent discomfort is the unsafe streets and alleys behind our building which have, of late, become increasingly raucous and dangerous. Gangs of men and boys, armed with clubs and machetes, commandeer the streets of the city under cover of darkness. Their anger at the "foreign devils", or *gwai-lou* (鬼佬, 'ghost-man') has mounted steadily. Each night, with police scarcely to be found, they rove the streets behind the European and American factory buildings and along the narrow passageways leading to the river, pounding on the walls and doors. Cries of *Gwai-lou! Gwai-lou!* reverberate through the night air and into our offices, dormitories and dining halls. God help the poor European who might find himself accidentally caught up in such a mob scene.

Death and destruction have become increasingly commonplace, here. More than one poor local, believed to be in the employ of Western interests, and thus pitted against the powerful clans, is found hanged or with a cut throat in a conspicuous public location, when dawn arrives in the streets of Canton. These deaths and open display of corpses are intended to send messages to those merchants, suppliers and translators who cooperate with the agents and company men—like me and mine—connected to the sale of opium.

Fueled by official government pressure to limit opium sale and use, several edicts recently arrived from Beijing, declaring the growing volume of *yāpiàn* 'a scourge on Chinese culture, productivity and well-being.' The emperor's official delegation to the provinces along the coast, including Canton, Hong Kong, and Shenzhen, have ordered local and regional authorities to quell the illicit opium trade wreaking havoc among the population. The volume of opium brought into the Pearl River, then dispersed through runners pulling up alongside foreign ships in "fast crabs" and "scrambling dragons" has grown yearly. What once were mere cautionary notices have now become threatening demands, with the careers and very lives of those tasked with enforcement now on the line.

Despite the escalating demands to control the flow of opium into the country, admonitions have gone largely unheeded; principally because those public figures being asked to set limits on trafficking are the very same ones profiting handsomely from the transfer, sale, and distribution of *yāpiàn*. The British and American business interests (including my own Russell & Company) operate with impunity, even in the face of one constricting clamp-down after another. Fortunes made (and lost) in the opium business have proven to be far more lucrative than other commodities—cotton, tea, or furs, with their own supply limits—and *no one*, except for the emperor and his high-born sycophants, want to see that kind of commerce come to an end.

The recent rise in violence came to a head at the American factory in early May of '32. I believe we were specifically targeted because of our nationality, even though access to other nations' long-established factories along the row are just as vulnerable as ours to disruption. Those same roving gangs from the streets the night before, continue agitating in the morning hours. They have somehow been emboldened by something or someone—perhaps another of those night-time lynching—and feel no particular need to dissolve into the shops, sampans and houses lining the waterfront at sunrise. Ironically, within hours, these are probably the very men to be found, sooner or later, semi-conscious in local opium dens throughout the Old City.

≈

ON THIS DAY, my men are hard at work: some engaged in record-keeping; others in communication with our regular translators and hoppos; still more reconciling the week's transactions. Suddenly, a great thud sounds at the rear door opening onto Thirteen Factories Street. The door is violently stoved in, nearly knocking it off its hinges. A dozen angry men erupt into the room, clubs raised, screaming, *Gwailou Huí jiā! Gwailou Huí jiā!* go home, go home! My men are shocked, but not unprepared. The possibility of such incidents had been discussed, and rehearsed: they know to offer no resistance, dropping to the floor. Still, the Chinese mob surges forward, overturning tables and desks, running arms along the shelves, spilling ledger books, dishes, and glassware to the floor. Shards of porcelain and glass soon litter the room, heaps of debris...and blood!

Knives secreted under loose fitting shirts, and wooden clubs are wielded against the men huddled on the floor. Chaos reigns amid shouts and sounds of flesh-against-flesh, as my men rise to defend themselves. My pocket pistol will be no match for this angry crowd. But, I reach for it anyway, aiming blindly in the direction of a dark-shirted attacker. Just then, as he raises an arm to strike another blow, he glances in my direction. I pull the trigger and watch in horror—as if in slow motion—as my projectile enters his right eye, bursting it like a grape in a spray of blood. He falls lifelessly to the floor. He may well have been leader of the group, for when his fellow attackers witness this event, the pent-up violent energy and anger are suddenly siphoned from the room, and the gang of men leaves the building as abruptly as they had arrived, dissolving into the streets of the city.

A long silence follows, as the shock and horror of the event sink in. Two of my men are apparently dead: my Scottish assistant, Lindsay Andrews and company writer, Asha Gardner. Two more will require immediate medical attention for their wounds but are likely to survive. And the assailant lay where he fell, blood and brain matter spilling from his head wound. The derringer is still in my hand, trembling as though I still believe it might be of use.

I stare out the window, taking stock of the ordered world beyond this one, the embankment and the river scene, bustling as always. The sun, now high above us, shines as brightly as ever.

I move to kneel at Lindsay's side, surveying the distorted, blood-soaked visage of the man I had come to depend on for so much. He stares back at me with lifeless eyes. I look away in shock and disbelief. Beyond the confines of the factory building, a faded green lawn extends to the fence separating the compound from the broad esplanade bordering the river. Farther out, countless vessels move in every direction, oblivious of the horrific scene that has so suddenly and fatally disrupted our well-ordered world.

The men slowly gather strength, administering to the wounded, calling for authorities and medical assistance, and righting furniture, as though by doing so, they can somehow erase the trauma of events that has befallen us all here today. Amid the confusion, I direct two men to proceed to our nearby warehouse to retrieve two canvas sails and cordage to wrap the bodies of Andrews and Gardner. They'll be stored in the cool cellar, our building's 'go-down,' where camphor wood storage racks will protect the remains from vermin and other invaders, until I can plan for their burial.

45. Morpheus Dreams

LATER IN THE DAY, after some semblance of order returns to the counting room, and local authorities have completed their reports and removed the body of the gang leader, I call the men together.

"Gentlemen, I fear for our safety. This office will remain vulnerable for the foreseeable future. We have no way of knowing what those hooligans might be planning next. They were frightened off by the fatal wounding of their leader but may be reorganizing at this very moment. I suspect I was their ultimate target, but the tables were turned, and events played out otherwise."

"We're not afraid of those bastards, Mr. Russell...excuse my French," one man offers. We beat them back when they tried to kill Sun-shing, and we got 'em where they slept after that heist at Lintin. Let us at 'em, Mr. Russell.

"Yah, Lindsay was such a nice, hardworking kid, and Asha, just doing his job. They didn't deserve to die," another adds.

My new colleague, William Lowe, then pipes in, "Gentlemen, we know emotions are running high. But we can't let emotions trump reason. We have a business to run, yes, but extreme measures must be taken to prevent further injury and loss of life. I'll be accompanying you for the next phase. Our time away will be temporary. If we're lucky, you'll be back here at your desks in a week."

"Hear me out," I say at that point, hoping to appeal to reason at a moment of heightened emotion. "As Mr. Lowe indicated, I've decided we're going to vacate the office for a few days, until I can talk to some people and learn more about the how and why of this incident. I've already spoken to our friends at the English factory next door, and they will loan us a couple of vessels to move all of us to Whampoa for the time being. You'll pack a bag and pull together the necessary papers to stay productive. Be ready to go at six tonight. The tide will have turned and there'll be enough daylight to see you all safely to *Pilgrim*, a Brown and Ives Company brig, at anchor there."

William adds, "so look sharp men. You've got two hours to get ready to leave."

As the men begin to stir, I raise my hand with an additional thought. "Besides, I want you all in Whampoa in the morning. I've asked Li-Min to contact the undertaker here in the Old City to provide me with two coffins, as soon as possible. They'll be modest—just pine boxes, really—less that each of these men deserve, but time is of the essence. I'll not be far behind you heading down river. The second loaner from the Brits will carry me, a missionary from our program and the two bodies, all under cover of darkness to Whampoa, as well. A couple of armed English security men have offered to come along for protection from God-who-knows-what."

"Beg pardon," says one young man, so fresh from the states that I don't yet know his name. "Asha bein' a good friend a' mine since I got here, and Lindsay such a gentleman to us all, I'd kinda like t' keep them company, goin' home, an' all."

I hesitate for a minute, then say, "Alright, I'll allow for two men, including you, mister...?"

"Bell, sir, William Bell."

"Very well, Mr. Bell, select another to accompany us, based on what you know of friendships among you, and we shall be off at nine, tomorrow night. Be prepared to put your backs to the oar if the evening winds die on us. We must be at Whampoa by sunrise on Thursday. And one more thing: for the men departing at six today, ask the master of *Pilgrim* if he would kindly dispatch a contingent of five men to the Protestant cemetery on Dane's Island at daybreak to pay for and prepare two fresh graves for our men. Your combined presence there two days hence will do these two men a great honor as we lay them to rest."

And with that, knowing the staff will be secure elsewhere tonight, I remain behind to tend to affairs and, and as a matter of honoring and ensuring the safety of the bodies, I chose to remain in the presence of the departed. My task, while I await word from Li-Min regarding delivery of the coffins tomorrow, is to write to the families of these two men. Of Asha Gardner's location, I am certain my sources in Providence will be able to trace survivors, as he was a local boy who signed onto a company vessel only recently arrived from there.

Lindsay Andrews' origins in Edinburgh will prove to be more difficult. He came to me like a bolt from the blue, having traveled on an Indiaman from Calcutta. I will do all I can, relating his story after he came to me, and then placing the letter in the hands of an East India Company vessel bound for London, in the hopes that a conscientious ship's master will take it upon himself to blaze a trail to the north and eventually to his family of origin. They must be left with so many questions as this young man set out so unexpectedly on life's adventure, leaving what must be a giant void behind.

After spending hours completing a carefully worded document for what I imagine a concerned family halfway around the world, I sign with my name and, 'May God speed this tome to its source.'

~

IT IS NEAR midnight as I complete my task. I impulsively decide for my own safety to spend the night on the roof of the factory. That will place me three stories above the street, giving the impression the building is empty and well out of harms' way, especially as I can configure an outside barrier to the stairway. Once I ascend, I select a sheltered spot for blanket and pillow, away from the precipitous drop to the street below, and with the full benefit of a brilliant night sky and cool breezes streaming down from the mountains.

Even though I'm emotionally and physically exhausted, sleep does not come easily. I am fitful and haunted by images from the previous day, and by many more from recent weeks, for that matter. All seems in turmoil around me, the fabric of what I have so hard to create, torn irreparably. I close my eyes, hoping that the numbness of Morpheus's welcome spell will overtake me. In my state of half-consciousness, the specter of Li-Min appears in the darkness before me. He stands over me, silent for what seems an eternity. A short, shadowy figure is just behind him, motionless and silent, as well.

Finally, he speaks to me, in slow, measured tones such as I haven't heard before. "Sam, I am sorry to come to you so late. It is the Hour of the Ox, but there is someone I want you to meet. This is my cousin, Lim-pai, who was once an addict, but now a recovered opium smoker. I want you to go with him tonight. I think you can learn much in the company of this man. Li-Min extends his hand to me, as I lie startled and uncertain of the unfolding events. But I take his hand and rise to my feet. I explain that I am now unshod and disheveled after a harrowing day. Yet, without speaking, he urges me to come to the light where I adopt a disguise he brought—a dark, nondescript shirt and loose trousers, a broad-brimmed hat pulled down to hide my white face.

I now find myself at the back door of the factory, where Li-Min and his man, Lim-pai, and I slip out into the night and the depths of Old Canton, an area strictly forbidden to Westerners at most times, and particularly this time of night. Once inside the walls of the old city, though. Li-Min, bids us goodbye. Old Canton at night—the part few Westerners ever see—is alive with shadowy figures standing or sitting in front of their stores or houses, darting noiselessly about in thick, felt-soled shoes, or leaning from the windows of their lodge-rooms and restaurants. Some are quietly smoking small tobacco pipes in doorways, the sweet smell lingering in still night air; others are wildly gesticulating and conversing in Cantonese; while still others disappear into dim alleys, as the raspy tone of a gong announces the opening of the many gambling saloons coming alive at this hour.

Descending a few steps into the basement of one of the houses, Lim-pai and I come into a small open space containing a table, a chair, a stool, and a small stove of peculiar design. Nearby are two small roughly constructed square rooms. A curtain is draped across a rude window on one. Pungent clouds of smoke emanated from the darkness within. In the small room to the left, I observe a crowd of men excitedly clustered about a high table covered with matting. The light of a single oil lamp shines upon their shadow-mottled faces, revealing all eyes fixed upon an old man, deftly manipulating some metal game pieces. They are playing a game of chance known as *fai-tan* or tan, *Lim-pai* explains.

The keeper of the table has a pile of bright coin before him. He takes a double handful, lays them on the table, then covers them with a bowl. Those standing outside the rail are to guess the remainder left there on the table after the pile has been divided by four, whether 1, 2, 3, or nothing. The guess and stake of each person is first recorded by a clerk. The keeper then carefully picks out the coins, four-by-four. The raucous, inebriated crowd watches this man's movements carefully. Cheating is almost impossible, as twenty very vigilant players, or as few as two will be scrutinizing the old man's every move. Tobacco smoke wafts to the ceiling as everyone grows silent, awaiting the final tally. The winners—there appear to be several, based on who comes closest—erupt in jubilant cries and laughter as the pot is divided up. The process is then repeated, with men spilling more coins on the table, hoping or more luck in the next round.

We find yet another room, farther into the bowels of the cavernous space. It is boarded halfway up in front, from which point small wooden bars run to the ceiling, separating it from the boisterous gaming anteroom. Behind the bars stands a pleasant-faced man who, with scales in hand, is weighing out some opium. In the dim light, I can make out a single wooden bunk covered with matting, upon which a group of three younger men are engaged in smoking their pipes. In a long a narrow passage running between the two rooms we come upon a small, pillared altar on which a light and some sweet smelling pastils are burning. Turning to the right we feel our way in the darkness along a damp stone wall, and through a low doorway, to find ourselves in yet another smoking-room.

Within a few moments, after our eyes have adjusted to the semi-gloom, we realize the low-ceilinged room is made of rough-hewn boards, around three sides of which run low wooden bunks, some four feet in width. In the back part of the room there are two tiers of bunks. Close to the ceiling is a narrow, grated window, the only means of ventilation. Upon these bunks are stretched transversely, in parties of two or three, some twelve men and women—Chinese, and from appearances, some Westerners—all engaged in cooking and smoking opium. The scene is rank with the acrid, vinegary odor of opium. The recumbent forms, quiescent faces half lit by small opium lamps, subdued conversation, sizzling and bubbling of the pipes, all impress me with an astonishment suggesting something uncanny or other-worldly.

This decrepit, subterranean warren is like many others we visit that night, cleverly hidden behind shop façades, densely packed into poor neighborhoods. It is in these opium houses where most Cantonese smoke, and from one-to-twenty may be found here during the afternoon, night, and until early the next morning (after 3 a.m., the Hour of the Tiger). Besides these 'joints,' there are multitudes of others scattered around the market district, posing as ordinary businesses by day, and devolving into opium dens by night. Some even smoke in the back rooms of Chinese laundries by day, where the prevailing smells of lye and laundry soap masks more nefarious activities; while others, provided they have the resources, gather, fully outfitted, to smoke together in private rooms. These dens and private spaces are ubiquitous throughout the city—too numerous to count—where even transient strangers can gather.

In our travels on one narrow street, there is a doorway presided over by a woman and her two daughters—whom I recognize from my time by the river—appearing to wave us in. The gently fluttering banner hanging overhead reads, 'baskets and cooking pots,' which Lim-pai demonstrates for me with hand gestures. Two women approach from the other direction and turn to enter, dipping their heads beneath the banners, to be swallowed up by the darkness within. "Many females are so sexually excited when first smoking opium," Lim-pai explains, again with a smattering of English and elaborate pantomime, "Older smokers beckon them in, to ruin them by turning to crime and prostitution. For this, they receive money, too. Many innocent girls have been seduced by this drug at the hands of these women," he expresses with difficulty, to which I nod assent.

The last opium-house we enter is situated mere paces from the entrance to the Governor-General's palace. Four or five rooms, in different parts of a square court, are occupied by men stretched out on crude couches of various types, on which lay a head-pillow, with lamps, pipes, and other apparatus for smoking opium. In one part of the largest room the proprietor stands apart. overseeing a small table with delicate brass balances. He is weighing out small portions of a dark, thick, semi-fluid the consistency of molasses on scraps of paper. The proprietor then transfers a small spoon's worth of the black paste to a silver pipe, lighting it with a certain flourish—enough to attract the attention of a few bystanders. This small company of opium-smokers gathers closer to indulge in the expensive fumes. Except for the most affluent, increasing poverty has placed this concentrate and its effects beyond their reach. The chance to cluster around the smoking embers of this concentrated drug keeps them coming back for more of what they can afford.

Seeing a familiar face in the person of Lim-pai, a group of men soon gathers around us, entering animated conversation. And while I couldn't understand what was being said, my guide's hand gestures, and vigorous shaking of his head tells me they're inviting him back into the fold of addiction. To his credit, he remains resolute, even while surrounded by a motley group of sallow, sunken cheeked, glassy-eyed compatriots, apparently regaling the specifics of their own degradation.

We sit and speak in rapt attention while another man, Heh-ven, who never stops conversing. His hands are busy, and his eyes are fixed on what he is doing—knitting I thought at first—wondering why nobody had ever mentioned this craft was practiced by Chinese men? Then I see what I had taken for yarn woven between the two needles he manipulates is a kind of gummy stuff, dark and thick. As he rotates the needle ends about each other, the stuff behaves like taffy in the act of setting; it changes color, too, slowly evolving from its earlier dark brown to tan. At a certain moment, just as it seems about to stiffen, he wraps the whole wad around one needle end and picks up a pottery object about as big around as a teacup. It looks rather like a cup, except it was closed across the top, with a rimmed hole in the middle of this fixed lid.

Heh-ven then plunges the wadded needle into this hole, withdrawing it, leaving the wad sticking up from the hole, and modeling the rapidly hardening stuff so that it sits on the cup like a tiny volcano. He then picks up a piece of polished bamboo with a large hole near one end, edged with a band of chased silver. Into this he fixes the cup, placing the opposite end of the bamboo into his mouth, holds the cup with the tiny cone suspended above the lamp flame, and inhales deeply. The stuff bubbles and evaporates as he does so, until nothing of it is left, a cloud of blue, gauzy smoke rises from his mouth, enveloping me in a dizzying haze.

I can feel myself being guided through this dark, cramped space, into clear night air. Focus and attention to my surrounding slowly returns. Once again Li-Mĭn has joined us and we begin to walk, a waxing moon casting its cold yellow light on the cobbled streets of the Old City.

≈

"I FIND MYSELF barely able to deal with the horrors I've witnessed tonight," I say to Li-Mĭn. "But Lam-pai showed amazing strength and courage to resist the temptation we encountered out there. I am so thankful to him for taking me on this journey."

Li-Min interprets for Lam-pai's benefit. Lam-pai hesitates for a moment. "I see too much bad when I had *yāpiàn* in my life. It was making me an old man, before I am ready for that time. They die young, those people we saw, the ones I talk to...they will die if they don't stop," he explains through Li-Mĭn. "They want to be free, but cannot escape that place, their friends who do it too."

"It is all over this city, even in the shadow of the governor-general's palace," I say to Li-Mĭn.

"I know. That's why I wanted you to see this for yourself," he says.

Lam-pai speaks at length to Li-Mĭn, appearing to count on his fingers. "You understand, Sam, Lam-pai was a dealer once. Had a shop like the ones you visited. Believed it couldn't touch him. Then he fell in, fell prey himself. He explains to me the six evils of opium-smoking." With that, Li-Mĭn takes Lam-pai's hand, signaling him to raise one finger at a time while he explains. Holding up trembling fingers, Li-Mĭn slowly counts them off, one-by-one: "1. Loss of appetite. 2. Loss of strength. 3. Loss of money. 4. Loss of time. 5. Loss of longevity. 6. Loss of virtue, leading to recklessness and gambling...the insidious effects of temptation, like a drunkard's life... worse than drunkenness, extreme dizziness and vomiting, unbearable cravings early in the morning...an early death."

"No desire to return," I say, a statement, rather than question, by way of expressing my understanding of Lam-pai's struggle and determination to recover. "You saved yourself," I say reassuringly.

Li-Mĭn translates. "Yes, no one would," according to Lam-pai, "but no one can save those people tonight unless they can escape, themselves. Each day, more give up, die. Many ships come. They bring more and more *yāpiàn*. The police they do nothing. The merchants just buy more, and it goes out into the countryside."

≋

SUDDENLY, I FIND myself back on the rooftop just as the sun is rising, wrapped in my blanket, and shaking from the morning's chill. Even as I pull open the fire door to descend the stairs, I imagine hearing a handful of men already arriving in the counting room. I can so envision Andrew in the center of it all, organizing papers at his desk. "Give me a few minutes," I'd say from across the room. "I've had a bit of a night. Will fill you in later." Andrew always seemed to understand.

The events of the night are deeply disturbing. To think of it abstractly is one thing... being transported into the very underbelly of the city to witness the pain, hardship and sacrifice of young lives fills me with disgust...not for them, but for myself and all I must represent in their eyes. It is just dawn as I stumble to my room. Still reeling from the nightmarish odyssey, and knowing I still must arrange for the bodies in the go-down to be brought to Whampoa for burial today, I fall on my unmade bed, my eyes red-rimmed and fixed on a small crack in the ceiling. Fully clothed, I soon fall into fitful sleep, briefly dreaming of a day—I might have been nine-or-ten—when I witnessed my father slaughter a pig for Christmas dinner.

46. Fugitive

THREE DAYS AFTER THE attack on our offices and following the burials of Andrews and Gardner in the Danes Island cemetery, I make plans to return to the factory in Canton. Before I depart the deck of *Pilgrim*, I offer sincere thanks to the vessel's master for his assistance in funeral plans. I promise my staff, now displaced from their usual workstations, that they must make every effort to keep current their records under these extreme circumstances, with the understanding that they will all be back on site, once I get a measure of the dangers, if any, awaiting us.

Once again, I travel north from Whampoa by night, with *Pilgrim's* first officer and a crew of two to accompany me on a gaff rigged sloop under the Brown & Ives Company ensign. We tie up at Jackass Point three hours later, and I'm relieved to see Respondentia Way nearly deserted, except for a few inebriated sailors lying about and a scattering of Chinese merchants setting up their stands for the new day's trade. I ask the crew if they'd be willing to stand by until I can garner more information. We agreed they would move the vessel to an anchorage one-hundred yards offshore to await a signal from me as to how to proceed: one candle in the factory's first floor window would mean, 'depart'; two closely placed candles, come retrieve me. I suggested they may have to wait for some hours before a signal might come. Given the life-and-death nature of the situation, they readily agreed, cautioning safety on my part, above all.

Placing the key into the garden-level door, I enter the now-empty counting room. I remain in the shadows beside the door to the kitchen for some time, not able to bring myself to stand on the bloodstained spot where Lindsay's body once lay. A quick glance in the crazed, discolored mirror over the sideboard and I barely recognize myself: face drawn and haggard; hair still tussled from a paucity of sleep for three straight nights; a mind dulled by lingering images of vivid dreams invading my senses whenever I briefly close my eyes, however briefly.

I stare blankly out the factory windows, beyond the balustrades and yellowing lawn, the gardens, and fences, to focus at last on the river, itself. I muse that traffic on the Pearl is heavier than usual for this time of night. I consider the disastrous events of previous days—my opium-ridden nightmare, the deadly raid on our offices, my role in the death of the gang leader, Andrews untimely loss and burial. I had come to think of him as a son, like my own so many miles away. I find myself hoping the violence taking place in my counting room will go unnoticed, absorbed like so much else of the teeming life in this city. But, in consultation with Li-Min and fearing arrest by local authorities for possession of a weapon in the confines of the factory, to say nothing of the shooting, a *murder* charge—justifiable or not—he's telling me I might be apprehended at any moment!

"Mr. Russell...Sam," Li-Min later comes to explain, "I have just spoken with Howqua and the other influential hongs, and they are saying that the authorities are in an uproar. Word is on its way to Beijing, and if it hasn't reached there already, a directive will certainly come down that may jeopardize your safety. The emperor knows of your extensive reputation with the *yāpiàn* trader, and he will not be merciful. You will become *un mùbiāo*, you know...a target, what you English call a scape goat."

"If I remain here in Canton, can you mount a defense for me? You know this side of the law as well as anyone.

"It will be difficult. You were justified in your actions, yes? We know that. You would be tried in the court of public opinion, though. Things are very negative right now. Feelings of resentment running deep. The governor-general is gathering his people to meet later today. You may have just a few hours to make a decision."

"Suggestions?"

"Retreat...for a while. Do what any smart military general might do when threatened. Go to a neutral place where you aren't well known. Not Macao. Maybe Shanghai, Bombay, with your friend Jeejeebhoy, Hawai'i, even Valperese. Wait some time. I will advocate for you in your absence. Say it was business that took you away. Let the passions die down."

"I'm needed here, though."

"You have men here, more than most operations. There's William Low and Augustus Heard, now. You have a company that they can carry on. Your life is in danger, this I know. Everything is getting more dangerous. Not what you bargained for, yes?"

"How will I know...?"

"I will make a point of communicating...reports, updates. I'll see to it that you stay informed. You can decide when its safe to come back."

"Can you stay? I want to call my men together. Make a plan."

"Yes, I can stay. But, let me go to meet with Howqua. Tell him of our conversation. He might be able to get us some additional time."

"Yes, please. Kindly be back to me in two hours, though. I've a boat standing by awaiting word of my plans, and I have accommodations with my staff at Whampoa if it's not safe to remain here."

47. Flight

BEFORE DAY'S END, I'm able to signal the crew waiting on Pilgrim's sloop to return to Whampoa. I decide it would be an act of cowardice to leave immediately for Whampoa, and the safe harbor afforded by Pilgrim and her captain. Instead, I explain to Li-Min that I want to opportunity to meet with Howqua and the other hongs to explain the circumstances under which I decided to use a firearm during the office invasion. I'm convinced that reason can win out over emotion in this case, and that I might be able to safely return to business as usual. The Canton System under which we'd been functioning since the day I arrived—a kind of unwritten rule book—allowing for fairness in negotiations, taxation favoring all levels of government, unwritten financial arrangements with key officials and a willingness to comply with more obvious local and regional regulations during business, has served as an unwritten guide.

Howqua, clearly agitated by my request to draw him into this conflict, upbraids me when we finally meet. Speaking through Li-Min, he says, "Mister Sam, you have always understood that the system has allowed for two kinds of trade with Chinese merchants, the kind that is allowed under the Old Canton System—American goods in trade for our silks and teas. The other kind of trade involving opium is prohibited at Canton, something you knew to be true. Yet, you persisted...yes to our mutual benefit, but also at the expense of our reputation. Your actions drew the attention of local hooligans, but they also exposed us all and our arrangement in the process."

"Howqua, there is no evidence this attack was prompted by anger over opium. Temperatures have been rising in the city for months now, even years. They resent our presence, all of us. Mine was an easy target because I am one of the busiest. My Chinese runners, compradors and others working for me are always visible in the warehouses and on the waterfront. The taxes I pay at customs house must be known to others...a real cause for anger, I would guess."

"Perhaps," says Howqua, "with the result that you are too large for your own good..."

"...For your own *safety*," Li-Min adds, further clarifying where he believes Howqua is going with his argument.

"I am told your Li-Min has advised you leave for a while, to allow from things to return to normal, to what we've had as our arrangement, which your men will know how to carry on, yes?"

"Yes, I suppose so..."

"I have learned that the authorities, Viceroy Li Hungpin, Governor Lu K'un, and the lead hoppo, Yen-lung, have been examining the books of the other hongs—one by one—and finding discrepancies in the totals of exports and import revenues for recent years," Li-Min says. "The only explanation for the difference is illicit income from undocumented opium. Howqua has been spared this indignity thus far. Your absence will be useful, for me to dissuade the authorities from taking up Howqua's books, saving him the embarrassment and possibly his position—one always helpful to you and your company, yes?"

"Yes, and *yes,*" I say, my voice raised in frustration, as the inevitability of what I must do becomes clearer by the minute. After a minute-or-two of contemplation, eyes lowered, thoughts rushing, I say, "I must meet with my men, first."

"Excellent," says Li-Mîn, as he speaks to Howqua, who smiles with approval. "I will arrange passage for you to Whampoa on a local fishing vessel. Dress unobtrusively and be ready to depart at midnight. You will never be detected."

≈

I DECIDE IN the unobstructed silence of my dormitory room at the factory, that if I'm to leave Canton, it will be best to return all the way to New England. There, I can assess my best next step, addressing all those matters that have lain unattended for the last four years: marriage, family, homestead, community. I hastily pack my duffle with little more in the way of possessions than when I first arrived, twelve years ago. My accumulated worldly goods are precious and few.

What I have of genuine value resides one story below in the form of my company ledges, and the assets I have amassed through my company. Careful documentation already exists. I have kept immaculate books in duplicate. It will remain for my counsel in Connecticut to coordinated with my partners here, to insure a steady flow of income once back in Middletown. Nearing the appointed time, I throw my bag over my shoulder and head for the garden door. One last look around and I step out into the cool night air for one last trip to Jackass Point, where Li-Mîn and his transport, a two-masted salt junk are already waiting. I bid Li-Mîn an emotional farewell and ask that, in my absence, he stand ready to lend his assistance on any legal matters that may arise when lawyers back home eventually correspond with my partners here. Naturally, he agrees.

As I step aboard the salt junk, with its fully battened brown sails, the crew of three Cantonese offer silent bows of greeting and we are soon underway, down river. I settle into the rush bench under a broad mat arch, subtly patting my breast pocket, reassured that the one document I needed to create before leaving the factory—one long overdue and that I am entitled to as company owner—is still neatly tucked away. It is a draft drawn against our accounts at Russell & Company's New York bank in the amount of $50,000; enough, I believe, to address my immediate needs once I return to Middletown.

≈

SHIPS OF ALL nations are anchored at Whampoa, some newly arrived and laden with goods to be sold to merchants in Canton, others, their bellies empty and awaiting delivery of tea, porcelain and silks from factories and looms in the countryside, others about to depart, once their holds were sufficiently packed with product, awaiting inspection and taxing by the hoppo, before being approved for departure.

It was my good fortune, after relying on *Pilgrim* for so much in previous days, to have our company vessel, *Providence,* lying nearby at anchor for weeks there, preparing for imminent departure. It was under the command of the capable, Obadiah Meeke. It's cleared with customs to depart for Boston on the next morning's tide —fully loaded with eighteen-hundred cases of Oolong and Black teas, sugar, cassia, silks, ribbons, fans, chinaware, mats, window blinds, rice paper umbrellas, firecrackers, and sweetmeats.

It was not so much that I fear justice for the events of the previous day, but I dread the form of Chinese justice that would likely be meted out to me as a wealthy

Westerner. Any trial—even one with Li-Min's intersession—would be conducted in a highly public setting, presided over by a team of Manchu judges and one officer serving under a Western flag. There would be no jury, merely a final majority pronouncement from the bench.

Any witnesses called, except for my own men, would likely support the perpetrators' side of the story, with little or no allowance for self-defense as a reasonable claim. A capital sentence would almost certainly result in a death sentence of one form or another, not-so-swiftly delivered. Any thought of a mitigated ruling, based on the idea of being a foreign national, would be hard to find. The history of past altercations in China proves Western business interests will always favor maintaining the tenuous *status quo.* No single American life is worth the millions to be made by stirring a Chinese hornet's nest, further threatening the fragile, unspoken alliances undergirding the opium trade.

≈

ON MAY 1, 1832, I am safely underway aboard *Providence,* bow pointed to the open Pacific. Any risk of a forced boarding by harbor authorities as we're piloted down river to Macao Narrows has passed. I am presently taking pen to journal, to carefully document this recent series of events. I hope it serves others as a cautionary tale to the dangers while in service to corporate interests in the 'Celestial Kingdom.' In my imagination, China can seem so far removed from the realities of business life back home; but, as I have learned, it can become its own form of hell.

As the Pearl's estuary broadens near Lintin Island, we take note, though, of a large junk man-o-war shadowing us a thousand yards off our starboard beam. Before breaking off, however, a single cannon report resounds from the vessel, with the resultant splash well ahead of our intended course. This threatening gesture by government authorities is likely intended to avoid any direct confrontation, while communicating their awareness of my presence on board. The message: 'fare thee well, not to return.'

Fame and fortune can be gained in many ways. My choice, for myself, family and partners, thousands of miles—and a world away—was to come to Canton to accomplish just that. In that limited sense, I have succeeded. Addiction is a disease that enslaves the mind; but it is no *less* dangerous, or fatal, than the epidemics of alcohol and tobacco prolific in society. Have we, as Westerners, been complicit in its promulgation? Yes, but are we singularly responsible for its effects on the population of China and other parts of the world? Perhaps, although the opium blight has existed as part of civilization for millennia. Can we stop this poisonous flow by virtue of any single individual's actions? The answer there, too, is that *that* time has long since passed.

I accomplished what I came to do, create a successful company at the far edge of the Pacific. What I found there was an existing culture and a business model adopted by many others before me. I simply took what I found—at great personal risk—and made it my own. That was my obligation to myself, my partners and banking interests, those who invested in me. I believe I left the company in good hands, to continue prospering for all involved, including myself.

But I must return to my home and family, to seek opportunity in a world that has undergone dramatic transformations since my departure in '19. Technology and western expansion will offer me new opportunities. I will apply my new-found fortune and hard-won skills to take advantage of those developments.

I assure myself I did not venture out from my Connecticut home, so many years ago, with malicious intent. As a young man, I did not view China so much as a destination, rather as a mystical state-of-mind, shaped by exotic images of ancient, narrow streets and splendid, golden temples. I arrived at the far margins of the world in '19, filled with well-intentioned plans to sell miscellaneous goods and slowly accrue my fortune. What I discovered after just a few weeks shocked my senses and good judgment. I witnessed young men, like me, making spectacular fortunes, at little risk to themselves or their sponsors back home. I learned from the British, Indian, and Chinese businessmen, alike—so many clever and engaging personalities—how to act in the service of those ambitions. We worked in concert at the expense of the nameless, faceless throngs I would never have to confront.

I can recall, years ago, standing in John Jacob Astor's library, as he explained to me the key to wealth: 'Read the future by reading the facts in front of you,' he told me. I'm afraid I missed the wisdom in his comment at the time. I was still young and brash, loaded with more principle than experience. My determination had not yet been tested in the real world. Once in China, did I succumb to temptation? Yes, more quickly than I ever imagined I would. My usual level head was flooded—like a hapless creature in a rapidly rising, swift current—lured by a promise of riches with no upper limit. I was quickly swept away in that raging tide, just as certainly as any stray creature finds itself overwhelmed in a deluge. Caught up in those opportunities, I immediately wrote to persuade my employers in Providence to alter our business plans...our fortunes *surely* lay in the opium trade. I made that determination deliberately, with a free and open mind. It is a choice I shall quietly and solemnly abjure, for the remainder of my life.

≈

AFTER THAT FATEFUL meeting, when Li-Min encouraged me to leave Canton for the sake of my own life and the company's future, he apparently left the American factory, bypassing his own quarters, going directly to the house of the governor-general. Howqua was there, as well. "He's leaving within a few hours," he told them. "I've placed the fear of his god into his heart. He believes he's about to be arrested, and he's planning to flee to avoid a trial. We should allow this to happen. Let him believe he's made fools of us by escaping justice. We have finally succeeded in chasing this *gong-gōng*, this copper-headed dragon, out of town."

It will be years before I would learn of his deception and betrayal from a company employee. In the years that follow my return to America, good fortune continues to favor me and that of Howqua, further adding to his enormous wealth and influence with the men I left behind to run my company. War for the Chinese would eventually— inevitably—erupt with Britain over the opium question, and the mystery of Li-Mǐn's identity, his carefully orchestrated role in my story, and his tragic demise would be fully revealed.

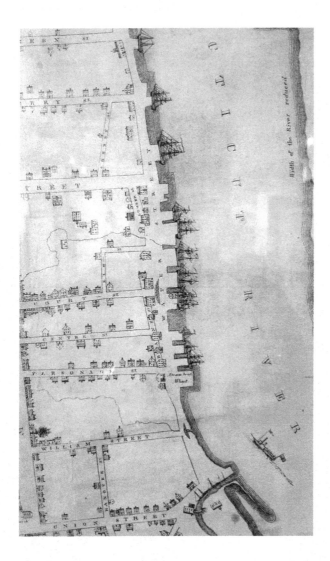

CLOCKWISE FROM TOP LEFT:

A youthful Samuel Russell (1789-1862).

A mature portrait of Russell, hanging in the Russell House, Wesleyan University, Middletown, Connecticut. *Property Wesleyan University*

Aerial view (partial) of Middletown's streets and riverfront docks (1851) *Collection, Russell Library, Middletown, CT.*

Ad for families to work in New England fabric mills, a staple of 19th c. regional economy (note factory owned by Samuel Colt's father)

Watercolor of Middletown, Conn.'s busy waterfront and docks (c. 1800) *Collection, Middlesex County Historical Society, Middletown, Connecticut*

CLOCKWISE FROM TOP LEFT:

Succession of Qing Dynasty emperors engaged with opium trade crisis:

Qianlong [Hongli] (1735-96)

Jaiqing [Jai] (1796-1820)

Paoguang [Minning] (1820-50)

Procession of Emperor Hongli to meet English delegation (1793), on Summer Palace hunting grounds, in futile attempted to negotiate China trade deal.

In this late 18th c. English caricature, Macartney and his delegation's gifts, meant to entice a deal, are slighted as unneeded 'toys.'

George Macartney, 1st Earl Macartney headed the mission to China to personally engage the emperor, requesting expanded trade with England. *Lemuel Francis Abbott, Portrait of Lord George Macartney (c. 1777). National Portrait Gallery, London*

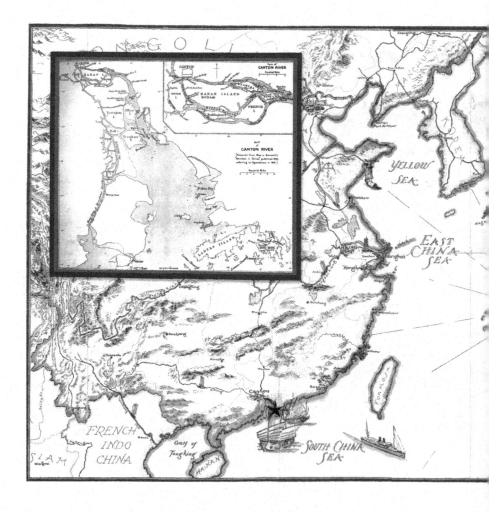

CLOCKWISE FROM TOP LEFT:

Map of Chinese mainland, with insert, featuring Macao, Hong Kong, the Pearl River, Lintin Island and Canton, all located on southeast coast. Beijing, nation's capital is 1200 miles to the NNE.

Lintin Island and harbor in Pearl estuary, north of Macao. Arriving Western vessels were expected to anchor here, awaiting Chinese tax man and river pilot for transport upriver to Whampoa. British & American "go-down" vessels sold opium, directly off ships to local opium runners on, 'crab boats' and 'scrambling dragons.'

Chinese artist, An unusual view of the Praya Grande at Macao, ca. 1830. Oil on canvas, 25 1/2 x 34 x 3" Gift of Russell Sturgis Paine, 1958, M9751.1. *Courtesy of the Peabody Essex Museum*

CLOCKWISE FROM TOP LEFT:

View up the Pearl toward 'Boca Tigres,' heavily Chinese fortified narrows leading to large boat anchorage and eventually, to Canton and the Thirteen Factories.

Chinese artist, View of Guangzhou (Canton), ca. 1800. Watercolor and gouache on paper, China, 24 1/2 x 47" *Museum purchase with funds donated anonymously, 1975, E79708 Courtesy of the Peabody Essex Museum*

Anchorage at Whampoa, where Western vessels were required to anchor, avoiding shallow waters on Canton harbor. Goods were off-loaded here to smaller vessels for transport to warehouses upriver near Western factories. Delays of months to first sell cargo, and bring Chinese goods aboard meant upper rigging was removed to prevent weathering, damage. Note utility sheds and well-known temple landmark in distance. Detail, Whampoa Anchorage (from Dane's Island, with British, American, Portuguese, French, Swedish, Danish, and Dutch shipping), Chinese School (c. 1810). *Private collection*

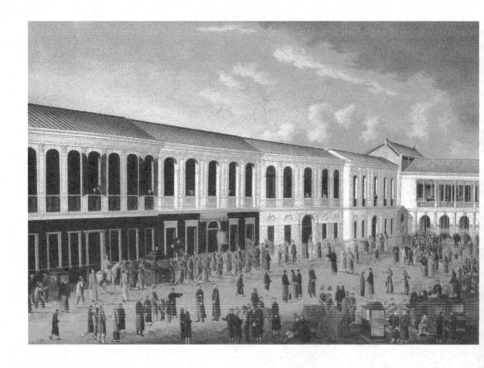

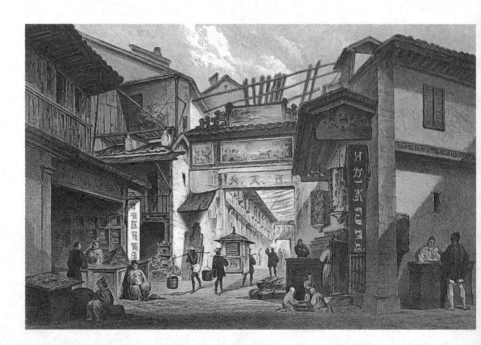

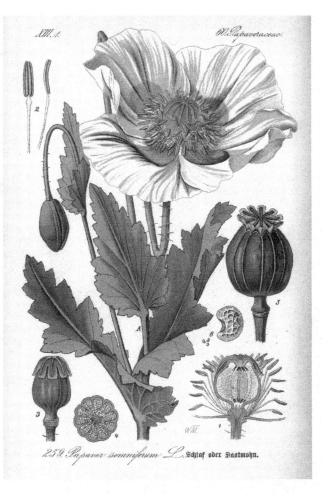

CLOCKWISE FROM TOP LEFT:

Another view of Thirteen factories, with wide, Respondentia Walk between buildings and river front. "Close View of the 13 Factories of Canton" (c. 1807). Hong Kong Museum of History.

18th c. illustration for *Papaver somniferum* (L.), and its extract, opium, which eventually replaced silver as the medium of exchange, reversing wealth flow out of England, U.S.

Spanish silver '8-reale' coin, profiling King Carlos IV, served as international currency in 18-19th c. Millions' worth flowed into China, purchasing teas, silks and porcelain, disrupting global balance of trade. Note: multiple 'chops' signify not counterfeit. Transactions using parts of a reale called, "pieces of eight."

Romanticized view of 'Streets of Canton' (1830). Westerners complained of "filth in streets" behind factories, despite daily clean up, particularly "stench from butcheries and fish mongers." Lithograph from illustrated text, 19th c., Collection British Library

CLOCKWISE FROM TOP LEFT:

Chinese trade agent (Hong), Howqua [Wu Bingjian] (1769-1843), one of many go-betweens (Co-hongs), needed for Westerners to sell to merchants. Howqua worked closely with Samuel Russell, earning mutual trust. In his day, Howqua was one of the wealthiest men in the world, estimated at $2B, by today's standard. *George Chinnery, Portrait of Wu Bingjian (Howqua) (1830). Metropolitan Museum of Art*

Opium production facility in India, geared for massive exports of the drug via English and American companies to China. Opaque poppy seed sap was collected, dried in balls, cured, and packed in chests for export. Thousands of peasant farmers, whose lands were appropriated for opium production, worked the factories. *British Library/Science Photo Library*

An example of a luxurious 'hong' property, on Honan Island, across the pearl from Canton. Thomas Allom, "House of Consequa, A Chinese Merchant, in the Suburbs of Canton" (c. 1842). *Beinecke Library, Yale University, New Haven, Conn.*

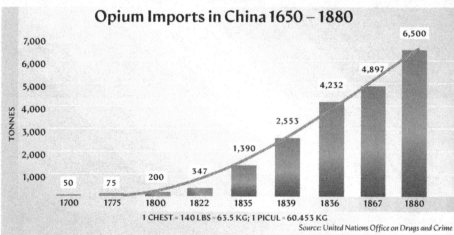

Opium Imports in China 1650 – 1880

1 CHEST = 140 LBS = 63.5 KG; 1 PICUL = 60.453 KG

Source: United Nations Office on Drugs and Crime

TOP: Studio of Guan Lianchang, also known as Tingqua (Chinese, active dates 1830–1879), Mandarin Boat, ca. 1855. Gouache on paper, 7 7/8 x 9 13/16" Gift of Mr. Charles H. Taylor, 1932. E83547.12. *Courtesy of the Peabody Essex Museum*

BELOW: Chart of opium sales into China from 1650-1880, in "thousands of chests." Each chest equaled 140 lbs. Chinese records accounted for volume in 'piculs,' equivalent to approx. 125 lbs. Payment in Chinese 'teal,' the silver tael = 40 grams (1.3 oz).

LEFT: Lithograph showing interior of Chinese opium den. The devastating effects of the drug on human behavior was aggressively portrayed and widely distributed, as a means of dissuading Westerners from succumbing to opium addiction. Nevertheless, opium dens soon appeared in major Western cites, like New York, San Francisco and London, introduced by returning sailors. Opium Smokers in an Opium Den. Credit: *George Bernard/Science Photo Library. Over the course of the 19th c., opium was soon being processed into morphine (key in the American Civil War), a common pain medication, Laudanum (a favorite among artists, writers), codeine and eventually, heroin.*

ABOVE: Lin Zexu, was retained by Emperor Minning to bring the opium problem under control. In 1838, he confiscated and destroyed over 20 tones in Canton (TOP RIGHT), prompting the British to threaten reprisals. The arrival of their naval fleet in 1839 triggered the First Opium War ('39-42). Considered a national hero as "Drug Fighter" by Chinese Americans, a Lin Zexu likeness stands in NYC's Chinatown today (RIGHT).

TOP: The power of British naval forces was no match for Chinese military. A one-sided was nevertheless resulted in substantial loss of life on both sides. Here, steamship Nemesis destroys Chinese junk, 2nd Battle of Chuenpi, 1841. E. Duncan, *Destroying Chinese war junks* (1843), *oil on canvas. Collection, Williamson Art gallery at Birkenhead, England.*

ABOVE: Treat of Nanking (1842), in which China paid reparations, ceded Hong Kong to Britain as cost of war. Captain John Platt, "The Signing and Sealing of the Treaty of Nanking in the State cabin of H.M.S. Cornwallis, 29th August 1842." *Anne S.K. Brown Military Collection, Brown University Library* [1846_TreatyNanking_Brown].

RESIDENCE OF S.̲ RUSSELL

Frances Osborne Russell (LEFT, *Collection Wesleyan University*) was Samuel's second wife. In her lifetime, she gave birth to their third son, Samuel Wadsworth Russell, oversaw the completion of their neoclassical home in Middletown (1827-29), (TOP, *Russell House Lithograph, Collection Russell Library, Middletown, Conn.*), designed by Ithiel Town (ABOVE, RIGHT) and, following her husband's death in 1862, directed family funds for the construction of the city library and chapel at Indian Hill Cemetery.

WATER WITCH.

TOP LEFT: By late 1830s, larger, faster boats were being designed/built. 'Tea Clippers' could complete 3 round trips from the east Coast/year, not two.

Like Russell, other Americans made fortunes in the opium trade. Returning home to cities like Boston, New York, Philadelphia, they applied their fortunes to public and educational causes, like the Bunker Hill Monument (TOP RIGHT), Mass. General Hospital (RIGHT), land tracts and railroads in the mid-West (LEFT), even contributing to the North's Civil War effort, itself.

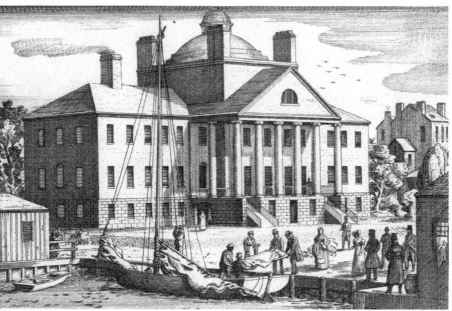

BOOK V
LION AT
THE GATE

48. Lion at the Gate

AUGUST 29, 1842: According to Zhengrui, Grand Minister to Daoguang Emperor, Minning, Seventh in Succession to the Manchu Qing Dynasty, Son of Heaven, Reigning over the Celestial Empire.

At dawn, a great white-tailed eagle soars upward on rising zephyrs, drifting in slow circles high above the fragrant hills of the Jingming Palace gardens. It loops nine times and counting, always returning to that place in the still blue air above Minning, who sits in lotus posture, alone and motionless, eyes rolled skyward behind closed lids. In this state of heightened awareness, he can sense the eagle's blazing yellow eyes focused on the ground below as he, a small, gold and scarlet-robed figure, sits unmoving in the precise center of his lush, well-ordered retreat. For the emperor, now in his fiftieth year, the appearance of this majestic bird has always signaled an auspicious promise of longevity, *chángshòu* (長壽), for his reign and for that of his eleven-year-old issue, Yicong, Prince Dunqin of the First Rank.

For as many years as he can recall, Minning has retreated here, away from the Winter Palace in Beijing, with its vast open spaces, to this summer retreat of his ancestors of centuries ago, surrounded by the cooling effects of a series of gardens and lakes. There, he and his consorts have traditionally offered prayers and sacrifices in remembrance of his departed father, Jiaqing Emperor, Yongyan, and to his continued joyous presence on their ancestral mountain top, along with all who have gone before, in the long Reign of Qing.

His annual retreat to this reputed '*gardens of gardens*,' has always been just that—an escape from the grief and burdens of decades on the throne that have always weighed heavily on his shoulders. On this, the twenty-ninth day of the eighth month, of the Year of the Tiger, (王), a year intended to symbolize the bravery and power of the king of animals, becomes instead, a victorious year—1842—for China's Western invaders. Despite his persistent efforts, and those of his dear father before him, to ward off the pernicious influence of greedy British and American merchants, his power and position—and that of the Celestial Empire—are being significantly compromised.

For centuries China has had little contact with the outside world. Various European nations, "foreign devils," had tried to foster commercial relations with generations of Minning's predecessors, but to no avail. Far from simply eschewing all things Western, Chinese authorities, acting on behalf of our self-sufficient nation, regarded—and continue to regard—foreign visitors to our shores as a danger to our lives and lifestyle. Adding to own long standing resistance in dealing with foreign traders, there underlies a traditional view of 'merchants' falling on the lowest rung of Chinese caste system— beneath craftsmen, civil servants, soldiers and priests. Merchants, themselves do not 'produce any useful goods or services,' we believe, but merely trade—*and profit*—from the labor and sacrifice of others.

In 1793, England sent Lord Macartney as ambassador to call on Minning's grandfather, Qianlong Emperor, sixth in the Manchu-led Qing dynasty, with hopes of establishing safe, reasonable relations of trade. Even as Macartney and his huge entourage's four-month long journey delivered them to the gates of the Celestial Kingdom, alarms were being raised across the land. Even as our very own ships carried him and his delegation up the Pei Ho River to the heart of Běijīng, we cleverly raised a flag on the vessel announcing, "Tribute-bearer from England." This greeting in our language was quite in accordance with the Chinese custom of claiming all gifts to the emperor as tribute, a highly visible gesture in direct defiance of the English, who hadn't a clue what the banner signified.

Another expectation dictated that whoever approached the throne of the emperor must perform the kowtow, kētóu (磕頭), kneeling three times, each time bowing three times till the head touches the floor. This is the manner great idols in the temples are approached, the practice signifying that the emperor is also a god. Lord Macartney told the Chinese legate he would not perform the kowtow unless a high officer of the Chinese state would indeed kowtow before a picture of the King of England. The emperor finally agreed to admit the ambassador, who consented he would merely bend his knee, as he would have done before his very own sovereign, the English king.

Nevertheless, in response to that meeting with Lord Macartney, Qianlong demanded that a letter be carried to George III, King of Britain, chastising the English delegation for their arrogance and presumptuous behavior. There is no evidence that letter was ever delivered to the king.

Despite these firm warnings by the emperor's father to a foreign royal he'd wished to subjugate, a series of events and military conflicts at the hands of the "foreign devils' has transpired, finally bringing Minning to this moment of quiet contemplation. When he had finally had enough of Western abuses, my emperor tasked Viceroy Lin Zexu to go to Canton to halt the opium trade completely. Lin wrote an open letter to Queen Victoria which she never saw, appealing to her moral responsibility to stop the opium trade. Lin then resorted to using force in the western merchants' enclave. He confiscated all supplies and ordered a blockade of foreign ships on the Pearl River. Lin also confiscated and destroyed tons of European opium. The British government responded by dispatching a military force to China and in the ensuing conflict, the British navy used its ships and firepower to inflict a series of decisive defeats on our greatly outnumbered forces. We are now being humiliated and forced to sign a settlement agreement, the so-called, Treaty of Nanking, an unequal treaty which forces us to pay reparations and open five ports to British merchants, and cede the fishing village of Hong Kong Island to them, as well. As he awaits word from the entourage traveling with great haste from Nanjing, where a treaty of surrender is currently being signed with the British, Minning— even as he is surrounded by the beauty of the gardens—solemnly considers his fate, and his future on the throne.

After decades of faithful service in the Qing succession, years ago I was finally elevated to the position of Grand Minister, what the English would call prime minister. My role allows me to freely roam the emperor's private quarters, as his companion and confidant. On this day, I find him seated in the garden with a scroll, a sacred document more than fifteen-hundred years old in hand. As I approach and sit nearby, he slowly pulls at the delicate red ribbon securing the ancient treasure, to reveal columns-upon-columns of ancient characters laid down on rice paper in delicate patterns of black ink. These are the words of third-century sage and Confucian devotee, Mengzi, second only to Confucius in his wisdom and importance during China's long-ago Warring Period. Mengzi wrote extensively on Confucian values, espousing those certain failures of virtue worse than death, rendering suicide morally permissible, or even praiseworthy, in some altruistic contexts.

As tears fill his eyes, Minning recalls that Confucius wrote, "For gentlemen of purpose and men of *ren* 仁—a virtue denoting the good feeling arising from the human expression of altruism—while it is inconceivable that they should seek to stay alive at the expense of *ren*, it may happen that they have to accept death in order to have *ren* accomplished."

Turning to Mengzi's scroll, Minning reads aloud to me:

"Fish is what I want; bear's palm is also what I want. If I cannot have both, I would rather take bear's palm than fish. Life is what I want; yi, faithful performance of one's specified duties to society, is also what I want. If I cannot have both, I would rather take yi than life. That is why I do not cling to life at all costs. On the other hand, though death is what I loathe, there is something I loathe more than death. Yet there are ways of remaining alive and ways of avoiding death to which a person will not resort. In other words, there are things a person wants more than life and there are also things he or she loathes more than death."

To me, Minning seems to be speaking in riddles. Yet, his choice to meditate on these words is deeply troubling. The emperor's face is pale and drawn, as though forces of gravity are descending on his features. Mengzi's ancient text is profound in its intent: to have his followers contemplate the value of life without dignity—*ren*—over death, death over the choice to live. To discover that life without dignity is worse than death is the central lesson of Mangzi's teaching.

Yi, a dignified death, swirls through Minning's mind; the choice to die, rather than live with the indignity of humiliating defeat. In the decades I have been in the service of the imperial throne, I have come to understand more of the Western mind. Many centuries ago, their Englishman, a scholar named Shakespeare, posed this very dilemma, spoken by their emperor-king, Lear: 'To be or not to be?' The terms and conditions under which one chooses to live or die, he teaches, rest with each of us. The difference between East and West is that the *gwai-lou* often chose a bloody end, as evidence of their courage to confront death in battle.

The Chinese, on the other hand, are averse to physical mutilation, from a belief that the body was a gift from one's parents and desecrating it therefore, an unfilial act. The preferred methods—as recorded in the twelfth century record, *The Book of Han*, by the court official, Ban Gu—appear to be those that do not leave the corpse significantly disfigured, notably hanging or strangulation. These teachings of the Confucian apostles Mengzi and Ban Gu guide our lives, even in death.

The years have been hard for my emperor. Defeat confronts him from many sides. Modern times and its temptations, forced on our People by a century-long Western invasion, have weakened the throne, and that of the long-standing Manchu-Qing dynasty in the eyes of his subjects, and in the opinion of the world. Master Mengzi advises those in positions of influence to favor righteousness over power.

In so many ways, this powerful man appears to be slowly succumbing to the ravages of time and duty to his throne. My sympathy for him is heart-rending, but my duty rests in service to my emperor. I must finally bring myself to speak up, with news from Beijing...

After what seems an eternity, then finally: "Excellency, I am sorry to distract you."

Slowly his attention returns to me. His eyes slowly focus, as though surfacing from beneath the dark waters of his thoughts. "Yes, Zhen?"

"The delegation from Beijing has arrived with news of the English treaty and reports from the front. They wish an audience."

Hesitating, after a long, deep breath, he says, "Yes...yes, have them convene in the Great Temple of Gratitude and Longevity. There is little there in the way of convenience to invite a lengthy visit, so they can soon be on their way."

≈

MINNING GATHERS HIMSELF for the long walk past Phoenix Pier and the Wangchan Pavilion to the austere, columned building where official receptions are held. The contingency is gathered and waiting and, as tradition dictates, Minning is last to enter the room. A single, elevated chair bearing a crimson cushion has been placed nearby in anticipation of this assembly of mid-level dignitaries from Canton's coastal Guandong province.

The group of a half-dozen men cluster at some distance from the seated emperor. Remote footsteps and the long groan of hinges on a massive door resound from the stark, high walls of the temple's marble corridors. Finally, after my signal, Second Provincial Executor, Cáo Gāng steps forward. In his hands, a crudely drawn map of the Pearl River, Canton, Macao, Hong Kong and the surrounding region, including site locations of key past battles of the so-called Opium War, marked with bold, red circles. In a tremulous voice, Cáo Gāng provides a rundown of the latest encounters with British forces, on sea and land, citing casualties on both sides.

"Excellency, our troops fought valiantly in battles on the north coast's Yellow Sea. But, by firepower alone, the British were able to eventually declare victory. With temporary peace secured with our admiralty, the barbarians then sailed south, allowing them to move their marine forces and gun boats well up into the Pearl River. The British launched an amphibious attack against us in the Humen strait, sinking eleven of our junks and capturing the city of Chinkiang and forts on the islands of Chuenpi and Taikoktow. Our cannon disabled, our soldiers lying dead or dying, the English forces overran fortifications that have stood for centuries. English troops quickly gained control of large swaths of riverfront territory. Canton is now effectively shut off from the sea by a British blockade."

My emperor listens in silence. I can only imagine what he is thinking, wishing more than anything, to be sitting once again beneath that circling eagle in the tranquility of his garden.

Gāng then carefully rolls the chart and hands it back to a member of the party. A long silence ensues. "I have yet more to tell you, Excellency." Second Provincial Executor, Cáo Gāng's hands tremble as he speaks, hoping not to evoke the ire of his emperor and his own expulsion from the palace...or worse, imprisonment or calls for his suicide—a failure of yi—faithful performance of his duties. "Sad news from the battle with the foreign devils at Chinkiang, Excellency. Among the bodies of your loyal Han Bannermen, was discovered that of your dear brother, Miankai, Prince Dun. He was not one of the many who committed suicide for failing to defend the city, but bore wounds of battle. He was likely fighting bravely in defense of your name and honor. British cannon fire almost certainly cut him down."

Despite Gāng's assurances that Miankai must have died bravely, a look of shock and dismay settles the emperor's face as he receives the news. "My brother, dead!? Didn't they know him? Didn't they recognize him as one who traveled among them for so many years?" Minning rises, striding to a window with a view of his distant sprawling gardens—so well-ordered and groomed. He stares vacantly, silent for a long moment, as though the tranquility of the scene might offer some escape from his slowly unfolding disbelief.

"We believe he must have finally left Canton and the factories of the barbarians and their atrocities to join the resistance...not able to tolerate their compliance in crimes against our people," Gāng continues, a tone of pleading and consolation in his voice, as if attempting to ease the emperor's grief and perhaps, spare his own life, as well. "The prince died a hero for the throne, Excellency."

"Years of training," Minning calls out to no one in particular, arms outstretched in a vain effort to plead his case to the divine for safe return of his brother's remains to the confines of the palace and the embrace of his family. "I arranged with the court's Catholic missionaries here in Beijing to have him become proficient in English; then with that Jesuit emissary from the Vatican, arranging for him to read in English law. Years of grooming in English dress, English manners, ample study of books and Western art, all aimed at allowing Miankai to move seamlessly in their midst, reporting on their actions, their plans, the fortunes they've made on the backs of our people."

"Yes, Excellency, he moved among them for years as Zhang Li-Mǐn, a commoner, yet a prince among men," Gāng added, "and they *never* suspected. For the translators who worked with the Americans and others, they knew him as Li-Mǐn, 'brave-clever,' a signal to those who could understand, that he was to be relied upon. Your brother was a hero who died in your service, Excellency."

"For years, the invaders took him into their confidence," Minning shouts aloud, as if offering himself small consolation. "Russell, Perkins, Delano, Jardine, Matheson, all of them came to trust his advice. Foolishly, they shared their plans with him. He offered his help and advice...all so that he could send information home to me by way of the swiftest messengers.

Gāng now seems a bit more at ease, as it becomes clear the emperor's preoccupation with the details of the plot might spare his life in the wake of this tragic news. He watches and listens attentively as Minning reminisces to no one about Prince Man's accomplishments in the guise of a Chinese confidant, trained in Anglo ways.

"Howqua entered the inner circle of the most powerful of them, Samuel Russell, at Li-Mǐn's urging," the emperor cries out. "Russell sought his legal counsel, hatching plans to bleed my people of their strength and treasure in the name of *yāpiàn*. Li-Mǐn was my eyes and ears in Canton. He served his brother well for all these years," speaking, as he sometimes did, in the third person. "He tracked all those chests of opium smuggled on the river ships, into the city, so that Lin Zexu knew where to strike when I assigned him Imperial Commissioner three years ago. Twenty-five thousand chests destroyed. *Hah!*

"And after that insult, war was inevitably to follow, Excellency. Especially when provoked by your decision to enlist the services of Viceroy Lin Zexu to go to Canton to forcibly halt the opium trade completely, destroying such large quantities of *yāpiàn*...

which was your absolute right to do," he hastily adds. "What was Prince Miankai to do, once rebellion had fomented, but join His Excellency's forces to defeat the enemy?" Gāng asked rhetorically. "The prince chose death with dignity in the face of enemy fire, rather than perpetuate the sham and risk being exposed and disgraced in the service of your name." Gāng's voice was pleading, as he senses the emperor's attention now turning away from the recitation of events and back to the messenger who'd borne the news.

"And how do you know so much of this tragic story, Gāng?" Were you there with the prince when he met his end? I can assure you I have ways to discover the answer, from others who answer to me in Canton and the province."

"Excellency, I can explain my role here." Gāng's gestures grow frantic, as he assumes a posture of submission before Minning—a partial kowtow reflecting an act of sup- plication that might help to spare his life. "I was one intended to be that of protector and servant to the prince; to accompany him wherever he intended to go in that time of great stress, and to do as he ordered."

"And where were *you* in the heat of battle? I caution you, my generals will tell me the facts of the matter," Minning demands.

"I was at the prince's side, Excellency. In the heat of the moment, with the smoke and noise, the falling bodies, the blood; but we became separated."

"And you went...*where?*"

"To the rear of the action, behind a wall yet standing. We ran together, but when I crouched behind the shelter of the wall, he was no longer with me," Gāng pleads. "When I returned to find my prince, he was among the dead, barely visible beneath heaps pf bodies...those killed in the bombardment and the many Cantonese and Mongols who then killed themselves." Gāng's voice is now shrill and pleading.

Minning is silent for what seems an eternity, his brow deeply furrowed, his mood one of silent rage. Without standing, or even looking at Gāng, with an open hand he gestures toward a nearby table, indicating that he should go to it. On it sits a single rosewood box about the size of a tea casket. On its highly polished lid appears the inlaid image of the Great Qing dragon, its pointed tail curled into a loop, its open mouth, its claws raised toward a blood-red sun. Gāng approaches it slowly and unsteadily, fearing what it holds.

"Open it," says Minning. "Its content will speak for itself."

Gāng is very familiar with this part of court proceedings—one as old as the Chinese culture, itself. He slowly raises the lid, to find a length of blue silk rope neatly coiled inside. His immediate association is its resemblance to a python, ready to strike. And its clear intent, for this devoted servant of the Qing Court is no less ominous than if it were, indeed, a snake. Gāng lifts the cord and holds it, draped across his open palms. He turns to the emperor, tears flowing down his face. Through quivering lips, his request of his emperor is simple, and barely audible: "Will you care for my family? My many children have barely come to know me."

"Your wife and issue can remain in the Forbidden City for as long as they care to," Minning replies, his eyes remaining averted. "Their every need will be met. They will be told that you acted heroically, but went in search of *yi*, because of your master's loss in the fiercest of battles. They will henceforth know you as Li Jié , "brave" (李杰), and I'll speak often of your actions, so that your children will offer incense and sake at the altar of your memory and at your grave, for all time."

Later that evening, in the Hour of the Ox, when all his family are retired to their sleeping chambers, Gāng calmly secures one end of the silken cord to a low willow branch in the garden behind the guard house. The other, he loops around his bare neck. As he steps off the chair to swing in the cool night air, his last sensation is the dense perfume of white jasmine draped over a nearby garden wall. Guards will find his body in the morning, alerting his family and the emperor.

BOOK VI
INDIAN HILL

49. BATHED IN SUNLIGHT ~ Mary's Epic

I JOIN SAM, to lie beside him once again.
No shared embrace this time.
  No lingering kisses to greet me.
Passion for life and each other once defined us—
  Now long forgotten.
Once, long ago, he awakened something special in me,
A certain desire that I could not yet name
In my youthful exuberance for life.
I was charmed, as we first met in New York,
  His eyes intently focused,
My hand trembling to balance a teacup,
  The world falling away around me
As he asked, "How did I not know you back home before now?"
I recall his attentive gaze:
  Eyes nearly matching the distant blue sky that framed his face.
We met again—and again—and each time his attentions
  Were to me like bathing in sunlight.
My midnight appeals to God, my silent prays to heaven,
  For some version of a happy life, seemed possible now.
A frail child of nineteen, pale translucent skin
  revealing blood and bone beneath,
I finally yielded my heart to this man, saying,
  "Yes, I will be your wife."
Confident in our union, his arms and vision
  for our future together encompassed me,
  As only he knew how to persuade.

We married on a Friday in October.
  I moved to the Russell homestead,
My sister, Frances, also orphaned, moved in with us.
Soon, Sam would be leaving me for months at a time,
  Gone to Europe on company business—stacking up profits and experience,
  "For our future," he would say.
On one of his absences, I brought our son, George into the world,
  But with greatest difficulty.
I sought to ease the burden and awkwardness
  Only my sister could provide.
I recall birthing pains and fever afflicting me for hours, days
Before I finally lay on the kitchen table, quickly draped with white sheets
  Pulled fresh from the clothes line outside.
I prayed the baby would come soon
  Delivering me from my agony.

Honey-gold morning light slanted in through the kitchen window,
As Frances applied cool compresses to my forehead and neck,
The midwife, stooped and intent, groped and coerced
  A squirming, living being into the world.
Moments later, that mewling, bloodied child was laid on my chest,
My eyes too tear-filled from joy and exhaustion to see clearly

That our son had joined the Russell household.
George Osborne Russell proved to have strength-of-character matching his father.
And despite an extra mouth to feed,
     Our family thrived in those early years.
But not for long.

I recall the day I lost Sam,
     Or rather the moment his eyes drifted from mine,
As he yearned for another life,
     One so distant and alien to my heart.
He led me to the garden, offering me a small bouquet of daisies,
     Gathered at the river's edge.
He took my hand briefly,
     Regarding me in the old way.
"They've asked me to sail to China," he said, "to open a business for them."
Feelings of panic and abandonment washed over me.
     I held back tears, pleading,
"It's just been four years, Sam. We've only been together for four years."
My sensibilities shocked,
I can still recall the smell of a nearby rain-soaked hayrick
     As my vision narrowed to a single golden blossom
     In our sunlit garden.
Nausea, a familiar sensation, overwhelmed me.
I fell silent.
"Just for a while, maybe two years. A chance to make enough money, so we needn't worry."
I pleaded, "This is not like Europe. China is a world away!"
"I want this for us. I've worked for it...earning their trust and confidence."
"How can I know you'll be safe?
     Will we be able to correspond?"
"Company ships from Providence and others from Boston travel back and forth all the time.
     "We'll write."
I sat silently beside him for an eternity.
     "What if I lose you...to a storm, to some pirate or angry mob, to your passions?"
'My heart and devotion reside here, with you," he said tenderly,
     My hand resting in his.
His eyes were fixed on some faraway detail,
     His heart's desire made clear.
In spite of my misgivings, I said, 'Go,"
     Not knowing it would be farewell.
"I am an 'Osborne' and I will survive," I told myself,
     Surrounded then, as now, by my kin.

A month later, Sam departed from Providence, bound for Canton, China,
Even as we learned that I was with child once again.
"You'll have your sister's help and support," he assured me.
     "I'll write each week."
Now I clearly see this abandonment,
     This ignoble purpose served up as love.
Necessity of purpose had its time and place in those days.

A man's prerogative,
    His guiding *credo*.
But, only two letters in as many months,
    By way of returning ships from Europe and South America.
I allowed myself to acquiesce,
    And paid most dearly.

All too soon, another feverish episode on the kitchen table,
    Shock and fear flood my consciousness,
Because this next birth felt different...
    Ominous, threatening,
    Sam's absence,
As though an evil force had come over my body.
The child, a boy to be named John Augustus,
    Burst on the scene.
    No coaxing this time.
Never to be laid on my bosom,
    Cascades of dark blood, instead,
    Drenching the white sheets.
Alarm for those gathered around me,
    Frantically sending for the doctor.
As I plunge into an icy realm of shivers and delusion,
    Struggling to remain conscious, alive.
Two days pass,
    Hovering between life and death,
    Pain replaced by complacency.
"This is not what we want to see," the doctor explains,
    "Giving up the ghost."
I linger for three days more,
    Dazed, sipping water,
Dreaming of being adrift in a small boat,
My face turned upward toward a brilliant sun
    And that same blue sky
    Framing Samuel's face on the day we met.

These bones, laid to rest far too soon, now molder in darkness,
    Beneath towering oak, maple and pine,
Under heaps of ashen snow and ice,
    Having lost track of the years.
    Awaiting Sam's return and our final resting place.
Surveying my funeral, I see my young son
    Close by the coffin,
Stunned, not fully understanding.
Frances holding my newborn, John, in her arms,
    He would never know his mother,
    A boy frail and prone to fever from the beginning.
Family and friends, too, weeping for their loss,
As prayers and exaltations are offered up to Heaven.

In the years that follow, I gain wisdom and understanding
    In ways only the dead can know.
I can explain:
In time, knowledge comes to the deceased

Devoid of emotion...no anger; jealousy or contempt.
No vengeful impulses; or thoughts of possession.
These are earthly responses reserved for the living.
We care little for these diversions, approaching human drama dispassionately,
But with kindness and empathy for the struggles sustained by those
Still cursed with living flesh, inflicted by bruises, wounds and indignities
They are forced to endure.

I watched as Sam realized his chosen ambitions in far-away China,
    Weeping over the letter from Frances describing my death.
Then, gathering resolve to succeed in business,
Pumping tons of opium into the heart of the Chinese spirit,
    Over the objection of imperial authorities.

He was briefly seduced by a beautiful Indian woman,
    Doe-eyed, subservient, Chavvi,
    Who intrigued him with her exotic ways.
    His passions whetted for the moment.
Then falling in love with a Portuguese girl, Isabella,
    In a garden behind the Church of Saint Paul,
    Later destroyed by typhoon and fire in '35,
    Its hollowed-out façade left standing
    As a monument to imperial ambition,
    And Sam's search for love, doomed by family alliances.
She captured his heart with her spirit and youthful abandonment.
When she left Macao to return to her native Portugal,
    Sam's fruitless pleas to marry,
    Left him heartbroken.
Once home again, she married a member of Portuguese nobility,
    On to London as part of the diplomatic corps.
    Once there, she would have three children,
    Only to perish at fifty in the city's cholera epidemic of `53.

In Isabella's absence,
His thoughts turned to my sister, Frances,
As feelings of love, need, and regard for her grew,
    Considering her role in caring for our two boys.
Dreams of a life with Isabella that could never be realized
Soon drove him briefly home to Middletown,
    To construct the house befitting his accomplishments,
    Signaling power and status to other men in town,
    A trophy he coveted for his lifetime.
And to marry my sister, Frances Ann,
    As China would again lure him back,
    More accounts, influence, wealth beyond imagining.

Some years later, though, Samuel returned home,
Beleaguered and emotionally distant,
    A steady diet of danger and death there
    Cooling his ardor and lust for ill-gotten fortune.
This time, in `32, returning home for the last time.
    Some years later, another son, Samuel Wadsworth Russell.
In the end, Frances, the three boys and he lived in that beautiful house

So well designed, including a new wing for the children.
Tragically, our second child, John Augustus, died a young man
From a condition arising from his epilepsy.
Eldest, George Osborne, would soon follow him to the grave,
A mere 33 years on this earth.

Years after Sam chose to leave Canton,
   In the face of rising violence,
   And his near escape from a pending murder charge,
War broke out with the British.
The first of two Opium Wars was a one-sided affair.
   The Chinese were soon defeated
   by the Crown's commanding naval forces.
As a result, Hong Kong was ceded to English hands,
   Where it remained for decades to come.
   For the West, fresh opportunity to open another opium-laced vein,
   Poisoning another generation of the Chinese nation.

A second war with British forces ensued some years later.
Blood was spilled again in the name of opium.
   More death, more destruction.
This time, the immaculate eleventh century Summer Palace,
Known as the 'Gardens of Perfect Brightness,'
   In the hills north of Beijing.
Was rendered asunder, burned, and ransacked to rubble.
   No strategic value...just spite.
   Precious objects looted, carried home to London museums,
   Satiating the appetites of the curious and ignorant.
The Chinese have not forgotten,
   nor will they ever forgive this insult.

Long after Sam returned to Middletown, taking up his respectable life
As business investor and part-owner of his China-based company,
Wreaking the ravages of opium on a nation, while reaping its rewards,
   He received shocking news,
   From a partner half-way around the world.
That his Chinese ally and confidant, Zhang Li-Min, was not, on his face,
   A well-intentioned English-trained lawyer
   Intent on helping Sam find his way
   through the maze that was Chinese culture,
But Miankai, Prince Dun, younger brother of Emperor Minning.
He had thus leagued himself with the hong, Howqua, and others,
Planted in Canton to spy on Sam and others' efforts,
   With relays back to the throne in Beijing.

Despite those feelings of outright betrayal,
Sam—always the pragmatist—nevertheless invested
   Howqua's millions into American land and railroads.
And through his bankers in London,
His favorite hong was directed to send similar millions
Into the welcoming hands of the Rothschilds,
   Whose landed interests in Europe meant more millions
   For one of the world's wealthiest men.

Others too, in Sam's employ, carried the Russell & Company banner
    For several more years after his departure,
    Turning fortune into 'good works,' once home.
Thomas Perkins, a Russell employee,
    whose family trafficked in slaves
Later turned to opium and feigned talk of abolition,
Perkins hired those who would later become
Boston's powerful 'Brahmins':
The Cabots, Cushings, Welds, Delanos (grandfather of FDR).
Their millions went to support institutions of higher learning and libraries:
    MIT, Princeton; Massachusetts General Hospital,
    McLean Psychiatric Hospital, the Boston Athenæum
    and Perking School for the Blind.
    Public monuments like Bunker Hill,
    and the one on Washington, D.C.'s Mall,
And countless steamship companies, mines, railroads, schools,
    and libraries, including Middletown's very own.

Today, their homes stand high on the cliffs of Newport, the Hudson River,
    Secure in New York City's mid-town
    and tucked away on Boston's Beacon Hill.
Sam's loyal minion, John Forbes and the family members,
    Who followed him to China in later years,
Included Robert Bennett Forbes,
    Who denied opium involvement for years afterward,
    fearing social retribution,
    Even as he built faster opium clippers
    for the next generation of so-called Chinese 'low and unprincipled,'
    Seeking to engage in a questionable trade
    plagued by "the convenience of forgetfulness."

Not every China trader engaged in ready-made fortune,
choosing a narrower path.
New York fabric merchant David Olyphant
    refused to trade opium, calling it *"an evil of the deepest dye."*
For this he was derided, according to a Forbes family member:
    "God protect me from ... Holy Joe,
    His ships are all commanded by JC,
    officered by angels and manned by saints."

Recalling that slave revolt in Peru, the brave Senegalese, Shodreny?
    He wasn't hanged after all.
Some thought it was too high a price spent for him,
    to be wasted like that.
    Whipping and branding were the ways lessons were taught.
He and the rest hauled off to the remote Pallancata silver mine
    in high altitude Ayacucho,
As more than a hundred souls died of exposure,
    Starvation and hard work.
Months later Shodreny revolted again.
    Many joined his cause, but had nowhere to go, really.
    They were finally slaughtered, to a man,
    in their mountain redoubt,

At the hands of company men and soldiers.

One bright winter day in '42,
    when Sam was well-along in years,
A messenger boy from town came to the door to say
    A Negro man was looking for him.
Sam slowly rose from his desk and ledgers to inquire.
On the portico, behind the nervous boy,
    A stooped, but elegantly dressed Black man
    Stood in the cold.
"Mister Russell, It's Adam...D'ya recall anything 'bout me,
    That boy from the ship some years ago,
    Sent out west with those men?
Seems you weren't nothin' but a far-away glimmer
    in yo' daddy's eye back then."

My Samuel was thunderstruck.
    He gripped the porch rail,
    As he searched for words.
'Adam, you're *alive!* We always believed you dead."
"Lucky, I guess. 'Cause a' th' English tongue your ma taught me,
    My master eventually set me to work in his house,
    Tendin' his two boys."

Sam brought Adam into the grand, long dining room; a fire lit for warmth.
    Up from the kitchen, long-time cook, Mary,
    known in the family—but not to her face—
    as 'Scary Mary,' brought warm biscuits
    And tall glasses of sparkling gold, Philadelphia *Yuengling.*
"Mr. Russell, I kep' my eyes and ears open durin' their schoolin',
Learnin' their lessons, right along with 'em.
Taught some of the other Coloreds, too—on the sly.
    Earned my freedom in '38."
"How? How is it...?"
"...Thet I'm here, y'ask? Master Swinton's ship come from Charleston t' New York.
Gave me passage 'cause I was yearnin' to come back here and find the *Russells.*
To say, much obliged for whach'a pa and momma did for me."

Adam and Sam sat and talked for hours,
    Across the hall in the high-ceilinged 'ship' room
    Filled with boat models, paintings, and artifacts from the China years.
    Two lives long-ago intertwined in unlikely ways.
Adam spent the night in John Augustus's old bedroom.
The following day, Sam paid for Adam's carriage passage to New York City,
    With a letter addressed to Mr. John Astor, himself,
    And directions to his office.
    'Help this man if you can,' it said.
Fate and good fortune's wheel soon turned for him.
As a teaching position was found in a fine Negro school for boys
    In the heart of the city.

During the final years
Many notables came to call.

Governor Edward Everett, of Gettysburg Address fame, for one.
He later out-talked Lincoln by two hours,
    Scant time for Honest Abe to get in his 'Four score and seven...'
Called Sam's house a *palace*.
Once told friends Sam made 'guineas by the barrel and shovel full.'
Partook of Sam's celebrity status,
    With his well-worn 'Washington' speech.
    'Well received' at their church in town, the papers said,
    Despite his self-proclaimed diffidence.
"Slept well in Middletown. Into the arms of Morpheus," he told his wife,
Before again departing for Washington.

What became of the 'Thirteen Factories'
Symbol of Western exploitation on Chinese soil?
Nothing remains of them today.
Once prominent on a reclaimed Pearl River mud bank,
    They burned to the ground one last time, in '56,
    Never to be rebuilt.
Cantonese shops and homes quickly reclaimed the land.
Now, just a memory and unwelcomed legacy for a few.

Sam passed quietly in '62.
Laid to rest on a peaceful crest of Indian Hill Cemetery.
Now, I am finally by his side,
    To be joined many years later by Frances,
    Who outlived most of our kin —
    Sons, their wives, and grandchildren, like.
The Russell family plot generously made room for all.
Nearby, Middletown 'prominents': Alsops; Müdders, Chaunceys
    And my own Osbornes,
    Among many other souls.

The slaves from the city, of which there had been many,
Lie mostly in unmarked graves
    In a remote section of the old Vine Street cemetery
    Near the new men's college,
    Founded by John Wesley's Protestants.

What has Sam shared with me since arriving?
Like so many others, newly arrived,
    He has not yet learned the lessons of patience and forgiveness.
He speaks in that stern voice he often used to rail against the fates,
    Those that finally delivered him to this quiescent resting place:
    Why am I here on this deserted hill?
    Rendered unable to reach into the world
    To shape a version of myself.
I cannot accept my misfortune, my stolen breath,
My bones entangled with the massive oak
    Thriving and swaying in the breeze overhead.
Shading those who come here to bear witness,
    Without ever fully knowing my name.

Slipping away from seasons
  I can never know again.
Vanity was my name in previous years
And for as long as I can recall, ambition drove me.
Yet, only now, to lie unmoving before
  Autumn's shimmering mantle,
  Winter's fierce leaden skies,
  Constellation Hydra's spring blossoms,
And great eagles high aloft on spiraling zephyrs
  Over my beloved Algonquin, Mattabesset,
  The river's, 'end of the carrying place.'

I watch as decades speed by,
Amid a world I helped shape with my own hands
  Over too many years to count.
  Now, eternity plays its inevitable role
  Melding my spirit and flesh
  In this dark, eternal New England soil.
No living man will know me again,
But may recall the ways in which
  I loved and was loved,
  Endeavored to make a better world.
  Of devotion and obligation,
  Chastity and passion,
  I lived as any human would—
  To the very best of my ability.

May God forgive my failings.

~ FINIS ~

EPILOGUE:
SAM RUSSELL'S AMERICA

"It seemed as if New England was a region given up to the dreams of fancy and the unrestrained experiments of innovators."
~Alexis de Tocqueville, Democracy in America, Vol. 1 (1813)

SAMUEL RUSSEL WAS a product of his time and place. He was born in 1789, at the height of the Enlightenment period and its thinking. This was a newly-formed American nation, as yet a high-risk experiment in a self-proclaimed, 'pursuit of happiness' and its corollary, self-determination. The Founding Fathers had not yet crafted the Bill of Rights, and anxieties were running high as to whether this fragile democratic republic could stand on its own. It was only two years prior to Russell's birth that Benjamin Franklin, in response to a question about his preferred type of government, was purported to say, "A republic if we can keep it."

Russell lived his childhood in a time when the newly-formed states—of which there were only a handful—were in a continual state of flux. Slavery was a thriving national enterprise. It was never successfully addressed by the Continental Congress, whose members only tabled the charged topic of indentured servitude for some future discussion. Not unrelated to this conundrum, States' Rights were also being hotly debated, as some with strong allegiance to their home turf were reluctant to cede governmental control to a central, but distant national legislative and administrative seat-of-power, then located in Philadelphia. Under the proposed model of representation, the northern states, with their disproportionate population and higher industrial output, put southern states at risk of having their legislative influence weakened on important matters of regional concern, particularly slavery.

In 1800, Connecticut's population numbered 250,000 (with nearly 1,000 'freed' slaves laboring in households and on farms), across more than one-hundred communities. At that time, ninety percent of the general population was engaged in farming of various kinds. This meant that any young man coming of age at the dawn of the nineteenth century, had little opportunity besides working the soil. By the end of the second decade of the 19th century, however, important changes were taking place in the American economy—namely, the gathering momentum of the Industrial age.

Historian, Jamie Eves, of the Windham Textile and History Museum, cites three periods in New England economic growth, the first being that of Farm and Sail (1630s to early 1800s); the second, Industry and Rail (1840s to mid-twentieth century); and the last, that of the automobile (1950s to present). I would view that same shift from agrarian (Age One), when farming practices had remained largely unchanged for centuries, to industrial (Age Two), as a shift from archaic to early modern technology, with its reliance on improved machinery and tools, with a corresponding migration away from farming to city-based economies.

As we consider this model to better understand the life and times of Samuel Russell, he would be coming of age on the cusp of the first and second periods (he would turn eighteen in 1807). Middletown at that time was prospering as a center for shipping to-and-from many parts of the world. Its safe harbor, away from busier, but more vulnerable open water ports, like New York, Newport and Boston, made it an ideal destination for ships trading farm product to the West Indies, in support of the slave trade. Markets were expanding in Europe, as well. where demand for manufactured goods from expanding Connecticut factories, and processed goods (principally cotton fabrics from southern plantations) was growing. Russell would invariably have been part of this scene, either because of his father and grandfather's purported role as ship captains;

or because of Middletown's vital role in trade and its impact on local businesses he came to know; or perhaps, his wanderlust as a young man sitting on busy Middletown docks, imagining a life somewhere beyond the borders of this small New England town.

It is important to recognize that Russell's role in economic and cultural events of the early nineteenth century, ideally positioned him to escape the likelihood of a life as farmer or sailor, to become a functionary of emerging mercantile opportunities on a broader scale. International markets were opening for American tradesmen at a rapid pace. The rate of trade growth with European interests was only partially impacted by the War of 1812-14, when shipping routes between the Northeast and Western Europe were temporarily affected by hostilities. Interest in U.S. goods had been so firmly established before the war, that soon after peace was declared, international trade resumed and grew rapidly. Companies in Providence, New York, and Boston, long established before Russell was old enough to be involved, had established trade routes for manufactured goods and farm products, in countries like Spain, England and Holland, and in Gibraltar, the gateway to Mediterranean markets.

Ships were available, built to make the trip and return safely, products were available in abundance, as manufacturing had steadily moved from home-based looms and bespoke workshops to water-powered mills and dedicated employees, sometimes entire families finding work on rows of high speed factory 'mules,' or looms. Still needed, however, at this point in history, were reliable men to accompany goods to Europe, sell them at a profit, and then return—body, spirit and cash intact. These men were called 'supercargoes,' agents traveling on behalf of shipping companies, responsible for the goods eventually sold to the highest bidder at the end of a trans-Atlantic crossing. They had to be reliable and trustworthy; willing to travel the dangerous oceans; be absent from family for months at a time; and intelligent enough to outwit an experienced merchant or reseller once tying up at a foreign port.

Enter an ambitious young Middletown man well suited to the task, Mr. Samuel Russell.

Russell had earned the trust of local trade merchants in Middletown, and, at the age of thirty-one, was recommended for the role of supercargo by a family member to a company in New York City, that of Hull & Griswold. In two trips to Europe aboard company vessels loaded with goods, he earned the admiration of his employers, returning with handsome profits and tales of his business encounters with men more than twice his age, who acquiesced in the face of his carefully guided negotiating style.

But, to truly understand the controversial actions and choices Sam Russell made over the course of his eventual career in China, we must look beyond his opportunistic placement at a critical time in the economic history of his town, nation, and global marketplace, in the process of transitioning from agrarian to modern. Russell's influences ran broader and deeper than mere luck and skill. His mode of thinking, about himself, his place in the world, and his obligations to family and society, writ large, were being shaped by forces likely well beyond his awareness. These principles must be explored and understood if we are to ever understand what drove him to adopt such extreme—even inhumane—choices he made as he developed and expanded his company in Canton. He returned to the United States in 1832, after just twelve years in Canton, China, with fortune enough for a lifetime, but at what moral and societal cost to himself and others?

The reader may recall early on in his career, while meeting with potential partners in New York City, this fictional account of his life has him meet and talk with John Jacob Astor at a reception. It was there, also, that he first encountered his wife-to-be, Mary Osborne. In private discussion with Astor, they discussed John Locke, an eighteenth-century English philosopher. Locke's influence on Enlightenment thinking is well documented, particularly as it pertains to our Founding Fathers and their intention to incorporate some of his thinking into the American Declaration of Independence. There, Declaration authors, Jefferson, Franklin, Adams, and others posited that *"...all people are entitled to life, liberty and the pursuit of happiness."* In fact, Locke's original wording specifically referenced "property," not "happiness.". This alteration in wording was necessitated by the issue—widely debated at the time—of slavery. If property were guaranteed in this key document, where does that leave the controversial issue of human ownership and its possible future abolition?

Locke's argument, that 'property' was an innate human right was, for all time, obfuscated in the original Declaration. In fact, Locke stated that each person owns his or her own body, and all the labor performed with the body. When an individual adds their own labor, otherwise termed their own *property*, to a foreign object or good, that object becomes theirs because of the added labor. This was known as Locke's, "labor theory of property." Thus, happiness, in Locke's view, as underscored by a core American founding document, places 'property possession' on an plain equivalent to individual liberty. Without being fully aware, or even cognizant of Locke's popularized "liberal" philosophy, prevailing views of the American experiment, as understood in those early days of nationhood, might have led to Russell's conclusion that 'effort equals ownership.' There was likely a shared consensus within a subset of the business community at the time, of heightened awareness of our revolutionary founding language, that this distorted rationale offered inherent permission to seek and declare ownership of property (read, *slaves*, as well), without consideration for those being afflicted by such action.

When Astor handed Russell his spare copy of Locke's *Second Treatise on Government* (1689) in his study that day, he was encouraging Russell to do well, but be certain to use any future wealth for the common good. Astor's understanding likely arose from a careful reading of Locke's writings which, unlike Locke's contemporary, John Calvin, heaped praise on human nature and the natural inclination to seek 'right and order' in the community of man. Locke asked by what right an individual can claim to own one part of the world, when, according to the Bible, God gave the world to all humanity in common? He answered that although persons belong to God, they *own* the fruits of their labor. When a person works, that labor enters into the object. Thus, the object becomes the property of that person. However, Locke held that one may only appropriate property in this fashion if the Lockean *proviso* held true, that is, "... there is enough, and as good, left in common for others."

It is unlikely that Russell would have encountered any version of the *Second Treatise* but might have taken to heart the core concept that labor equates to ownership. This would have been timely, particularly at a time in American history when unbridled expansion westward translated to laying claim on property (land), just as entire communities of Native Americans and their cultural heritage were being actively discriminated against. This idea of Manifest Destiny, though, would not be fully codified until the arrival of President Andrew Jackson in Washington's corridors of power, from 1829-37. Claiming to represent the common man, Jackson adopted his Indian Removal Act of 1830, shaping a public view of Native-Americans as less than human (from benign, to savage, "children in need of guidance"), deserving of displacement from their lands, abdication of any treaties and prior agreements, even subjection to wholesale slaughter. The profile of the entitled American male of European extraction was being encouraged, if not obligated, to exercise free will, acting on his own behalf. This cultural norm gained traction very quickly following the War for Independence, a view persisting even to the present day.

Nor was possession of foreign lands and natural resources an impulse limited to Jackson and his newly-formed Democratic Party. Colonialism and the racist views underpinning it were a worldwide phenomenon. By the mid-1700s, England had already laid claim to the Indian subcontinent. Traders and military forces saw opportunity in India's scattered, disorganized provincial model of governance, as they eventually gained control of the entire nation under the banner of Queen Victoria's benign, 'Sun Never Sets' global manifesto. As foreign lands and cultures in Africa and Asia were being explored and newly revealed to a curious Western European public, pseudo-science was quick to step forward and declare white, Greco-Roman somato-types superior in intelligence, accomplishments, and every other way, to lesser breeds of far-flung black, brown, red and yellow-skinned peoples. This impetus for racial stereo-typing became the basis for the study of eugenics, a discredited 'science' holding a grip on the imaginations of many, even today. Politicians, military opportunists, industrialists, and others soon wrapped themselves in this cloak of racial profiling to their own advantage, invading, conquering, and exploiting these so-called underclass societies. By the mid-to-late 1800s, large swaths of coastal Africa and the Pacific archipelago were controlled by one country or another, orchestrating events from far-away Europe.

And while the United States never professed colonial ambitions as other nations did, prevailing views of racial inferiority nevertheless allowed for exploitation of foreign nations. The increased dependence on an enslaved workforce of millions—particularly, but not exclusively in the south—meant that regular supplies of Blacks, captured and removed by force from Western European-controlled countries along Africa's west coast, continued unabated. This Triangle Trade route, relying on a transfer of goods and human trade between continental Africa, Western-occupied West Indian islands, and American ports along the eastern seaboard. This transactional economy continued unabated, well into the second half of 19th century.

Recall again, Astor's imagined conversation with Russell, as they stood on the banks of his property, overlooking Hudson River's outer harbor. There, an active, dark-of-night exchange of funds for slaves bound for the West Indies was taking place. Complicit financial institutions in the City of New York and dedicated slavers allowed for decades-old anti-slavery laws to be flouted, as long as no chattel touched foot on American soil during these illicit dealings. The historical record would show that Astor was actively engaged in this arrangement for a limited period, as well as conducting opium business with Russell, himself, once he (Russell) had arrived in Canton and realigned his business priorities beyond cotton trading.

Russell is portrayed here as driven to despair by moral dilemma. How could he explain to himself, and others, that his fortune as an opium trader was achieved on the backs of a nameless, faceless, and geographically distant population? But, within that conundrum lay his unsettling answer: the very exploitation of a non-Western population, especially given the broad indifference surrounding the chronic use and dependence on opium as a cultural norm for 'someone else,' made it an acceptable pursuit in his day.

≈

EARLY EVIDENCE OF the emergence of unique American character traits of free-wheeling autonomy can be found in a series of published essays by the Frenchman, Alexis de Tocqueville, *Democracy in America* (1833). His cogent observations of the American character shed light on the argument that a national character profile was already emerging, even as the principles—and very survival—of republicanism and representative democracy, were still being hotly debated. Of his nine-month long

American tour, he wrote: *"Americans believe their freedom to be the best instrument and surest safeguard... to secure for themselves a government which will allow them to acquire the things they covet, and which will not debar them from the peaceful enjoyment of those possessions."* Here, the Lockean 'labor theory of property' is being played out in real world terms, with a newly minted American nation serving as its laboratory.

Also, *"As one digs deeper into the national character of the Americans, one sees that they have sought the value of everything in this world only in the answer to this single question: how much money will it bring in? [...] In no other country in the world is the love of property keener or more alert than in the United States, and nowhere else does the majority display less inclination toward doctrines which in any way threaten the way property is owned."*

Given that de Tocqueville's published works did not appear on the American scene until well after Russell returned from China to his home in Middletown, he may not have been aware of them until he was already well-established in his community. However, de Tocqueville's objective view of prevailing American personality traits and the impulse within our culture to achieve greater-and-greater personal success than had gone before, is telling. It is a narrative time capsule offering insight into how men who lived two-hundred years ago viewed the world around them and choices afforded them in that time and place.

Men, in their role as ultimate providers, were permitted—even encouraged—to take whatever steps within the loose confines of domestic law and pre-antitrust corporate practice to amass tax-free fortunes. Unconstrained by international law, overseas adventurism in the early nineteenth century became a game that men of wealth and influence could indulge. Large ships, foreign offices and staff, wildly fluctuating markets, piracy and double-dealing, large cash reserves and good credit, and the willingness to risk it all became the rules to live by in international trade...as seen in today's venture capitalists.

Russell, a man who came from modest means, was fortunate enough to find a group of men specializing in this high-flying marketplace who wished to have him on their team. He was, therefore, able to step into the rarified world of high finance and anything-goes trade negotiations as an agent, i.e.- with little of his own wealth at risk, in a risk-prone business climate. Relying on business acumen, accounting skills acquired in his private endeavors, and a reputation for honesty and integrity, Russell was able to move into a crowded Cantonese trade setting and emerge the winner. We can only surmise that what he packed for the journey, apart from clean clothes, a grooming kit, and a barrel of common sense, also included a propensity to think of himself, firstly, as an American. Embodied in that perception came the uniquely American traits so brilliantly summarized by de Tocqueville, here:

"It is strange to see with what feverish ardor the Americans pursue their own welfare; and to watch the vague dread that constantly torments them lest they should not have chosen the shortest path which may lead to it. [...] ...few men are idle in democratic nations; life is passed amid noise and excitement, and men are so engaged in acting that little remains to them for thinking. I would especially remark that they are not only employed, but that they are passionately devoted to their employments. They are always in action, and each of their actions absorbs their faculties: the zeal which they display in business puts out the enthusiasm they might otherwise entertain for idea."

≈

TO MAKE THE perilous case for delving into the mind of an early nineteenth-century man, it is perhaps better to consider his motivation to action. For the bulk of this narrative, Russell is based in Canton, China. There, he spent twelve years amassing a fortune, while selling quantities of opium to thousands of drug dependent Chinese citizens, over the objection of the emperor and other authorities. We are confronted by the challenge, attempting to understand Samuel Russell's business and moral choices, as he ramped up his businesses, various iterations of 'Russell & Company,' until he quickly became one of the largest traffickers of the Turkish and Indian opium in that part of the world. Ironically, we come to understand him as a compassionate man, prone to emotions of love, loss, guilt, and anger—though all in moderation. We see him confront challenges, setbacks, dangers, opportunities, and crises, all with the same level-headed resolve. He is, after all, a man on a mission: to earn his competency and return home to Connecticut as soon as was practicable. And yet, he gets caught up in the prolonged, dangerous game of opium dealing, a victim of his own success. Why, might we ask, does he persist in the face of these challenges?

In summary then, the answers might be found in examples set forth by some of the major influences shaping the attitudes and behavior of men like Russell, and others so inclined for business on an international playing field. The American Revolution and its resolve on behalf of 'everyman' was an Enlightenment era exercise in free will and self-governance. This crucial period in our development as a nation, together with the simultaneous arrival of the Industrial revolution, set the stage for men like Samuel Russell to break the bonds of a rural, agrarian lifestyle, and begin to think globally, with expanded American industrial output as 'currency for trade' on the world stage. Distant horizons rather than domestic markets, became a new, realistic business objective.

Next, philosophers like John Locke, whose vision for the interplay of property and 'happiness,' as spelled out in the nation's founding documents, cleared the way for the belief—one adopted as a uniquely American one—that effort expended equals possession. This paradigm was quickly incorporated into the American ideal, as thousands set out into newly available western lands, cleared of Native American tribes, with long term 'possession' in mind. For Russell and others influenced by this same logic, capturing distant markets meant being able to own the means to achieve those profits, an entitlement distinct from any moral constraints; arising by logical extension from the Lockean concept of 'possession.'

Lastly was the prevailing belief, reinforced by ill-conceived versions of scientific inquiry, that European Whites were biologically superior to all other races. This abomination set the stage for a protracted period of racially motivated colonialism, involving many European nations; and America, by extension, as it sought a rationale to keep enslaved Black populations confined at hard labor on farms and plantations across an ever-expanding national landscape. This view of racial inferiority was exported by American businessmen, including Russell, who could rationalize their treatment of the Chinese as a nameless, faceless nation of heathens, suffering from an addiction no worse that alcohol or tobacco dependence, found in the West.

So, understanding an historical figure like Samuel Russell means setting aside twenty-first century biases, to insert our understanding of motives and actions into a time and place influenced by mores and standards different than our own. The last word may go to Alexis de Tocqueville, who described that generation of Americans as he saw it, as, "However energetically society in general may strive to make all the citizens equal and alike, the personal pride of each individual will always make him try to escape from the common level, and he will form some inequality somewhere to his own profit."

APPENDIX 1:
Afterward

THIS IS A work of historical fiction. Much of what you will read here of Sam Russell's daily activities, emotional and moral choices, and high seas adventures, are fictional, his ethical dilemmas a matter of conjecture. Accounts of his time spent in China, his role in promoting the consumption of opium and its sale in record quantities, as well as business legacy and that of others similarly engaged in the practice, are factual. When the narrative can be grounded by a family interview, rarely found personal document, or matter-of-historical record, it has been so accounted for.

During his international travels, Russell surely would have encountered numerous cultures and indigenous languages. For purposes of authenticity, words and phrases in Portuguese, Hindi, Scottish, Spanish and other Western languages appear in true form. Mandarin Chinese (traditional ideograms and pinyin phrasing) and Arabic are presented as transliterations. These words and phrases are initially employed in context, then repeated in other settings to promote comprehension and enhanced realism for the reader.

Pidgin English is a generic term for a mixture of English and local tongues, enabling those who do not share a common language to communicate. The previously noted decision to make use of various languages throughout the text also includes Pidgin English, as it would have been spoken by local Chinese, regularly in contact with foreigners. By twenty-first century standards, incorporating these terms and phrases certainly fails the racial sensitivity test. But they nevertheless represent documented, 19th century contemporaneous accounts of actual verbal interactions. For purposes of authenticity, historical realism, and accuracy, it was determined that examples of these documented exchanges should, by necessity, be included in this story.

≈

THE INTERNAL FORCES that drove Russell's desire to succeed were not without conflict. In this fictional account, he regularly fell into periods of despair, loneliness, guilt, and self-doubt. Always focused on his goals of immediate wealth and the esteem of his peers, he rarely revealed his emotional struggles to others—let alone to himself. He sought the solace of his ledgers to speak for his success, even while unremittingly searching for meaningful human connections. Ordinarily risk-averse in his business dealings, over the course of his life, Russell appeared surprisingly willing to reveal his heart and emotional vulnerability to a small handful of people, those who touched him personally.

With scant evidence found in available records—except for those reams of fastidiously- maintained ledgers and brief personal notations—this fictional treatment of Russell's life finds him committed to the cause of emancipation (later called abolition), a deep revulsion of slavery held by his father before him. And while there is no discernible evidence that he, or his family directly interceded on behalf of slaves in the Middletown, Connecticut community, historical documentation reveals slavery and its horrors to be alive-and-well in the region during his years. A handful of Middletown residents actually established and maintained onsite slave importation and sale businesses during the late 18th century. And while many of the town's wealthiest families owned and engaged in exploiting slaves, there is also no proof that most

Middletown families, including the Russells, dealt directly in human trafficking. Many shipping companies, though, operating as provisioners of farm goods to West Indian Island plantations, would have continued to benefit financially from the practice, during the same period around the turn of the late 18th and early 19th centuries, just as slavery was being incrementally outlawed in the northern states.

≈

WHILE NUMEROUS TRADE concerns of the era—both British and American—openly exploited the Chinese population by supplying them with voluminous quantities of opium, it was explained away at the time as 'no worse than alcohol,' or the alternate claim—'what harm for a faceless race?' Sailors returning to ports-of-call like London, New York, and San Francisco, with stores of opium, though, were instrumental in spreading its devastating effects to uninitiated Western, urban population. The growing plague of addiction in Western cities drew wide condemnation at the time.

In the nativist, colonialized world of the 19th century, however, lines of distinction were frequently drawn between the inherent worth of entire races and cultures, where errant notions of racial "superiority" and a pseudo-scientific rationale for inferiority and servitude aimed at the 'Other' were widely held. The men portrayed in this narrative, whether fictional or real, were deeply indoctrinated with this immersive culture of exploitation, so much so that, in their day, racial inferiority was commonly viewed merely as a self-evident reality.

It is also important to remember that, at the time, while excessive use of opium was scorned as a condition of dependence and debauchery, affecting only the weak, it was also widely touted as an effective pain killer, aphrodisiac and mental stimulant. By the mid-19th century, opium had been chemically processed into the drug, morphine (from the Greek god of sleep, Morpheus), proving indispensable as a pain killer on the Civil War battlefield and in operating rooms.

Another opiate derivative was laudanum (laud=praise; anum=worthy). It was an alcohol and herbal preparation containing 10% opium. Called the 'aspirin of the nineteenth century,' laudanum was a popular painkiller and relaxant, recommended for all sorts of ailments including coughs, rheumatism, 'women's troubles' and, perhaps most disturbingly, as a soporific for babies and young children. And as twenty or twenty-five drops of laudanum could be bought for just a penny, it was also affordable. As a children's cough syrup, it appeared on druggists' shelves well into the 20th century. It was also the drug-of-choice for 19th century artists, poets, composers and other 'highly creative types'.

Codeine, as well, has remained a chemical element in many modern medications. Heroin, with all its addictive and deleterious effects, is also an opium derivative. Synthetic versions of opioids, namely Vicodin and OxyContin, are no less a scourge on contemporary society than yāpiàn was on the Chinese of two centuries ago. Public shaming and threats of prosecution for those directly involved in the unlawful promotion and sale of addictive substances remain a remedial course of action, today.

≈

HOW DO WE understand Samuel Russell's motivation during those formative years, 1820-40? He was a complex man—a devout Christian, civically aware, and devoted family man—very much a 'man of his time.' By today's standards, the brutality and mindlessness with which the Chinese community (and other minority nations) were treated, would be termed callous, if not criminal. Colonialism was on the rise in the 19th century, when men and nations deemed those less fortunate and culturally disconnected by Western standards as 'in need of salvation and redemption,' even as their very nations' resources and labor forces were being exploited for profit. "We could do no worse than introduce 'these people' to our way of life," was a familiar refrain.

And, while there is no evidence that Samuel Russell viewed his Chinese clientele in this way, he nevertheless pursued a business strategy over several decades aimed at the exploitation of a nation's population—far removed from his own—in the name of his 'competency.' It was procured through the sale of an illicit substance ('mud,' yāpiàn) to as many people as could be identified through a complex network of shippers, runners, and quasi-official accomplices. The pervasive problem of controlling opium in-flow was a pernicious reality. Except for the emperor and a handful of dedicated Beijing administrators, nearly everyone else, up and down the Chinese administrative chain-of-command, was receiving payouts from Western interests, or from powerful hongs, complicit in the business of opium smuggling.

≈

EUROPEAN TASTE FOR tea had been well established since the Dutch introduced the Chinese delicacy to Western palates in the 18th century. Consumer passion for Asian porcelain and silks would soon follow. But what did the cryptic Chinese desire in exchange from Western merchants? They were, after all, a nation whose culture and norms had lain obscured behind a wall of self-imposed isolation —indecipherable to foreign sensibilities—for centuries.

One of the largest problems faced by foreign traders in Canton was finding a reliable medium of exchange that would enable sustainable trade with the Chinese. The lack of interest in trade goods from Western factories arose from an insulated Chinese nation's belief in its self-sufficiency, with no desire for "foreign baubles."

Chinese merchants, though, were always willing to accept silver bullion or coins issued by silver-rich Spain, 'reales' (known as specie), in exchange for teas, silks, porcelain and other products. The continued, expanded use of specie to purchase these items during the period 1650-1810 made silver coinage expensive to acquire, difficult and dangerous to transport across open seas. Also, supplies of the precious metal flowing into global markets from South America fluctuated, given the ongoing political conflicts and supply issues in that region.

The high volume of goods demanded by markets in Western nations eventually drove British, Dutch and American traders to seek alternatives to these cash-based transactions. Unable to affordably sustain high-level trading in specie, British merchants eventually turned to the lucrative drug trade. Beginning in 1767 and rapidly expanding through the early 1800s, English cotton goods were first traded in Turkey and India for opium, then delivered to China, where it was used as the medium of exchange for tea and other goods for importation back to European markets.

Once they entered the scene in the 1780s, Americans had less difficulty finding a variety of products to barter for tea. The Empress of China, the first American vessel to enter Chinese waters in 1784, and other vessels that followed, transported native ginseng root (used to strengthen the immune system and help fight off stress and disease), in trade for tea. The market for ginseng was small, however, so Americans soon began trading sea otter pelts with Indian tribes in the American Northwest, which were sold for specie in Canton, then used, in turn, to purchase tea. By 1812, as sources for seal skins were depleted, demand by Chinese merchants for these also waned. New products had to be found. In the Pacific Islands, merchants evaded cannibals to trade with natives, acquiring sandalwood and sea slugs for use in trade for specie. But those items also soon ran their course, and by 1814, specie-based sales had risen to nearly seventy percent of total American exports. A global imbalance of trade soon emerged, with China controlling large quantities of the world's silver.

The eventual introduction of the British bank's credit system and willingness to issue bills-of lading, allowed both English and American traders, along with their Chinese merchant counterparts (hongs), to carry debt thousands of miles away in London, without any onsite exchange of tangible currency. Once goods were sold and credits applied to accounts, all parties on both sides of the transaction could order payment of both principal and interest on their loans through these British banks. From 1830 to 1850, faster and larger tea clippers were also introduced, replacing the earlier, smaller privateering vessels, some still being vestiges of the American Revolution. As a result, all Western parties could scale their businesses with the combination of high-speed clippers (three roundtrips/year, rather than two), along with the convenience of British bank credit. Tea could now be transported to American markets in less time than ever, with greater freshness, translating into higher profits. By 1834, tea accounted for over 80% of American trade from China.

≈

HAVING SECURED THEIR fortunes in the Chinese opium market, many of these men returned to the United States, intent on 'doing good,' after having done so 'well.' Since most of the Canton merchants came from influential, well-established families in the American Northeast, much of their attention was directed at cultural, historical, and educational endeavors within that region of the country. Once home, they planned and built luxury estates on the banks of the Hudson (Warren Delano), 'cottages' on the cliffs of Newport, Rhode Island (Wm. King, Wm. Wetmore) and elegant mansions in and near Boston (Perkins family, John P. Cushing), and the Washington, D.C. area, among others.

Many returning entrepreneurs contributed financially in support of prominent national landmarks, hospitals and higher educational institutions. Among them: Massachusetts General Hospital, McLean Psychiatric Hospital, Perkins School for the Blind, the Boston Athenaeum, Bunker Hill Monument, Massachusetts Institute of Technology, Princeton University (partial endowment), many factories, mines, the expanding railroad system, university buildings, high schools, public libraries (Samuel Russell's widow endowed the city library in Middletown, CT), and an orphanage, were made possible with proceeds from opium smuggling. When the Civil War erupted (1861-65), many turned their support and funds to sustain and expand the resources necessary for a Union victory.

Broadly speaking, proceeds from the China opium trade allowed the transfer of that nation's wealth to fuel, at least in part, the second American industrial revolution of the late 19th century.

APPENDIX 2:
References

Allen, Nathan, *The Opium Trade*, James P. Walker, Lowell, MA, 1853.

Bello, David Anthony, *Opium and the Limits of Empire: Drug Prohibition in the Chinese Interior, 1729–1850*, Harvard University Asia Center, Cambridge, MA (and London), 2005

Chung, Tan, *China and the Brave New World*, Carolina Academic Press, Durham, NC, 1978.

Collins, Maurice, *Foreign Mud: Being an account of the Opium Imbroglio at Canton in the 1830s and the Anglo-Chinese War that followed*, Faber and Farber, Ltd, London, 1956.

Crossman, Carl, *The Decorative Arts of the China Trade*, The Antique Collectors Club, Suffolk, England, 1991

Downing, C. T., *The Fan-Qui in China in 1836-1837*, citation...

Downs, Jacques M., *The Golden Getto: The American Commercial Community at Canton and the Shapping of American China Policy, 1784-1844*, Associated University Presses, Cranbury, NJ, 1997.

Eves, Jamie H. "Population Growth and Urbanization in Connecticut During the Industrial Age," The Windham Textile and History Museum- The Mill Museum. Online blog, https://millmuseum.org/population-growth/, date unknown.

Fay, Peter Ward, *The Opium Wars, 1840-1842*, University of North Carolina Press, Chapel Hill, NC, 1975.

Forbes, H. A. Crosby, ed., *The China Trade: Romance and Reality*, an exhibition organized by the Decordova Museum, Lincoln, MA & The Museum of the American China trade, Milton MA, 1979

Hahn, Emily, "The Big Smoke," Times and Places, New York: Thomas Y. Cromwell Company, 1937; the article also appeared in the *New Yorker* magazine.

Hamilton, Peter E., May Holdsworth & Christopher Munn (ed.). Dictionary of Hong Kong Biography. Hong Kong University Press (2012).

He, Sebing, *Russell and Company, 1818-1891: America's Trade and Diplomacy in Nineteenth Century China* (1997 Thesis). ProQuest Dissertations Publishing.

Holt, Edgar, *The Opium Wars in China*, Dufour Editions, Chester Springs, PA, 1964

Hunter, William C., *The 'Fan-Kwae' in Canton before Treaty Days* (1825-1844), Reprint under the title, *An American in Canton* (1825-1844), Derwent Communications, Hong Kong, 1994.

Latourette, Kenneth Scott, *A History of Christian Missions in China*, London 1929

Lubbock. Basil, *The Opium Clippers*, Brown, Son and Ferguson, Ltd., Glasgow, 1933

Munkintrick, Alain, *Samuel Wadsworth Russell (1789-1862): A Study of Ordered Investment*, (1973). An honors thesis submitted in fulfillment of a B.A., Wesleyan University, Middletown, Conn.

Ujifusa, Steven, *Barons of the Sea, and the race to build the world's fastest clipper ship*, Simon & Schuster, New York, NY, 2018

Van Dyke, Paul A., *The Canton Trade: Life and Enterprise on the China Coast, 1700-1845*, Hong Kong University Press, Hong Kong, 2005.

Walley, Arthur, *The Opium War through Chinese Eyes*, The Macmillan Company, New York, 1958

Whitehall, Walter Muir, ed., "'Remarks on the Canton Trade and the Method of Transacting Business,' from a Manuscript in the Peabody Museum of Salem." EIHC 73 no. 4 (October 1937): 303-10.

Yheng Yangwen, *The Social Life of Opium in China*, Cambridge University Press, Cambridge, UK, 2005

*MASQUERADE: This chapter is based on a real-life incident, occurring in 1833, and documented in several texts. Harriet Low lived in Macao from 1828 to 1833 as guest of her uncle, a senior partner in the Russell & Co. trading firm. One night in 1830, Harriet and her aunt disguised themselves as boys and snuck into Canton—then strictly forbidden to foreign women. Harriet marveled in her diary that it was "more Chinese than anything I had ever seen." Although Chinese officials threatened to shut down trade with all Americans until the two departed, Harriet concluded, "I have enjoyed it all very much, and have not yet repented that I came."

**A PERUVIAN UPRISING: This chapter is based on an actual captain's log entry from February 5, 1824, located at the Phillips Library at the Peabody Essex Museum (MA). An American vessel sailed into the Peruvian port city of Callao, only to learn of a slave revolt involving 600 African slaves who were holed up in the nearby Real Felipe Fortress. Led by a slave named Shodreny, they demanded $100,000 and two ships to carry them home to Africa. The record shows that by the time the Americans arrived, communications with the group had already ceased. The following day, a British vessel in the harbor agreed to fire on the fortress, and the vessel they arrived on, "on pain of death" if they did not surrender. The ship's log ended at that point, with no indication of outcome. This fascinating entry became the basis for a dramatization of Shodreny's heroic role in the real-life, but likely doomed-to-fail, incident.

APPENDIX 3:
1879 Correspondence Regarding History of Russell & Co.*

"Many of us were caught up in this accident of history—becoming one with both fortunate and tragic consequences for those who strived to become involved...the only thing I fear is that in giving a sketch of the causes & effects of the opium traffic & and our imprisonment I may say too much & and so when somebody goes into the history..."
~ Robert Bennett Forbes

THOSE FOUNDERS OF American companies engaged in the China Trade of the early 1800s returned home wealthy men. From their luxurious homes in cities like New York and Boston, and other Northeast cities, a select group calculated, decades later, it might be useful to record for the history books something of the events that transpired there. What follows are excerpts from 1879 correspondence between former Russell & Co. partners (its founder, Samuel Russell (deceased in 1862), regarding the merits and risks of such an undertaking:

26 FEBRUARY, 1879: [*In preparing a history of the period*] *"...the only thing I fear is that in giving a sketch of the causes & effects of the opium traffic & and our imprisonment I may say too much & and so when somebody goes into the history...he may spin out more than I want to print, as I must wait for responses from [the principles in] China...to make an interesting pamphlet."*

28 FEBRUARY 1879: *After seeing the objections of [several principles involved in trade]...it suggests that when we get answers from all survivors at home & in China, we can determine...if it will be advisable to print anything or not."*

9 MARCH 1879: *"John (Forbes) [Russell & Co. partner 1834-39]...entered a solemn protest against my printing & circulating anything like a history of Russell & Co....to give up any idea of printing anything. But I shall go on and collect & arrange my facts for anyone who may be sufficiently interested my (sic) read it, or take notes."*

12 MARCH 1879: *"Joshua Hubbell, supercargo in the 1830s-40s...says that the first opium troubles began at the time a sailor was executed at Whampoa and that at the time Turkey opium smuggling was not rare...During my early visits to Whampoa I never heard of any opium smuggling there & I suppose it was on a small scale & and not countenanced by regular houses."*

31 MARCH 1879: *"Since my last...John offers me $500 for the copyright of my personal reminiscences & wants me to prepare my R & Co. sketch to add to it...and along with fair royalty on sales, the condition that he is to use a pair of scissors wherever he chooses in cutting out objectionable parts. I have accepted his offer."*

4 MAY 1879: *"...I have done nothing of late in writing up the sketch [of R & Co.] because John has not been well enough to look at what I have written. I suppose I have informed you of my bargain with him—& I do not desire to waste pen, ink and brains unless he approves of the matter already written."*

13 JULY 1879: *I believe I have informed you that J[ohn] M. Forbes has bought the copyright of my memoir not to destroy the plates as one would have suppose[d] who knows he is dead-set against the printing of anything having to do with Russell & Co., but in order to add a chapter on that renowned house. His only condition is that he may use scissors in cutting out what he calls irrelevant private matters. I know not when he will submit them to any other of the old members."*

≈

THE ANXIETY AND concerns reflected in the exchanges noted above, between Forbes and Delano, get to the heart of the challenge I faced as a cultural historian and historical fiction writer. I was tied, by choice, to the original records and documents pertaining to the life and activities of Samuel Russell, those surrounding his life and work while in China. As you might expect, the available records are largely opaque regarding much of the trading activity involving opium acquisition, smuggling and sales—not only for Russell's enterprise—but for most of the shipping, sale and management of clandestine goods being brought into the Pearl River by American and British traders during that time. Any direct reference to the word, 'opium,' in the thousands of preserved shipping logs and records available to researchers, is rare indeed.

*Excerpts from a series of 1879 letters from Robert Bennet Forbes, to Warren Delano, grandfather of Franklin Delano Roosevelt, now on file at Hyde Park (Frederick A. Delano Collection)

APPENDIX 4:
Where Are They Now?

Thirteen Factories

THE THIRTEEN FACTORIES, was a two-hundred yard long strip of neo-classical styled buildings constructed outside the old walled city, along the banks of the Pearl River's upper reaches, in southwestern Canton (now Guangzhou). Western traders occupied these building during the Qing Empire (1757 to 1842). These warehouses and stores served as the principal business and residential location for most Western traders, who were not permitted to freely mix with the city population, of conduct business with any other that licensed Chinese trade intermediaries (Co-hong). The "factories" were not workshops or manufacturing centers but the offices, trading posts, and warehouses of foreign factors, mercantile fiduciaries who bought and sold goods on consignment for their principals. The word derives from "feitoria" which means trading post in Portuguese (the first westerners to engage in trade with China).

The factories were destroyed by fire which swept through neighboring buildings in 1822; again in 1841 amid the First Opium War; and finally, in 1856 at the onset of the Second Opium War. The factories' importance diminished after the opening of additional ports under the terms of the 1842 Anglo-Chinese, Treaty of Nanking. After the Second Opium War, Western offices were relocated to fashionable first to Henan Island across the Pearl River and then to Shamian Island south of Guangzhou's western suburbs. Their original site is now part of Guangzhou Cultural Park.

Qing Dynasty

THE QING DYNASTY succeeded the Ming dynasty, which had spent hundreds of years fortifying the Great Wall and strengthening the navy in hopes of preventing foreign invaders from overthrowing Han Chinese rule, as had happened two dynasties prior. In the 17th century, the Ming emperor formed an alliance with Manchu tribes to China's north to suppress rebellion from within resulting in being conquered by the Manchus themselves.

The Manchus then established the Qing dynasty, maintaining the capital at Beijing, and changing little about the Ming order. While the dynasty ensured that half of all higher-level officials were Manchu, it pacified its constituents by adopting a traditional Confucian approach to leadership and continuing to employ Ming officials.

In 1839, 40 years after the Qianlong Emperor's death (Hongli), the British incited naval warfare on China over the opium trade, and China's "Century of Humiliation" began. The First Opium War, as the three and a half years of battles between the Chinese and British were called, spurred the forced opening of China's ports to international trade. The First Opium War, of course, was followed by the Second Opium War, but not before the Qing endured another major humiliation known as the Taiping Rebellion.

Though preceding dynasties had nearly all suffered rebellions, the Taiping Rebellion was unprecedented in its scale and impact. Believing he was the brother of Jesus Christ, Hong Xiuquan, a failed civil servant, started the rebellion. Seeking a more Christian nation, beginning with the overthrow of the Manchus, Hong gathered sympathetic followers throughout China's south, and together, this army waged a 14-year-long civil war against the Qing. The Qing won in the end, but not before severely weakening itself and losing an estimated 20–30 million civilians and soldiers.

The cracks in the dynasty were really beginning to show by this point, and the "Century of Humiliation" was just getting started. In 1894, the Qing began another war, this time with the Japanese over influence in Korea, and through it, revealed their inability to fight off modernity. Inspired by this defeat and Japan's Meiji Restoration, the Qing's Empress Dowager Cixi attempted similar reforms in China but missed the mark, particularly failing when she decided to support the Boxer Rebellion, with the result that hundreds of foreign missionaries and others were killed.

By this point, the Qing had little hope of turning itself around, and finally, a republican revolution in 1911 forced the abdication of China's last emperor, the boy, Puyi, and imperial China had to step aside in the new century, setting the stage for the Communist nation we know today.

Russell & Company

RUSSELL & COMPANY was the largest American trading house of the mid-19th century in China. The firm specialized in trading tea, silk and opium and was eventually involved in the shipping trade. In 1818, Samuel Russell was approached by Providence merchants Edward C. Carrington, Cyrus Butler and Benjamin and Thomas Hoppin to be an employee of their new resident commission firm in Canton under the name of Samuel Russell & Company. The contract would expire after five years and the profit accumulated would be split between all parties. Russell arrived in Canton in 1819 and established Samuel Russell & Co. The company and its strong working relationship with hong, Howqua, and other Co-hongs, allowed the organization to grow rapidly in the early years. A series of high-level staffing changes strengthened Russell's business model, even further.

Following the acquisition of Perkins & Co. in 1829, Russell and Co. inherited their extensive opium trading connections from across the globe. In 1833, the East India Company's monopoly on the British China Trade came to an end and Russell & Co. entered into an unofficial partnership with two British firms, Jardine, Matheson, & Co. and Whiteman & Co., to further expand the opium trade with India. From 1834-36, the company saw an annual net profit of over $400,000 ($8.7 million in 2021). By the early 1840s, Russell & Co. had become the largest American trading house in China and maintained that position for decades.

During the 1850s, Russell & Co. would expand its operation, with headquarters in Shanghai and branches specializing in tea trade in Fuzhou, Hong Kong and several other Chinese cities In the following decade, they would diversify into international shipping, employing the latest in steamship technology.

In the 1860s, the China trade underwent a series of transformation which was the result of more competition from their British rivals and the shortened length of time that was needed to commute to locations with the opening of the Suez Canal in 1869. By the 1870s, Russell & Co. were forced to cease their banking operations, as the lucrative importing of precious metals were eventually overtaken by newer commission firms and professional banks. Initially, Shanghai S. N. Co. was established to counter their losses, however their rates of return would continue to decrease and in 1877 they were acquired by the China Merchants Steam Navigation Company along with their various properties. Facing further financial difficulties, the company sold remaining assets and stopped operations in 1891

The Russell Company Upper Mill is an historic structure in Middletown,

Connecticut, built in 1836 by Samuel Russell (after his return from China), and Samuel Hubbard (contractor for Russell House during construction), and others, and is listed on the National Register of Historic Places. This factory was designated as the Russell Manufacturing Company and is the oldest surviving textile mill building in the city of Middletown. In 1841, the company was the first to produce elastic webbing on power looms. By 1896, it manufactured a wide variety of woven products and was the nation's largest manufacturer of suspenders. Approximately 900 workers were employed in the company's seven mills.

Samuel Russell House

THE SAMUEL WADSWORTH RUSSELL HOUSE is a neoclassical house at 350 High Street in Middletown, Connecticut, built in 1827-8 to a design by architect Ithiel Town. Many architectural historians consider it to be one of the finest Greek Revival mansions in the northeastern United States. In 1827-8 when his house was built, Russell was in Canton. He had briefly returned from China to initiate planning for the siting and building of the property, and to marry his second wife (sister of his first, deceased wife, Mary). His friend Samuel D. Hubbard worked with his wife, Frances Russell, to supervise the construction of the house. The house has the form of a Greek temple with six full-height Corintian columns obtained from a New Haven bank that closed before renovations could be completed. The six columns were transported by barge to Middletown for incorporation into the new structure. In 1832 Russell returned to Middletown and his new home, where he resided until his death in 1862

The house was listed on the National Register of Historic Places in 1970, and designated as a National Historic Landmark in 2001. After the Russell family retained the house for five generations, in 1937 Thomas Macdonough Russell, Jr. deeded it to Wesleyan College. The building was used as Honors College until 1996. The building is currently used as a special events facility and as the home of the University's Philosophy department.

APPENDIX 5:
Full Texts of Qing Emperors' Letters to British Crowns (1783, 1839)

PARTIAL TEXT of letter from Emperor Hongli to George III, King of England (1783)

You, O King, live beyond the confines of many seas, nevertheless, impelled by your humble desire to partake of the benefits of our [Chinese] civilisation, you have dispatched a mission [led by George McCartney] respectfully bearing your memorial. Your Envoy has crossed the seas and paid his respects at my Court on the anniversary of my birthday. To show your devotion, you have also sent offerings of your country's produce.

I have perused your memorial: the earnest terms in which it is couched reveal a respectful humility on your part, which is highly praiseworthy. In consideration of the fact that your Ambassador and his deputy have come a long way with your memorial and tribute, I have shown them high favour and have allowed them to be introduced into my presence. To manifest my indulgence, I have entertained them at a banquet and made them numerous gifts. I have also caused presents to be forwarded to the Naval Commander and six hundred of his officers and men, although they did not come to Peking [Beijing], so that they too may share in my all-embracing kindness.

As to your entreaty to send one of your nationals to be accredited to my Celestial Court and to be in control of your country's trade with China, this request is contrary to all usage of my dynasty and cannot possibly be entertained.

It is true that Europeans, in the service of the dynasty, have been permitted to live at Peking, but they are compelled to adopt Chinese dress, they are strictly confined to their own precincts and are never permitted to return home. You are presumably familiar with our dynastic regulations. Your proposed Envoy to my Court could not be placed in a position similar to that of European officials in Peking who are forbidden to leave China, nor could he, on the other hand, be allowed liberty of movement and the privilege of corresponding with his own country; so that you would gain nothing by his residence in our midst.

Moreover, our Celestial dynasty possesses vast territories, and tribute missions from the dependencies are provided for by the Department for Tributary States, which ministers to their wants and exercises strict control over their movements. It would be quite impossible to leave them to their own devices. Supposing that your Envoy should come to our Court, his language and national dress differ from that of our people, and there would be no place in which to bestow him. It may be suggested that he might imitate the Europeans permanently resident in Peking and adopt the dress and customs of China, but, it has never been our dynasty's wish to force people to do things unseemly and inconvenient. Besides, supposing I sent an Ambassador to reside in your country, how could you possibly make for him the requisite arrangements? Europe consists of many other nations besides your own: if each and all demanded to be represented at our Court, how could we possibly consent? The thing is utterly impracticable. How can our dynasty alter its whole procedure and system of etiquette, established for more than a century, in order to meet your individual views? If it be said that your object is to exercise control over your country's trade, your nationals have had full liberty to trade at Guangzhou for many a year and have received the greatest consideration at our hands.

Missions have been sent by Portugal and Italy, preferring similar requests. The Throne appreciated their sincerity and loaded them with favours, besides authorising measures to facilitate their trade with China. You are no doubt aware that, when my Guangzhou merchant, Wu Chao-ping, was in debt to the foreign ships, I made the Viceroy advance the monies due, out of the provincial treasury, and ordered him to punish the culprit severely. Why then should foreign nations advance this utterly unreasonable request to be represented at my Court? Peking is nearly two thousand miles from Guangzhou, and at such a distance what possible control could any British representative exercise?

If you assert that your reverence for Our Celestial dynasty fills you with a desire to acquire our civilisation, our ceremonies and code of laws differ so completely from your own that, even if your Envoy were able to acquire the rudiments of our civilisation, you could not possibly transplant our manners and customs to your alien soil. Therefore, however adept the Envoy might become, nothing would be gained thereby.

Swaying the wide world, I have but one aim in view, namely, to maintain a perfect governance and to fulfill the duties of the State: strange and costly objects do not interest me. If I have commanded that the tribute offerings sent by you, O King, are to be accepted, this was solely in consideration for the spirit which prompted you to dispatch them from afar. Our dynasty's majestic virtue has penetrated unto every country under Heaven, and Kings of all nations have offered their costly tribute by land and sea. As your Ambassador can see for himself, we possess all things. I set no value on objects strange or ingenious and have no use for your country's manufactures [the McCartney mission brought wool socks as an offering]. This then is my answer to your request to appoint a representative at my Court, a request contrary to our dynastic usage, which would only result in inconvenience to yourself. I have expounded my wishes in detail and have commanded your tribute Envoys to leave in peace on their homeward journey. It behoves you, O King, to respect my sentiments and to display even greater devotion and loyalty in future, so that, by perpetual submission to our Throne, you may secure peace and prosperity for your country hereafter. Besides making gifts (of which I enclose an inventory) to each member of your Mission, I confer upon you, O King, valuable presents in excess of the number usually bestowed on such occasions, including silks and curios-a list of which is likewise enclosed. Do you reverently receive them and take note of my tender goodwill towards you! A special mandate.

Yesterday your Ambassador petitioned my Ministers to memorialise me regarding your trade with China, but his proposal is not consistent with our dynastic usage and cannot be entertained. Hitherto, all European nations, including your own country's barbarian merchants, have carried on their trade with our Celestial Empire at Guangzhou. Such has been the procedure for many years, although our Celestial Empire possesses all things in prolific abundance and lacks no product within its own borders. There was therefore no need to import the manufactures of outside barbarians in exchange for our own produce. But as the tea, silk and porcelain which the Celestial Empire produces, are absolute necessities to European nations and to yourselves, we have permitted, as a signal mark of favour, that foreign hongs [merchant firms] should be established at Guangzhou, so that your wants might be supplied and your country thus participate in our beneficence.

But your Ambassador has now put forward new requests which completely fail to recognise the Throne's principle to "treat strangers from afar with indulgence," and to exercise a pacifying control over barbarian tribes, the world over. Moreover, our dynasty, swaying the myriad races of the globe, extends the same benevolence towards all. Your England is not the only nation trading at Guangzhou. If other nations, following your bad example, wrongfully importune my ear with further impossible requests, how will it be possible for me to treat them with easy indulgence? Nevertheless, I do not forget the lonely remoteness of your island, cut off from the world by intervening wastes of sea, nor do I overlook your excusable ignorance of the usages of our Celestial Empire. I have consequently commanded my Ministers to enlighten your Ambassador on the subject, and have ordered the departure of the mission. But I have doubts that, after your Envoy's return he may fail to acquaint you with my view in detail or that he may be lacking in lucidity, so that I shall now proceed ... to issue my mandate on each question separately. In this way you will, I trust, comprehend my meaning....

[a list of answers to particular requests follows:]

Your request for a small island near Chusan, where your merchants may reside and goods be warehoused, arises from your desire to develop trade. As there are neither foreign hongs nor interpreters in or near Chusan, where none of your ships have ever called, such an island would be utterly useless for your purposes. Every inch of the territory of our Empire is marked on the map and the strictest vigilance is exercised over it all: even tiny islets and far-lying sand-banks are clearly defined as part of the provinces to which they belong. Consider, moreover, that England is not the only barbarian land which wishes to establish ... trade with our Empire of Guangzhou [Canton]: supposing that other nations were all to imitate your evil example and beseech me to present them each and all with a site for trading purposes, how could I possibly comply? This also is a flagrant infringement of the usage of my Empire and cannot possibly be entertained.

Regarding your nation's worship of the Lord of Heaven, it is the same religion as that of other European nations. Ever since the beginning of history, sage Emperors and wise rulers have bestowed on China a moral system and inculcated a code, which from time immemorial has been religiously observed by the myriads of my subjects. There has been no hankering after heterodox doctrines. Even the European (missionary) officials in my capital are forbidden to hold intercourse with Chinese subjects; they are restricted within the limits of their appointed residences and may not go about propagating their religion. The distinction between Chinese and barbarian is most strict, and your Ambassador's request that barbarians shall be given full liberty to disseminate their religion is utterly unreasonable.

... Should your vessels touch the shore, your merchants will assuredly never be permitted to land or to reside there but will be subject to instant expulsion. In that event your barbarian merchants will have had a long journey for nothing. Do not say that you were not warned in due time.

SOURCE: E. Backhouse and J. O. P. Bland, *Annals and Memoirs of the Court of Peking* (Boston: Houghton Mifflin, 1914), pp. 322–331

FULL TEXT OF "Letter of Advice to Queen Victoria"

Letter to Queen Victoria (1839) from: Lin Tse-Hsu, Imperial Commissioner, Guangdong (Canton) and Guangxi, the "Dual-expanses" 兩廣 (liǎng guǎng).

A Communication:

"The Way of Heaven is fairness to all; it does not suffer us to harm others to benefit ourselves Magnificently our great Emperor soothes and pacifies China and the foreign countries, regarding all with the same kindness. If there is profit, then he shares it with the peoples of the world; if there is harm, then he removes it on behalf of the world. This is because he takes the mind of heaven and earth as his mind.

But after a long period of commercial intercourse, there appear among the crowd of barbarians both good persons and bad, unevenly. Consequently there are those who smuggle opium to seduce the Chinese people and so cause the spread of the poison to all provinces. Such persons who only care to profit themselves, and disregard their harm to others, are not tolerated by the laws of heaven and are unanimously hated by human beings. His Majesty the Emperor, upon hearing of this, is in a towering rage. He has especially sent me, his commissioner, to come to Kwangtung, and together with the governor-general and governor jointly to investigate and settle this matter.

All those people in China who sell opium or smoke opium should receive the death penalty. We trace the crime of those barbarians who through the years have been selling opium, then the deep harm they have wrought and the great profit they have usurped should fundamentally justify their execution according to law. We take into to consideration, however, the fact that the various barbarians have still known how to repent their crimes and return to their allegiance to us by taking the 20,183 chests of opium from their store ships and petitioning us, through their consular officer [superintendent of trade], Elliot, to receive it. It has been entirely destroyed and this has been faithfully reported to the Throne in several memorials by this commissioner and his colleagues.

We find your country is sixty or seventy thousand li [three li make one mile, ordinarily] from China Yet there are barbarian ships that strive to come here for trade for the purpose of making a great profit The wealth of China is used to profit the barbarians. That is to say, the great profit made by barbarians is all taken from the rightful share of China. By what right do they then in return use the poisonous drug to injure the Chinese people? Even though the barbarians may not necessarily intend to do us harm, yet in coveting profit to an extreme, they have no regard for injuring others. Let us ask, where is your conscience? I have heard that the smoking of opium is very strictly forbidden by your country; that is because the harm caused by opium is clearly understood. Since it is not permitted to do harm to your own country, then even less should you let it be passed on to the harm of other countries—how much less to China!

Of all that China exports to foreign countries, there is not a single thing which is not beneficial to people: they are of benefit when eaten, or of benefit when used, or of benefit when resold: all are beneficial. Is there a single article from China which has done any harm to foreign countries? Take tea and rhubarb, for example; the foreign countries cannot get along for a single day without them. If China cuts off these benefits with no sympathy for those who are to suffer, then what can the barbarians rely upon to keep themselves alive? Moreover, the woolens, camlets, and longells [i.e., textiles] of foreign countries cannot be woven unless they obtain Chinese silk. If China, again, cuts off this beneficial export, what profit can the barbarians expect to make? As for other foodstuffs, beginning with candy, ginger, cinnamon, and so forth, and articles for use, beginning with silk, satin, chinaware, and so on, all the things that must be had by foreign countries are innumerable.

On the other hand, articles coming from the outside to China can only be used as toys. We can take them or get along without them. Since they are not needed by China, what difficulty would there be if we closed our frontier and stopped the trade? Nevertheless, our Celestial Court lets tea, silk, and other goods be shipped without limit and circulated everywhere without begrudging it in the slightest. This is for no other reason but to share the benefit with the people of the whole world. The goods from China carried away by your country not only supply your own consumption and use, but also can be divided up and sold to other countries, producing a triple profit. Even if you do not sell opium, you still have this threefold profit. How can you bear to go further, selling products injurious to others to fulfill your insatiable desire?

Suppose there were people from another country who carried opium for sale to England and seduced your people into buying and smoking it; certainly your honorable ruler would deeply hate it and be bitterly aroused. We have heard heretofore that your honorable ruler is kind and benevolent. Naturally you would not wish to give unto others what you yourself do not want.

We have further learned that in London, the capital of your honorable rule, and in Scotland, Ireland, and other places, originally no opium has been produced. Only in several places of India under your control such as Bengal, Madras, Bombay, Patna, Benares, and Malwa has opium been planted from hill to hill, and ponds have been opened for its manufacture. For months and years work is continued to accumulate the poison. The obnoxious odor ascends, irritating heaven and frightening the spirits. Indeed you, O King, can eradicate the opium plant in these places, hoe over the fields entirely, and sow in its stead the five grains [millet, barley, wheat, etc.]. Anyone who dares again attempt to plant and manufacture opium should be severely punished. This will really be a great, benevolent government policy that will increase the common weal and get rid of evil. For this, Heaven must support you and the spirits must bring you good fortune, prolonging your old age and extending your descendants. All will depend on this act.

Now we have set up regulations governing the Chinese people. He who sells opium shall receive the death penalty and he who smokes it also the death penalty. Now consider this: if the barbarians do not bring opium, then how can the Chinese people resell it, and how can they smoke it? The fact is that the wicked barbarians beguile the Chinese people into a death trap. How then can we grant life only to these barbarians? He who takes the life of even one person still has to atone for it with his own life; yet is the harm done by opium limited to the taking of one life only? Therefore in the new regulations, in regard to those barbarians who bring opium to China, the penalty is fixed at decapitation or strangulation. This is what is called getting rid a harmful thing on behalf of mankind.

May you, O King, check your wicked and sift out your wicked people before they come to China, in order to guarantee the peace of your nation, to show further the sincerity of your politeness and submissiveness, and to let the two countries enjoy together the blessings of peace How fortunate, how fortunate indeed! After receiving this dispatch will you immediately give us a prompt reply regarding the details and circumstances of your cutting off the opium traffic. Be sure not to put this off.

The above is what has to be communicated.

ACKNOWLEDGMENTS

THIS PROJECT WAS spurred on by a growing curiosity, as I so often passed by a beautiful building on our Wesleyan University campus, the Samuel Russell House. It goes by many other names here, including Honor's College. Its splashy white façade and stand of six regal Corinthian columns supporting a jutting cornice are memorable. But, equally intriguing is the story of the man who once occupied this property on the corner of Washington and High Streets, in Middletown, Connecticut. An early 19th century entrepreneur and world traveler, Samuel Russell earned the fortune that allowed for the construction of this building through the wholesale distribution of the illicit drug, opium, during his years as part of the China Trade.

A cursory glance at the historical record yields troves of ledgers and records maintained by Russell and his staff during the early 1800s. They principally account for his business as an agent in the fabric trade, first at home in Middletown, then as he traveled to Europe and China, and again, as a prosperous resident of his hometown in Connecticut.

It was quite by accident that I noted a small, footnoted reference in a routine Google search under Russell's name. It was by a Wesleyan undergraduate, dated 1973, entitled "Samuel Wadsworth Russell (1789-1862), A Study in Ordered Investment," by Alain Munkittrick. This senior thesis, completed to satisfy requirements for an B.A. with honors, in English, quickly came to serve as a touchstone for me in my efforts to better understand the motivations and actions of Samuel Russell, the man. No small accomplishment for an undergraduate, his research was carefully detailed and referenced; the document itself, 181-pages of double and single-spaced narrative, painstakingly hammered out on an IBM Selectric typewriter, over what was likely, days of labor.

I am indebted beyond words to Alain for his Herculean effort, undertaken nearly fifty years ago, as his otherwise long-lost thesis became a principal source of reference for me, as I endeavored to inject points of realism and authenticity into my fictional storytelling. His effort to rise to the task of putting flesh and bones on this 19th century "ordered investor" succeeded beyond expectation.

I am also grateful to the institutions that have made it their responsibility to carefully preserve the ledgers, letters, images, and ephemera from that period in our history. Colorfully illustrated ships logs carefully executed daily records of sea conditions, cargoes, personalities involved and descriptions of early 19th century sailing vessels served to animate period history for this struggling writer. The National Archives (D.C.), Mystic Seaport's (CT) archival library, Middlesex County Historical Society's records (CT), and the Phillips Library at the Peabody Essex Museum (MA) proved invaluable, as did the resources of the Russell Library ((gifted by Frances Russell to the city) and my port-graduate alma mater, Wesleyan University, in Middletown, CT, who renewed my reference texts repeatedly, in order that I may have vital material at my fingertips during the process of writing this book.

I was thrilled to meet direct descendants of Samuel Russell, including Samuel Russell IV, who could recall living in the Russell House in the 1930s, and cousin, Tom MacDonough. Sam's recollections of the layout and furnishing in the property before it was gifted to the university, and family lore about previous generations, proved entertaining and invaluable. Our visit to Indian Hill Cemetery, and to the Russell family plot, brought the reality of succession of generations to life for me, in ways that would otherwise not be possible.

I am also indebted to Debbie Shapiro and Jesse Nasta, past and present directors of the Middlesex County Historical Society, and their permanent exhibit, "A Vanished Port: Middletown and the Caribbean, 1750-1824"; Anne Farrow, noted author on the topic of Northern slavery; and author, Diana Ross McCain, with her perspective on the early abolitionist movement. Lastly, to Anne Marcotty, with her keen designer's eye and expert guidance in helping to realize the book you now hold in your hand.

TITLE PAGE: Drawn by Auguste Borget, lithograph by Eugene Ciceri - Auguste Borget (1842). *Sketches of China and the Chinese / from Drawings by Auguste Borget.* London: Tilt and Bogue. Plate 23.

RIGHT: Map of the Canton [Pearl] River (1845) showing main features, including Macao (lower left); Hong Kong (lower right); Lintin Island; Boca Tigres; Whampoa and Canton (upper left).

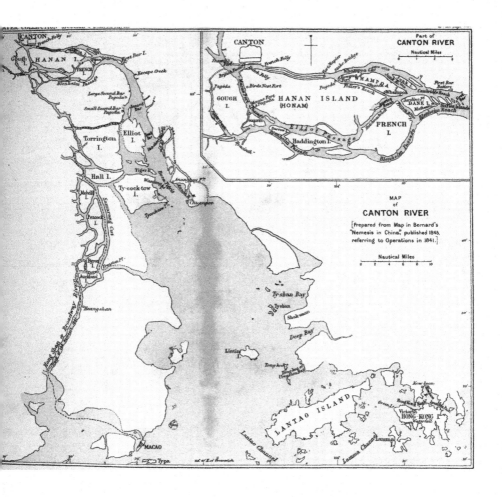

ABOUT THE AUTHOR

RICHARD J. FRISWELL, is a cultural historian and Wesleyan University Visiting Scholar. There, he directs the Wesleyan Institute for Lifelong Learning, an adult education program.

He is publisher and managing editor of ARTES, a fine arts online magazine (artesmagazine.com) and an elected member of the International Association of Art Critics, as well as an award-winning writer in the field of art journalism, with over 400 published articles.

In 2016, Hammonasset House Books published a collection of his essays, *Balancing Act: Postcards from the Edge of Risk and Reward*. In 2018, an historical fiction tale of Hudson River School of painting founder, Thomas Cole, entitled, *Hudson River Chronicles: In Search of the Splendid & Sublime on America's 'First' River*.

He lives in southern Connecticut, where he lectures widely on topics related to the visual arts and cultural history in the modern era.

ABOUT THE TYPEFACE

SERIF:

Artifex CF was chosen for being reminiscent of early 19th-century lead type.
It is a text-friendly serif that's easy on the eyes. Subtle serifs help the flow of reading
without being ornate or stiff, and *a near-upright italic* adds emphasis without distraction.

SANS SERIF:

Artifex Hand CF is a humanist sans-serif variation on the original Artifex typeface; its
serifs replaced with a subtle flare, lending a calligraphic feel and warm tone.